Power-Sharing

Power-sharing is an important political strategy for managing protracted conflicts and it can also facilitate the democratic accommodation of difference. Despite these benefits it has been much criticized, with claims that it is unable to produce peace and stability, is ineffective and inefficient, and obstructs other peacebuilding values, including gender equality.

This edited collection aims to enhance our understanding of the utility of power-sharing in deeply divided places by subjecting power-sharing theory and practice to empirical and normative analysis and critique. Its overarching questions are:

- Do power-sharing arrangements enhance stability, peace and cooperation in divided societies?
- Do they do so in ways that promote effective governance?
- Do they do so in ways that promote justice, fairness and democracy?

Using a broad range of global empirical case studies, it provides a space for dialogue between leading and emerging scholars on the normative questions surrounding power-sharing. Distinctively, it asks proponents of power-sharing to think critically about its weaknesses.

This text will be of interest to students, scholars and practitioners of power-sharing, ethnic politics, democracy and democratization, peacebuilding, comparative constitutional design, and more broadly Comparative Politics, International Relations and Constitutional and Comparative Law.

Allison McCulloch is Associate Professor of Political Science at Brandon University, Canada. Her research explores the processes and institutions that facilitate the building of democracy and stability in deeply divided places, with a particular emphasis on power-sharing.

John McGarry is Professor of Political Studies and Canada Research Chair in Nationalism and Democracy in the Department of Political Studies, Queen's University, Kingston, Canada. His academic work is mainly concerned with the design of political institutions in deeply divided places.

Routledge Studies on Challenges, Crises and Dissent in World Politics

Series editors:
Karoline Postel-Vinay
Centre for International Studies and Research (CERI), France
and
Nadine Godehardt
German Institute for International and Security Affairs, Germany

This new series focuses on challenges, crises and dissent in world politics and the major political issues that have surfaced in recent years. It welcomes a wide range of theoretical and methodological approaches including critical and postmodern studies, and aims to improve our present understanding of global order through the exploration of major challenges to inter/national and regional governability, the effects of nationalism, extremism, weak leadership and the emergence of new actors in international politics.

1   **Empires of Remorse**
    Narrative, Postcolonialism and Apologies for Colonial Atrocity
    Tom Bentley

2   **Crisis and Institutional Change in Regional Integration**
    Edited by Sabine Saurugger and Fabien Terpan

3   **Violent Non-State Actors**
    From Anarchists to Jihadists
    Ersel Aydinli

4   **Power-Sharing**
    Empirical and Normative Challenges
    Edited by Allison McCulloch and John McGarry

5   **Hegemony and Resistance around the Iranian Nuclear Programme**
    Analysing Chinese, Russian, and Turkish Foreign Policies
    Moritz Pieper

Power-Sharing
Empirical and Normative Challenges

**Edited by
Allison McCulloch
and John McGarry**

LONDON AND NEW YORK

First published 2017
by Routledge
2 Park Square, Milton Park, Abingdon, Oxon OX14 4RN

and by Routledge
711 Third Avenue, New York, NY 10017

Routledge is an imprint of the Taylor & Francis Group, an informa business

© 2017 selection and editorial matter, Allison McCulloch and John McGarry; individual chapters, the contributors

The right of Allison McCulloch and John McGarry to be identified as the authors of the editorial matter, and of the authors for their individual chapters, has been asserted in accordance with sections 77 and 78 of the Copyright, Designs and Patents Act 1988.

All rights reserved. No part of this book may be reprinted or reproduced or utilized in any form or by any electronic, mechanical, or other means, now known or hereafter invented, including photocopying and recording, or in any information storage or retrieval system, without permission in writing from the publishers.

Trademark notice: Product or corporate names may be trademarks or registered trademarks, and are used only for identification and explanation without intent to infringe.

British Library Cataloguing in Publication Data
A catalogue record for this book is available from the British Library

Library of Congress Cataloging in Publication Data
Names: McCulloch, Allison, editor. | McGarry, John, 1957– editor.
Title: Power-sharing : empirical and normative challenges / edited by Allison McCulloch and John McGarry.
Description: Abingdon, Oxon ; New York, NY : Routledge, 2017. | Series: Routledge studies on challenges, crises and dissent in world politics ; 4 | Includes bibliographical references and index.
Identifiers: LCCN 2016048764| ISBN 9781138640368 (hardback) | ISBN 9781315636689 (ebook)Subjects: LCSH: Coalition governments–Case studies. | Political stability–Case studies. | Conflict management–Case studies. | Peace-building–Case studies. | Democratization–Case studies.
Classification: LCC JF51 .P666 2017 | DDC 324–dc23
LC record available at https://lccn.loc.gov/2016048764

ISBN: 978-1-138-64036-8 (hbk)
ISBN: 978-1-315-63668-9 (ebk)

Typeset in Times New Roman
by Wearset Ltd, Boldon, Tyne and Wear

Contents

Lists of illustrations   vii
Notes on contributors   viii
List of abbreviations   x

Introduction: contemporary challenges to power-sharing theory and practice   1
ALLISON McCULLOCH

1 Centripetalism, consociationalism and Cyprus: the 'adoptability' question   16
JOHN McGARRY

2 Power-sharing in Kenya: between the devil and the deep blue sea   36
NIC CHEESEMAN AND CHRISTINA MURRAY

3 Power-sharing executives: consociational and centripetal formulae and the case of Northern Ireland   63
JOHN McGARRY AND BRENDAN O'LEARY

4 Consociationalism in the Brussels Capital Region: dis-proportional representation and the accommodation of national minorities   87
THIBAUD BODSON AND NEOPHYTOS LOIZIDES

5 Mandatory power-sharing in coup-prone Fiji   103
JON FRAENKEL

6 Ethnic power-sharing coalitions and democratization   124
NILS-CHRISTIAN BORMANN

7	**Lebanon: how civil war transformed consociationalism** MATTHIJS BOGAARDS	148
8	**Power-sharing in Burundi: an enduring miracle?** STEF VANDEGINSTE	166
9	**Mostar as microcosm: power-sharing in post-war Bosnia** SUMANTRA BOSE	189
10	**Power-sharing and the pursuit of good governance: evidence from Northern Ireland** JOANNE McEVOY	211
11	**Good fences make good neighbours: assessing the role of consociational politics in transitional justice** KRISTIAN BROWN AND FIONNUALA NÍ AOLÁIN	229
12	**Gendering power-sharing** SIOBHAN BYRNE AND ALLISON McCULLOCH	250
	Conclusion: what explains the performance of power-sharing settlements? JOHN McGARRY	268
	Index	293

Illustrations

Figure

4.1   The Belgian federal structure   89

Tables

2.1	Distribution of ministers and assistant minister under power-sharing in Kenya	48
3.1	Applying the Jefferson–d'Hondt Divisor with ten ministries in a hypothetical 100-seat legislature	65
4.1	Election results in the Brussels Capital Region, 2004 to 2014	95
6.1	Theoretical link between ethnic representativeness and diversity, and the likelihood of democratization	131
6.2	Democratic transitions in the Polity IV and GWF sample, 1946 to 2009	132
6.3	Polity IV democratization and ethnic power-sharing, 1946 to 2009	136
6.4	GWF democratization and ethnic power-sharing, 1946 to 2009	138
6.5	GWF model predictions: successes and failures	140
7.1	Consociationalism in Lebanon from the National Pact to the Ta'if Agreement	152
8.1	Power-sharing dimensions in Burundi	168

Contributors

Thibaud Bodson, PhD Candidate, Freie Universität Berlin, Germany and Hebrew University of Jerusalem, Israel.

Matthijs Bogaards, Visiting Professor, Political Science, Central European University, Hungary.

Nils-Christian Bormann, Lecturer, Politics, University of Exeter, UK.

Sumantra Bose, Professor, Department of Government, London School of Economics, UK.

Kristian Brown, Lecturer, Transitional Justice Institute, Ulster University, UK.

Siobhan Byrne, Assistant Professor, Political Science, University of Alberta, Canada.

Nic Cheeseman, Associate Professor of International Development, Birmingham University, UK.

Jon Fraenkel, Professor in Comparative Politics, Victoria University of Wellington, New Zealand.

Neophytos Loizides, Professor in International Conflict Analysis, University of Kent, UK.

Allison McCulloch, Associate Professor, Political Science, Brandon University, Canada.

Joanne McEvoy, Senior Lecturer, Department of Politics and International Relations, University of Aberdeen, UK.

John McGarry, Canada Research Chair in Nationalism and Democracy, Queen's University, Canada.

Christina Murray, Professor, Department of Public Law, University of Cape Town, South Africa, and Director of the Bingham Centre for the Rule of Law, British Institute of International and Comparative Law, London, UK.

Fionnuala Ní Aoláin, Robina Chair in Law, Public Policy, and Society at the University of Minnesota Law School, USA, and Professor of Law, Ulster University, UK.

Brendan O'Leary, Lauder Professor of Political Science, University of Pennsylvania, USA.

Stef Vandeginste, Lecturer, Institute of Development Policy and Management, University of Antwerp, Belgium.

Abbreviations

AKEL	*Anorthotikó Kómma Ergazómenou Laoú*/Progressive Party of Working People (Cyprus)
AMISOM	African Union Mission to Somalia
AV	Alternative vote
BCR	Brussels Capital Region (Belgium)
BiH	Bosnia-Herzegovina
BINUB	United Nations Integrated Office in Burundi
BNUB	United Nations Office in Burundi
CAMV	Conservative Alliance – *Matanitu Vanua* (Fiji)
CIRA	Continuity IRA (Northern Ireland)
CKRC	Constitution of Kenya Review Commission (Kenya)
CNARED	National Council for the Respect of the Arusha Agreement and the Rule of Law (Burundi)
CNDD-FDD	National Council for the Defense of Democracy – Forces for the Defense of Democracy (Burundi)
CRC	Constitutional Review Commission (Fiji)
CTP	*Cumhuriyetçi Türk Partisi*/Republican Turkish Party (Cyprus)
DFM	Deputy first minister
DIKO	*Dimokratikó Kómma*/Democratic Party (Cyprus)
DISY	*Dimokratikós Sinagermós*/Democratic Rally (Cyprus)
DPA	Dayton Peace Agreement (Bosnia-Herzegovina)
DRC	Democratic Republic of the Congo
DSG	Dutch-speaking Group (Belgium)
DUP	Democratic Unionist Party (Northern Ireland)
ECHR	European Convention on Human Rights
ECHR	European Court of Human Rights
EPR	Ethnic power relations database
EU	European Union
EUAM	European Union Administration of Mostar (Bosnia-Herzegovina)
FAP	Fijian Association Party (Fiji)
FBiH	Federation of Bosnia-Herzegovina
FLP	Fiji Labour Party (Fiji)
FM	First minister

FPTP	First-past-the-post
FRODEBU	Front for Democracy in Burundi (Burundi)
FSG	French-speaking Group (Belgium)
GWF	Geddes, Wright and Frantz database
HDZ	Croatian Democratic Union (Bosnia-Herzegovina)
HR	High Representative (Bosnia-Herzegovina)
ICC	International Criminal Court
ICTY	International Criminal Tribunal for the former Yugoslavia
IDP	Internally displaced persons
IIBRC	Interim Independent Boundaries Review Commission (Kenya)
IICD	Independent International Commission on Decommissioning (Northern Ireland)
IIEC	Interim Independent Electoral Commission (Kenya)
IMC	Implementation Monitoring Committee (Burundi)
IMC	International Monitoring Commission (Northern Ireland)
IMF	International Monetary Fund
IPTF	International Police Task Force
IRA	Provisional Irish Republican Army (Northern Ireland)
KACC	Kenyan Anti-Corruption Commission (Kenya)
KADU	Kenya African Democratic Union (Kenya)
KANU	Kenya African National Union (Kenya)
KNCHR	Kenya National Commission on Human Rights (Kenya)
LRA	Lord's Resistance Army (Uganda)
LVF	Loyalist Volunteer Force (Northern Ireland)
MDC	Movement for Democratic Change (Zimbabwe)
MEP	Member of European Parliament
MIAB	Inter-African Mission in Burundi
MLA	Member of Legislative Assembly
MP	Member of Parliament
NaRC	National Rainbow Coalition (Kenya)
NATO	North Atlantic Treaty Organization
NFP	National Federation Party (Fiji)
NGO	Non-governmental organization
NPS	National Police Service (Kenya)
NPSC	National Police Service Commission (Kenya)
NS-RzB	People's Party-Progress Through Work (Bosnia-Herzegovina)
ODM	Orange Democratic Movement (Kenya)
OFMDFM	Office of the First Minister and Deputy First Minister (Northern Ireland)
OHR	Office of the High Representative (Bosnia-Herzegovina)
ONH	Óglaigh na hÉireann (Northern Ireland)
ONUB	United Nations Operation in Burundi
OSCE	Organization for Security and Cooperation in Europe
Palipehutu-FNL	Party for the Liberation of the Hutu People – National Liberation Forces (Burundi)

xii *Abbreviations*

PANU	Party of National Unity (Fiji)
PfG	Programme for Government (Northern Ireland)
PIC	Peace Implementation Council (Bosnia-Herzegovina)
PNU	Party of National Unity (Kenya)
PR	Proportional representation
PSNI	Police Service of Northern Ireland
RHC	Red Hand Commando (Northern Ireland)
RS	Republika Srpska
RUC	Royal Ulster Constabulary (Northern Ireland)
SDA	Party of Democratic Action (Bosnia-Herzegovina)
SDL	Soqosoqo Duavata ni Lewenivanua/United Fiji Party (Fiji)
SDLP	Social Democratic and Labour Party (Northern Ireland)
SDP	Social Democratic Party (Bosnia-Herzegovina)
SPA	Sequential portfolio allocation
STV	Single transferable vote
SVT	Soqososo ni Vakavulewa ni Taukei/Fijian Political Party (Fiji)
TJ	Transitional justice
TRNC	Turkish Republic of Northern Cyprus
UBP	*Ulusal Birlik Partisi*/National Unity Party (Cyprus)
UDA	Ulster Defence Association (Northern Ireland)
UN	United Nations
UNFICYP	United Nations Peacekeeping Force in Cyprus
UNHCR	United Nations High Commissioner for Refugees
UNIFEM	United Nations Development Fund for Women
UNMiBH	United Nations Mission in Bosnia-Herzegovina
UNSC	United Nations Security Council
UNSCR	United Nations Security Council Resolution
UPNI	Unionist Party of Northern Ireland
UPRONA	Unity and National Progress (Burundi)
USAID	United States Agency for International Development
UUP	Ulster Unionist Party (Northern Ireland)
UVF	Ulster Volunteer Force (Northern Ireland)
VAT	Value-added tax
VLV	Veitokani ni Lewenivanua ni Vakarisito/Christian Democratic Alliance (Fiji)
WPS	Women, peace and security
ZANU-PF	Zimbabwe African National Union – Patriotic Front (Zimbabwe)

Introduction

Contemporary challenges to power-sharing theory and practice

Allison McCulloch

This collection investigates the empirical and normative challenges of power-sharing, an institutional design often recommended by national and international actors in war-torn and other deeply divided societies. All forms of democratic politics involve some degree of shared power, but this volume focuses on arrangements which move beyond simple majority rule towards a more inclusive form of decision-making. Power-sharing, as we understand it, relies on some form of joint political decision-making between the major ethno-political groups in divided societies. This collection considers different models of power-sharing, including consociationalism and centripetalism, and their implications for the pursuit of political stability, for effective governance and for justice and fairness.

In this introduction, I review the different institutional forms power-sharing can take, the various challenges to power-sharing as a democratic model of governance in deeply divided societies, and where the contributors to this collection stand in relation to these challenges. In taking the empirical and normative challenges to power-sharing seriously, we nonetheless argue that it is integral for building peace and consolidating democracy. As the chapters make clear, while this does not make it a panacea, there are compelling reasons to share power in deeply divided places. Our intent is to enhance our understanding of the utility of power-sharing in deeply divided societies by subjecting power-sharing theory and practice to careful analysis and critique. We focus on three overarching questions:

- Do power-sharing arrangements enhance stability, peace and cooperation in divided societies?
- Do they do so in ways that promote effective government?
- Do they do so in ways that promote justice, fairness and democracy?

Designing power-sharing

Power-sharing is, broadly speaking, committed to the representation and participation of all major ethno-political actors in key decision-making channels. Institutionally, power-sharing consists of "those rules that, in addition to defining how decisions will be made by groups within the polity, allocate decision-making rights, including access to state resources, among collectivities competing for power" (Hartzell and Hoddie 2003, 320). To assess the stability, effectiveness and fairness of power-sharing institutions, it is important to understand the range of ways by which power is shared. Caroline Hartzell and Matthew Hoddie (2003, 2007) conceptualize power-sharing along four dimensions. The political dimension "details the distribution of political power among the parties to the settlement," primarily through electoral, administrative and executive proportional representation at the centre (Hartzell and Hoddie 2003, 320) while the territorial dimension considers autonomy arrangements in either federal or regional form. Military and economic forms of power-sharing, respectively, distribute the state's coercive power and economic resources among key groups. Many of the cases considered in this volume combine certain dimensions. In Burundi, military and political power-sharing coexist; addressing the ethnic imbalance of the military, previously composed almost entirely of Tutsi, was a central component of the Arusha Accords (2000) and subsequent agreements. The political arrangement would arguably have been impossible without major security sector reforms (see Chapter 8). Similarly, in Northern Ireland, major reforms to the police, which prior to the 1998 Good Friday Agreement had been overwhelmingly Protestant, have proven vital to the pursuit of political stability and perceptions of fairness (see Chapter 10). Many political power-sharing arrangements also include a territorial dimension, such as in the Brussels Capital Region or Bosnia's entities and cantons. This volume is principally concerned with political power-sharing (i.e., the institutional rules that distribute state power and the incentives they provide for stability, effectiveness and fairness) but we nonetheless recognize that the political dimension of power-sharing intersects with and cuts across the other dimensions.

In terms of political power-sharing's institutional design, there are three further distinctions that matter: whether the agreement to share power is formal or informal, whether power is shared directly or indirectly, and whether it is based on a corporate or liberal understanding of power-sharing.

Formal vs. informal

Political institutions, which have a constraining effect on political behaviour, operate either formally or informally. Formal rules operate within official channels and are often embedded in the legal and constitutional framework of the state (Koneska 2014, 33), whereas informal rules are "created, communicated and enforced outside of official sanctioned channels" (Helmke and Levitsky 2004, 725). As with other institutional frameworks, power-sharing arrangements may be the result of formal rules, either temporary or permanent, that are constitutionally enshrined or formalized as part of a peace agreement, or they may be a matter of political conventions and other informal practices. As the case of Lebanon demonstrates, both formal and informal rules can be enduring. The National Pact, a post-independence "gentlemen's agreement" [*sic*], governed the country's politics for three decades (1943–1975). Unwritten rules dictated that the position of president, which included wide discretionary powers, would be permanently reserved for Maronite Christians while the post of prime minister was to be filled by a Sunni Muslim and the role of speaker by a Shia Muslim. Power-sharing rules, including rules on parity legislative representation between Christians and Muslims, were later formally institutionalized in the 1989 Ta'if Agreement, which ended the 15-year civil war. This reflects a larger trend to formalize power-sharing rules, particularly when they are adopted as part of a peace agreement. For more on Lebanon, see Chapter 7.

For many power-sharing advocates, such as Arend Lijphart, the preference is for informal arrangements. In a democratic setting, informal power-sharing provides a level of flexibility that allows the polity to respond to shifting demographic and voting trends. In Switzerland, the 'magic formula' for appointments to the Swiss Federal Council operates on an informal basis. Between 1959 and 2003, it divided the seven executive seats between the four main parties; the formula was later modified to accommodate shifts in voting patterns. Informal agreements also suggest the presence of mutual trust and the "spirit of accommodation" that is so important for effective power-sharing (Lijphart 1977). This was the case in the Netherlands, which, as the political salience of pillarization declined, was able to move away from consociationalism in part because the informal nature of its arrangements already suggested sufficient levels of trust and cooperation. However, informal arrangements are not always appropriate. They make it difficult for groups excluded from the initial informal pact to access political power and their 'behind-closed-doors' nature brings a lack of transparency that might facilitate corruption, clientelism and other illicit activities (Spears 2013; Koneska 2014). Moreover, because of the lack of trust that characterizes divided societies, minorities are reticent to accept informal arrangements and will use whatever bargaining power they have to push for strong guarantees and protections (see Chapter 1 on Cyprus for an example).

As power-sharing theory and practice evolve, there has been a notable shift in where the model is applied. While Switzerland and the Netherlands are plural societies, they do not exhibit the violence and fractiousness of contemporary power-sharing cases, such as Bosnia, Burundi or Lebanon. This shift implies the adoption of power-sharing, often on a coercive basis, amid conditions of a profound lack of trust or even a willingness to cooperate. Under such conditions, "there is probably no alternative to formal constitutional and legal rules to govern power-sharing and autonomy in deeply divided societies" (Lijphart 2002, 54). Moreover, how these formal and often highly contentious arrangements fare is contingent on two further distinctions in power-sharing theory: whether power is shared directly or indirectly, and whether it is premised on liberal or corporate rules.

Direct vs. indirect

Power-sharing arrangements can be designed with the direct representation and participation of all major groups in government in mind, or they may be designed indirectly by having victorious political parties seek support from across the ethno-political divide. The former arrangement is referred to as consociationalism, whereas the latter is called centripetalism or the integrative approach. Consociationalism begins from the principle of inclusivity; its ultimate goal is to ensure the widespread inclusion of all ethno-political groups in governing processes and that they are included on their own terms. This means direct political representation for all groups, regardless of whether they elect moderates or extremists to represent them. Consociationalism is a form of direct power-sharing as the groups participating in the joint decision-making process are often clearly identifiable; that is, the different groups serve as 'building blocks' in the design of political institutions.

Consociationalism is associated with four key institutions, all of which can be designed in multiple ways: executive power-sharing, proportionality, veto rights and autonomy arrangements. Executive power-sharing can function in both presidential and parliamentary systems and grand coalitions can include varying levels of group support. As Brendan O'Leary suggests, power-sharing coalitions can be complete (all major segments are included), concurrent (majority support from each segment) or weak (at least one segment has only plurality support) (O'Leary 2005, 12–13). The proportionality principle is intended to ensure the widespread inclusion of all ethno-political groups in the processes of "executive, legislative, judicial, bureaucratic, military [and] cultural power" (O'Leary 2013, 4). One mechanism for this is the use of proportional representation (PR) electoral systems. Lijphart (2008) has strongly advocated for a closed-list PR electoral system while others have advocated the single transferable vote, the electoral system used in Northern Ireland (McGarry and O'Leary 2006). In other cases, such as Bosnia, an open-list PR system is employed. Veto rights are also incredibly diverse. They can be enacted in the legislature, the executive or both; a veto may prompt an immediate suspension of the proposed legislation or it may defer the vote and refer the issue to committee for further consideration; the issue areas to which veto rights pertain may either be constitutionally prescribed or open-ended (McEvoy 2013). Autonomy provisions are often associated with territorial rules, such as pluralist federalism, but may also be implemented in non-territorial fashion through cultural autonomy arrangements in areas that relate to a group's exclusive domain, such as education and cultural affairs, regardless of where in the polity they reside (McGarry and O'Leary 2014). There is thus no singular way to design consociational institutions.

Centripetalism starts from a principle of "making moderation pay" (Horowitz 1990). It is primarily focused on forging reciprocal relations between groups by making politicians appeal across ethnic lines in order to get elected. If election is only possible by appealing for the second and lower order preference votes of different ethnic groups, then politicians, it is said, will need to present themselves as moderate and cooperative, particularly on ethnically contentious issues. While centripetalism is designed in such a way as to necessitate cross-community appeals, it does not ensure that the representatives of minority groups will actively participate in power-sharing. Minorities may exert influence on the majority through pre-election pacts, but there is no guarantee that they will help form the government post-election. To this end, power is shared only indirectly.

Centripetalism is meant to encourage electoral incentives for moderation, arenas of cross-ethnic bargaining and centrist, aggregative political parties (Reilly 2001, 11); its supporters suggest that a range of institutions can accomplish these goals, though they tend to most often recommend the use of majoritarian-preferential electoral systems, the creation of centrist coalitions of commitment, distribution requirements in presidential elections and administrative federalism. Majoritarian-preferential voting rules allow voters to rank the candidates in order of preference and require candidates to obtain 50 per cent + 1 in order to get elected. This includes, with minor variations, the alternative vote, used in Fiji's parliamentary elections between 1999 and 2006, the supplementary vote, used in Sri Lankan presidential elections since 1983, and the limited preferential vote, used in Papua New Guinea's legislative election since 2007. While there is thought to be a close connection between centripetal electoral rules and moderate parties – the electoral system will produce victorious centrist parties who form coalitions of commitment based around their shared desire for inter-ethnic cooperation – centripetalists support the creation of centrist coalitions regardless of how they come about. The point of such coalitions is to ensure that moderates prevail at the executive and legislative levels. Distribution requirements are meant to ensure that the winning candidate's support is evenly distributed across the country (e.g., in Nigeria, the winning candidate needs a plurality at the national level, as well as a minimum of 25 per cent of the popular vote in at least two-thirds of the federal states; a similar strategy has been used in Kenya: see Chapter 2). While it is difficult to share power between divided communities in a single office, it is thought that candidates will need to appeal for pan-ethnic support in order to win, thereby encouraging indirect power-sharing. Administrative federalism designs heterogeneous constituent units by cutting across group lines and dispersing power away from existing ethnic divisions. This is thought to "lower the high temperature of politics at the center by reducing the all-or-nothing nature of the stakes at that level" and to further socialize norms of inter-ethnic cooperation (Horowitz 1991, 222; 2008, 1218).

There is a long-standing debate between the advocates of direct and indirect power-sharing (McCulloch 2014). Consociationalists argue that centripetal guarantees are simply not strong enough; what groups want is to represent themselves, not to indirectly influence majority decisions. This makes centripetalism particularly difficult to adopt, as John McGarry demonstrates in Chapter 1. Both Greek Cypriots and Turkish Cypriots have strong incentives to seek direct power-sharing provisions, including bicommunal executive power-sharing and a form of bizonal federalism that avoids cutting across group lines. Moreover, the moderate parties at the centre of the centripetal model are rarely elected with sufficient support to form government and, when they are, they find it difficult to consolidate political stability, as Jon Fraenkel demonstrates in the case of Fiji, covered in Chapter 5 (see also Fraenkel and Grofman 2006). Instead, what tends to happen is that it is the majority groups which benefit most from centripetalism, whereas minority groups find it difficult to elect their own representatives (even moderate ones) and must hope that their lower order preference votes induce majority parties to treat them favourably. As O'Leary notes (2013, 36), "centripetal vote-pooling institutions unfairly privilege the majority or largest group; politicians from such groups have to pool fewer votes to win office than do politicians from smaller groups." Even if elected, centrist coalitions have to be strong enough to withstand the outbidding, opposition and potential reactionary violence of omitted extremists. As a result, consociationalists see centripetal arrangements as neither stable nor fair.

Centripetalists, in contrast, argue that consociational guarantees are too strong; as a result they entrench divisions and reward extremism. Centripetalists further claim that it is consociationalism which suffers from an adoption problem; consociational arrangements are said to be "as rare as the arctic rose" (Horowitz 2002, 197). Moreover, when adopted, as a system that requires parties to be the most vocal and robust defenders of the group cause (Mitchell *et al.* 2009), consociationalism encourages parties to adopt more extreme positions in order to retain this mantel. This culminates in what Horowitz (2014) calls the "immobilism problem." Consociationalism often leads to protracted decision-making; this can manifest at both the executive coalition-building stage and in the legislature. Voluntary inter-ethnic coalitions are difficult to form, reserved seats are difficult to fill, and such negotiations can take a long time. The legislative agenda may also be limited. As Joanne McEvoy demonstrates in Chapter 10 on Northern Ireland, policy innovation can be in short supply, as parties struggle to reach agreement on a shared future. Even if adopted, centripetalists see consociations as neither effective nor stable.

Liberal vs. corporate

This distinction, which applies to direct or consociational power-sharing, begins from the assumption that ethno-political inclusion can be facilitated in two main ways: by predetermining which groups ought to share power or by allowing groups to determine the terms of their participation. Power-sharing modelled on a logic of predetermination, what McGarry and O'Leary have called corporate consociation, "accommodates groups according to ascriptive criteria, such as ethnicity or religion" (McGarry and O'Leary 2007, 675). As a result, it privileges certain identities by guaranteeing specific proportions of power in governing institutions to specific groups, such as the requirement that Bosnia's three-person presidency contains one representative from each of the three constituent groups (Bosniaks, Bosnian Croats, Bosnian Serbs) or the use of ethnic quotas such as the 6:4 ratio of Hutu to Tutsi in Burundi's legislature.

Self-determination, or liberal consociation, "rewards whatever salient political identities emerge in democratic elections, whether these are based on ethnic or religious groups, or on subgroup or transgroup identities" (McGarry and O'Leary 2007, 675). Examples include Northern Ireland's use of sequential portfolio allocation to form its power-sharing governments, which relies on the share of legislative seats gained by parties for the distribution of cabinet positions, and

Fiji's stipulation on parties with 10 per cent of seats being able to join cabinet. These rules are discussed in Chapters 3 and 5 respectively. Under liberal consociational rules, group members are able to self-identify and are not constitutionally constrained into rigid identity categories. This ability to self-identify could potentially encourage the growth of trans- or even non-ethnic parties over time (McGarry and O'Leary 2007).

It is also possible for countries to display a mixture of liberal-corporate, indirect-direct and/or formal-informal arrangements. Fiji, for example, while typically assessed as a centripetal case due to its use of the alternative vote, displays direct power-sharing features as well. The mandatory power-sharing rule, in making no guarantees as to which parties would share power at the executive level, embodied a liberal consociational approach, whereas the reserved seats for indigenous Fijians and Indo-Fijians in the legislature reflected a corporate bias (see Chapter 5). Sometimes, a single institutional rule may embody both liberal and corporate values. In the Brussels Capital Region, voters decide whether to belong to the French-Speaking Group or the Dutch-Speaking Group (a liberal slant) but, once elected, party representatives can only sit in one of the language groups and must protect the rights and interests of that group (a corporate perspective) (see Chapter 4). The hybrid nature of many power-sharing cases speaks to Horowitz's point about the "oxymoron" of constitutional design. Because it is often difficult to reach any kind of agreement on institutional rules in deeply divided settings, "only partial measures that are doomed to fall short of the coherent package stand a real chance of adoption most of the time" (Horowitz 2000, 262). The upshot of power-sharing hybridity is that it cautions against making sweeping generalizations about the stability, effectiveness and fairness of power-sharing arrangements writ large. Instead, careful case analysis – or even single-institution analysis – is required.

Debating power-sharing

Power-sharing advocates, including many of the contributors to this volume, make the pragmatic argument that broad inclusion is needed when groups are deeply or violently divided; in such circumstances political exclusion represents too high a cost. Power-sharing is seen as a critical political strategy for dealing with protracted conflicts: conflict parties are more likely to accept settlements when they are included in power-sharing institutions (Walter 2002), and external mediators are increasingly likely to promote the adoption of power-sharing deals as a way of ending war and building peace (Vandeginste and Sriram 2011). Beyond these short-term considerations, power-sharing is believed to offer a "parity of esteem" between groups – to use the language of Northern Ireland's agreement – which suggests that the state is obliged to treat both majorities and minorities in a reasonable and respectful manner in exchange for the acceptance of the legitimacy of political institutions (Thompson 2002). Moreover, its proponents emphasize its ability to democratically accommodate linguistic, religious, ethnic and national differences. Sid Noel notes, "power-sharing mechanisms are intended to serve the dual purpose of promoting post-conflict peace building and serving as a foundation for the future growth of democratic institutions" (Noel 2005, 1). Nonetheless, power-sharing has been subject to intense scrutiny and criticism. As proponents of power-sharing, we do not shy away from these critiques.

The first line of critique is centred on the alleged inability to produce peace and stability, either through perverse incentives or through an "adoption problem." Rupert Taylor (2009) laments the "injustice" of a consociational system premised on what he sees as a kind of systemic sectarianism that only serves to entrench and exacerbate divisions, thereby denying citizens in divided societies both peace and justice. Philip Roeder and Donald Rothchild (2005, 37, 29) argue that consociational practices entail a perpetual "game of brinkmanship" and "empower ethnic elites from previously warring groups, create incentives for these elites to press radical demands once the peace is in place, and lower the costs for these elites to escalate conflict in ways that threaten democracy and peace." Dennis Tull and Andreas Mehler (2005) warn that reaching power-sharing deals which bring former combatants to power only teaches would-be insurgents that violence has its rewards. Donald Horowitz (2014) meanwhile suggests that power-sharing suffers an "adoption problem." Ethnic minorities do not want to settle for anything less than consociationalism, while ethnic majorities prefer majoritarian rules but may be willing to settle on centripetal arrangements. The intractability of positions means that any agreement may be difficult to achieve, which prolongs conflict and instability. The instability critique stems from an underlying belief that consociational power-sharing in particular simply entrenches and exacerbates divisions.

The collection begins with this important, if neglected, question of adoptability: which power-sharing institutions are likely to be agreed to in the first place? If, as Horowitz suggests, the adoption problem is "so intractable that many troubled states in need of conciliatory institutions and inclined toward democracy will have great difficulty adopting either consociational or centripetal institutions," then we might anticipate few power-sharing arrangements in practice (Horowitz 2014, 17). Yet, as this collection demonstrates, power-sharing has been adopted in settings that are both geographically and culturally diverse from one another. In Chapter 1, John McGarry offers a more nuanced assessment of the adoption problem through the lens of the protracted Cypriot peace process. His analysis, drawn from his first-hand knowledge of the UN-mediated peace process, finds that centripetal arrangements are far more difficult to adopt than consociational institutions. This has important implications for the stability, effectiveness and fairness of different power-sharing designs. As McGarry suggests in his chapter, while researchers have tended to focus on functionality, divided societies would be better served by a prior focus on adoptability. Indeed, it hardly matters whether an institution is functional if it cannot be agreed to. In Chapter 2, Nic Cheeseman and Christina Murray offer a detailed account of the temporary power-sharing provisions adopted in the wake of severe electoral violence in Kenya in 2007 and 2008, and the effect of those provisions on political stability. They find the record of temporary executive power-sharing to be mixed: while the power-sharing rules that brought the country's two major political groupings, namely the Party of National Unity and the Orange Democratic Movement, into a coalition government contributed to the cessation of short-term violence by giving both groups a stake in the system, it had an ambivalent effect on security sector reform, and had little to no impact on curtailing impunity or corruption. The temporary power-sharing arrangement also set the country on the path to a new constitution, adopted in 2010, which, while it moved away from direct power-sharing, nonetheless provides some incentives for political cooperation.

Another line of criticism focuses on the governability of power-sharing systems. Executive formation is frequently a protracted affair as parties bargain for a share of power. It can often take months – even more than a year – to agree to a cross-community coalition amenable to all sides. Bosnia, Lebanon and Belgium have all struggled with prolonged executive formation whereas executive formation in Northern Ireland benefits from the automaticity of sequential portfolio allocation (SPA) procedures. In Chapter 3, McGarry and his long-standing co-author Brendan O'Leary consider the stability and adoptability of executive power-sharing arrangements from the perspective of the consociationalism–centripetalism debate. They make the case that SPA rules have clear constitutional advantages over centripetal and other consociational coalition-building strategies. SPA rules support adoptability and functionality, and, by being "party- and ethnicity-blind," they also encourage fairness. Once formed, power-sharing coalitions also face several legislative challenges. Veto rights run the risk of thwarting the legislative agenda and bringing it to a standstill (Bieber 2005; McEvoy 2013). Even without vetoes, it is alleged that power-sharing may result in a dearth of policy innovation with parties only able to agree to lowest common denominator strategies. Particularly in its consociational guise, power-sharing has been accused of overemphasizing constitutional issues, keeping ethnonationalism alive and bread-and-butter issues off the agenda (Hulsey 2010, 1139). The effectiveness of power-sharing governance is thus called into question.

This focus on governability continues in Chapters 4 to 6, which offer detailed analyses of specific institutional rules. "Institutional design," it is noted, "is often viewed as something opaque"; as a result, greater clarity of how institutions work in practice and the impact they have on inter-ethnic relations is needed (Bieber 2012: 530). This is precisely the motivation here; the authors shed light on the intricacies of power-sharing institutions, finding that they often work in ways unanticipated during initial constitutional negotiations. In Chapter 4, Thibaud Bodson and Neophytos Loizides investigate the little-studied mechanism of protective disproportional representation in the regional power-sharing arrangement in the Brussels Capital Region. Situated within Belgium's larger consociational setting, this mechanism challenges the traditional association between consociationalism and proportionality. When a polity consists of a large majority and one or more small minorities, as is the case with Brussels' French and Dutch speakers, the proportional representation of groups may not offer sufficient protection. Disproportional representation is instead an important way to ensure that small groups "reach a level of equality with the majority or the largest group" (Lijphart 1977, 41). While Bodson and Loizides raise the question of the fairness of over-representation, they – and the Belgian Constitutional Court – ultimately contend that it is a stabilizing device whose benefit works in tandem with other power-sharing rules in Belgium as a whole.

In Chapter 5, Jon Fraenkel assesses the functionality of Fiji's mandatory executive power-sharing rules which, under the terms of the now-defunct 1997 constitution, stipulated that any party with a 10 per cent seat share was entitled to cabinet posts. The extent to which an institutional rule can facilitate stability is, of course, contingent on parties abiding by it, which did not happen in Fiji. Over the course of three election cycles, Fraenkel details how the parties circumvented the power-sharing rule, how the courts intervened to implement it, and how this contributed to the tense conditions which ultimately led to a military coup and the abrogation of the constitution. Fraenkel's chapter, in challenging both the consociationalists' and centripetalists' claim to Fiji as confirming their respective positions, is an important contribution to the power-sharing debate, particularly on mandatory power-sharing provisions.

In Chapter 6, Nils-Christian Bormann takes a large-N statistical perspective to consider whether ethnic power-sharing coalitions can hasten the transition from authoritarian to democratic decision-making. Making the distinction between representativeness (i.e., what proportion of the population shares an ethnic identity with political leaders in the coalition?) and diversity (how many ethnic groups are represented in the coalition?), his analysis suggests that, in authoritarian settings, the more representative and the more diverse a power-sharing coalition is, the more likely it is to increase prospects for democratization. Bormann's findings suggest a critical role for ethnic power-sharing not just in maintaining democracy in divided societies, but in introducing the political space for democratization in such settings in the first place.

Chapters 7 to 10 consider the values underpinning power-sharing as a whole, either in a specific polity or more broadly across divided societies. These chapters take up the question of how war and ethnic violence impact the functionality of power-sharing in the post-conflict period. In Chapter 7, Matthijs Bogaards confronts the question of whether the "new wave" of power-sharing (Taylor 2009) – cases where power-sharing is adopted as part of larger peace processes aimed at ending large-scale ethnic violence or war – operate differently from the classic cases where power-sharing was adopted in more democratic and less divided settings. In his case study of Lebanon – the only country to adopt consociationalism in both its classic and new-wave configurations – Bogaards finds that the 1989 Ta'if Agreement did not, contrary to common assumption, pick up where the National Pact (1943–1975) left off. Instead, as he details, there are significant differences between the two power-sharing periods, which fall along seven dimensions: the stakes, favourable factors, incentives, institutions, domestic actors, external actors and the role of the military. The lesson here is that the timing of power-sharing – whether it is adopted before or after war – matters for whether it contributes to stability, effectiveness and justice. Post-war power-sharing is a decidedly more difficult undertaking.

In Chapter 8, Stef Vandeginste assesses whether power-sharing is compatible with encroaching single-party government in Burundi, a country that also adopted consociationalism following war. He emphasizes several features of Burundi's political culture, including its long tradition of single-party rule, to make sense of contemporary events, including the adoption and survival of power-sharing amid ongoing insecurity and rising violence. Making the distinction between power-sharing between ethnic groups and power-sharing between former military opponents, he explains the "miraculous" survival of power-sharing in Burundi in terms of the complex confluence of the different dimensions of sharing power. The CNDD-FDD's rise to dominance and de facto authoritarian rule undermines democratization and limits opportunities for political power-sharing between former combatants. However, due to electoral rules on the ethnic diversity of political parties and ethnic quota provisions for the composition of the military, this has not yet undone the sharing of power between the country's Hutu and Tutsi communities. While peace and stability face an increasingly uncertain future in Burundi, the overlapping dimensions of power-sharing may yet prove critical to the country's restabilization.

In Chapter 9, Sumantra Bose explores the challenges of bringing power-sharing to the local level, with a nuanced case study of the divided city of Mostar, Bosnia-Herzegovina. Despite the interventions of international actors to reconfigure the city council along more integrative lines, the city remains as divided as ever. His analysis presents a stark reminder that post-war tensions play out in daily, face-to-face interactions and that the local takes on heightened salience in divided settings. While most research on power-sharing focused on its initial capacity to facilitate stability, in Chapter 10 Joanne McEvoy focuses on the medium term with an analysis of governance as performance, or how well power-sharing governments deliver on the provision of public goods. Reviewing the case of Northern Ireland, arguably the most stable 'new-wave' consociation, McEvoy highlights how power-sharing can positively influence security considerations in the post-conflict period while finding that deep divisions can still frustrate policy formulation, innovation and implementation.

As to whether power-sharing is fair, some critics have argued that power-sharing obstructs the politics of class or gender, and therefore makes it more difficult to confront these inequities. The final two chapters take up the question of how power-sharing intersects with other peacebuilding objectives, including the women, peace and security agenda and transitional justice processes in the new wave of power-sharing. Both use the lens of ethnonationalism to make sense of power-sharing's relationship to these normative ambitions. Power-sharing deals struck during a peace process are increasingly expected to entail further provisions on the establishment of human rights institutions, including protections for women's rights, as well as mechanisms designed to "undo the legacy of conflict," such as provisions on the release of political prisoners, the return of refugees, and the creation of truth and reconciliation commissions (Bell 2005, 97). A growing body of literature, discussed further in Chapter 11, examines the tensions between judicial processes, human rights and power-sharing (e.g., McCrudden and O'Leary 2013;

Bell 2013; Aroussi and Vandeginste 2013). Many scholars perceive power-sharing to be in tension with the normative pursuit of transitional justice; Vandeginste and Sriram (2011) go so far as to suggest that power-sharing and transitional justice may represent "a clash of paradigms." Part of the issue is that "those who are given the greatest benefits in power-sharing arrangements are usually those who engaged in armed violence; they are also highly likely to have engaged in human rights abuses" (Sriram 2013, 275). As a result, the protection of human rights and the prosecution of past wrongs may not receive adequate attention at the peace table. Power-sharing, it is claimed, may be required for peace but that peace comes at the cost of justice. While this may satisfice in the short term, it is unlikely to facilitate stability, effectiveness or fairness over the long term (Zahar and Sriram 2009). Vandeginste and Sriram note that there has been little attempt at the global level to either reconcile transitional justice and power-sharing, or to at least prioritize one over the other (Vandeginste and Sriram 2011, 498). Kristian Brown and Fionnuala Ní Aoláin begin this important work of reconciling the approaches in their chapter wherein they propose an agonistic approach, which highlights the complementarity of transitional justice and power-sharing practices. The agonistic approach called for by Brown and Ní Aoláin draws together the elite institutional focus of consociationalism with the narrative sensitivity of transitional justice. While recognizing that the two approaches do not always fit together neatly – indeed, as they detail, there are both positive and negative interactions between power-sharing and transitional justice – they suggest that a reorientation towards the local can facilitate the complementarity of the approaches. In so doing, they effectively challenge the position that consociationalism and transitional justice are necessarily in conflict.

Another normative line of inquiry, highlighted in Chapter 12, suggests that power-sharing scholarship sets gender aside as an identity or social location that does not motivate people in the same way as ethnonationalism does. From a feminist perspective, such thinking serves the interests of ethnicized elites while continuing to exclude women and other marginalized communities from key sites of political power (e.g., Rebouché and Fearon 2005; Deiana 2015; Ní Aoláin *et al*. 2011). By being fair to one identity grouping – ethnic and ethnonational groups – power-sharing manifests a form of unfairness for others. This also impacts upon power-sharing's ability to provide the conditions under which justice may be pursued. Siobhan Byrne and Allison McCulloch begin with the argument that the frustrating gender-blindness in power-sharing theory and practice is untenable in a context where power-sharing and gender-mainstreaming proposals, such as those at the heart of UN Security Council Resolution 1325 on Women, Peace and Security, are being applied simultaneously to conflicts around the world. To this end, they ask what would a model of consociationalism that takes gender seriously look like? While we may still be a long way off from a feminist theory of power-sharing, Byrne and McCulloch emphasize that there are several key points of alignment between the women, peace and security agenda and power-sharing theory and practice.

The allegations against power-sharing – on stability, effectiveness and justice – merit serious attention but, as John McGarry demonstrates in the Conclusion, blanket critiques of power-sharing are unsustainable. Rather, we should focus on the variables that explain the variance in power-sharing practice. He highlights four factors that account for power-sharing's mixed record: the role of external actors, provisions on security matters, the treatment of self-determination claims and the precise institutional rules in place.

By and large, our contributors support power-sharing governance, though some do so more than others. However, each takes seriously the empirical and normative challenges to power-sharing theory and practice. The collection asks the contributors to think critically about the fragilities and limitations of power-sharing along with its dividends. The collection is methodologically diverse, including single case studies, large-N statistical analysis and broad conceptual analyses. There are a number of case studies of leading consociational cases, including Bosnia-Herzegovina, Northern Ireland, Belgium, Burundi and Lebanon; for each one of these polities, however, the authors focus on less-studied features of these common cases, such as the local power-sharing arrangements in Belgium and Bosnia. Also covered are cases that have undertaken major power-sharing reforms in recent years, such as in Fiji and Kenya, and cases where power-sharing designs are being actively considered and debated as part of a larger peace process, such as in Cyprus. Finally, certain chapters assess how power-sharing intersects with some of the other normative ambitions of peacebuilding and statebuilding in divided societies, such as democratization, gender equality and transitional justice. This diversity in perspective and scope allows us to underscore the complexities and challenges of sharing power while nonetheless recognizing the import of power-sharing to stability, effectiveness and justice in deeply divided societies.

References

Aroussi, Sahla and Stef Vandeginste. 2013. "When Interests Meet Norms: The Relevance of Human Rights for Peace and Power-Sharing." *International Journal of Human Rights* 17, no. 2: 183–203.

Bell, Christine. 2005. "Women Address the Problems of Peace Agreements." In *Women, Peacemaking and Constitutions*, edited by R. Coomeraswamy and D. Fonseka. New Dehli: Women Unlimited, Transitional Justice Institute Research Paper No. 11-03.

Bell, Christine. 2013. "Power-Sharing and Human Rights Law." *International Journal of Human Rights* 17, no. 2: 204–237.

Bieber, Florian. 2005. "Power-Sharing After Yugoslavia: Functionality and Dysfunctionality of Power-Sharing Institutions in Post-War Bosnia, Macedonia, and Kosovo." In *From Power-Sharing to Democracy: Post-Conflict Institutions in Ethnically Divided Societies*, edited by Sid Noel, pp. 85–103. Montreal: McGill-Queen's University Press.

Bieber, Florian. 2012. "Reconceptualizing the Study of Power-Sharing." *Südosteuropa* 60, no. 4: 528–537.

Deiana, Maria-Adriana. 2015. "To Settle for a Gendered Peace? Spaces for Feminist Grassroots Mobilization in Northern Ireland and Bosnia-Herzegovina." *Citizenship Studies* 20, no. 1: 99–114.

Fraenkel, Jon and Bernard Grofman. 2006. "Does the Alternative Vote Foster Moderation in Ethnically Divided Societies? The Case of Fiji." *Comparative Political Studies* 39, no. 5: 623–651.

Hartzell, Caroline and Matthew Hoddie. 2003. "Institutionalizing Peace: Power Sharing and Post-Civil War Conflict Management." *American Journal of Political Science* 47, no. 2: 318–332.

Hartzell, Caroline and Matthew Hoddie. 2007. *Crafting Peace: Power-Sharing Institutions and the Negotiated Settlement of Civil Wars*. University Park: Penn State Press.

Helmke, Gretchen and Steven Levitsky. 2004. "Informal Institutions and Comparative Politics: A Research Agenda." *Perspectives on Politics* 2, no. 4: 725–740.

Horowitz, Donald L. 1990. "Making Moderation Pay: The Comparative Politics of Ethnic Conflict Management." In *Conflict and Peacemaking in Multiethnic Societies*, edited by Joseph Montville, pp. 451–475. Lexington, MA: Lexington Books.

Horowitz, Donald L. 1991. *A Democratic South Africa? Constitutional Engineering in a Divided Society*. Berkeley: University of California Press.

Horowitz, Donald L. 2000. "Constitutional Design: An Oxymoron?" In *Designing Democratic Institutions*, edited by Ian Shapiro and Stephen Macedo, pp. 117–147. New York: New York University Press.

Horowitz, Donald L. 2002. "Constitutional Design: Proposals versus Processes." In *The Architecture of Democracy: Constitutional Design, Conflict Management and Democracy*, edited by Andrew Reynolds, pp. 15–36. Oxford: Oxford University Press.

Horowitz, Donald L. 2008. "Conciliatory Institutions and Constitutional Process in Post-Conflict States." *William and Mary Law Review* 49: 1213–1248.

Horowitz, Donald L. 2014. "Ethnic Power Sharing: Three Big Problems." *Journal of Democracy* 25, no. 2: 5–20.

Hulsey, John. 2010. "'Why Did They Vote for Those Guys Again?' Challenges and Contradictions in the Promotion of Political Moderation in Postwar Bosnia and Herzegovina." *Democratization* 17, no. 6: 1132–1152.

Koneska, Cvete. 2014. *After Ethnic Conflict: Policy-Making in Post-Conflict Bosnia and Herzegovina and Macedonia*. Farnham, Surrey: Ashgate Publishing.

Lijphart, Arend. 1977. *Democracy in Plural Societies: A Comparative Exploration*. New Haven, CT: Yale University Press.

Lijphart, Arend. 2002. "The Wave of Power-Sharing Democracy." In *The Architecture of Democracy: Constitutional Design, Conflict Management and Democracy*, edited by Andrew Reynolds, pp. 37–54. Oxford: Oxford University Press.

Lijphart, Arend. 2008. *Thinking about Democracy: Power Sharing and Majority Rule in Theory and Practice*. New York: Routledge.

McCrudden, Christopher and Brendan O'Leary. 2013. *Courts and Consociations: Human Rights versus Power-Sharing*. Oxford: Oxford University Press.

McCulloch, Allison. 2013. "Does Moderation Pay? Centripetalism in Deeply Divided Societies." *Ethnopolitics* 12, no. 2: 111–132.

McCulloch, Allison. 2014. *Power-Sharing and Political Stability in Deeply Divided Societies*. London: Routledge.

McEvoy, Joanne. 2013. "'We Forbid! The Mutual Veto and Power-Sharing Democracy." In *Power-Sharing in Deeply Divided Places*, edited by Joanne McEvoy and Brendan O'Leary, pp. 232–252. Philadelphia: University of Pennsylvania Press.

McGarry, John and Brendan O'Leary. 2006. "Consociational Theory, Northern Ireland's Conflict, and its Agreement. Part One: What Consociationalists Can Learn from Northern Ireland." *Government and Opposition* 41, no. 1: 43–63.

McGarry, John and Brendan O'Leary. 2007. "Iraq's Constitution of 2005: Liberal Consociation as Political Prescription." *International Journal of Constitutional Law* 5, no. 4: 670–698.

McGarry, John and Brendan O'Leary. 2009. "Power Shared after the Death of Thousands." In *Consociational Theory: McGarry & O'Leary and the Northern Ireland Conflict*, edited by Rupert Taylor, pp. 15–84. London: Routledge.

McGarry, John and Brendan O'Leary. 2014. "Territorial Pluralism: Taxonomizing its Forms, Virtues, and Flaws." In *Assessing Territorial Pluralism*, edited by Karlo Basta, John McGarry and Richard Simeon, pp. 13–53. Vancouver: University of British Columbia Press.

Mitchell, Paul, Geoffrey Evans and Brendan O'Leary. 2009. "Extremist Outbidding in Ethnic Party Systems is not Inevitable: Tribune Parties in Northern Ireland." *Political Studies* 57, no. 2: 297–421.

Ní Aoláin, Fionnuala, Dina Francesca Haynes and Naomi Cahn. 2011. *On the Frontlines: Gender, War and the Post-Conflict Process*. Oxford: Oxford University Press.

Noel, Sid. 2005. "Introduction." In *From Power-Sharing to Democracy: Post-Conflict Institutions in Ethnically Divided Societies*, edited by Sid Noel, pp. ix–xiii. Montreal: McGill-Queen's University Press.

O'Leary, Brendan. 2005. "Debating Consociational Politics: Normative and Explanatory Arguments." In *From Power-sharing to Democracy: Post-Conflict Institutions in Ethnically Divided Societies*, edited by Sid Noel, pp. 3–43. Montreal and Kingston: McGill-Queens University Press.

O'Leary, Brendan. 2013. "Power Sharing in Deeply Divided Places: An Advocate's Introduction." In *Power Sharing in Deeply Divided Places*, edited by Joanne McEvoy and Brendan O'Leary, pp. 1–66. Philadelphia: University of Pennsylvania Press.

Rebouché, Rachel and Kate Fearon. 2005. "Overlapping Identities: Power Sharing and Women's Rights." In *Power Sharing: New Challenges for Divided Societies*, edited by Ian O'Flynn and David Russell, pp. 155–171. London: Pluto Press.

Roeder, Philip and Donal Rothchild. 2005. "Power Sharing as Impediment to Peace and Democracy." In *Sustainable Peace: Power and Democracy after Civil Wars*, edited by Donald Rothchild and Philip Roeder, pp. 29–50. Ithaca, NY: Cornell University Press.

Spears, Ian. 2013. "Africa's Informal Power-Sharing and the Prospects for Peace." *Civil Wars* 15, no. 1: 37–53.

Sriram, Chandra Lekha. 2013. "Making Rights Real: Minority and Gender Provisions and Power-Sharing Arrangements." *International Journal of Human Rights* 17, no. 2: 275–288.

Taylor, Rupert. 2009. "The Injustice of a Consociational Solution to the Northern Ireland Problem." In *Consociational Theory: McGarry & O'Leary and the Northern Ireland Conflict*, edited by Rupert Taylor, pp. 1–11. London: Routledge.

Thompson, Simon. 2002. "Parity of Esteem and the Politics of Recognition." *Contemporary Political Theory* 1, no. 2: 203–220.

Tull, Denis and Andreas Mehler. 2005. "The Hidden Costs of Power-Sharing: Reproducing Insurgent Violence in Africa." *African Affairs* 104, no. 416: 375–398.

Vandeginste, Stef and Chandra Lekha Sriram. 2011. "Power-Sharing and Transitional Justice: A Clash of Paradigms?" *Global Governance* 17, no. 4: 489–505.

Walter, Barbara. 2002. *Committing to Peace: The Successful Settlement of Civil Wars*. Princeton, NJ: Princeton University Press.

Zahar, Marie-Joëlle and Chandra Lekha Sriram. 2009. "The Perils of Power-Sharing: Africa and Beyond." *Africa Spectrum* 44, no. 3: 11–39.

1 Centripetalism, consociationalism and Cyprus

The 'adoptability' question[1]

John McGarry

Cyprus has been partitioned since 1974, and a political settlement there requires agreement between its two communities, the Greek Cypriots and Turkish Cypriots, as is acknowledged in the explicit understanding of both communities' leaders, and the United Nations. Any settlement must initially be agreed between the respective leaders and then ratified by both communities' voters in separate and simultaneous referendums (Joint Declaration 2014). This equality of veto power over a settlement exists even though the Turkish Cypriots comprise around only 20 per cent of the island's population, with the rest Greek Cypriots. The Turkish Cypriots' negotiating clout is owing to Turkey's backing of the Turkish Cypriots, and has existed since 1974, when Turkey partitioned the island, carved out a self-governing zone for the Turkish Cypriots in the north and stationed over 40,000 troops there.[2]

This chapter is concerned with the relative adoptability of two alternative models of power-sharing in Cyprus, based on centripetalism and consociationalism, respectively. The former aims to promote a politics that strengthens political moderates, seen as likely to compromise with ethnic rivals, over political hardliners, seen as likely to be intransigent, and is associated with three particular institutional forms. The first of these forms involves a presidential executive system, which centripetalists believe can produce a leader who transcends ethnicity or at least can exercise moderation on ethnic issues. The second is a 'vote-pooling' electoral system that gives moderate candidates for office an edge over their hardline rivals. The third is a particular form of federalism that seeks to "fragment" ethnic identities while promoting a more fluid form of cross-cutting politics that softens divisions (Horowitz 1990, 163–126; Horowitz 2007). Consociationalism, in contrast, focuses on collegial executives that are built around the existing leadership of ethnic communities. It champions electoral systems that permit the election of elites representing the salient political cleavages, and it supports segmental autonomy, i.e., cultural self-government for those communities that seek it. According to one leading authority, centripetalism and consociationalism are the two main forms of power-sharing, and the choice between them constitutes the "most fundamental" decision in institutional negotiations in deeply divided places (Horowitz 2002, 213).

'Adoptability' refers to the prospects of centripetal or consociational institutions being acceptable to both parties and communities in Cyprus, rather than the prospects of these institutions being 'adopted,' i.e., put in place. For power-sharing institutions to be adopted, a settlement is needed which may require agreement on additional matters not directly related to power-sharing institutions (in Cyprus's case, agreement on security and property matters). Settlements also require motivational elements that are distinct from their substantive content, such as may arise from external pressures, demographic change, economic opportunities or hurting stalemates. As has often been said of the Palestine/Israel conflict, it is possible to have a reasonable consensus on what is adoptable, but not the circumstances in which it may be adopted. But clearly adoptability is a prerequisite for adoption.

Two important caveats are necessary at the outset. First, this is a single case study, an 'N' of one. It lacks the breadth that large-N quantitative analyses or multiple case study qualitative analyses can provide. On the other hand, it provides a reasonably in-depth study of the adoptability question in a setting where two sides need to agree. While Horowitz stands out as one of the very few political scientists to have broached the adoptability question (Horowitz 2002, 2008, 2014), his treatment is general in nature, and there is as yet no focused case study on the subject. This chapter also makes arguments that are generalizable from Cyprus to all deeply conflicted places where settlements require agreement. Quantitative and other comparative scholars are invited to examine these arguments and test them in other cases.

Second, Cyprus is a partitioned polity, which currently lacks any common power-sharing institutions. Indeed, no functioning common institutions have existed in Cyprus since its consociational arrangements collapsed in December 1963, 11 years before Turkey's partition in 1974. Cyprus, in fact, is a clear example of the 'primacy' of the functionality question in academic writings: whenever Cyprus is mentioned, it is generally to illustrate the failings of consociational power-sharing once implemented (e.g., Horowitz 2014, 13; Polyviou 1975, 26). Nonetheless, there is a significant body of agreement between the two communities, and between them and the United Nations, on the sorts of institutions that are adoptable in a reunited Cyprus. There are also long-standing and clearly articulated positions from the two sides on which institutions are and are not acceptable to each of them.

This chapter proceeds by examining the position of the parties in Cyprus according to the three institutional axes identified above: (1) presidentialism vs. collegial executives; (2) electoral systems that favour moderate elites vs. those that do not; and (3) a form of federalism that fragments ethnic communities vs. a form that does not. In outlining the reasons why the parties in Cyprus adopt the positions that they do, this chapter seeks to draw lessons that may be applied elsewhere.

A presidential executive vs. a collegial executive

Donald Horowitz, the doyen of centripetal theory, prefers a presidential executive for divided polities, combined with an electoral system that requires or encourages candidates to reach out to (pool votes from) all salient communities (Horowitz 1990, 1991, 205–214; see also Brancati 2009, 16; Wimmer 2003, 122). The presidential executive he has in mind is conventional, i.e., a single-person executive comprising a strong president and a weak, dependent vice-president and cabinet. This prescription may reflect Horowitz's provenance: the USA has such a presidential executive and an electoral college that requires candidates to appeal to different regional constituencies instead of simply trying to pile up winning coalitions on head counts alone. A presidency with its state-wide campaign plus a vote-pooling electoral system is said to make possible a pan-ethnic, moderate, political leader who can build national unity and transcend his or her own ethnic affiliations (Horowitz 1991, 206–207).

A second claimed advantage of presidentialism is that it provides for a separation of powers, which makes it "impossible" for a single ethnic group to capture the state "by merely winning a majority in parliament" (Horowitz 1991, 205; 1985, 636). The separation of powers means that minorities excluded from a parliamentary majority may become part of the president's winning coalition, or vice versa: "who owns the state [under a presidential regime] is a question no longer answered simply by looking to ascriptively based parliamentary majorities" (Horowitz 1991, 206; see similar arguments in Roeder 2005). Horowitz's writings are replete with the advantages of presidential systems in Nigeria and Sri Lanka, and the multiple problems attached to parliamentary regimes throughout Africa and Asia (Horowitz 1991, 205–214; 1985, 647). They have been seen as a significant corrective to Juan Linz's influential writings on the perils of presidentialism (Elgie 2005, 110).

Consociationalists, in contrast, support collegial executives that permit power-sharing among representatives of different ethnic communities. Arend Lijphart, the leading scholar of consociational theory, supports parliamentarianism over presidentialism on the grounds that the former facilitates power-sharing coalitions of political parties that represent the polity's different communities (Lijphart 2004, 49–51). The key difficulty with presidentialism in deeply divided places, from the perspective of consociationalists, is that it is an indivisible good (see Lijphart 1977, 56–57, 170–171; Stepan *et al.* 2011). The president, even if a moderate, will represent only one community, irrespective of whatever electoral system is used. Other consociationalists have pointed out that presidentialism – an institutional arrangement whereby the executive is not responsible to the legislature – is compatible with consociationalism as long as it is 'collegial' in nature, involving multiple persons, and not the conventional or single-person presidency supported by Horowitz. Thus, collective or rotating presidencies of the sort that are found in Bosnia-Herzegovina, Switzerland and even the European Union are consistent with consociationalism (McGarry 2013).

The main difficulty with a conventional presidency in Cyprus is that it is completely unacceptable to the Turkish Cypriots. As a minority of 20 per cent in a divided polity where voters may be expected to vote ethnically, Turkish Cypriots fear that a conventional presidency would result in them being governed for the foreseeable future by a Greek Cypriot. Turkish Cypriot politicians have consistently opposed a conventional presidency whenever it has been proposed, and they have not changed their minds in spite of recent reassurances from the Orthodox Archbishop of Cyprus that if the USA can elect an African American, then why shouldn't Cypriots be able to elect a Turkish Cypriot?[3] This is possibly because it took 200 years for Americans to elect an African American to their highest office, and because it does not look likely to be a regularly recurring phenomenon. Nor are Turkish Cypriot elites persuaded by the possibility raised by centripetalists of a compensating pivotal position for Turkish Cypriots in a legislative coalition, as they plausibly believe the legislature would also be dominated by Greek Cypriots, unless there were offsetting consociational rules (quotas and minority vetoes) of which centripetalists disapprove. While centripetalists are correct that it would be 'impossible' for Greek Cypriots to capture the state under a presidential regime 'merely' by winning a parliamentary majority, the Turkish Cypriots know that the large Greek Cypriot majority would still be easily able to capture the state by winning both the legislature and presidency and by then appointing the judiciary, bureaucracy, soldiers and police.

Turkish Cypriot opposition to a conventional presidency is clear from the historical evidence. Since Cyprus gained independence in 1960, Turkish Cypriot negotiators have consistently insisted on a formally collective, or consociational, executive, although the precise type of collective executive they have sought has varied. The Turkish Cypriots strongly supported the de facto *co*-presidency created by the 1960 independence constitution. This executive is usually, and confusingly, described as presidential, because it included a (Greek Cypriot) president and (Turkish Cypriot) vice-president, and because the executive was not responsible to the legislature. But unlike in the USA, for example, the president and vice-president were independent political figures, elected separately by Greek Cypriots and Turkish Cypriots, rather than on a joint ticket. Each was mandated to appoint proportions of the cabinet from their respective communities, with the president able to appoint seven Greek Cypriots and the vice-president three Turkish Cypriots. Each was able to veto any cabinet or legislature decision on matters of foreign affairs, defence or security. One Greek Cypriot critic exaggerated when he described the 1960 executive as "vice-presidential" (Polyviou 1975, 26), but it was clearly not a conventional single-person presidency.

Following the partition of Cyprus in 1974, and during negotiations on the UN's 'Annan Plan' (2001–2004), Turkish Cypriot negotiators proposed a formal 'co-presidency' of equals (UNSC 2003, para. 81). Bargaining from a stronger position after Turkey's intervention, the Turkish Cypriots were no longer satisfied with the 'symbolic' subordination suggested by the 1960 Constitution's president/vice-president model. The emphasis on equality in a co-presidency also accorded with Turkish Cypriots' traditional view of Cyprus as a partnership between two communities, and with their then-leader Rauf Denktash's preference for a confederation of two states. In the referendum on the Annan Plan in 2004, however, Turkish Cypriot voters overwhelmingly endorsed a settlement that included a compromise option put forward by the UN in which there was to be an indirectly elected "presidential council," one-third of whose members were to be Turkish Cypriots, and which permitted a Turkish Cypriot member of the Council to be head of state/president for one-third of each term (UNSC 2003, para. 84).

The current clear preference of the Turkish Cypriot public is for a co-presidency of equals. Indeed, a 2009 poll indicates that a majority of Turkish Cypriot respondents see a presidential council, comprised equally of Turkish Cypriots and Greek Cypriots, as "absolutely essential" (Lordos et al. 2009). It is possible that, as in the 2004 referendum, Turkish Cypriots will in the future endorse a more proportionally comprised (collective or rotating) presidency; it is less likely that they will accept the 1960 model of a permanent and powerful Turkish Cypriot vice-president; and it is unthinkable that they will agree, in any realistic time horizon, to the conventional single-person presidency advocated by Horowitz.

The fact that the Turkish Cypriot minority prefers a consociational collegial executive to a centripetal conventional presidency will not surprise centripetalists. Minorities are likely to prefer consociational guarantees that put their representatives into positions of power (Horowitz 2014, 8). It is also not surprising that the Greek Cypriot majority, including their current Archbishop, have a clear preference for Horowitz's conventional single-person presidency. A former Archbishop, Makarios, who was also the Greek Cypriot political leader and president of Cyprus, proposed a single-person presidency (indeed, one that even lacked the weak vice-president associated with the US or 'conventional' model) in 1968, during the first inter-communal talks that took place in Cyprus after the breakdown of the consociational government in 1963 (Clerides 1992, 464; Pericleous 2009, 105–106; Polyviou 1980, 69). Makarios proposed this weakening of the Turkish Cypriots' position in the 1960 Constitution because the latter were seen as in a weak and isolated position, scattered in fortified enclaves throughout the island and dependent on the UN for food and other supplies.

Since Turkey's intervention in 1974, the bargaining position of the Turkish Cypriot minority has improved significantly. Turkish Cypriots, comprising one-fifth of the island's population, currently hold 36 per cent of its territory, and 60 per cent of its coastline. There is also a massive Turkish armed presence in the Turkish Cypriot part of the island, with a mere 900 UN peacekeepers separating them from the Greek Cypriots. During the partition, 160,000 Greek Cypriots, around a quarter of the total Greek Cypriot population, were forced to abandon their property in the north. Since a settlement is the only realistic way for Greek Cypriots to get some of their territory and property back, and to get Ankara's troops out, they have come to accept that any executive in a united Cyprus must be collegial or consociational. In the 'High Level Agreement' of 1977, the Greek Cypriot leader Makarios accepted that "all" the political institutions of a reunified Cyprus, including the executive, must be "bicommunal" in nature, and this has since become unquestioned orthodoxy among Greek Cypriot leaders. They have generally supported a variant of the 1960 presidential-vice-presidential model, in which a Greek Cypriot president and Turkish Cypriot vice-president would appoint a cabinet, approximately 30 per cent of which would be Turkish Cypriot, but in which there would be no presidential or vice-presidential veto (e.g., National Council 1989).[4] To address Turkish Cypriot concerns that the permanent vice-presidency of the 1960 model implies their symbolic subordination, some Greek Cypriot leaders have gone further and endorsed 'collective' and 'rotating' presidential models in which a Turkish Cypriot politician would become president of Cyprus for a set proportion of time, though not an equal proportion. In 2002/2003, Glafkos Clerides, then the Greek Cypriot leader and president of Cyprus, supported the UN's proposal for a Swiss-style presidential council in which Turkish and Greek Cypriot members would rotate as president/head of state, with the former serving for one-third of each term. When new inter-communal negotiations began in 2008, the Greek Cypriot leader and president of Cyprus, Demetris Christofias, abandoned the Annan Plan's presidential council but retained the core concept of a two-person 'rotating' presidency in which a Turkish Cypriot would hold the presidency for one-third of each term, although, as we shall see, he tied this to a particular type of electoral system. The current Greek Cypriot leader and president of Cyprus, Nicos Anastasiades, favours the 1960 president/strong vice-president model adopted by the National Council in 1989, but is under pressure from AKEL, the main Greek Cypriot opposition party, to embrace Christofias's rotating presidency.[5] No serious Greek Cypriot politician favours a conventional unicommunal presidency.

The need for a reunited Cyprus to have some form of consociational or bicommunal executive is also the clearly expressed view of the international community and the United Nations. Since the early 1960s, the UN's proposals for the island's executive have all been based on consociational principles (UNSC 2003, para. 80), and the UN's parameters have also been backed by the EU. This international consensus behind bicommunal (consociational) institutions is more a consequence of an understanding that the island's power balance calls for consociation than it is a cause of the sides' preference for consociation. The international community would likely support any arrangements acceptable to the Cypriot communities.

Electoral systems that privilege moderate politicians vs. non-discriminatory electoral systems that permit the election of ethnic elites

Centripetalism's key prescriptive institutional mechanism involves an electoral system that rewards candidates who reach out to (pool votes from) all salient ethnic communities (Horowitz 1991, 163–214; see also Brancati 2009, 16; Wimmer 2003, 122; Reilly 2006). Horowitz recommends two particular electoral systems. The first involves distributive requirements, is generally used for country-wide presidential elections and is recommended where ethnic communities are territorially concentrated. The winner must win a plurality or majority of votes overall as well as a certain modest percentage in different regions of the country. Distributive requirements are used for presidential elections in Nigeria, Kenya and Indonesia. The second electoral system is the alternative vote (AV), a majoritarian and preferential electoral system that may be used for either presidential or parliamentary elections, and which is said to encourage inter-ethnic voting in lower preferences. While AV would seem most likely to produce inter-ethnic voting in a divided polity that has multiple communities with none in a majority, Horowitz argues that it may also do so in a bipolar divided polity with a large majority community, such as Cyprus or Sri Lanka, as long as there is party proliferation in the majority group.[6] In such cases, Horowitz argues, politicians from the majority community have incentives to reach out to minority voters to defeat rivals from their own (majority) community. Vote-pooling electoral systems advantage moderates over hardliners, since the former are more likely to make appeals across ethnic lines. Such electoral systems have been described by one centripetalist as "one of the most feasible paths" to inter-group accommodation (Reilly 2001, 8). In contrast, consociational electoral systems allow ethnic politicians to win office by appealing exclusively to their own ethnic community, while not mandating such behaviour. Consociationalists aim at election results which 'represent' the divisions in the polity, and then seek to ameliorate these divisions through power-sharing among elected ethnic representatives. The most commonly preferred consociational electoral system is party-list proportional representation.

As we have seen, Horowitz recommends a conventional (single-person) presidential executive, which is not feasible in Cyprus, but his preferred electoral systems are detachable from this style of executive. In Cyprus, either of Horowitz's centripetal electoral systems could be used to elect a bicommunal (consociational-style) presidency, such as a co-presidency, a presidential council, the president/strong vice-president model of 1960, or a two-person rotating presidency, in which Greek Cypriot and Turkish Cypriot candidates would stand for office individually or on a joint ticket.

The problem is that even when used to elect a bicommunal presidential executive, neither of Horowitz's electoral systems is likely to be agreed to in Cyprus, for the same reason that his conventional presidency is unlikely to be agreed to. Both electoral systems are decisively biased in favour of the larger (Greek Cypriot) community, in a context where a balance of negotiating power between the two communities has given the smaller (Turkish Cypriot) community a veto. With Greek Cypriots comprising around 80 per cent of the electorate, either of Horowitz's electoral systems would mean that the election of the winning candidates, including the Turkish Cypriot member(s) of the bicommunal presidency, would be far more dependent on Greek Cypriot votes than on Turkish Cypriot votes. Under AV indeed, any Turkish Cypriot candidate who won 62.5 per cent of the Greek Cypriot vote (assuming a 80:20 GC/TC electorate) would be elected as the Turkish Cypriot 'representative' in the presidential team, even if that candidate received no support from Turkish Cypriots.

What if distribution requirements were used to elect the Turkish Cypriot member(s) and the Greek Cypriot member(s) of a presidential team? For instance, what if the winning candidates would have to obtain a plurality or majority in Cyprus *and* at least 20 per cent of the vote in each of the Greek Cypriot and Turkish Cypriot federal regions? This would mean that the winning Turkish Cypriot candidate would need some Turkish Cypriot votes, given that the two regions are currently ethnically homogeneous, but she or he would be more dependent on Greek Cypriot votes than on Turkish Cypriot votes to pass the twin thresholds. Moreover, if, as it is reasonable to expect, the Turkish Cypriot region was to become more heterogeneous over time,[7] the requirement of a plurality or majority throughout Cyprus as well as at least 20 per cent in each region would, like AV, allow the Turkish Cypriot candidate to be elected with little or no support from Turkish Cypriots. This possibility could be prevented by raising the distribution threshold in the Turkish Cypriot region above the percentage of Greek Cypriot voters there, but this manoeuvre would increase a problem present in every electoral system with a formal distribution requirement: it may produce no winner, unless there was a default election rule, presumably one that did not require the winning candidate to have a minimal level of support in two regions. Horowitz's electoral systems have never been put forward in negotiations in Cyprus, but whenever Greek Cypriot elites have proposed that a bicommunal presidential executive be elected by related conventional majoritarian electoral systems (i.e., by majority vote in an integrated all-island election), the Turkish Cypriots have consistently rejected these systems, and countered that each community's representatives in the presidency be elected communally (i.e., on separate electoral rolls).

Centripetalist-minded thinkers in Cyprus are perfectly well aware that any electoral system that gives the Greek Cypriot majority the dominant role in selecting the Turkish Cypriot member(s) of the presidency will be unacceptable to Turkish Cypriots, but are also unwilling to accept separate electoral rolls, since these preclude inter-ethnic voting with its anticipated advantages for moderate politicians. This has led local 'centripetalists' to propose a *sui generis* centripetal electoral system, designed to advantage moderates, but consistent with the need to win the agreement of Turkish Cypriots.[8] In this Cypriot variant of a centripetal electoral system, known locally as 'weighted cross-voting,' the key principle is that each community should have a *small* and *equal* degree of influence over the election of the other community's candidate(s). Greek Cypriots and Turkish Cypriots would each have two votes, one for a Greek Cypriot member of a two-person rotating presidency, and one for a Turkish Cypriot member. Greek Cypriot votes cast for the Turkish Cypriot position would then be 'weighted' to constitute exactly the same proportion of votes cast for the Greek Cypriot position by Turkish Cypriots. Since Turkish Cypriots comprise approximately 20 per cent of the electorate, the effect of this would be to give each community's voters an approximately 20 per cent say in the election of the other community's candidate.

Weighted cross-voting has been recommended for Cyprus since the mid-1990s by a moderate British-based NGO called the Friends of Cyprus. Its rationale, though applied to a consociational-type bicommunal presidency, is squarely centripetal: it would, in the minds of its backers, "make it advisable for politicians of both communities to appeal also to members of the other community for their votes" (Friends of Cyprus 1995). Indeed, weighted cross-voting would seem to provide something close to a 20 per cent start for moderate politicians from each community, as voters from the other community could be expected to support these moderates over hardliners. This weighted cross-voting proposal was put forward by the Greek Cypriot leader and President of Cyprus Demetris Christofias during inter-communal negotiations in 2008 to 2010 (with the stipulation that the elected Greek Cypriot, being from the larger community, would be president for two-thirds of each term, while the elected Turkish Cypriot would be president for the remaining one-third). This was accepted by Christofias's interlocutor, Mehmet Ali Talat, the Turkish Cypriot leader and president of the unrecognized Turkish Republic of Northern Cyprus, in January 2010.[9] Unfortunately for supporters of weighted cross-voting, Talat faced re-election in April 2010, before a comprehensive settlement incorporating the electoral system could be agreed on and ratified by referendums. He was defeated by Dervis Eroğlu, a hardline nationalist. Eroğlu promptly rejected the weighted cross-voting proposal and returned to his community's traditional insistence on separate electoral rolls.

How should the rise and rapid demise of this modest centripetal electoral proposal be explained? The proposal was made necessary by a balance of power between the two Cypriot communities that ruled out majoritarian electoral proposals of the sort suggested by Horowitz or previously proposed by Greek Cypriot leaders. However, as weighted cross-voting was biased in favour of moderates, to be put on the negotiating table and agreed to, it required an *intra*-communal *imbalance* of power that favoured moderates. No hardliners, after all, could be expected to favour an electoral system that made it difficult or impossible for them to be elected. This requirement was a tough one to satisfy in a deeply divided polity, as moderation is not normally plentiful in such contexts, but it was seemingly met between 2008 and 2010 when the two communities were led by Christofias and Talat. Both were communists who wanted to transcend ethnicity, and each led the most moderate major parties in their communities, AKEL and the CTP. Christofias and Talat accepted weighted cross-voting because they believed it would promote moderation in a united Cyprus, but also because they led the two parties that were most likely to benefit from it.

The problem Christofias and Talat faced was that the apparent strength of moderates within both communities that had produced an agreement on weighted cross-voting was superficial and ephemeral. This was most evident on the Turkish Cypriot side. Although Talat had been elected president of the TRNC in 2005 with 55 per cent support in the first round, economic decline and disillusionment with the pace of the inter-communal negotiations had led to his CTP receiving just 29 per cent of the vote in the TRNC parliamentary elections of 2009. In contrast, a right-wing nationalist party, the UBP, won the 2009 elections with 44 per cent of the vote, making its leader, Dervis Eroğlu, prime minister of the TRNC, while the Democratic Party, another hardline nationalist party, won 11 per cent of the vote. Effectively, although Talat was the sitting president, his moderate Turkish Cypriot party, the CTP, was in a weak minority position within the Turkish Cypriot bloc at the time cross-voting was being negotiated. Talat's endorsement of weighted cross-voting caused a predictable backlash from the UBP. Eroğlu denounced weighted cross-voting as posing an "existential threat" to Turkish Cypriots, because it raised the possibility of a Turkish Cypriot supported by Greek Cypriot votes defeating the most popular politician among Turkish Cypriots (UNFICYP Media Monitoring, 8 March 2012). Eroğlu formed an anti-weighted cross-voting pact with Serdar Denktash, the leader of the Democratic Party. This pact helped Eroğlu defeat Talat in the Turkish Cypriot presidential elections of April 2010, during which weighted cross-voting was one of the most salient election issues.

Christofias could have arguably strengthened Talat's chances of being re-elected by publicizing the progress that had been made in the closed-door negotiations, or he could have agreed to a settlement entrenching weighted cross-voting before Talat faced re-election. Instead, he opposed a proposed joint declaration with Talat, failing "to take advantage of the golden opportunity to announce progress in the negotiations" (Iacovidis 2011). He felt unable to act because he was in a relatively weak position within his own community. There was (and is) a reasonably stable three-way balance of power within the Greek Cypriot community among the left (AKEL), centre-right (DISY) and nationalist right (DIKO and an assortment of smaller parties). Christofias depended for his election as president in 2008 on the support of DIKO in the second round of a two-round run-off. In the first round, Christofias won 33 per cent of the vote, compared to 32 per cent for the hardline nationalist DIKO candidate Papadopoulos, and 33 per cent for the centre-right DISY's Kassoulides. With Papadopoulos eliminated, DIKO switched its support to Christofias, which allowed Christofias to defeat Kassoulides in the second round by 53 per cent to 47 per cent. Similarly, between 2006 and 2011, AKEL held only 18 of 56 seats (with 31 per cent of the vote) in the Republic of Cyprus (Greek Cypriot-controlled) legislature, and depended on a coalition with the hardline DIKO (11 seats and 18 per cent of the vote) for a governing majority. Christofias's intra-communal weakness, and his dependence on a nationalist coalition partner, help explain his failure to assist Talat. Following Talat's defeat, Christofias decided not to run for re-election when his term ended in 2013, his decision reinforced by a serious economic crisis. He was replaced by DISY's Nicos Anastasiades, who was also put into power with DIKO's help, and who rejects weighted cross-voting because it favours the left.[10]

The experience of Cyprus suggests that any need for agreement between majority and minority makes it difficult to find sufficient support for the majoritarian electoral rules that Horowitz proposes. The adoption of these rules would seem to require a reasonably strong majority that can act on its own, but this raises the question of why such a majority's leaders would then opt for centripetal vote pooling over straightforward majoritarianism and domination.[11] More strikingly, the Cyprus experience suggests that the adoption of an electoral system that advantages moderates needs an *intra*-communal *imbalance* of power in all relevant communities, one that favours moderates. This condition is unlikely to be common in deeply divided polities. In contrast, consociational power-sharing with its emphasis on proportionality looks feasible in a context where agreement is needed, and more feasible than centripetal power-sharing in all intra-communal power configurations except possibly those in which moderates are durably dominant on all sides.[12]

Centripetal federalism vs. consociational federalism

Centripetalism's third institutional prescription is a particular type of federation, aimed at unlocking the fluidity and "sub-ethnic and non-ethnic complexity" that Horowitz believes exists in deeply divided polities (Horowitz 2007, 961). Among the benefits of federations, Horowitz argues, is that they allow conflict to be quarantined within regions rather than infecting the whole state (as has happened with conflicts over Sharia law in Nigeria). Federations also provide a training ground for aspiring 'national' politicians to engage in ethnic bargaining at the local level, inhibit authoritarianism by dispersing power from the centre, and offer the opportunity for state-wide minorities to become regional majorities (Horowitz 1985, 1991, 2007).

The key perceived advantage of a 'centripetal federation' lies in its potential for 'fragmenting' divisive ethnic cleavages, i.e., for splitting solidary and divisive ethnic identity groups into multiple sub-ethnic and non-ethnic components (Horowitz 1985, 646; 2007, 108; see also Wippman 1998, 222–223). A centripetal federation would produce fragmentation, in Horowitz's view, because politically relevant group identities respond to a territorial context (1985, 589; 2007, 961). An ethnic group that appears monolithic in a unitary state will, when assigned territorial self-government, split into different factions, as different interests emerge on parochial issues. If the group is divided across multiple self-governing regions, its regional sub-components will come to have at least some different interests (intra-ethnic divisions), and interests in common with sub-components of other ethnic groups (cross-ethnic alliances). Horowitz imagines, for example, that regions that are resource poor or resource rich will combine across ethnic lines on grounds of economic interest (Horowitz 1985, 612; 2007, 960). Fragmentation also facilitates vote pooling, since it promotes party proliferation within ethnic communities. It helps resolve the 'domination' problem posed by large ethnic majorities by dividing the majority in question (Horowitz 1985, 597–598; 2007, 961). Overall, the multiplication of identities and fluidity induced by fragmentation is said to make less likely the stark polarization that we associate with two- or three-sided conflicts, and to reduce conflict as a whole (Horowitz 2007, 961). Given fragmentation's multiple benefits, Horowitz argues that federations should have as many regions as possible, and more regions than groups (Horowitz 2007, 964):

> [T]he more states there are, the greater will be the tendency of ethnic and sub-ethnic groups to be concerned with parochial alignments and issues, and

the greater will be their difficulty of combining across state lines to make coherent and divisive claims at the center.

(Horowitz 1985, 621)

Nigeria is offered as the prime example of (successful) centripetal federalism at work (Horowitz 1985, 602–613; 2000, 259–260). The first Nigerian republic comprised three large regions, each dominated by a particular ethnic community (Ibo, Yoruba and Hausa-Fulani), and collapsed into coups d'état and secessionist war between 1966 and 1969. The victorious federal Nigerian generals, acting like centripetalists, redivided the federation during and after the Biafran war into 12 and then 19 and eventually 36 regions, which had the effect of dividing each of the three main communities across several regions. This territorial engineering apparently made it much more difficult for the dominant Hausa-Fulani community to dominate, and opened up "considerable intra-ethnic tension" within the three large communities, particularly in the Muslim North, where the existence of one region had muted latent intra-Muslim diversity (Horowitz 1985, 605–606). Inter-ethnic politics was replaced by inter-regional politics, at least on a few all-Nigeria issues (ibid., 612). Nigeria's multiple regions promoted party proliferation, and augmented the vote-pooling incentives produced by the 1979 Constitution's centripetalist presidential electoral system (ibid., 606). The Nigerian precedent, and Horowitz's work on federalism, led one of his close academic supporters, in the context of post-invasion Iraq, to warn against a tripartite federation made up of Kurdish, Shia Arab and Sunni Arab regions, and instead to recommend a federation based on Saddam's 18 administrative provinces, or 'governorates,' the presumed effect of which would have been to subdivide each of Iraq's three large communities across multiple regions (Wimmer 2003, 124).

Consociational federalism takes a different approach. With common matters assigned to power-sharing institutions at the federal level, consociational theory calls for 'segmental autonomy' on matters that are not common. When the segments, or communities, are territorially concentrated, segmental autonomy may take the form of territorial self-government, including federalism. The emphasis in consociational theory is on autonomy for whatever durably mobilized communities or segments exist in the divided polity (Lijphart 1977, 41–42; McGarry and O'Leary 2007). Consociationalists do not advocate dividing communities into different regions as a way to build cross-cutting cleavages and promote an integrated identity. Rather, they seek to promote such an identity, usually seen as a long-term project in a deeply divided polity, through the accommodation of the polity's segments in consociational institutions.

Centripetal federalism faces a number of difficulties in Cyprus. First, there is no serious prospect of Turkish Cypriots supporting it if it involves a division of their region, and there is no plausible democratic way to impose such a division upon the Turkish Cypriots. Turkish Cypriot leaders who support a united Cyprus reluctantly acknowledge that they will have to concede a substantial part of the territory they currently control to the Greek Cypriot region in the event of a settlement, but this is not the same as being prepared to divide the Turkish Cypriot community across two or more regions. The consensus among both Turkish Cypriot and Greek Cypriot political elites is that the vast majority of Turkish Cypriots (those who are not 'original owners') living in the 'territorially adjusted' zone that would be transferred to the Greek Cypriots will relocate to the Turkish Cypriot region. No Turkish Cypriot leader has ever suggested that this truncated Turkish Cypriot region could be subdivided, whether that implies two or more regions controlled by Turkish Cypriots, or a 'third' mixed region, perhaps under federal control. There are sound administrative efficiency reasons for their outlook. After the expected territorial adjustment, the Turkish Cypriot federal region will be only around 2,700 square kilometres in size, or 29 per cent of the territory of Cyprus. It will also be small in population (c.275,000), and in GDP. It will be difficult enough, though not impossible, for the Turkish Cypriots to achieve the economies of scale needed for the efficient production of public services within a region of this size, without its further subdivision.

More importantly, the Turkish Cypriots have consistently claimed that they are a people with a right not just to self-determination, but to 'collective' self-determination. In this respect, they are like other mobilized *national* communities, such as the Kurds in Iraq, the Québécois in Canada or the Scots in Scotland. Even when the Turkish Cypriots were dispersed across Cyprus, whether in ghettos and villages during 1960 to 1963, or in the scattered enclaves of the 1963 to 1974 period, they took the view that their security and cultural reproduction depended on 'collective' leadership. During the first intercommunal negotiations that took place between 1968 and 1974, Turkish Cypriot elites never wavered from an insistence on collective autonomy, and any proposals for Turkish Cypriot 'cantons' were put forward on the condition that they would exist under the rubric of a single Turkish Cypriot authority (Michális 2009, 32; Polyviou 1980, 71–72). Since Turkey's partition of Cyprus in 1974, the Turkish Cypriots have governed an undivided territory, and cantonization is no longer attractive. The Turkish Cypriot position is now roughly analogous to that of the Kurds in Iraq in 2003, who refused to divide their autonomous region when pressed, and threatened withdrawal from constitutional negotiations, a refusal that vetoed any prospect for an Iraqi federation based on 18 governorates. Indeed, the TRNC has had none of the serious territorially based intra-ethnic divisions which marked the Kurdish self-government era between 1991 and 2003, and which partly inspired the (mistaken) belief that a cantonization of the Kurdish region was feasible (Wimmer 2003, 124).

For Turkish Cypriots to abandon their single region would be to jeopardize not just collective self-determination but also their security, and would be seen as a step backward, reviving their traumatic memories of being enclaved. It would also create barriers, though not insurmountable ones, to the secession of the Turkish Cypriots should this be seen as needed in future. Nor are Turkish Cypriots likely to be inspired by the centripetalist argument that territorial division is needed to fragment the Turkish Cypriot identity, or to strengthen the unity of Cyprus, as opinion polls make clear that the first preference of most Turkish Cypriots is for their own independent state in the north of Cyprus (Lordos *et al.* 2009, fig. 5a). Moreover, if the Turkish Cypriots were somehow to agree to the territorial division of their own entity, it is doubtful that Turkey would follow. Turkey appears to see the security of Turkish Cypriots, but also its own strategic interests, as linked to a single, defensible Turkish Cypriot region.

Even if the Turkish Cypriots will not divide their region, it would still be possible to achieve a centripetal federation in Cyprus, though perhaps not an optimal one, if the Greek Cypriots were to divide their part of the island into several regions. Horowitz, after all, is usually careful not to insist that any particular type of community (minority or majority) should have its territory divided, only that there should be as many regions as possible and more regions than ethnic groups. In principle, a division of the Greek Cypriot majority into multiple regions could fragment Greek Cypriot identities in much the same way that several English-speaking provinces in Canada or German-speaking cantons in Switzerland have developed distinct provincial and cantonal identities. Such a division could arguably promote the sorts of rotating alliances between different Greek Cypriot regions and the Turkish Cypriot region that have occurred in Canada among different English-speaking provinces and Québec or in Switzerland among different German-speaking cantons and their Francophone or Italophone counterparts. A subdivision of the Greek Cypriot region would have the additional benefit of creating a more symmetrical federation, with more proximately sized regions, as a single undivided Greek Cypriot region would be more than twice the size of the Turkish Cypriot region, as well as far richer and nearly four times more populous. As Greek Cypriots are much more interested in Cyprus's unity than the Turkish Cypriots, and as they, as a large majority, may plausibly come to see their need for 'collective' self-determination satisfied within federal institutions, it may also be thought more feasible to seek a subdivision of the Greek Cypriot region.

The difficulty here is that while Greek Cypriots are indeed champions of Cyprus's unity, persuading them to divide their region into several parts would require them to see their territorial and political cohesion as an obstacle to this unity, and the division of their territory as a solution. But that is decidedly not how Greek Cypriots explain the Cyprus problem. The obstacle to unity, in their eyes, is Turkish Cypriots' insistence on self-determination (and, behind that, Turkey's historic aggression). This worldview has been mainstream among Greek Cypriots since at least 1960, when fear of Turkish Cypriot secession informed Greek Cypriots' refusal to countenance separate Turkish Cypriot municipalities. What Greek Cypriots fear about a bizonal federation, then, is not the existence of a united Greek Cypriot region, but the existence of a Turkish Cypriot region, particularly the united, ethnically homogeneous and sealed region that many Turkish Cypriots want. Thus, when Archbishop Makarios proposed 'cantonization' immediately after the Turkish partition of 1974, he had in mind the division of the region that was to be governed by the Turkish Cypriots, while the Greek Cypriot remainder of the island would remain intact. His motive was not the goal of unlocking sub-ethnic and non-ethnic cleavages, but the Hellenocentric goal of rolling back Turkish army territorial gains, preventing a strong united Turkish Cypriot region and minimizing the prospects of secession. Makarios gave up on the idea of cantonizing Turkish Cypriots when Glafkos Clerides, his chief adviser, convinced him that it was impossible given the new inter-communal balance of power established by the Turkish invasion of 1974. Since the late 1970s, the Greek Cypriots have accepted that the united Cyprus should be 'bizonal,' with two regions administered by the Greek Cypriots and Turkish Cypriots, respectively (although there remain complex disagreements on the political rights of future Greek Cypriot residents of the Turkish Cypriot region). The Greek Cypriots' reluctance to consider internal subdivision also stems from their own regional insecurities: a significant majority in Cyprus, they are a small minority in a region dominated by Turks and, therefore, like the Turkish Cypriots, see strength in numbers and communal solidarity (Clerides 1992, 463).

A multizonal federation that divides the Greek Cypriot part of Cyprus would be very difficult to sell to Greek Cypriots unless it also divided the Turkish Cypriot region. This, unsurprisingly, is what those few Greek Cypriots who tout the centripetal benefits of multizonality recommend (Iacovidis 2011; Theophanous 2004, 148–150).[13] Among the Greek Cypriot public, federal division of the island of any kind remains a distinct second preference, with unitarism as the first preference. Greek Cypriots regularly invoke the alleged inefficiencies (dysfunctionalities) of federations, in part because they have achieved, at least until recently, significant increases in their standard of living, including a high GDP, inward investment and successful tourism, through the functionally proven structure of a unitary state.[14] From this perspective, multizonality is worse than bizonality, because it would deepen the problems and costs that arise from multiple administrations and bureaucracies. Even a single Greek Cypriot federal region would be relatively small by international standards even if much larger than the Turkish Cypriot region.

A centripetal federation, then, would seem even less feasible in Cyprus than a centripetal electoral system. Unlike weighted cross-voting, multizonality has not been proposed by a serious politician on either side since the mid-1970s.[15] As with a bicommunal consociational government, a bizonal federation, based on the two mobilized communities and in broad keeping with consociational precepts, is not just the domestically agreed basis of negotiations; it is accepted by all relevant international principals, including Turkey, Greece, the UK, the EU, the USA and the UN, and is reflected in numerous Security Council resolutions going back to UNSCR 649 (13 May 1990). The international consensus behind bizonality may not itself be an insurmountable obstacle to centripetal federalism, because most internationals would almost certainly be prepared to support change if both the Greek Cypriots and Turkish Cypriots wanted it, but there is no sign of this happening.

Tentative lessons

It is likely that the most popular lesson to be drawn from the Cyprus stalemate is one in sync with some of Horowitz's recent and more pessimistic writings, i.e., that many conflicts are intractable, with parties that may agree on some things unlikely to reach overall settlements (Horowitz 2008, 2014). That conclusion may be right, but there were important signs in 2015/2016 that Cyprus's frozen conflict may be thawing (*Guardian* 2015; *New Europe* 2016). It is also incumbent even upon pessimists to have a sense of what is adoptable in case they are wrong about Cyprus or elsewhere.

While Cyprus is but one case, its experience suggests a number of generalizable hypotheses which need to be tested more broadly. First, it appears unlikely that the rival sides in a deeply divided or partitioned polity will choose a centripetal (conventional) presidency over a collegial consociational executive whenever agreement is needed, i.e., when there is a rough equality of veto power between the negotiating parties. One response to this is that such situations are rare and that Cyprus is *sui generis*, because of the particularly strong backing Turkey provides for the Turkish Cypriot minority. But there are other cases where minorities are in much stronger positions than their numbers suggest, because of external backing and other factors, and where consociational institutions are needed, including Burundi, and, perhaps in the future, Syria and Rwanda. An equality of veto power can exist not just where a strong minority confronts a majority, but when there is a small number of communities with none in a majority (e.g., Bosnia-Herzegovina in 1995), or when there are two communities of almost equal size (e.g., Northern Ireland in 1998). There are also a range of recent cases – Afghanistan (2014–), Kenya (2008–2012) and Zimbabwe (2009–2013) – when a rough equality of veto power among conflicting elites forced them to swop conventional single-person presidencies for more collegial executives, although not for comprehensive consociations. In all of these examples, the winner-takes-all single-person presidency is an unattractive institution. In contrast, single-person presidencies seem more feasible where dominant majorities or dominant minorities (in undemocratic and authoritarian settings like Baathist Iraq and Syria, or in Paul Kagame's Rwanda) can impose their preferences, or, as in Zimbabwe after its recent experiment in power-sharing, when authoritarian leaders are able to re-establish dominance. Conventional presidencies may also be agreed to in cases where there is very significant diversity, i.e., many groups, none of them in a dominant position. In this context there is less likely to be the bipolar or tripolar antagonisms that give rise to the discriminatory governments and civil wars that make power-sharing necessary, and groups may be too small to aspire to power-sharing. There is also likely to be a natural 'rotation' of the presidency in such places.

Second, centripetal electoral systems like the alternative vote or distributive systems are unlikely to be the first preference of political minorities. This is because both electoral systems are biased in favour of majorities. It is also unclear why majority elites would opt for such electoral systems instead of straightforward majoritarian electoral systems such as the two-round run-off system that is commonly used in presidential elections.

Third, and relatedly, moderates-advantaging centripetal electoral systems are likely to be proposed in negotiations only if moderates are involved, and are likely to be agreed to only if moderates dominate all of the veto-wielding negotiating parties. The electoral systems are likely to be implemented only if these moderates remain durably dominant. As we have seen in Cyprus, a centripetal voting system was agreed to in an unusual, indeed unprecedented, set of circumstances when moderate elites were in charge of both communities, but was quickly taken off the negotiating table as soon as one of these moderates was replaced by a hardliner. Consociational electoral systems (like collegial executives) seem more likely to be adopted where agreement between sides is necessary, as they are based on the principle of proportionality. They are more likely to match the political balance of power around the negotiating table and more likely to match the need for a solution that avoids winner-takes-all.

Fourth, centripetal federalism, with its emphasis on fragmentation, looks infeasible where minorities are nationally mobilized, already enjoy collective self-government, and are capable of resisting what they will code as 'partition.' In contrast, it looks more feasible where the communities in question are not collectively (nationally) mobilized, or where such communities are too weak to resist and/or where fragmented self-government represents the most attainable advance on a centralized status quo. Majority nations may be more open to fragmentation than minority nations, as they generally have more of an interest in the construction of the state-wide political identity that fragmented federalism is intended to secure, and because they may see their right to self-determination as fulfilled within common institutions. Majorities, however, may also oppose fragmentation, as do the Greek Cypriots and the UK's English. Consociationalism can accommodate both situations where communities are collectively mobilized and where they are not, since it does not seek to fragment or force together communities, but to accommodate them as they are.

This chapter has focused on the adoptability question, but it should be noted that what is adoptable is not necessarily what is optimally functional. Bizonal federations, of the sort that Cypriots are likely to adopt, have an unhappy track record (Vile 1982), and it would be better if Cyprus had more than two communities, each of which could have their own region, if the Greek Cypriot majority divided its region into two or three, or if the two communities agreed on a shared third region like the Brussels Capital Region in Belgium. Whether or not a consociational executive is functional, and not just adoptable, is likely to depend on its institutional design, including its ability to avoid the mistakes of Cyprus's 1960 Constitution, particularly its lack of agreed deadlock-breaking mechanisms, its divisive left-over business from the 1959/1960 negotiations and its sharing of power between two monolithic and adversarial camps (see McGarry and Loizides 2015).

Conclusion

There has not been enough research in comparative politics on the adoptability question, and much more of a focus on functionality. To the extent that this has led to prescribing arguably functional solutions that are not adoptable, it is time wasted. A line of research suggested by this chapter is that it may be better to approach research from the other direction, starting with adoptability and moving to functionality. For comparativists, this would mean more research on the politics of the particular case study rather than the more common approach of importing models from other cases that may not be relevant. As Horowitz has noted, there is a domestic path-dependency in the adoptability of institutions that is resistant to new imports (Horowitz 2002). Once researchers have limited their options to the possible, there is then a better foundation for approaching the functionality question, including borrowing information from outside on how similar institutions have worked or failed. In the case of Cyprus, this involves focusing on collegial decision-making, electoral systems that both communities can live with, and how to approach and offset the difficulties attached to a bizonal federation.

Notes

1 The original version of this chapter was published in Political Studies. Available at doi: https://doi.org/10.1177/0032321716666293.
2 Turkey's backing of the Turkish Cypriots also explains the existence of strong consociational provisions in Cyprus's 1960 constitution. The Turkish Cypriots' disproportionate strength in negotiations since 1974 is analogous to that of the Tutsi of Burundi during the Arusha negotiations of 1995 to 2000. The Tutsi comprised around 15 per cent of Burundi's population, but dominated its military.
3 "Archbishop Says He Will Take Position on 2013 Presidential Elections." *Alithia*, 13 June 2011.
4 The president and vice-president would appoint the Council of Ministers conjointly, or, in the event of disagreement, the Greek Cypriot president and Turkish Cypriot vice-president would separately appoint the ministers from their respective communities.
5 "We Cannot Avoid the Rotating Presidency." *Kathimerini*, 19 July 2015.
6 Indeed, Horowitz selects 80:20, the exact demographic mix present in Cyprus (and also roughly present in Sri Lanka and Israel within its 1967 boundaries) to illustrate how vote pooling works in such scenarios (see Horowitz 1985, 630).
7 Inclusion in the European Union will likely place limits on the Turkish Cypriots' ability to keep their region mono-ethnic, unless they are able to negotiate derogations from the EU's *Acquis Communautaire*, its body of basic laws, which promote freedom of movement of people, goods, capital and services throughout the Union.
8 Weighted cross-voting ideas are described, and its supporters listed, in Loizides and Keskiner (2004).
9 The details of Christofias's proposals on weighted cross-voting and Talat's acceptance of them were reported by Talat on his Facebook account in March 2012. See the media reports in *Yeni Duzen* and *Havadis*, covered in UNFICYP Media Monitoring, 8 March 2012.
10 DISY's vice-chair at the time and current leader, Averoff Neophytou, argued that weighted cross-voting had been concocted to "keep the left governing Cyprus forever." See "Resigning is Christofias's Only Option." *Phileleftheros*, 4 September 2011.
11 Horowitz's answer is that party proliferation in the majority bloc may lead a moderate party from the majority to seek votes from the minority to defeat its hardline opponents. The difficulty with this is that if the polity was deeply divided, the moderate party would risk losing more votes among its own (larger) bloc than it would reasonably expect to win from the other (minority) bloc.

12 Consociational power-sharing is even feasible in a scenario where moderates are in leadership positions in all relevant communities, as long as the moderates do not enjoy durably and clearly dominant positions (an unlikely scenario in a deeply divided polity). This is because moderate leaders may be open to 'inclusive' consociational power-sharing, including relatively hardline parties where they see this as necessary for peace and stability, or to prevent intra-ethnic outflanking. Northern Ireland's inclusive consociational executive was proposed and agreed to in 1998 by the moderate unionist and nationalist parties, the UUP and SDLP, respectively (see McGarry and O'Leary, Chapter 3, this volume).

13 The third-placed candidate in the Republic of Cyprus presidential elections of February 2013, the hardliner George Lillikas, supports a multizonal and non-ethnic federation on the "American, Australian or German" model that would divide both the Turkish Cypriots and Greek Cypriots. See "Towards a United States of Cyprus, fuelled by Natural Gas." *Kathimerini*, 27 January 2013.

14 There have been recent setbacks as a result of the post-2008 economic crisis.

15 Lillikas (see note 13) is the only candidate for the presidency of Cyprus since the 1977 High Level Agreement to reject its stipulation that a federation be bizonal.

References

Brancati, Dawn. 2009. *Peace by Design: Managing Intrastate Conflict through Decentralization*. Oxford and New York: Oxford University Press.

Clerides, Glafkos. 1992. *My Deposition (Volume 4)*. Nicosia: Alithia Publishing.

Elgie, Robert. 2005. "From Linz to Tsebelis: Three Waves of Presidential/Parliamentary Studies?" *Democratization* 12, no. 1: 106–122.

Friends of Cyprus. 1995. *Report No. 38*. Available at www.peace-cyprus.org/FOC/ (accessed 18 February 2012).

Guardian. 2015. "Cyprus Reunification 'Within Reach,' Claims John Kerry." 4 December.

Horowitz, Donald L. 1985. *Ethnic Groups in Conflict*. Berkeley: University of California Press.

Horowitz, Donald L. 1990. "Comparing Democratic Systems." *Journal of Democracy* 1, no. 4: 73–79.

Horowitz, Donald L. 1991. *A Democratic South Africa? Constitutional Engineering in a Divided Society*. Berkeley: University of California Press.

Horowitz, Donald L. 2000. "Constitutional Design: An Oxymoron?" In *Designing Democratic Institutions*, edited by Ian Shapiro and Stephen Macedo, pp. 253–284. New York: New York University Press.

Horowitz, Donald L. 2002. "Explaining the Northern Ireland Agreement: The Sources of an Unlikely Constitutional Consensus." *British Journal of Political Science* 21: 193–220.

Horowitz, Donald L. 2007. "The Many Uses of Federalism." *Drake Law Review* 55: 953–966.

Horowitz, Donald L. 2008. "Conciliatory Institutions and Constitutional Process in Post-Conflict States." *William and Mary Law Review* 49: 1213–1248.

Horowitz, Donald L. 2014. "Ethnic Power Sharing: Three Big Problems." *Journal of Democracy* 25, no. 2: 5–20.

Iacovidis, Savvas. 2011. "What Federation for Cyprus?" Available at: www.sigmalive.com/simerini/politics/interviews/369448.

Joint Declaration. 2014. www.uncyprustalks.org/media/Good%20Offices/Photos%20For%20Main%20Articles/FEBRUARY_2014_JOINT_DECLARATION_FINAL.pdf.

Lijphart, Arend. 1969. "Consociational Democracy." *World Politics* 21, no. 2: 207–225.

Lijphart, Arend. 1977. *Democracy in Plural Societies: A Comparative Exploration*. New Haven: Yale University Press.

Lijphart, Arend. 2004. "Constitutional Design for Divided Societies. *Journal of Democracy* 15, no. 2: 96–109.

Loizides, Neophytos and Eser Keskiner. 2004. "The Aftermath of the Annan Plan Referendums: Cross-Voting Moderation for Cyprus." *Southeast European Politics* 5, nos 2–3: 158–171.

Lordos, Alexandros, Erol Kaymak and Nathalie Tocci. 2009. *A People's Peace in Cyprus: Testing Public Opinion on the Options for a Comprehensive Settlement*. Brussels: Centre for European Policy Studies.

McGarry, John. 2013. "Is Presidentialism Necessarily Non-Collegial?" *Ethnopolitics* 12, no. 1: 93–97.

McGarry, John and Neophytos Loizides. 2015. "Power-Sharing in a Re-united Cyprus: Centripetal Coalitions vs. Proportional Sequential Coalitions." *International Journal of Constitutional Law* 13, no. 4: 847–872.

McGarry, John and Brendan O'Leary. 2007. "Iraq's Constitution of 2005: Liberal Consociation as Political Prescription." *International Journal of Constitutional Law* 5, no. 4: 1–29.

Michális, Michael. 2009. *Resolving the Cyprus Conflict: Negotiating History*. New York: Palgrave Macmillan.

National Council. 1989. *Greek Cypriot Proposals*. Nicosia: National Council.

New Europe. 2016. "European Parliament President Says There is 'Hope' for a Cyprus Solution." 31 March. Available at https://neurope.eu/article/european-parliament-president-says-hope-cyprus-solution/ (accessed 31 March 2016).

Pericleous, Chrysostomos. 2009. *The Cyprus Referendum: A Divided Island and the Challenge of the Annan Plan*. London: I.B. Tauris.

Polyviou, Polyvios. 1975. *Cyprus: The Tragedy and the Challenge*. Washington, DC: The American Hellenic Institute.

Polyviou, Polyvios. 1980. *Cyprus: Conflict and Negotiations 1960–1980*. London: Duckworth.

Reilly, Benjamin. 2001. *Democracy in Divided Societies: Electoral Engineering for Conflict Management*. Cambridge: Cambridge University Press.

Reilly, Benjamin. 2006. *Democracy and Diversity: Political Engineering in the Asia-Pacific*. Oxford: Oxford University Press.

Roeder, Philip. 2005. "Power-Dividing as an Alternative to Ethnic Power-Sharing." In *Sustainable Peace: Power and Democracy after Civil Wars*, edited by Donald Rothchild and Philip Roeder, pp. 51–82. Ithaca, NY: Cornell University Press.

Stepan, Alfred, Juan Linz and Yogendra Yagav. 2011. *Crafting State-Nations: India and Other Multinational Democracies*. Baltimore, MD: Johns Hopkins University Press.

Theophanous, Andreas. 2004. *The Cyprus Question and the EU: The Challenge and the Promise*. Nicosia: Intercollege Press.

Vile, Maurice. 1982. "Federation and Confederation: The Experience of the United States and the British Commonwealth." In *Political Cooperation in Divided Societies: A Series of Papers Relevant to the Conflict in Northern Ireland*, edited by Desmond Rea, pp. 216–228. Dublin: Gill & Macmillan.

Wimmer, Andreas. 2003. "Democracy and Ethno-Religious Conflict in Iraq." *Survival* 45, no. 4: 111–134.

Wippman, David. 1998. "Practical and Legal Constraints on Internal Power-Sharing." In *International Law and Ethnic Conflict*, edited by David Wippman, pp. 211–241. Ithaca, NY: Cornell University Press.

2 Power-sharing in Kenya
Between the devil and the deep blue sea

Nic Cheeseman and Christina Murray

Introduction

Kenya's 2007 elections led to unprecedented ethnic violence in which over 1,000 people died and more than 600,000 were displaced. The crisis was resolved when the main parties agreed to a new form of power-sharing to tide the country over until new elections could be held. President Kibaki, the incumbent who was accused by his main opponent of stealing the election with the assistance of a corrupt electoral commission, agreed to share executive power with a 'prime minister' and to establish a coalition cabinet in which the positions were split equally between the two sides. Although it included an executive president and a prime minister, this model of power-sharing, soon to be followed in Zimbabwe, should not be confused with the semi-presidential systems of the Francophone world and Eastern Europe. In Kenya, executive power was not divided between an executive president, on the one hand, and a prime minister and cabinet accountable to Parliament, on the other. Instead, it involved the inclusion of a prime minister and some opposition ministers in what remained, essentially, the president's government. Moreover, the fact that this arrangement was only temporary meant that it had a limited direct impact on the way in which politics subsequently unfolded in the run-up to the next election campaign.

At the same time, the Kenyan model should not be confused with the full 'consociational' model advocated by Arend Lijphart, in which political inclusion is far-reaching and constitutionalized. The deal struck in Kenya was temporary, expiring at the end of the parliamentary term, and so failed to reduce the stakes of political competition. As we explain below, it therefore provided little incentive for the elite accommodation that we argue is necessary for long-term stability in Kenya.

What the arrangement did do was to bring the two main political parties – Mwai Kibaki's Party of National Unity (PNU) and Raila Odinga's Orange Democratic Movement (ODM) – into government. In doing so, it gave them a stake in maintaining the political system and hence demobilizing political violence. The nature of the two parties, which were in effect electoral coalitions of prominent leaders from some of the country's various ethnic groups,[1] ensured that the largest communities, such as the Kamba, Kalenjin, Kikuyu, Luhya and Luo, were all represented within the government. Although the importance of ethnicity to Kenyan politics is at times overstated, many Kenyans think and vote 'ethnically' and so the increase in political accommodation gave a degree of legitimacy to the government. It also dealt with a major criticism of the elections – that they had resulted in the exclusion of many groups that felt that it was their "turn to eat" (Branch *et al.* 2010).

The power-sharing deal ended the period of election-related political violence and Kenya remained stable up until the next general election. It also facilitated important processes of constitutional review and reform of the security forces. However, the coalition was troubled by infighting and corruption accusations throughout its five-year existence, and paved the way for the emergence of an 'anti-prosecution' alliance across party lines between leaders seeking to escape accountability for the role they played in organizing and funding the post-election violence (Lynch 2008). The emergence of this 'alliance of the accused' ensured that no domestic prosecutions of senior political leaders would take place, and also made it more difficult to tackle corruption effectively. These and other developments led to widespread rejection of any form of executive power-sharing government in the future. Instead, Kenya's leaders chose to revert to a strong system of presidential government in the new constitution. This is balanced, to some extent, by a relatively strong system of devolution that, as we explain below, has diffused political tensions at the national level. However, whether the constitutional and other institutional and political arrangements adopted during the period of power-sharing are an adequate foundation for longer term stability is not clear.

Thus, the legacy of power-sharing in Kenya is complex. On the one hand, the passage of the new constitution in 2010 represented a major achievement that many commentators doubted was possible (Kasfir 2014). On the other hand, the new arrangement did little to end Kenya's culture of impunity and created the conditions within which two of the leaders accused of committing crimes against humanity by the International Criminal Court, namely William Ruto and Uhuru Kenyatta, could not only forge a political alliance, but win the 2013 general elections and ultimately escape responsibility for the violence. The model that the Kenyans adopted may have struck some of the negotiators as the only one possible given their circumstances, but it is far from obvious that other countries should be encouraged to embrace it.

Among other things, this chapter draws upon Cheeseman's fieldwork and interviews in Kenya before, during and after the implementation of the power-sharing government and Murray's involvement in the constitution-making process.[2] It begins by setting out the historical and constitutional background to the power-sharing agreement, before explaining the roots of the 'Kenya crisis' of 2007/2008. The second part of this chapter evaluates the successes and failures of the power-sharing deal, including the 2010 Constitution, and reflects upon what lessons other countries can learn from the Kenyan experience.

Background

The 'Majimbo' constitution

Upon achieving independence in 1962, Kenya had two main political parties: the Kenya African National Union (KANU) and the Kenya African Democratic Union (KADU). The prohibition of colony-wide parties during the Mau Mau rebellion of the 1950s meant that these parties were effectively coalitions of local political bosses whose authority was rooted in a combination of anti-colonial rhetoric, personal charisma, ethnic sentiment and patron–client relations (Cheeseman 2015). Since no ethnic group represents more than 20 per cent of the population, multi-ethnic coalitions are needed to secure power. In the 1950s, KANU represented two of the larger ethnic groups upon which colonial rule had had the greatest economic impact: the Luo and the Kikuyu.

Although the Kikuyu had lost land as a result of colonial displacement, they also had greater access to missionary education and colonial jobs. Heading one of the largest ethnic groups in the country, Kikuyu leaders therefore had most to gain and least to fear from the end of colonial rule. For their part, the Luo community had emerged as one of the most educated and also occupied many colonial jobs. KANU's vision of post-colonial Kenya therefore focused on the maintenance of a strong, centralized government. By contrast, KADU represented many of the country's smaller ethnic groups (Anderson 2005). These more economically and politically marginal communities feared that the end of colonial rule might lead to domination by the Luo and Kikuyu, and so, in the negotiations for independence, they sought to persuade Britain to safeguard their interests by supporting their demands for a decentralized constitutional system.

Led by Jomo Kenyatta, KANU emerged as the most popular movement. However, the colonial regime had good reason to try to strengthen the position of KADU and, at the Lancaster House independence negotiations, an alliance of European settlers, moderate Asians and conservative African groups – who favoured a gradual transition in which they could benefit from the protection of colonial oversight – were able to push through what became known as the 'majimbo' (regionalist) constitution. This established a devolved system with provincial governments that would have enjoyed considerable control over resources. At the national level the country was to be governed by a parliamentary system, with elections on a first-past-the-post basis, mimicking the British model (Ghai and McAuslan 1970).

However, any hope that the majimbo system would check the power of the central state evaporated shortly after independence. KANU used both carrots and sticks to force KADU to dissolve itself, leading to the creation of a one-party state.[3] At the same time, Kenyatta used his legislative dominance to push through constitutional changes that removed the decentralizing aspects of the constitution, downgraded democratic institutions, and transformed him from a prime minister to a president with few checks on his authority. A form of hyper-presidentialism was the result, in which a strong presidency was grafted on to a parliamentary model. This had the effect of centralizing power and effectively eliminating the checks inherent in a parliamentary regime without adding those characteristic of a balanced presidential system. Among other things, the president enjoyed a considerable legislative role, with a cabinet that was drawn from and sat in the National Assembly, and the power to dissolve Parliament at any time. Although President Kenyatta sought initially to form a relatively ethnically inclusive government, over the next three decades the concentration of power in the executive and the marginalization of excluded groups increased steadily (Widner 1992).

The politics of participation and control

What political contestation did exist in the 1960s and 1970s largely occurred within the single party. It did not follow the cleavages that one might have expected, as KADU leaders quickly assimilated into the upper echelons of KANU. Instead, the battle within KANU was fought between its founders. On the one hand, a more economically conservative group around Kenyatta defended the status quo, concerned that redistributive politics would undermine the benefits it had accrued from control of the state. On the other hand, a left-leaning group led by the influential Luo leader Oginga Odinga and the *Mau Mau* veteran Bildad Kaggia argued for land redistribution and campaigned against inequality (Cheeseman and Larmer 2015).

During Kenyatta's time in office, the more progressive elements within KANU were gradually forced out. To avoid party dissidents, Kenyatta ruled through the Provincial Administration, the prefectural bureaucratic system established under British colonial rule. This enabled him to extend political control from the centre to the periphery while bypassing representative political institutions. At the same time, Kenyatta was careful to sustain the popular legitimacy of the regime by holding regular one-party elections that gave voters the opportunity to select their own representatives (Hyden and Leys 1972). A key feature of this system was that it channelled resources to those who supported the government and away from those who did not, generating a classic winner-takes-all model of politics.

Key positions in the state were increasingly awarded to Kikuyu figures or to those related to the president through marriage. Although Kenyatta was careful to maintain a degree of ethnic balance in the cabinet, the growing centralization of control around the president and his allies led to an increasing perception that power lay predominantly in the hands of a small Kikuyu elite. When Moi succeeded Kenyatta in 1978, he pursued a similar strategy, albeit one that became increasingly authoritarian. However, the social basis of the government shifted radically: Kenyatta's Kikuyu allies were gradually edged out, replaced by members of Moi's Kalenjin community and allied groups (Widner 1992). During both eras, the politicization of ethnicity increased, sowing the seeds of future election disputes.

Subverting democracy

By the end of the 1980s, the political landscape had shifted radically. Domestic pressure, particularly from elites who had been manoeuvred out of formal politics, had grown and, post-Cold War, the international community was less compliant. In 1991 Moi finally acceded to the removal of the 'one-party state' provision in the constitution and, in 1992, faced a multi-party election. Yet despite deep popular frustration at his rule, he proved able to retain power in the elections of 1992 and 1997 (Throup and Hornsby 1998). It was only the new presidential term limit that forced him to stand down in 2002.

Moi's electoral success owed much to four main factors. First, a consistently divided opposition enabled him to win with less than 50 per cent of the vote. Second, he resisted demands for constitutional review, so that the presidential executive remained as powerful as ever. Third, the KANU government created an atmosphere of fear that intimidated the supporters of rival parties, including the deployment of allied militias. Fourth, the international community consistently pulled its punches, worrying that declaring elections were not free and fair would trigger civil unrest and destabilize the region.

The strategies deployed by Moi in the 1990s had a profound influence on the way in which Kenyan politics evolved thereafter (Branch and Cheeseman 2009). By manipulating ethnic tensions to retain power, and creating semi-autonomous militia groups to do the state's dirty work, he laid the foundations for the ethnic clashes of 2008. The worst of the violence following Kibaki's disputed 2007 win occurred in the Rift Valley area, and was committed by the militias that Moi's government had unleashed a decade earlier. Moreover, by legitimizing his actions through the language of majimbo, invoking the principle of community-based self-government, Moi refocused attention on local struggles over land and power. The combination of an increasingly violent political system, ethnic polarization and historical grievances over the distribution of resources and government positions interacted to create a 'perfect storm' when combined with a controversial election outcome.

In part because of the poor quality of elections and the tight restrictions on political space, the demands of the opposition and civil society for fundamental constitutional change became increasingly difficult to resist. By 2001, Moi had approved an ambitious and inclusive process to review the constitution and had installed a commission to initiate it. In 2002, the Constitution of Kenya Review Commission (CKRC) produced a draft constitution that resembled a modernized version of the independence constitution. Like the independence constitution, it provided for parliamentarianism and a strong system of devolution (now to regions, districts and locations), with mechanisms to secure the equitable distribution of resources. To this it added, among other things, a strong emphasis on accountability and inclusiveness, an ambitious bill of rights, provisions to secure the independence of the judiciary and fair elections, and a set of institutions intended to protect democracy. It seems likely that KANU leaders would ultimately have sabotaged this process as they sabotaged others before it – in any case, KANU lost power at the next election (Anderson 2003).

The 'second coming'

In the knowledge that the new term limit required him to stand down in 2002, Moi began to look for a successor. His choice of Uhuru Kenyatta, son of Jomo, was designed to harness the youth vote and to demonstrate that KANU was willing to share power across ethnic lines. It proved to be a serious mistake. On the one hand, it split the governing party when other KANU leaders, frustrated at being overlooked, joined the growing ranks of the opposition. On the other, Kenyatta proved unable to mobilize adequate support even in his own Kikuyu areas because he was seen as a stooge of the Moi government and lacked the political networks to effectively mobilize the vote (Cheeseman 2010a). At the same time, a moment of opposition unity saw many of the country's most authoritative leaders coalesce behind the newly formed National Rainbow Coalition (NaRC). The sight of senior Kikuyu leaders lining up alongside high-profile figures from the Luhya and Luo community generated a sense of unity and momentum among the opposition that culminated in an embarrassing defeat for the ruling party.

Following the transfer of power, Kenyans were the most optimistic people in the world, with over 80 per cent of people believing that the next year would be better than the last. It was easy to see why (Branch and Cheeseman 2005). Moi and KANU had been replaced by a multi-ethnic alliance promising constitutional reform and an anti-corruption drive. Moreover, NaRC's leadership – President Mwai Kibaki, a Kikuyu, and Raila Odinga, the Luo son of Oginga – generated nostalgic comparisons to the initial KANU coalition. However, it was not to last. Just two years later, Kenyans were among the most pessimistic people in the world. Between these two points, the NaRC government had fragmented into its ethnic components, in large part because President Kibaki proved to be unwilling to deliver the constitutional change he had lauded in opposition, and reneged on a promise to create the post of prime minister to reward Odinga for his electoral support (Murunga and Nasong'o 2006).

The 2002 elections had interrupted the process of constitutional review. When it was revived, a 628-member National Conference debated the CKRC's draft constitution and approved a revised version. The Conference's draft was in essence the same as that of the CKRC, again parliamentary, again with strong provisions concerning devolution and inclusion. However, despite extraordinary public support for the entire process, it lacked elite agreement: the government walked out of the Conference mainly in objection to proposals concerning devolution and the format of the executive, both of which threatened to change existing power relations (Kasfir 2014). The draft that Parliament approved and that was finally put to a national referendum in 2005 had effectively been hijacked by senior Kibaki advisers. Consequently, it did little to curb the powers of the president, providing for hyper-presidentialism, and failed to offer a serious system of devolved government.

Odinga and his allies moved into opposition to campaign against the proposed draft, with resounding success. The proposed constitution was rejected in the referendum by 57 per cent of the voters. Out of this success, the Orange Democratic Movement (ODM), was born. The formation of the ODM represented another dramatic shift in ethnic political alignments. Odinga was able to knit together a diverse multi-ethnic alliance, complete with a 'pentagon' of leaders from all parts of the country within which he pitched himself as the first among equals (Cheeseman 2008). By contrast, Kibaki's alliance, now rebranded the Party of National Unity (PNU), relied disproportionately on Kikuyu support.

This set the fault lines for a bitter electoral campaign in 2007 that quickly became depicted as a contest between 'the Kikuyu' and 'the rest.' In a bid to unify his broad patchwork quilt of a coalition, push forward constitutional reform and capitalize on the 2005 'No' campaign, Odinga fell back on the call for majimbo. This represented an effective slogan because, by promising communities self-government, it represented something that everyone in his movement could support. However, for Kibaki's supporters who remembered their experiences under Moi, and the debates over the issue during the divisive 2005 referendum, majimbo bore connotations of ethnic chauvinism and ethnic cleansing. The combination of a history of winner-takes-all politics, personal rivalries and clear ethnic cleavages set the scene for 'the Kenya crisis' (Mueller 2008).

The 'Kenya crisis'

When Odinga and Kibaki went to the polls in 2007 the weaknesses of the Kenyan political system were clear. The problem was not the system for electing the legislature, although this may not have been ideal. The first-past-the-post (FPTP) system used in Kenya often exaggerates the majority of the winning party and, when KANU was in power, the gerrymandering of seats in the Rift Valley gave the ruling party a built-in advantage. However, this ceased to be significant following the NaRC victory in 2002 and the FPTP results did not represent a major deviation from what a proportional system would have delivered. Thus, despite evidence of widespread corruption in the 2007 general elections, an outcome in which the National Assembly was roughly evenly split between the two coalitions was credible enough to stand.

Instead, the problem lay in the concentration of power in the presidency, the failure of successive leaders to share power with others and the 'winner-takes-all' attitude so characteristic of a neo-patrimonial state (wa Gĩthĩnji and Holmquist 2008). Successive presidents had appointed leaders of various ethnic groups to the cabinet, but because their own communities often saw them as stooges, this did little to make minorities feel that they had a stake in the political system. At the same time, Kibaki enjoyed a vast array of powers, including the right to appoint the electoral commission and the High Court. In the build up to the 2007 election, he used these powers to pack the Commission and the bench with allies, eroding the trust of the opposition in key democratic institutions yet further. It was for this reason that Odinga and the ODM were unwilling to trust what they called "Kibaki's courts" once it became clear that the electoral process had gone horribly wrong (Branch and Cheeseman 2009).

Thus, the Kenya crisis had six different causes: three long term, two medium term and one short term. First, the combination of political exclusion and a history of winner-takes-all politics meant that no leaders or communities trusted their rivals to look after their interests in the case of electoral defeat. Second, decades of experience had taught Kenyan leaders that political institutions would not deliver fair outcomes. Third, historical grievances and mistrust between rival communities had been stoked by land struggles and the strategies used by Moi to retain power in the 1990s. Fourth, the shifting nature of political alliances meant that many of the figures who had allegedly organized the violence of the 1990s in the Rift Valley, such as William Ruto, had left the government and were now part of the opposition. Fifth, the nature of the 2007 contest, which pitted a Luo leader against a Kikuyu, and came to be interpreted as a contest between the 'haves' (represented by the Kikuyu) and the 'have nots' (represented by the Luhya, Luo and others), increased the stakes of the election. Finally, the poor performance of the Electoral Commission, and the fact that Kibaki was eventually declared the winner although Odinga had led in the opinion polls and the early results, was the short-term trigger that catalyzed these overlapping factors into an explosion of political unrest (Throup 2008).

The violence unfolded in a series of iterations. Once Kibaki was hastily sworn in, opposition supporters targeted communities that were assumed to have voted for the president, such as the Kikuyu. In response, state police repressed protests and attacked Odinga supporters, including members of the Luo and Kalenjin communities, while groups allied to senior Kikuyu leaders committed revenge attacks. By this point, a generalized atmosphere of fear and instability had gripped the country, which did not end until the relevant parties signed the power-sharing agreement on 28 February 2007. Exactly what proportion of the violence was premeditated is difficult to discern, but it is worth noting that far more Kenyans were displaced (around 600,000) than were killed (just over 1,000). This suggests that land capture and not killing political rivals was a key motivation in many areas. At the same time, the Waki Commission set up to investigate the clashes found that around one-third of those who died did so at the hands of the police, not other civilians (Waki Commission 2008). Similarly, the subsequent International Criminal Court proceedings against Ruto and Kenyatta presented considerable evidence of elite orchestration. Taken together, these factors suggest that the proportion of truly spontaneous violence that occurred between individuals from different ethnic groups may have been relatively low. If this is true, it demonstrates the centrality of inter-elite accommodation to political stability in Kenya (Branch and Cheeseman 2009).

The power-sharing agreement

The mediation of the crisis in 2007/2008 has been well documented (e.g., Cohen 2008; Lindenmayer and Kaye 2008; Juma 2009; Griffiths 2009). In summary, following a regional initiative that contained the violence temporarily, Kofi Annan arrived in Nairobi to head the group of eminent Africans who were to carry the process further in an African Union-mandated process. Exercising considerable persistence, Annan's team persuaded the principals, Kibaki and Odinga, to call for an end to the violence and to enter into an executive power-sharing agreement.

The mediation agenda was agreed relatively quickly. It was headed by three urgent items: the violence and breaches of rights (Agenda One), the humanitarian crisis (Agenda Two) and the political crisis (Agenda Three). Agenda Item Four balanced these short-term concerns with a list of longer term problems such as constitutional and land reform, on which proposals were to be made within a year. While Agenda Items One to Three were critical in bringing the violence to a timely end, the matters listed under Agenda Item Four were considered key to future stability.

By 14 February, an initial agreement reflecting significant concessions on both sides had been reached. Most importantly, instead of revisiting the election results or running new elections, an independent commission of Kenyan and non-Kenyan electoral experts would investigate the 2007 elections. On 28 February, the resolution of the interim governance arrangement was captured in an agreement headed "Acting Together for Kenya: Agreement on the Principles of Partnership of the Coalition Government," and signed by Odinga and Kibaki. The Agreement purported to reflect consensus on a short-term Grand Coalition government, a 'holding operation,' to last until the next general elections. It speaks of power-sharing and, in the preamble, the signatories boldly assert: "As partners in a coalition government we commit ourselves to work together in good faith as true partners, through constant consultation and willingness to compromise." News of the deal led to a global sigh of relief and celebration in Kenya, but well-grounded concerns remained. Domestically, the agreement was widely criticized both for compromising democracy – by enabling Kibaki to stay in power – and, more seriously given the context, for its vagueness. As soon became apparent, this reflected very limited consensus between the parties, a lack of goodwill and the refusal of the Kibaki camp to make genuine concessions. In turn, the combination of a flimsy deal and limited commitment to power-sharing heralded difficult years ahead.

The inclusive arrangements in the agreement were relatively narrow, restricted to executive power-sharing.[4] No other elements of a consociational model were included. Instead, broader elite accommodation and consideration of other mechanisms that are often argued to be necessary for long-term stability in divided societies such as devolution (segmental autonomy in the language of consociationalists) and a fairer distribution of resources and positions in the public sector was left to the constitution-making process to be set up under Agenda Item Four. Moreover, the provisions on executive power-sharing were themselves sparse. The deal involved the now-familiar device of creating space in a presidential system for a prime minister who is given some executive authority. As noted above, this did not follow a 'semi-presidential' format, with the prime minister elected by, and accountable to, the legislature. Instead, Mwai Kibaki remained president and a new post of prime minister was created for

Odinga absent any broader constitutional changes to set out the distribution of power between the two positions.

Thus, although Odinga was granted the right "to co-ordinate and supervise the execution of the Government, including those of Ministries," his authority rested on shaky foundations that reflected the PNU's determination not to create an "executive prime minister."[5] The decision to establish a prime minister whose role was primarily to assist the president, rather than to operate as an equal to the head of state, is reflected in the amendment to Article 17 of the 1963 Constitution intended to secure the arrangement. The text accommodated the new composition of the cabinet but retained in clause (2) the old description of the function of the cabinet (now including the prime minister), which was to "aid and advise the President in the government of Kenya." On this basis, the PNU soon argued that, in the absence of clear language suggesting anything else, "[u]nder both the Accord and the Constitution, the coalition government must be based on the principle that the President holds ultimate executive authority and presides over one government" (Kibwana 2008).

In addition to the creation of the position of prime minister, each side was to appoint a deputy prime minister. These leadership positions were secured under the Agreement: as long as the power-sharing arrangement was in place, only Parliament, by an absolute majority of its members, could remove the new prime minister and deputy prime ministers. The arrangements for the rest of the cabinet were less secure. It was to be constituted in a manner that "*at all times*" reflected the representation of each party in Parliament and took account of "portfolio balance." Ministers and assistant ministers were to be chosen by leaders of the parties to the Agreement but, for later replacements to these positions, the president appeared to have something close to a veto.[6] Moreover, despite the notorious fluidity of political party formations, there was no mechanism for discouraging ministers and MPs from deserting their leaders. However, while dismissal of ministers and assistant ministers was in the hands of the president, it did require the written consent of the leader of his or her party (National Accord and Reconciliation Act Art 4(5)). Thus, although the Agreement described the arrangement as a 'coalition' and partnership, it did little to translate this into reality other than creating positions for people from the opposition. Indeed, on a number of occasions, decisions made by Odinga were overruled by Kibaki, and, despite the clear language in the amended constitution, some PNU leaders even argued that the president retained the right to dismiss the prime minister should he so wish. Moreover, in reality PNU-allied leaders held two-thirds of the executive positions,[7] as Kalonzo Musyoka, the vice-president and leader of ODM-K – a splinter party formed after Musyoka had failed to secure the ODM presidential nomination – promised his loyalty to the president in return for his unexpected promotion (Cheeseman 2008).

Moreover, although the power-sharing arrangement was intended to continue until the next elections, Clause 6 provided for its earlier dissolution on agreement of the parties or if one party withdrew. As a Kenyan scholar put it, if the ODM were to walk out "the coalition will collapse but not government" (Gekara and Kumba 2010). The overall imbalance was reflected in the fact that President Kibaki signed the Agreement on behalf of 'the government' and the PNU, while Odinga signed only as the ODM. This generated a number of further criticisms of the deal. First, by fixing the positions of prime minister and deputy prime minister in stone, it undermined legislative oversight, and so further weakened democratic accountability. Second, by linking the holding of posts to the status of the power-sharing government, it 'locked in' opposition leaders, who could not leave the unity government for fear of losing their posts because the agreement contained no provisions for renegotiating the terms of the deal in the event of a government breakdown. Combined with Kibaki's retention of the presidency, this oversight effectively empowered the PNU to make life difficult for the ODM, safe in the knowledge that only the opposition stood to lose if the coalition government collapsed. Third, the legal framework developed around the deal clearly protected the interests of President Kibaki at the expense of Odinga and the ODM. As a number of commentators noted, this meant that under the power-sharing arrangement power was not really shared at all.

More practically, neither the brief National Accord and Reconciliation Act nor the Constitutional Amendment that followed it contained any provisions to establish or facilitate future decision-making in the 'coalition' (Cheeseman 2015). For instance, no mechanism for allocating cabinet portfolios was included; no decision-making procedures or mechanisms for resolving deadlocks were agreed; and nothing was said about the senior departmental appointments or appointments to most other public positions. A secondary coalition agreement, setting out shared goals of the government, decision-making procedures including structured consultations between coalition members and other practical arrangements, might have eased matters later on. However, although a Kenyan participant in the negotiations proposed one, neither side was prepared to sign on (information from a member of Kofi Annan's team).

The ODM did secure influence in the composition of seven commissions and a special court established as part of the overall package of agreements. First, with the exception of the Interim Independent Electoral Commission (IIEC) and the Interim Independent Boundaries Review Commission (IIBRC), each of these bodies included foreigners, an arrangement intended to ensure impartiality and objectivity and that ethnic politics were not played out again in their deliberations. Second, the National Assembly, in which the ODM was strongly represented, had most say in the appointments.[8] ODM influence is also evident in the constitutional amendment that required a replacement constitution to be approved in a referendum and that also tightened up the process of parliamentary approval (Constitution Article 47 A).

The first sitting of Parliament after the Agreement was signed offered an early indication of the weakness of the partnership. Kibaki's PNU occupied the traditional 'government' seats to the right of the speaker. Their coalition partners, the ODM, including Raila Odinga, sat across the floor, capturing, for the nation to see, the traditional antagonism between government and opposition. Shortly after this, an acrimonious protocol dispute erupted publicly when the vice-president was placed second to the president with Odinga third, again undermining Odinga's assertion that the Partnership Agreement had created an equal partnership, and sending strong signals that President Kibaki considered himself to be in charge.

It took six weeks of haggling, considerable international pressure, a drop in the value of the Kenyan Shilling and a fresh wave of protests in the streets before the membership of the coalition cabinet was settled. However, the division of portfolios that was announced hardly achieved the 'portfolio balance' required by the agreement. Instead, it favoured the president's party and those allied to it. Broadly speaking, a balance of portfolios would usually see both of those positions that have political and coordination authority and those that have spending power shared. Examples of the former include the ministries of finance, foreign affairs and the interior (defence), and, of course, the presidency (Cheeseman and Tendi 2010). These positions are significant in that the individuals and parties that hold them are able to determine the core pillars of government policy and, via the control of both the purse and the sword, constrain or open the space for political debate and the opportunities for opposition parties. Examples of the spending portfolios include the ministries for education, health and roads. Those in charge of these ministries can control the location of spending, through which they can reward their supporters and construct patron–client relations. However, they must operate within limits set by those who control the political and coordination ministries.

Instead of a balanced outcome, the intransigence of President Kibaki and the hardliners that formed a core part of his team ensured that the most significant political and coordination ministries were retained for his allies. Indeed, Kibaki had already publicly announced 17 ministers before the power-sharing agreement was sealed (Reuters 2008). Thus, the PNU held the ministries of finance, foreign affairs and the interior. Odinga's ODM had to be content with the 'spending ministries,' which it accepted in the hope that it could use these positions to deliver services and generate funds for future election contests, thus leveraging the power-sharing deal to increase its prospects of victory in 2013 – although this hope proved to be overly optimistic.

The 'deal' was ostensibly sweetened by an agreement that if Kibaki's side held the position of minister, the positions of deputy minister and permanent secretary would go to the other side and vice versa. This arrangement (like that in South Africa 15 years before) was a potential basis for working in partnership and greater openness, but instead it often resulted in disputes and dysfunctionality. Moreover, the need to accommodate leaders from both sides led to a hugely bloated and expensive cabinet with 40 ministers and 50 deputies (see Table 2.1). As part of this process, many existing ministries were split and, as with other executive matters, it was Kibaki who decided what departments fell under which new ministry. The one major positive outcome from the negotiations was that the inclusion of both coalitions ensured that leaders from all of the country's main ethnic groups were represented at cabinet level, albeit not all in positions of equal significance.

Table 2.1 Distribution of ministers and assistant minister under power-sharing in Kenya

Party	Ministers		Assistant ministers	
	N	%	N	%
ODM	20	50	22	44
PNU	14	35	11	22
ODM-K	3	7.5	3	6
NARC-K	1	2.5	2	4
Others	2	5	12	24
Total	40	100	50	100

Source: Horowitz (2008).

The mediators had attempted to include a formal monitoring mechanism in the Agreement but neither side took up the idea. Instead, the Annan team established an external monitoring project, commissioned a Kenyan consultancy firm to report on progress on a quarterly basis and regularly reconvened in Nairobi to engage with the parties to the agreement, civil society and other actors on the implementation of the Agreement. Despite the initial antipathy of the parties, the monitoring process influenced the Serena Dialogues – the meetings of the four ministers from each side mandated to deal with matters arising from the Accord. According to participants, the progress reports kept the Dialogues focused and increased pressure on them to find solutions to the policy gridlock and political disputes that characterized coalition relations (Schreiber 2016, 20). Nonetheless, problems in the coalition are referred to in every report of the monitoring project, starting in 2009 with the simple statement that "[t]he coalition government lacks cohesion. The dominant perception is that there are 'two-governments-in-one'" (Kenya National Dialogue and Reconciliation Monitoring Project 2009).

More dramatically, *The Economist* (2009) referred to "feuding ministers" in a "crumbling government" and the *New York Times* described a dispute between the president and prime minister in February 2010 as a "poisonous, seemingly ego-driven standoff" (Gettleman 2010b). Senior appointments and corruption scandals caused continuous disputes (Gettleman 2010a; Mathenge 2012). Later in the term, among other things, International Criminal Court charges against senior members of both parties, disagreement about implementing the 2010 Constitution and the lack of agreement about the election date exacerbated tensions yet further. The constant squabbling between the coalition partners affected the attitude of Kenyans to the government. Although most people recognized that the coalition had brought peace, Juma reports that, by March 2009, opinion polls put confidence in the Government of National Unity at less than 15 per cent (Juma 2009, 425).

The acrimonious coalition relationships that dismayed Kenyans and presumably disappointed the mediation team were not unexpected. Political and social divisions in Kenya are deep. Moreover, the power wielded by

President Kibaki simply by virtue of remaining in office was unlikely to be radically modified by any deal, even a high-profile one. However, a more specific and tighter agreement may have eased matters. The question then is why was the power-sharing agreement so slanted to the PNU, and why did it lack detail? The answer lies in the balance of power at the time of the negotiations. Kofi Annan's own account is revealing. He suggests that a subordinate role in government for Odinga and the ODM was all that the PNU was prepared to concede. Using the word "supervise" to describe the prime minister's role provided the key to reaching agreement because it avoided saying outright that there would be an executive prime minister. However, in Annan's view and presumably that of the ODM, it was acceptable because it also expanded the powers of the prime minister over the cabinet beyond those that the PNU was initially prepared to accept.

Ultimately, it was President Kikwete of Tanzania who persuaded Kibaki that power-sharing under these conditions would be acceptable, arguing that the prime minister would have less power than in Tanzania (Griffiths 2009). The analogy is surprising. Unlike Kenya, Tanzania is a one-party dominant system, which means that the Tanzanian prime minister is completely under the control of the president. Although President Kibaki must have realized that the arrangement would work rather differently at home where the ODM was much stronger in Parliament, the model was apparently reassuring. For its part, the ODM was under huge pressure not to be cast as the spoiler, while its slight majority in Parliament offered it some protection against presidential excess.

The performance of power-sharing

The power-sharing deal had both short- and long-term aims. In the short term, it was intended to end the violence. In turn, it was hoped that an end to the conflict would lead to an immediate improvement in the economic situation, create a degree of political stability and, for some, also create the conditions for the longer term elite accommodation that appeared to be necessary for ongoing stability and development. Opposition supporters hoped that this would include the reform of the security forces, which were implicated in some of the post-election violence, and a national debate on the appropriate distribution of wealth and resources to reduce the level of regional inequality. For their part, civil society groups argued that the most important challenges included restoring the public's faith in key political institutions and reducing corruption. Thus Agenda Item Four expressed commitment to the following:

> 1) undertaking constitutional, legal and institutional reform; 2) tackling poverty and inequity, as well as combating regional development imbalances; 3) tackling unemployment, particularly among the youth; 4) consolidating national cohesion and unity; 5) undertaking land reform; and 6) addressing transparency, accountability and impunity.
>
> (Annotated Agenda)

Evaluating the performance of power-sharing against these complex goals is challenging because of their breadth. Even an extremely successful and effective period of power-sharing in a highly democratic and functional state could not have dealt with all of the major issues in just one parliamentary term. We therefore focus our analysis on three of the most significant long-term goals: the drafting of a new constitution, ending the culture of impunity and the reform of the security forces.

Before we move to these issues, however, a comment on the impact of the power-sharing arrangement on day-to-day politics in Kenya and on its political evolution is necessary. It is clear that the period of power-sharing was successful in a number of important ways, leading to a period of political stability and ushering in a new and much improved constitution. It also had an immediate and positive impact upon security and the economy. Almost as soon as it was signed, the ethnic clashes ceased and the country quickly moved into a period of uneasy peace. In the four years to the next general elections, there was no significant episode of inter-ethnic violence related to the 2007 elections. Moreover, despite constant rumours that it was on the brink of collapse, the power-sharing government itself survived intact, providing some much-needed political stability as the country began the difficult task of national reconciliation. This had a positive impact upon the state of the economy. Economic growth fell from over 7.1 per cent in 2007 to 1.6 per cent in 2008, but rebounded to 2.6 per cent in 2009 and had recovered to more than 6 per cent by the end of the power-sharing period as business confidence strengthened.

However, power-sharing was also problematic because it blunted the capacity for political competition to act as the motor of democratic reform (Cheeseman 2015, Conclusion). Towards the end of Moi's presidency and during President Kibaki's first term in office, opposition legislators successfully campaigned to free Parliament from its financial dependence on the executive, and used their powers of scrutiny to expose government abuses. These reforms only scratched the surface of the corruption at the heart of Kenyan politics, but they did suggest that those in power would have to be more careful in the future. However, following the creation of the power-sharing administration in which everyone was formally in government, there were no parties to play this role. One reason for this was the remarkable fluidity of Kenyan politics, which led to the rapid breakdown of party identities. This had both positive and negative consequences. On the positive side, Kibaki and Odinga were able to put aside their differences to briefly share a platform in support of a new constitution that significantly reduced the powers of the president.

On the negative side, by incorporating the opposition in government, power-sharing also exacerbated the tendency for Kenyan politicians to protect their own interests at the expense of the public (Cheeseman and Tendi 2010). As we explain further below, because representatives from both of the main parties were implicated in the post-election violence, a broad range of MPs had an interest in maintaining the country's culture of impunity. Most notably, in the shadows of the power-sharing deal, two leaders who feared that they would be prosecuted for their role in the clashes, namely PNU leader Uhuru Kenyatta and ODM leader William Ruto, formed an anti-reform alliance. Thus while the two parties traded accusations of corruption, little was actually done to hold ministers to account. Instead, Kenyatta and Ruto marshalled MPs from both sides of the house to protect their allies. This may have happened even if Kenya had not pursued power-sharing. But the formation of a government of national unity exacerbated this tendency because so many MPs benefited from being 'in government' – and hence were unwilling to speak out against their colleagues – that there was never a serious attempt to challenge this development.

At the same time, the unbalanced distribution of ministries placed the ODM in a difficult position. On the one hand, the lack of key coordinating ministries meant that it was difficult for former opposition parties to demonstrate a clear impact upon major policy issues and ensure high-quality elections. On the other hand, gaining control of expenditure ministries facilitated higher levels of patronage politics and a growing sense that the ODM was in fact just as corrupt and inefficient as the parties they were seeking to displace. As a result of the combination of these two developments, the ODM struggled to mobilize support in the post-power-sharing elections. This failure had two dimensions. First, as with the National Party in South Africa more than a decade earlier, and the MDC in Zimbabwe, the ODM struggled to take credit for the accomplishments of the power-sharing government while dissociating itself from its failures. Second, the perception that corruption was pervasive undermined its reform credentials, which in turn undercut the public zeal that Odinga had benefited from in 2007. Thus, the impact and legacy of power-sharing in Kenya was complex and uneven.

The culture of impunity

The high degree of elite cohesion witnessed in Kenya, where politicians have a history of swapping alliances between elections, facilitated the emergence of an anti-reform alliance (Cheeseman and Tendi 2010). As early as February 2009, rumours began to circulate that the PNU's Uhuru Kenyatta had engaged in talks to establish a behind-the-scenes pact with the ODM's William Ruto, whose relationship with party leader Raila Odinga deteriorated throughout the year. Such an alliance was remarkable for bringing together leaders from the Kikuyu and Kalenjin communities that were at the forefront of the inter-communal violence in 2008 (Cheeseman 2011). The Kenyatta/Ruto coalition owed much to the fear of both leaders that they would be prosecuted as part of the investigations into post-election violence, and represented a complex realignment of anti-reform forces under the cover of the unity government (Brown and Sriram 2012). By forming a cross-party alliance, the two leaders secured enough votes within Parliament to effectively control the reform agenda and ensure their interests. This was significant, because when the Commission of Inquiry on Post-Election Violence – better known as the Waki Commission – reported its findings, it placed the names of high-profile suspects in an envelope. This was then handed over to Kofi Annan, who was tasked with making the names public when a process had been agreed for prosecuting those concerned – or handing the envelope to the ICC if a domestic process was not established.

When the National Assembly rejected the Special Tribunal for Kenya Bill, 2009 by 101 votes to 93 on 12 February, it became impossible for Kenya to meet Annan's 1 March deadline for the creation of a domestic tribunal. In frustration, he handed over the envelope to the ICC, which ultimately began proceedings. Allies of Kenyatta, acting with the support of President Kibaki, immediately began to mobilize to undermine the process. This strategy comprised two strands: 'shuttle diplomacy' to strengthen bilateral relations with potential allies and intense lobbying of the African Union to build pressure on the ICC by depicting it as a Western imperial imposition. Both strategies strengthened the government's position on the world stage and increased the pressure on the ICC to compromise – eventually agreeing to postpone the cases until August 2013 so that the proceedings would not directly interfere with the April 2013 elections.

However, the ICC did have a major impact on the outcome of the polls. Kenyatta and Ruto formalized their coalition in the shape of the Jubilee Alliance and used their prosecution on crimes against humanity to their own advantage (Lynch 2014). They did this by cultivating a siege mentality in their home areas, accusing Odinga of being part of a plot devised by foreign governments and the ICC to undermine Kenyan sovereignty. Together with the advantages of incumbency (as President Kibaki's favoured successors), the vast resources at Kenyatta's disposal and Odinga's failure to reinvigorate his own supporters, this message propelled the "alliance of the accused" into State House (Cheeseman *et al.* 2014). In this way, power-sharing facilitated the opportunity for the leaders who allegedly helped to fund and organize some of the worst political violence in the country's history to come to power.

The failure to tackle the culture of impunity extended to corruption. In February 2009, accusations of illegal maize trading had surfaced, and a subsequent independent audit by PricewaterhouseCoopers found that US$26 million had been lost when a government company illegally sold subsidized maize to a series of ghost companies. In December 2009, the education ministry was the object of similar allegations that US$1.4 million had gone missing from a fund dedicated to the government's flagship free education project (Cheeseman 2010b). These scandals led donors to halt funding, which in turn increased the pressure on Kibaki and Odinga to punish offenders. However, their well-publicized decision to clamp down on graft quickly became politicized, as each man manipulated corruption allegations to undermine the position of his rivals.

Later in the year, it looked as if things might change when the appointment of the 'activist' Patrick Lumumba as the new director of the Kenyan Anti-Corruption Commission (KACC) triggered a welcome spate of dismissals and resignations. However, when Lumumba, frustrated that his efforts were being blocked by senior government figures, went public with his concerns, the response of Kenya's political elite was predictable. Charity Ngilu, now Water and Irrigation Minister but formerly Minister for Justice and Controversial

Affairs, said that Lumumba's appointment "really was a big mistake" (Onyiego 2011). Thus, when constitutional change led to the creation of a new legal framework concerning ethics in public office, the power-sharing government took the opportunity to shut down the work of the KACC.

As a result, when Mwai Kibaki signed the Ethics and Anti-Corruption Bill into effect with unusual efficiency on 28 August, Lumumba was effectively sacked. The disembowelling of the KACC encouraged the abuse of public office by a political class that has systematically misused state funds. A Food Assistance Integrity Study conducted by Transparency International in late 2011 (in partnership with the United Nations and the Government of Kenya) found that much of the food aid intended for the 3.75 million Kenyans suffering shortages had been diverted to the supporters of political leaders, local elites and those in charge of local relief committees (Transparency International 2012). Thus, under the shelter of the power-sharing government, the rate of corruption accelerated.

Reform of the security forces

If power-sharing had a positive impact upon short-term violence and a negative impact upon the culture of impunity, progress towards the reform of the security forces fell somewhere in between. Both Western donors and the opposition understood the importance of building a more professional and independent police force – after all, Mohamed Hussein Ali, a former commissioner of police, was one of those initially charged by the ICC – but struggled to force the implementation of far-reaching reforms. This was despite considerable evidence of police wrongdoing. In February 2009, a visit by the United Nations Special Investigator, Philip Alston, to investigate extra-judicial killings by the police and security services revealed that the Kenyan police "frequently execute individuals and that a climate of impunity prevails." At a press conference in Nairobi on 25 February, Alston went further, claiming that "Kenyan police are a law unto themselves. They kill often, with impunity" (BBC News 2009).

The government's failure to respond to these criticisms, or to the assassination of two human rights activists shot and killed while on their way to a meeting at the Kenya National Commission on Human Rights (KNCHR), led to mass protests calling for Police Commissioner Hussein Ali to step down on 10 March. This forced the government to establish a National Taskforce on Police Reforms on 8 May. More substantial reform was to occur two years later in August 2011, when the government passed three key police reforms: the National Police Service Bill, the National Police Service Commission Bill and the Independent Policing Oversight Authority Bill, which transformed the formal rules governing the police force. Taken together, the legislation established the National Police Service (NPS), which merged the Kenyan Police and the Administration Police – a parallel force that is a legacy of the colonial period – and created a National Police Service Commission (NPSC) tasked with "overseeing recruitment and disciplinary matters and the vetting of the members of the National Police Service." It also provided for "the establishment of a specific body mandated to deal with complaints against the

NPS," thus generating a greater degree of checks and balances within the system (Mageka 2015). Following on from this, the improved performance of the police during the 2013 elections – when they generally showed a far higher level of restraint than in 2007 – suggested that at least some lessons had been learned (Noyes 2013).

However, the full implementation of the reforms was undermined by a lack of political will within both the government and police. As a member of the Police Reforms Implementation Committee, Odour Ong'wen, told the researcher Alex Noyes, "Organizational reforms, including administrative merger and vetting, have had limited impact" (2013), while "The merger of the Administration Police (AP) and the Kenya Police ... only partially succeeded" and so "human rights violation is still rampant within the police service" (Mageka 2015). As a result, the politicization and professionalization of the security forces remains a serious cause for concern.

The passage of the 2010 Constitution

The major achievement of the power-sharing government was the introduction of a new constitution in 2010. But, ironically, the carefully designed inclusive and balanced procedure that led to its adoption was the work of a parliamentary group and not the product of the coalition government itself. When the process of settling the new constitution-making procedure had stalled at cabinet level, a group of MPs from both sides who were committed to constitutional change took on the project and drove it through the National Assembly. The agreed procedure involved an extraordinary juggling act, designed to keep everyone on board. Respect for earlier constitutional proposals, strict time lines and protection of aspects of the process from political decision-making appeased the ODM; decision-making by politicians on the major issues reassured party leaders and made it more likely that the constitution would be passed in a referendum; and giving experts a central role on a committee that included three foreigners together with some public participation and a referendum brought most civil society actors on board.

Remarkably, despite the country's history of incomplete constitutional review processes, the procedure worked. In the face of considerable skepticism and obstruction from officials and others, a new constitution was put to the public in a referendum in August 2010 and passed with 68.6 per cent of the vote. As had been the case in 2005, the constitutional referendum campaign exposed ethnic and religious fault lines. However, despite the tensions that this generated, it did not split the power-sharing administration. Although neither side was particularly happy with the draft, the two principals, Kibaki and Odinga, put their differences aside and campaigned together for a 'Yes' vote (Kasfir 2014). This would have been improbable in the absence of the power-sharing arrangement, and was essential to the passage of the constitution. In this way, the elite cohesion that facilitated greater corruption also made possible constitutional reform. But has this laid the foundations for long-term political stability in Kenya?

The new constitutional dispensation

The 2010 Constitution established a presidential system and a relatively strong system of devolved powers with 47 counties comprising a subnational level of government. It retains the first-past-the-post electoral system, tweaked to provide for seats for women and certain other groups. The Constitution also includes an extensive bill of rights that permits (perhaps requires) affirmative action for disadvantaged groups and that has clear provisions concerning its enforcement; establishes a new Supreme Court and seeks to secure judicial independence through the creation of a new Independent Judiciary Service Commission with responsibility for the appointment of judges, designed explicitly to limit the ability of the executive to maintain a partisan bench; and, provides for a number of independent institutions intended, as in the CKRC draft, to protect democracy. In addition, a framework of principles including accountability, transparency and inclusiveness governs the exercise of public power.

The Constitution is detailed in its treatment of many matters that caused problems in the past such as elections, land, the representation of women and public finance. And, in relatively elaborate transitional arrangements, it requires judges to be 'vetted' for their suitability to remain on the bench, seeking to address the lack of legitimacy of the courts. These features, which emphasize democratic control of government power, nation-building, the protection of public space and full public participation in public affairs, have earned it the reputation of being the 'best' or at least one of the best constitutions in Africa. But, it is not a constitution designed primarily for power-sharing or elite accommodation, and it is not yet clear that the government arrangements it introduces are an adequate basis for ongoing political stability.

In particular, there has been considerable speculation around the deal struck by the politicians to reject a parliamentary system for presidentialism. The experience of the coalition government, which many Kenyans saw as dysfunctional and divisive, created considerable resistance to any form of executive power-sharing, but it did not lead to a general rejection of parliamentarianism. Indeed, for many, the acute danger of a majoritarian presidential election and the tendency for power to be captured by a small clique, especially in a system that works through patronage and patrimonialism, suggested that parliamentarianism would be a safer option. With the sole exception of the draft put to the referendum in 2005 by the Kibaki government, the earlier constitutional proposals had all made this choice: a parliamentary system, with the executive drawn from the legislature and accountable to it, and a figurehead president who, although directly elected, had no substantive executive power.

For those who had fought for parliamentarianism for decades, accepting a presidential system was a bitter pill to swallow – although this was mitigated to some extent by the agreement that the Constitution be "American style, with strong checks and balances." However, although the Constitution does contain some 'American-style' checks – most notably with the requirement of legislative approval of certain appointments, the creation of a second legislative chamber and the requirement that ministers (now called cabinet secretaries) may not be Members of Parliament – it is not clear that the president can be properly constrained given the great informal power of the position and the weakness of key political institutions.

The choice of presidentialism is therefore evidence of the resistance of party leaders to change and a lack of interest in more inclusive politics. Indeed, with the exception of devolution, there are no mechanisms in the new constitution to ensure that power is shared. Instead, the winner-takes-all logic of the previous political system has been reproduced. As a result, little has been done to reduce the stakes of electoral competition. The requirement that the cabinet "shall reflect the regional and ethnic diversity of the people of Kenya" (Article 130(2)) may seem to imply a commitment to inclusivity, but this provision is so ambiguous that it is likely to prove easy to evade. Similarly, new rules that the president must win 25 per cent of the vote in at least 24 of the 47 counties and an absolute majority (50 per cent + 1) of the vote to win power – necessitating a run-off if these conditions are not met – are designed to encourage coalition formation. However, it is not clear that these changes have significantly changed the 'ethnic maths' of Kenyan politics. First, if no candidate meets these requirements in the first round, the system reverts to a pure majoritarian one: a run-off is held with the two candidates who received the highest number of votes in round one competing. Second, the geographical requirement is very similar to the rules under the old constitution, when the president was required to win at least 25 per cent of the vote in five of the eight provinces, and President Kenyatta was able to secure a first-round victory in 2013 without securing support from a large number of historically marginalized ethnic groups (Kenya Const. Art. 138).

Changes to other parts of the system of representation have also had a limited effect on levels of political inclusion. Rather than moving to a system of proportional representation as some had proposed, a FPTP model was retained. Again, this is not a mechanism usually associated with power-sharing arrangements. However, in this case, the reasons for rejecting change were more compelling. First, of course, politicians themselves were unwilling to let go of the system that had served them. The most they could do was agree that the gross disproportionality in the size of electoral districts be curbed and that some attention should be paid to making the system more inclusive of women and other traditionally excluded groups. Second, FPTP elections generate a strong connection between the MP and their community, enabling effective communication between the centre and periphery. A number of scholars such as Joel Barkan have suggested that this plays an important role in maintaining a form of political accountability in Kenya (Barkan 1998). Third, a mixed system of proportional representation plus constituency representation, such as that used in Germany, was thought to be too complex and likely to facilitate electoral manipulation. Finally, proportional representation may have facilitated an even more fragmented set of voting alliances, further fracturing what limited party cohesion exists.

Thus, the most far-reaching change in the 2010 Constitution, and the reform with the greatest potential to support a more inclusive form of politics, is the system of devolved government. Although this is usually viewed in Kenya primarily as a mechanism for dispersing the power of the state, it also constitutes a form of power-sharing – for example, between the ethnic community/ies that win the presidency and those that do not, but win control of their county governments. For the first time in Kenyan history, national losers can be local winners. Although the powers granted to the 47 new counties are tightly constrained, and the Constitution vests great authority in the central government, county governors have already emerged as major players with considerably greater weight than Members of Parliament. This is because county governments receive far greater resources – around 22 per cent of government resources – and are responsible for delivering essential services such as healthcare. As a result, county government has truly come to life, and devolution remains highly popular with Kenyans from almost all ethnic groups, despite considerable evidence of corruption and financial mismanagement. The net effect of devolution has therefore been to give more Kenyans a sense that they have a stake in the system, and there is some evidence that this contributed to the peaceful elections in 2013 (Cheeseman *et al.* 2016).

This is not to say that the introduction of devolution has not also introduced its own complications. Indeed, many of the tensions and disputes that have previously played out at the national level are now being played out at the county level. This includes confrontations between Governors and the directly elected County Assemblies, directly elected Senators, and government-appointed County Commissioners. In the worst cases, such as Embu and Kericho, this has led to impeachment proceedings being brought against unpopular Governors – something that is remarkably easy under the new legal dispensation. These processes have been high profile, disruptive and destabilizing and have often intensified ethnic tensions. In turn, this has led to concerns that in the future there may be a greater risk of electoral violence at the county than at the national level.

Given this, it is significant that the need for elite or ethnic accommodation was not the central concern in the design of the counties. This is particularly clear in the way that the counties themselves were delineated. Although the constitutional objectives of devolution include "to foster national unity by recognising diversity" (Kenya Const. Art. 174(b)), "to recognize the right of communities to manage their own affairs" (Kenya Const. Art. 174 (d)) and "to protect and promote the interests and rights of minorities and marginalized communities" (Kenya Const. Art. 174(e)), the counties established under the Constitution are based on the 47 districts recognized in the 1992 Districts and Provinces Act. This configuration was adopted without any consideration of population movement, the ethnic dynamics of particular areas or the interests of particular communities. As a result, in some cases counties are dominated by a single ethnic group, in others not. In many cases, smaller groups that had managed to secure a level of autonomy in the past two decades became minorities in their new counties. Particularly in parts of the country in which there has historically been a divide between (often self-proclaimed) 'indigenous' and 'non-indigenous' communities, as in the Rift Valley, this has exacerbated existing tensions.

Presidentialism, a constituency-based electoral system and modest devolution are not the marks of constitutional arrangements concerned with power-sharing. But the Kenyan Constitution does pay careful attention to the historic problems of exclusion and marginalization in other ways. It requires a fair distribution of resources across the country, inclusion in public offices and, in security services, representation of the "diversity of the Kenyan people in equitable proportions" (Art. 238(2)(d)). It also requires political parties to have "a national character." In addition to these formal, institutional mechanisms of inclusion, the Constitution forefronts a diverse and active citizenry, enjoying equal dignity and respect, and it emphasizes constitutionalism and the rule of law, and the responsibilities of government towards the people.

These 'soft' provisions are intended to provide a framework for more inclusive public life and for citizens to deepen democratic government. However, their ambiguity and the fact that they go against the grain of Kenyan politics means that enforcement will depend on the active work of citizens and civil society organizations. There are already signs that this is occurring in some areas. For example, in 2015 the Governor of Kiambu was successfully taken to court for failing to comply with the constitutional requirement for public participation in the budget process. As a result, county governments across the country rushed to establish framework legislation, significantly increasing the quality of civic engagement. But in other areas, such as the composition of the cabinet, the formation of national priorities and employment in the security forces, it has so far been business as usual. In turn, this has led the opposition to once again complain about a lack of compromise and consensus building in the policy making process.

Conclusion

In short, the transition is no easier than might have been expected. The deteriorating domestic security situation, escalating Al-Shabaab terrorist activity and perceptions that the government is unable or unwilling to respond adequately have increased mistrust and compounded the difficulties. Moreover, there has been at best limited progress on land reform, and efforts to deal with the sense of historical injustices, exclusion and ethnicity have stalled. However, despite the enormous challenges and a lack of enthusiasm among significant sectors of the political elite for the new arrangements, the new political system is dynamic and vibrant. Although the introduction of repressive media legislation suggests that the new Jubilee Alliance government intends to reverse some of the recent democratic gains, coalitions of Governors have actively resisted efforts to recentralize power. Combined with strong public support for devolution, this has silenced those members of the elite who may continue to oppose it, leading analysts to conclude that some aspects of the new institutional arrangements are fast becoming entrenched. There are also other positive signs. Most notably, trust in public institutions more generally and in particular in the judiciary has improved since 2008 and the economy is growing slowly.

Major questions remain, of course. Most importantly, will the new institutional arrangements be sufficiently robust to provide a real basis for tackling the deep structural problems that Kenya faces, which are closely tied to the intertwined relationship between politics and the economy and "are rooted in land distribution and ethnicity"? Although the new Constitution has re-energized local politics, it has not transformed power relations at the heart of government. In large part, this is because the incumbent president retained strong overall control throughout the power-sharing process, from the negotiations through to the unity government and on to the constitutional drafting. As a result, the introduction of reforms was done on the basis of terms set out by the political establishment. This is clear both in relation to the distribution of ministries and the retention of a presidential system of government with no space for the position of prime minister. At the same time, the inclusion of the ODM within government meant that the former opposition subsequently struggled to distinguish its role from that of the former government. Combined with accusations of corruption stemming from the incorporation of opposition politicians in government networks of patronage and clientelism, this called into question the extent to which the ODM represented a genuine 'change' option. As a result, it was not surprising that Raila Odinga and the Orange Democratic Movement performed worse in the presidential and parliamentary 2013 elections than they had done in 2007, despite the new Constitution. In this way, power-sharing served to entrench existing political hierarchies.

It is worth noting that this reflects a general trend. In Zimbabwe, the only significant difference to the distribution of ministries in Kenya was that the country's

> desperate economic plight, combined with the clear preference of Western governments for the MDC, forced ZANU-PF to allow opposition leader Tendai Biti to take up the powerful position of Finance Minister in a bid to turn on the taps of international financial assistance.
> (Cheeseman and Tendi 2010, 219)

Similarly, the new Constitution in Zimbabwe does little to genuinely check the power of the president, while the elections that brought power-sharing to an end returned a ZANU-PF government with a greater majority. The Kenyan and Zimbabwean experience therefore highlights the tendency for power-sharing deals in civilian contexts to simultaneously facilitate processes of constitutional review while reproducing the hold of the government over the key strategic and coordinating positions, and undermining the capacity of opposition parties to hold the government to account.

Notes

1 Kenya is said to have over 70 ethnic groups but the exact number is controversial and subject to change as new communities seek to assert their own identities. The largest communities are the Kikuyu, Luo, Luhya, Kamba and Kalenjin, followed by the Meru and the Kisii. None of these groups comprises over 20 per cent of the population, and so political leaders cannot hope to win elections on the basis of support from one ethnic

group alone. As a result, Kenyan politics revolves around the formation of broad – and often fragile – electoral coalitions (Cheeseman 2008).
2 Cheeseman was an election observer in 2007. Murray was a member of the Committee of Experts, appointed in terms of the Constitution of Kenya Review Act of 2008 to prepare the Constitution.
3 With the exception of the short-lived Kenya People's Union, which split from KANU in 1966 and offered opposition until it was banned in 1969.
4 In addition, in a different type of power diffusion, a number of commissions and a special (newly established) court with exclusive jurisdiction to adjudicate matters concerning the constitution-making process were to include one-third foreigners, as discussed below. Incorporation of the agreement in the Constitution was a central element of the deal. The Constitution was duly amended (Act 3 of 2008) and the National Accord and Reconciliation Act 4 of 2008 (Accord Act) passed.
5 Nor do the "key points" set out in the Agreement. They are just the institutional arrangements and make no attempt to define the role of the new prime minister.
6 "Thereafter" there was to be "full consultation with the President on the appointment of all Ministers" (ACT), a provision that was easily interpreted to grant a veto power to President Kibaki. See also provision on dismissal of Ministers (ACT).
7 By which we mean the president, vice-president and prime minister.
8 Members of these commissions were to be selected by members of the ODM-dominated National Assembly and appointed by the president 'in consultation with' the prime minister.

References

Anderson, David M. 2003. "Briefing: Kenya's Elections 2002: The Dawning of a New Era?" *African Affairs* 102, no. 407: 331–342.

Anderson, David M. 2005. " 'Yours in Struggle for Majimbo.' Nationalism and the Party Politics of Decolonization in Kenya, 1955–64." *Journal of Contemporary History* 40, no. 3: 547–564.

Barkan, Joel. 1998. "Rethinking the Applicability of Proportional Representation in Africa." In *Elections and Conflict Management in Africa*, edited by Timothy D. Sisk and Andrew Reynolds, pp. 57–70. Washington, DC: United States Institute of Peace Press.

BBC News. 2009. "Kenya Police 'Ran Death Squads.'" 25 February. Available at http://news.bbc.co.uk/1/hi/world/africa/7909523.stm.

Branch, Daniel and Nic Cheeseman. 2005. "Briefing: Using Opinion Polls to Evaluate Kenyan Politics, March 2004–January 2005." *African Affairs* 104, no. 415: 325–336.

Branch, Daniel and Nic Cheeseman. 2009. "Democratization, Sequencing, and State Failure in Africa: Lessons from Kenya." *African Affairs* 108, no. 430: 1–26.

Branch, Daniel, Nic Cheeseman and Leigh Gardner. 2010. *Our Turn to Eat: Politics in Kenya since 1950*. Berlin: Lit Verlag.

Brown, Stephen and Chandra Lekha Sriram. 2012. "The Big Fish Won't Fry Themselves: Criminal Accountability for Post-Election Violence in Kenya." *African Affairs* 111, no. 443: 244–260.

Cheeseman, Nic. 2008. "The Kenyan Elections of 2007: An Introduction." *Journal of Eastern African Studies* 2, no. 2: 166–184.

Cheeseman, Nic. 2010a. "African Elections as Vehicles for Change." *Journal of Democracy* 21, no. 4: 139–153.

Cheeseman, Nic. 2010b. "Kenya in 2009." In *Africa Yearbook*, edited by Andreas Mehler, Henning Melber, Klaas Van Walraven and Rolf Hofmeier, pp. 343–357. Leiden: Brill.

Cheeseman, Nic. 2011. "Kenya in 2010." In *Africa Yearbook*, edited by Andreas Mehler, Henning Melber, Klaas Van Walraven and Rolf Hofmeier, pp. 240–252. Leiden: Brill.
Cheeseman, Nic. 2015. *Democracy in Africa: Successes, Failures, and the Struggle for Political Reform*. Cambridge: Cambridge University Press.
Cheeseman, Nic and Miles Larmer. 2015. "Ethnopopulism in Africa: Opposition Mobilization in Diverse and Unequal Societies." *Democratization* 22, no. 1: 22–50.
Cheeseman, Nic and Blessing-Miles Tendi. 2010. "Power-Sharing in Comparative Perspective: The Dynamics of 'Unity Government' in Kenya and Zimbabwe." *Journal of Modern African Studies* 48, no. 2: 203–229.
Cheeseman, Nic, Gabrielle Lynch and Justin Willis. 2014. "Democracy and its Discontents: Understanding Kenya's 2013 Elections." *Journal of Eastern African Studies* 8, no. 1: 2–24.
Cheeseman, Nic, Gabrielle Lynch and Justin Willis. 2016. "Decentralisation in Kenya: The Governance of Governors." *The Journal of Modern African Studies* 54, no. 1: 1–35.
Cohen, Roger. 2008. "Op-Ed: African Genocide Averted." *New York Times*, 3 March.
Gekara, Emeka-Mayaka and Samwel Kumba. 2010. "Accord Doesn't Expressly Provide for Equal Power: Unending Wrangles in the Grand Coalition between the President and the Prime Minister have Triggered a Fresh Debate." *Daily Nation*, 27 February. Available at www.nation.co.ke/News/politics/-/1064/870280/-/wqmfsnz/-/index.html.
Gettleman, Jeffrey. 2010a. "Kenyan President Blocks Prime Minister's Suspension of 2 High-Ranking Officials." *New York Times*, 15 February. Available at www.nytimes.com/2010/02/21/world/africa/21kenya.html?ref=mwaikibaki&pagewanted=print.
Gettleman, Jeffrey. 2010b. "Political Standoff Puts Kenyans' Rage in Focus." *New York Times*, 20 February. Available at www.nytimes.com/2010/02/21/world/africa/21kenya.html?_r=0.
Ghai, Yash P. and Patrick McAuslan. 1970. *Public Law and Political Change in Kenya: A Study of the Legal Framework of Government from Colonial Times to the Present*. Oxford: Oxford University Press.
Gĩthĩnji, Mwangi wa and Frank Holmquist. 2008. "Kenya's Hopes and Impediments: The Anatomy of a Crisis of Exclusion." *Journal of Eastern African Studies* 2, no. 2: 344–358.
Griffiths, Martin. 2009. "The Prisoner of Peace: An Interview with Kofi A. Annan." *Henri Dunant Centre for Humanitarian Dialogue*. Available at www.hdcentre.org/uploads/tx_news/74Kofi-interview.pdf.
Hyden, Goran and Colin Leys. 1972. "Elections and Politics in Single-Party Systems: The Case of Kenya and Tanzania." *British Journal of Political Science* 2, no. 4: 389–420.
Juma, Monica K. 2009. "African Mediation of the Kenyan Post-2007 Election Crisis." *Journal of Contemporary African Studies* 27, no. 3: 407–430.
Kasfir, Nelson. 2014. "Agency across Changing Sites: The Path to Kenya's 2010 Constitution." In *The Politics of Governance: Actors and Articulations in Africa and Beyond*, edited by Lucy Koechlin and Till Förster, pp. 52–74. Oxford: Routledge.
Kenya. *The Constitution of Kenya* [Nairobi, 1969].
Kenya National Dialogue and Reconciliation Monitoring Project. 2009. "Project Context and Summary of Findings." Available at http://south.co.ke/images/south/KNDR_Reports/Projectcontextandsummaryoffindings.pdf.
"Kenya's Crumbling Government: The Great Rift." 2009. *The Economist*. 23 April. Available at: www.economist.com/node/13527865.

Kibwana, Kivutha. 2008. "Kenya: There Can't Be Two Centres of Power in Any Country." *Daily Nation*, 9 April. Available at http://allafrica.com/stories/200804081161.html.

Lindenmayer, Elisabeth and Josie Lianna Kaye. 2008. "A Choice for Peace? The Story of 41 days of Mediation in Kenya." New York: International Peace Institute. Available at http://peacemaker.un.org/sites/peacemaker.un.org/files/KenyaMediation_IPI2009.pdf.

Lynch, Gabrielle. 2008. "Courting the Kalenjin: The Failure of Dynasticism and the Strength of the ODM Wave in Kenya's Rift Valley Province." *African Affairs* 107, no. 429: 541–568.

Lynch, Gabrielle. 2014. "Electing the 'Alliance of the Accused': The Success of the Jubilee Alliance in Kenya's Rift Valley." *Journal of Eastern African Studies* 8, no. 1: 93–114.

Mageka, Annie. 2015. "Police Reform in Kenya: Challenges and Opportunities." *Security Sector Reform Resource Centre*, 9 October. Available at www.ssrresourcecentre.org/2015/10/09/police-reform-in-kenya-challenges-and-opportunities.

Mathenge, Oliver. 2012. "Rift Looms over Appointments." Daily Nation, 26 January. Available at www.nation.co.ke/News/politics/Rift+looms+over+appointments+/-/1064/1314706/-/xe9c0v/-/index.html.

Mueller, Susanne D. 2008. "The Political Economy of Kenya's Crisis." *Journal of Eastern African Studies* 2, no. 2: 185–210.

Murunga, Godwin R. and Shadrack W. Nasong'o. 2006. "Bent on Self-Destruction: The Kibaki Regime in Kenya." *Journal of Contemporary African Studies* 24, no. 1: 1–28.

Noyes, Alexander. 2013. "Cleaning House in Kenya's Police Force." *Foreign Policy*, 30 December. Available at http://foreignpolicy.com/2013/12/30/cleaning-house-in-kenyas-police-force/#sthash.t8hBKcuT.dpbs.

Onyiego, Michael. 2011. "Kenya Corruption Chief Faces Backlash." *Voice of America*, 25 August. Available at www.voanews.com/content/backlash-against-kenya-corruption-chief-could-set-back-fight-against-graft-128474538/158751.html.

Reuters. 2008. "Timeline: Kenya in Crisis after Disputed Elections." 8 February. Available at www.reuters.com/article/us-kenya-crisis-events-idUSL0891082120080208.

Schreiber, Leon. 2016. "Making Power Sharing Work: Kenya's Grand Coalition Cabinet, 2008–2013." *Princeton University*. Available at http://successfulsocieties.princeton.edu/sites/successfulsocieties/files/LS_Kenya_Powersharing_FINAL.pdf.

Throup, David W. 2008. "The Count." *Journal of Eastern African Studies* 2, no. 2: 290–304.

Throup, David and Charles Hornsby. 1998. *Multi-Party Politics in Kenya: The Kenyatta and Moi States and The Triumph of the System in the 1992 Election*. Athens: Ohio University Press.

Transparency International. 2012. "Food Assistance Integrity Study." Available at www.tikenya.org/index.php/integrity-studies?download=204:ti-kenya-food-assistance-integrity-study-2012.

Waki Commission. 2008. *Report of the Commission of Inquiry into Post-Election Violence*. Nairobi: Government Printer.

Widner, Jennifer A. 1992. *The Rise of a Party-State in Kenya: From "Harambee!" to "Nyayo!"* Berkeley: University of California Press.

3 Power-sharing executives
Consociational and centripetal formulae and the case of Northern Ireland[1]

John McGarry and Brendan O'Leary

There is widespread if not universal agreement among political scientists that power-sharing, permanent or temporary, offers workable means to prevent, resolve or regulate violent ethnic conflicts. 'Proportional' democracies are less violent than 'majoritarian' democracies (Powell 1982, 2000) and consensual democracies, according to numerous criteria, outperform winner-take-all democracies (Lijphart 2008, 2012). The evidence on other criteria has not settled among political scientists or economists.[2] Using key developmental and stability indicators, it has been argued in a large-N study, supplemented by paired case studies, that all kinds of regimes, including non-democratic regimes, which exhibit some power-sharing institutions and practices, outperform those that do not (Norris 2008). More crucially for ethnopolitics, power-sharing provisions in the commitments of peace agreements appear to reduce the likelihood of violent conflict recurrence (Mattes and Savun 2009).

There is, however, much less consensus among political scientists on defining and operationalizing power-sharing, and about what types of power-sharing, particularly executive power-sharing, are most effective in inhibiting national, ethnic, racial, religious and linguistic conflict, or preventing its recurrence (O'Leary 2013). One expert identifies two principal approaches to inter-ethnic conciliation in severely divided places (Horowitz 2002). Whereas centripetalism encourages a coalition of moderate parties to "fend off the extremes," ideally undergirded by an electoral system benefiting moderates, consociation, by contrast, is said to emphasize a 'grand coalition' encompassing all segments within the polity, and may include both moderate and hardline parties. Donald Horowitz considers choosing between these alternatives to be the "most fundamental" decision in institutional negotiations in deeply divided places (Horowitz 2002, 213). He believes that the choice is straightforward: consociational grand coalitions are hard to compose, because they depend on hardliners cooperating across rival blocs; dysfunctional, because hardliners are inflexible; and undemocratic, because they dispense "with the idea of government on one side and opposition on the other" (Horowitz 2002, 194, 197). Moderate parties, by contrast, are more likely to accept and operate centripetal power-sharing; and moderate coalitions are consistent with the minimum-winning pacts that allow for opposition. He deems consociations "inapt to moderate conflict," perhaps suited only for moderately divided places where they are said to be not needed (Horowitz 2000, 56). Consociations in deeply divided places are said to be as rare as the Arctic Rose, likely the result of errors by international powers imposing them upon unwilling locals (Horowitz 2000, 56, 271; 2002, 197).

It is simply incorrect, however, to argue that consociations must be synonymous with grand or comprehensive coalitions (O'Leary 2005). Consociations typically require joint government, involving the polity's major communities, but do not require all parties to be in the executive. Consociations may either be 'complete,' that is, include all parties;[3] 'concurrent,' that is, restricted to parties commanding majorities but not total support within their respective segments; or 'weak,' that is, based on coalitions where at least one of the parties in office commands only plurality support within its group.[4] It is also possible to have dominant parties which monopolize the executive but which are internally consociational – as demonstrated in the experience of several post-colonial countries (Bogaards 2014). Here, however, the case of Northern Ireland will be used to assess the core centripetalist claim that executive rules which advantage moderates are superior to more inclusive consociational rules.

Northern Ireland experimented with a centripetal coalition in 1974, and since 1998 (punctuated by periods of suspension) it has had a consociational coalition government based on sequential and proportional allocation rules – which we will abbreviate to SPA. Northern Ireland's experience shows that SPA coalitions have clear advantages over both their centripetal and more conventional consociational counterparts. No sweeping claims can be made, or are made here, about the transferability of SPA rules to other deeply divided polities, or about the lifetime of the Northern Ireland settlement, but the merits of SPA rules are certainly worth considering, particularly in areas which approximate the conditions that contributed to their success in Northern Ireland. Before we lay out the case evidence, let us present some general arguments in favour of SPA rules.

General arguments

SPA rules for executive formation deserve more attention from the academic and policy-making communities than they have received thus far.[5] They contrast strongly with standard methods for allocating ministries in coalitions, such as agreements reached in inter-party negotiations; the assignment of portfolios by the party leader with most legislative support; or proposals by an executive president, a symbolic head of state, a formateur or a third party. SPA mechanisms are automatic rules applied to parties' shares of seats in a legislature. The party with the highest number of seats wins the first choice of ministry; the divisor is then applied to its seat total, and the next ministry allocated to the party with the highest remaining number of seats. This process is repeated until all ministries are distributed. The degree of proportionality in the executive is a function of the divisor used, and the number of ministries available.[6] To be determinate, the process requires a previous convergence on the division of functions among portfolios and their number – which may be embedded in the constitution, a law or a political agreement.

Holding the number of ministries constant, it follows from standard analyses of voting systems (Balinski and Peyton Young 1982; Taagepera and Shugart 1989) that the Jefferson d'Hondt divisor (1, 2, 3, 4 …) is more favourable to larger parties than Webster-Sainte-Laguë (1, 3, 5, 7 …), which, in turn, is more favourable to larger parties than the Danish divisor (1, 4, 7, 10 …).[7] Table 3.1 shows how applying the Jefferson-d'Hondt divisor would allocate ten ministries among parties in a hypothetical 100-seat legislature. The example assumes the following five-party configuration in a place dominated by two ethnic groups: a hardline party and a moderate party in each of two ethnic groups A and B, and a small non-ethnic (or inter-ethnic) party. The moderates from Group A are the largest party in the assembly, so it wins the first choice of ministry, and its seat total is then divided by 2 (M + 1), where M = number of ministries already held. In this case, the second pick goes to the hardliners from Group B, and so on. The outcome is an executive inclusive of parties from both Group A and Group B, but also of the hardliners and moderates in each group. In this example, no ministries are won by the small non-ethnic party.

Divisor mechanisms are usually used to allocate legislative seats to parties following elections using list proportional representation. However, as Table 3.1 suggests, they can also be used to fill committees and cabinets, to ensure both proportionality and sequential order of status. The d'Hondt divisor is currently used to allocate committee places and their chairs and deputy chairs in the European Parliament (Hix and Høyland 2011), committee places in the Scottish Parliament (and the time allowed in debates there), and to allocate executive and administrative offices in the Brussels-Capital Region in Belgium, in the four largest Danish municipalities of Copenhagen, Aarhus, Odense and Aalborg, and in executive formation in Northern Ireland (O'Leary et al. 2005).

Table 3.1 Applying the Jefferson–d'Hondt divisor with ten ministries in a hypothetical 100-seat legislature

Party/ (M + 1)	Hardliners of Group A		Moderates of Group A		Non-ethnic party		Moderates of Group B		Hardliners of Group B	
	S	M	S	M	S	M	S	M	S	M
1	22.0	3rd*	28.0	1st	5		22.0	4th*	23.0	2nd
2	11.0	7th*	14.0	5th			11.0	8th*	11.5	6th
3	7.3		9.3	9th			7.3		7.6	10th
Total M		2		3		0		2		3

Notes
S = seats in legislature.
M = ministries won in order of portfolio choice.
* = the number of total votes won by the party is used as a tiebreaker in cases where parties have identical numbers of legislative seats.

In evaluating different executive formation mechanisms, a critical issue is their respective likelihoods of being successfully negotiated by antagonists in severely divided places. We hypothesize that SPA mechanisms are broadly 'agreeable' in the same circumstances that produce grand coalitions, among which perhaps the most important facilitative condition is a balance of power that makes it difficult for one bloc to govern as a majority. Thus, for example, when an inter-bloc balance of power exists, and one party or coalition of parties represents each ethnic bloc, a grand coalition becomes feasible. Within the past 20 years, such balances of power have facilitated grand coalitions in Burundi (1999), Fiji (1997), Kenya (2008) and Zimbabwe (2009). Inter-bloc balances of power[8] have also facilitated super-sized coalitions in what today are less deeply divided places: in Switzerland, since 1959; in Austria, from 1945 to 1966; in Belgium, during one quarter of the years between 1918 and 1963; in Colombia, after its first major civil war, 1958 to 1974; and in Germany, from 1966 to 1969, 2005 to 2009 and 2013 onward.[9]

Often, however, an ethnic bloc has more than one significant party, and these parties are typically differentiated by whether they are moderate or hardline in their ethnic agenda. Negotiating a grand coalition may be facilitated among such blocs if there is both an 'inter-bloc' balance and an intra-bloc balance of power. For example, when an intra-bloc balance exists, it is difficult for one of the bloc's parties (moderates) to enter a coalition without the other (hardliners), primarily because of the threat (or manifestation) of outflanking from the hardline party.[10] It is also possible that the moderates, as well as parties from other blocs – and external powers – may believe that the hardliners' inclusion is necessary for stability and peace because they may credibly threaten violence if excluded. Lastly, moderates may believe that including their bloc's hardliners will strengthen their community's overall bargaining power within the coalition. All of these possibilities are empirically enhanced the stronger the hardliners are within their bloc. Such a confluence of both inter- and intra-bloc balances facilitated the creation of Northern Ireland's 1998 Good Friday Agreement (McGarry and O'Leary 2004a). Even though one large party, the Democratic Unionist Party (DUP), initially rejected the design, it came to work within it.

In sum, grand or super-sized coalitions, including those which use SPA mechanisms, are feasible when there is a balance of power between blocs, and where each bloc has either one dominant party or an internal balance of power. However, we believe that it is easy to see that exactly these same conditions would work against the formation of a centripetal coalition that would seek to exclude either a bloc, or a major party within one or more blocs, especially hardline parties. Agreement to form centripetal coalitions is facilitated by a condition likely to be rare in deeply divided places, namely a balance of power that favours moderate parties. A centripetal coalition requires that moderate parties be able to form a legislative majority. In Northern Ireland, that happened in 1973 when moderate parties, under British and Irish governmental coaxing, established the Sunningdale Agreement, named after the UK civil service college in which it was negotiated. The Sunningdale executive's period of office lasted from January until May 1974.

Horowitz has argued that the likelihood of a balance of power that favours moderate parties can be enhanced by adopting the alternative vote (AV).[11] Adopting such a system, however, requires moderates to be in a position of strength when the institutions are initiated. The same, of course, applies to statutes, constitutional provisions or peace agreements that give moderate parties an edge in executive formation. Our reasoning is based on the reasonable assumption that only moderate parties will back rules that benefit them, while hardline parties will oppose rules clearly designed to damage their own prospects. In Fiji, in 1997, a centripetal electoral system for the legislature was initiated and shepherded through constitutional review by moderate parties from the Indian and Fijian blocs, which then held key leadership positions in each bloc (Fraenkel and Grofman 2006a, 2006b). Fiji, however, is perhaps the world's sole example of a deeply divided place which has accepted a centripetal electoral system to undergird an executive coalition of moderate parties.[12] Yet, even in this singular case, the political classes hedged their bets by simultaneously adopting what is typically called a consociational grand coalition.

The key point is that centripetal executive coalitions are likely to precipitate outflanking pressures in direct proportion to the strength of excluded hardliners.[13] This is what recently happened in negotiations over the reunification of Cyprus almost immediately after moderate Turkish Cypriot and Greek Cypriot leaders agreed in January 2010 to propose a centripetal electoral system for a rotating presidency, one that would have favoured moderates. Three months later, Mehmet Ali Talat, the moderate Turkish Cypriot leader who negotiated the proposal, was defeated by a hardliner Dervis Eroglu in a presidential election within the 'Turkish Republic of Northern Cyprus' – in which the electoral system became a key issue. The result terminated for now the prospects of this centripetal proposal, an example of a "cross-voting scheme" (Loizides 2009).[14] Fiji's centripetal electoral system also resulted in immediate defeat for the moderate parties primarily responsible for its adoption (Fraenkel 2003). These examples suggest that even when centripetal arrangements can be agreed, their implementation and maintenance require moderate parties to enjoy 'stable' dominance in all relevant blocs (Nordlinger 1972).

SPA mechanisms, in contrast, proportionally reflect intra- and intercommunity balances of power among parties. They automatically reallocate executive ministries in response to shifting balances of support registered in elections. They are useful both in making agreement possible and for the subsequent implementation and maintenance of any such agreement, though, of course, they do not guarantee either goal. The inclusion of all sizeable parties which cross the relevant threshold – determined by the joint impact of the number of ministries and the divisor rule – may well strengthen stability by giving these parties a stake in the system, and parties with support below this threshold are arguably less capable of disrupting the political system. The critical democratic condition for inclusion should be each party's ability to win sufficient votes to be entitled to at least one ministerial portfolio, and all-round commitments to democratic and non-violent politics.

Executive formation through a sequential and proportional process therefore offers functionality enhancements. Hardline parties have incentives to enter government because failure to do so results in their ministerial entitlements going to rival parties, and not in an immediate failure to form the executive. They are also able to share power with rivals without having expressly to consent to the correctness of any of their rivals' convictions or policies. Executive formation follows an algorithm that is both party- and ethnicity-blind. Provided that the political settlement specifies ministerial portfolios and their numbers, executive formation occurs 'automatically' following elections to the legislature. Protracted negotiations on coalition formation, including which parties should be included, or on how many and which portfolios each should have, can be avoided. In principle, an investiture or ratification of the entire executive by the legislature need not be required. Hardline parties can point to the sequential proportional rules to persuade those of their supporters who oppose negotiations with rivals. And, with each party's share of ministries, and the order in which they win them, linked to its popular support, incentives exist for all parties to conduct themselves to broaden their electoral support. Since the obvious way for hardliners to expand support is at the expense of their moderate co-ethnics, strong incentives exist for them to moderate their platforms, as long as this can be achieved without an offsetting loss of votes to new parties emerging on the hardliners' flanks (Mitchell *et al.* 2009).

Typical centripetal rules, by contrast, may create serious executive formation problems. If the rules are formal – that is, the executive 'requires' cross-ethnic support in direct or indirect elections – the requirement may simply not be met. The UN 'Annan V' Plan for reunifying Cyprus in a federation, put to a referendum in 2004, had centripetal rules biased towards moderates: an executive council would be indirectly elected by a qualified majority of the Senate, including support from at least two-fifths of each of the two blocs of Greek Cypriot and Turkish Cypriot Senators (Loizides 2015). Bizarrely, the rule did not provide for a default outcome if the threshold was not met (United Nations 2004, Art 25.2. (e)). Annan V stated that any vacancy in the council would be filled by the same rule used to elect the executive as a whole, but did not stipulate what would happen if no one was elected (Art. 26.5). Therefore had the referendum passed, a reunited Cyprus may have begun life without a government, and with no constitutional way to form one, or to fill a vacancy if one occurred. Similarly, in Nigeria's presidential election of 1979, held under geographical 'distributive requirements,' a centripetal system, no candidate passed the requisite threshold of an overall plurality and a minimum of 25 per cent of the vote in two-thirds of the states (i.e., 13 out of 19). The Supreme Court resolved that a candidate with an overall plurality and 25 per cent of the vote in 12 states had 'passed' the threshold, thereby setting back the teaching of arithmetical rounding rules.

The quasi-automaticity of SPA mechanisms, and the fact that they deliver determinate outcomes, contrasts positively with centripetal, traditional consociational and other coalitions that rely on post-election bargaining to decide which parties will be in government, how many ministries and which portfolios each party will have. Even in mature and stable democracies, and even when there is some minimum ideological coherence among potential coalition partners, such negotiations may present a formidable task. Following the 2007 federal election in Belgium, it took 176 days to form a caretaker coalition that brought together enough parties to govern and that conformed to constitutional provisions on parity in the cabinet for Francophones and Dutch speakers (Deschouwer and van Parijs 2013). The problem was repeated in 2010/2011, when it took 541 days to form a cabinet, breaking the world record for the longest caretaker government in a democracy. After deadly riots following a disputed election in late 2007, Kenya's parties agreed to share power, with a rule to allocate ministries proportionally, but with no rule on how to allocate portfolios. Within three months, disputes over this matter threatened the agreement (Horowitz 2009). In the coalition formed in Zimbabwe in 2009, three parties agreed to share power, but under the agreement allocation was left to President Robert Mugabe, who gave the important ministries, particularly related to security, to his own party, rendering the original bargain a sham (Cheeseman and Tendi 2010). In Fiji, following the elections in 2001, in which the constitution mandated that every party with at least 10 per cent of the vote be included in the cabinet, the ethnic Fijian prime minister grudgingly offered token ministries to the main Fijian Indian Party, which declined the offer and moved into opposition instead: inter-ethnic distrust increased (Fraenkel and Grofman 2006a). Following the March 2010 elections in Iraq, it took until November, including a doubtful advisory opinion from a transitional Supreme Court with an expired mandate, before a coalition government was formed in principle, and even then, certain posts remained unfilled. Prime Minister Nouri al-Maliki imitated one of Mugabe's moves, with a twist, retaining the two most important security ministries within his own office, thereby deepening the alienation of Sunni Arabs. He had stoked up such rebellious violence by 2014 that his resignation was forced as his country threatened to fall apart (Romano 2014). More recently, the President of Afghanistan Ashraf Ghani and his chief executive Abdullah Abdullah took "more than three months of squabbles and infighting" to form a cabinet, a delay that caused the Taliban to 'tweet' that the cold in Kabul must have frozen cabinet formation.[15]

The automatic allocation of ministries distinguish the SPA model from the coalitions formed in Belgium in 2007, Kenya in 2008, Zimbabwe in 2009 and Iraq in 2010. The sequential process brings an enhanced element of fairness and choice, seen by coalition specialists as linked to system adoption and maintenance (Brams and Kaplan 2004; Brams and Kilgour 2010a, 2010b). The proportionality principle also avoids some of the serious problems attached to 'corporate consociations,' such as those in Lebanon and Bosnia, where the ethnic beneficiaries of power-sharing are specified in advance of elections through quotas or set-asides. Proportional sequential coalitions are compatible with 'liberal consociation'; that is, consociations which use impersonal and formally group-blind proportionality rules (McGarry and O'Leary 2007). The institutional design of liberal consociations should cope better with demographic and electoral change; that is, with changes in the balance of power. For example, a liberal consociation with SPA mechanisms would have helped address (if not definitively resolve) the problems that prompted civil war in Lebanon in 1975, when the Muslim population, especially the Shia, demanded a share of power that better matched their increased share of the population (Hanf 1993). Liberal consociations also permit non-ethnic parties, not just ethnic parties, to share power, in line with their popular support. Indeed, since non-ethnic parties are likely to be small in severely divided places, the combination of liberal consociation and inclusion offered by SPA mechanisms may be the only way for such parties to attain executive office. Liberal consociational institutions are also far less likely than corporate consociations to be challenged in courts as alleged violations of human rights (McCrudden and O'Leary 2013).

Inclusive coalitions, based on proportional and sequential mechanisms, have robust democratic credentials. They typically establish super-majority governments inclusive of all parties with significant mandates that are willing to take their entitlements to portfolios. This inclusiveness contrasts favourably with both centripetal minimum-winning coalitions, and single-party governments in plurality or majoritarian voting systems, each of which may enjoy power with the support of a bare legislative majority or just a plurality of voters. SPA mechanisms also prevent the policy distortions that may occur in minimum-winning coalitions where small parties exploit disproportionate pivotality because they hold the balance between large political blocs – as happens in Israel and Germany.

It is true that executives formed with SPA mechanisms and that serve fixed terms are not consistent with opposition in the form of 'governments in waiting.' This does not mean, however, that such governments cannot be changed, or that there is no accountability (Garry 2009, 2014). Voters remain free to punish or reward any party by increasing or decreasing its vote and therefore its share of ministries (or its place in the sequence of allocation), and to vote new parties into the coalition. The accountability of the executive to voters may be less clear than when a single party is in government, but it is not obviously less clear than under any multi-party coalition, which is the more frequent alternative in most democracies (Garry 2014). Given that parties in an inclusive coalition are likely to have policy differences, and will each be interested in increasing their respective shares of ministries after subsequent elections, dynamics exist to deliver competition and accountability, though they may also lead to deadlock. But centripetalists must choose their complaint: is it that grand coalitions lack opposition, or that such coalitions are likely to be mired in internal opposition?

Evidence from Northern Ireland, 1973 to 2015

Northern Ireland's last four decades help evaluate the debate over the merits of centripetal and consociational executives in deeply divided areas. Both modes of power-sharing have been tried there, and many other key variables regarding preferences and culture can be kept constant (including some key personnel). Since the subject was first debated (Horowitz 2002; McGarry and O'Leary

2004b; O'Leary 2004b), the region has had nearly a decade of experience of SPA mechanisms.

The key cleavage in Northern Irish politics has always been between nationalists who wanted a reunified and sovereign Ireland and unionists who wish to maintain the Union with Great Britain. The decision of both main moderate parties – the nationalist Social Democratic and Labour Party (SDLP) and the Ulster Unionist Party (UUP) – to negotiate SPA mechanisms in the Good Friday Agreement of 1998 was not just based on their calculations about their future interests. It reflected their evaluations of Northern Ireland's previous experience with power-sharing, the 'Sunningdale executive' of 1974, which was squarely centripetal.[16] John Hume, the SDLP leader in 1998, had served as Minister of Commerce in the Sunningdale executive, while David Trimble, the UUP leader in 1998, had begun his political career as a member of the Vanguard Unionist Party, which opposed the Sunningdale Agreement.

The Sunningdale executive comprised the moderate wing of the UUP led by Brian Faulkner as Prime Minister, the moderate nationalists of the SDLP led by Gerry Fitt as Deputy Prime Minister, and two small moderate non-ethnic parties, the Northern Ireland Labour Party and Alliance, which were not necessary for a minimum-winning coalition. Appointed by the UK Secretary of State William Whitelaw, the executive took office in January 1974, but collapsed less than five months later, largely because the inter-bloc and intra-bloc balances of power were unfavourable for centripetal power-sharing (for accounts see Fisk 1975; Kerr 2011; O'Duffy 2007). During these years, unionists had strong electoral dominance. The unionist:nationalist ratio of votes won in the June 1973 Assembly elections that preceded the Sunningdale Agreement was 62:25. Both blocs also lacked stably dominant moderate parties. Faulkner's pro-power-sharing unionists had won 24 seats out of the 78 available (25.3 per cent of the vote, 30.8 per cent of the seats), while unionists opposed to power-sharing won 25 seats (35.1 per cent of the vote, 32.1 per cent of the seats).[17] Thus pro-power-sharing unionists were highly vulnerable to outflanking. When the executive began life, supporters of the Sunningdale Agreement had become a minority among unionists even within the UUP, eventually forcing Faulkner to resign as party leader, and later to form his own party, the Unionist Party of Northern Ireland (UPNI). In February, the power-sharing executive suffered a critical wound. The Conservative Prime Minister Edward Heath called a snap election for the UK's Westminster Parliament. In Northern Ireland, it became a referendum on the Sunningdale Agreement. Hardline unionists opposed to power-sharing won 11 of the region's then 12 districts, and 51 per cent of the vote, compared with the 13 per cent received by pro-power-sharing unionists, who were comprehensively outflanked. The power-sharing agreement was also strongly opposed by loyalist militias, then engaged in the killing of Catholics and nationalist civilians. On the nationalist side, electoral data superficially suggested stable moderate dominance. The SDLP was the only significant party to contest the 1973 elections, and it received 22 per cent of the overall vote. But this picture was misleading. The nationalist bloc was close to one-third of the population. A significant republican (hardline nationalist) constituency had boycotted the elections, while militants in the IRA (Provisional Irish Republican Army) were waging a violent armed campaign to end British sovereignty.

Rather than successfully "fending off the uncompromising extremes" the centripetal coalition of moderates was on the defensive on both of its flanks from the outset. The coalition partners failed to cooperate to avoid vote splitting in the Westminster elections. The pathologies of winner-takes-all in single-member districts (O'Leary 2010) worked to hand at least three districts to hardline unionist rejectionists, even though a majority of the voters in these places supported power-sharing parties. Moderate nationalists were unable to address the concerns of their unionist partners on the all-Ireland dimensions of the Sunningdale Agreement, because republicans accused them of legitimizing hardline security measures, including detention without trial (Cunningham 1991, 56). An SDLP Assembly member, Hugh Logue, eager to compete with his party's republican rivals, told a Dublin audience in January 1974 that the Agreement was designed to "trundle unionists into a united Ireland," prompting unionist opponents of power-sharing to coin the effective slogan that "Dublin was just a Sunningdale away." Faced with what became a widespread strike, led by militant loyalists and their militias, and diminishing legitimacy in their bloc, the moderate unionists on the executive resigned in May 1974, ending the experiment.

The British government failed to take action against the strike partly because the internal bickering within the executive convinced them that power-sharing was doomed.[18] The fate of the Sunningdale executive led to 25 years of disillusionment with power-sharing, and to neo-colonial 'direct rule' from London. That said, it has to be admitted that agreeing a coalition based on SPA mechanisms would have been unlikely in 1974 because neither hardline republicans nor the majority of unionists were prepared to share power on mutually acceptable terms[19] – though the IRA was more flexible than imagined at the time (Ó Dochartaigh 2011). But, as we have seen, moderates certainly lacked the stable dominance to sustain a centripetal coalition.

The Good Friday Agreement of 1998, which provided for an executive based on the d'Hondt algorithm, was negotiated after an inter-community balance of power emerged between the region's two blocs. Unionist parties won 48 per cent of the vote in the 1998 elections to a new Northern Ireland Assembly while nationalist parties won 40 per cent. The combined unionist share of the vote had been steadily declining, driven by demographic change and the hardline Sinn Féin's successful mobilization of previous abstentionists in the nationalist community (O'Leary and Evans 1997). This new inter-bloc balance meant that power-sharing was necessary to govern any local assembly. It was also mutually desirable: nationalists, as a long-term minority, had an obvious interest in power-sharing, but unionists could see that a compromise was in their long-term interests, given their demographic decline.

In 1998, a clear intra-community balance of power existed in both communities. In the Assembly elections, the relatively moderate UUP and the hardline DUP led by Ian Paisley received 45 per cent and 38 per cent of the unionist vote, respectively, while the relatively moderate SDLP and hardline Sinn Féin received 56 per cent and 44 per cent of the nationalist vote, respectively. The moderate parties, the SDLP and UUP, were the leading parties in their blocs, and would have had the numbers in the Assembly to opt for a centripetal minimum-winning coalition, perhaps along with the small cross-ethnic Alliance Party, but this was not what had been negotiated.

Instead, in the agreement and before the elections, the SDLP had proposed a d'Hondt-based executive and their UUP counterparts had accepted. The hardline parties, minority parties in each bloc, were the main beneficiaries of this inclusive approach, even though they played no role in the key discussions on the rules of executive formation: the DUP boycotted the negotiations, while Sinn Féin focused on the release of IRA prisoners and other subjects. This result – where moderates with discretion opted for a consociational and probable grand coalition – was not one expected by centripetal theorists. How should this decision be explained?

The particular rule selected, d'Hondt, had been used in the European Parliament to allocate committee positions, where Hume and Paisley had been MEPs for nearly 20 years. Variations on the idea had also been discussed in the past (McGarry and Graham 1990; O'Leary et al. 1993; Rose 1976). The d'Hondt divisor was attractive to the SDLP and UUP because it benefited larger parties, the status held by these parties in 1998. The more fundamental decision to use the rule to allow for an inclusive grand coalition, however, flowed from the intra-bloc balance of power. Hume's SDLP faced a powerful rival in Sinn Féin, which raised the threat of successful outflanking if the SDLP participated in an executive that excluded Sinn Féin. In the early 1980s, Hume, along with the Irish and British governments, had sought to marginalize Sinn Féin through the Anglo-Irish Agreement, but it was clear by the late 1980s that this strategy had halted, but not marginalized, the party's support (O'Leary 2004a). Sinn Féin looked set to remain a significant electoral force, which helped precipitate controversial talks between Hume and the Sinn Féin leader Gerry Adams between 1988 and 1994. With the IRA's decision to declare a ceasefire from August 1994, and Sinn Féin's preparedness to accept constitutional politics, the party became increasingly attractive to SDLP voters (McLoughlin 2010, 186–187). Since Sinn Féin was the political wing of the IRA, Hume believed, along with the British and Irish governments, that its political inclusion was necessary to stop the violence. Hume's talks with Adams led the former to believe that an end to violence was possible, and that inclusion would strengthen the relative moderates in Sinn Féin's ranks against republican hawks. Hume thought that an end to violence was desirable not just for its own sake, but because a settlement with unionists would be impossible or unworkable without it.[20] He understood that Sinn Féin's participation in the executive would strengthen the overall nationalist position and give them a greater total share of ministries than in any coalition that excluded Sinn Féin, particularly if that coalition included both the UUP and DUP. And when the d'Hondt allocation was initially run in 1999, nationalists were able to win half of the ten ministries available, although after subsequent elections their total dropped to four of the ten.

Trimble of the UUP accepted the prospects of a grand coalition partly because he shared Hume's analysis that Sinn Féin's inclusion was necessary for peace: the SDLP alone could not deliver the legitimacy among nationalists required for stable power-sharing. Trimble was also sympathetic to the SDLP's fears about being outflanked. He told his biographer that he endorsed d'Hondt because he had succeeded in winning concessions in the negotiations on north–south institutions, and he believed that the SDLP needed a win on the executive in return:

> We can't push the SDLP to the limit. We'd then be doing to them what the SDLP and the Irish and Whitelaw did to Faulkner [at the Sunningdale Conference in 1973]. We had to give them enough [d'Hondt] to defend themselves [against Sinn Féin].
>
> (Godson 2004, 339)

Trimble's flexibility was also shaped by the UUP's intra-bloc position. He recalled Faulkner's fate, and could not sign up to a coalition with the SDLP and Sinn Féin that left the DUP free to outflank his party. He needed a mechanism that made all sizeable parties eligible for government, including the DUP, and d'Hondt met these requirements. Although it was risky for Trimble to accept d'Hondt while the DUP posed a powerful threat, the risk would be mitigated if the executive's formation rules induced the DUP to join.

The sole party that preferred a centripetal coalition of moderate parties was the small and moderate inter-ethnic Alliance, which won 6.5 per cent of the vote in 1998. It would have held a pivotal and disproportionate position in such an executive, but it risked not qualifying for a ministry under d'Hondt. Yet, Alliance accepted the possibility of a grand coalition based on d'Hondt, knowing that the mechanism would not perpetually exclude it, and it was eventually able to win a ministry under these rules in 2011. The DUP, in contrast, supported the d'Hondt proportionality principle as a fair basis for distributing offices, but, in 1998, it did not accept an executive which included ex-IRA personnel.

Conditions in Northern Ireland, then, were conducive to the establishment of a sequential and proportional coalition, but how did this coalition function, once agreed? The coalition's experience may be divided into two phases: from 1999 until 2007 and from 2007 until 2015. The first period was one of significant instability. The executive was not established until late 1999; it was then unilaterally suspended on four occasions by the UK government; the last suspension ran from late 2002 until March 2007 (McGarry and O'Leary 2006a, 2006b). For centripetalists, these problems had their roots squarely in institutional flaws; they were evidence that grand coalitions "just d'Hondt work."[21] Writing at the beginning of the last suspension, Horowitz explained that grand coalitions were inherently conducive to "immobilism"; Sinn Féin's inclusion had "perpetuated the appeal of rejectionist unionism," weakened Trimble and made it difficult for him to compromise. What was needed was an institutional and coalitional change, a centripetalist "compromising middle" that would undercut the extremes with progress on divisive issues (Horowitz 2001, 102; 2002, 194, 197).

This explanation was starkly different from Horowitz's account of the failure of the centripetal Sunningdale executive. The latter collapsed, in his view, not because moderates were too weak to sustain it – a view that would have suggested that successful centripetalism requires pre-existing moderation – but for two other reasons. The Sunningdale coalition, he argued, lacked the backing that a strong centripetal electoral system based on the alternative vote would have provided, a strongly counterfactual claim.[22] In addition, he observed that the coalition "was asked to take on too many contentious issues at once: the end of internment, a North–South Council, and the policy of the Republic towards self-determination for the people of the North." This agenda "was a great deal to put on the plate of a government while unionists were divided over whether it was possible to admit nationalists to government in the first place" (Horowitz 2002, 216). One problem with this explanation for the failure of the Sunningdale executive is that power-sharing governments in deeply divided places frequently confront contentious issues. Another is that the post-1998 executive has faced issues arguably just as divisive as those confronted by its 1974 predecessor. In 1998, unionists were also divided on the merits of admitting nationalists, especially republicans, into government, and rejected several of the Agreement's provisions including the North–South Ministerial Council, and more vehemently provisions for releasing convicted prisoners on licence. Even unionist supporters of the Agreement adopted radically different positions from their nationalist and republican counterparts on matters to be resolved by independent commissions or postponed under the provisions of the Agreement. Republicans insisted on the disbanding of the police and rapid demilitarization before the IRA decommissioned its weapons, while power-sharing unionists insisted on immediate decommissioning and opposed both demilitarization and policing reform. Yet, in spite of these divisive issues, the 1998 executive survived, unlike its Sunningdale counterpart, and if we count only the period from 2007 up until the time of writing, the new executive has lasted in office almost 20 times longer than its Sunningdale predecessor.

When Northern Ireland's parties and the British and Irish governments dealt with the post-1998 divisive issues through issue linkages, log rolls and reciprocity between 2003 and 2007, the bargaining ushered in a period of unprecedented stable and successful power-sharing that still continues, though the security of the institutions is certainly not set in stone, and progress remains fragile (McCrudden et al. 2016). Parties representing all 108 members of the Assembly, and 98 per cent of voters supported the executive that sat from 2007 to 2011, whereas parties representing 107 of 108 MLAs and 97 per cent of voters supported that elected in 2011.[23] In 2010, the leading parties in the coalition, the DUP and Sinn Féin, reached agreement on the controversial matter of the transfer of policing and justice powers. The first post-2007 FM and DFMs, Ian Paisley and Martin McGuinness, got on so well together that they became known as the "Chuckle Brothers." Paisley's successor, Peter Robinson, initially developed a working relationship with McGuinness: the former attended masses and Gaelic football games, while the latter shook hands with and then toasted the

Queen, previously unthinkable events. The two parties cooperated in 2007 and 2011 on the sharing of ministries – even agreeing to explain what portfolios they would pick in advance of the formal running of the d'Hondt allocation, although the process prudently remains as the legally mandated default to voluntary agreement on the allocation of particular ministries. By 2014, some of those who had earlier denounced Sinn Féin and the DUP's inability to compromise now accused them of cooperating too much, and of establishing a pact to 'carve up' patronage. Others shifted their criticisms from themes of instability and uncooperativeness to exaggerated complaints of inertia and inefficiency. Yet, other critics argued that Northern Ireland had so matured that it was now safe to envisage a return to normal "government and opposition" (for our reply see McCrudden et al. 2016).

Post-2007 power-sharing has not been without its difficulties – the latest in 2014/2015 involve how to deal with past crimes, enduring controversies over parades by the Orange Order and spending on the welfare state, and managing the repercussions of the London government's determination to cut Northern Ireland's block grant. One should never underestimate the problems confronting any power-sharing pact in a severely divided place. However, thus far, successive coalitions since 2007 have weathered the storms they have faced. We do not say that they are certain to survive all adverse conditions, but even if breakdown occurs, the arrangements have clearly been far more successful and stable than their centripetal predecessor.

Methodologically speaking, the d'Hondt (SPA) rule of executive formation cannot have been the major explanatory variable responsible for instability during the transition years of 1999 to 2007, because it remained in place after 2007. Arguably, however, the d'Hondt method was extended in the St Andrew's Agreement Act of 2006, because it now effectively applies to the election of the first minister (FM) and, in a qualified way, to the election of the deputy first minister (DFM). Before 2007, the FM and DFM had been elected by a concurrent majority of nationalists and unionists, but the FM is now the nominee of the largest party in the Assembly, the equivalent of a first pick under d'Hondt. The DFM is now the nominee of the largest party in the largest designation other than the FM's – rather than, as would happen under unqualified d'Hondt, the nominee of the second-largest party. This qualification was necessary to prevent the possibility of unionists or nationalists winning both posts.

Indeed, a fair case can be made that the d'Hondt rule contributed to the moderation of the hardline parties after 1998, and the stability of the institutions after 2007. Sinn Féin's strategy for winning over their own hardliners, and isolating those who could not be won over, stressed that inclusive institutions offered an alternative way to advance its political agenda. Therefore, d'Hondt, in combination with other factors of course, helps explain the relative peace after 1998. Initially, the DUP's moderation was far less obvious. In 1998, the DUP sought to renegotiate the Agreement, opposed it in the May referendum, and appeared keen to outflank Trimble's UUP. However, the fact that the d'Hondt rule provided no incentive to refuse office helped persuade the DUP to take up and retain its seats on the executive (Mitchell *et al.* 2009).[24] Had the possible exit of the DUP brought about the executive's destruction, as the resignation of Faulkner's moderate unionists ended the Sunningdale Agreement, the new institutions would have been less stable. While there was little trust among the parties, both the DUP and UUP could explain to their supporters that sharing government with Sinn Féin was not of their volition, but rather imposed upon them by the d'Hondt rule.[25] This fact explains why the politically useful but legally inaccurate phrase 'mandatory coalition' has been a steady refrain in discontented unionist discourse. Parties are free not to take up their ministerial entitlements, but the SPA mechanism strongly encourages them to do so. After 1998, DUP supporters, previously habituated to their party refusing to enter the same buildings as republicans, became used to joint membership of the executive with Sinn Féin, making the 2006/2007 pact between the parties imaginable. The fact that the d'Hondt organized executive does not rely on conventional principles of collective cabinet responsibility also meant that it was capable of withstanding the lack of cooperation that marked the immediate post-Agreement years –another constructive contrast with the Sunningdale executive.

The d'Hondt rule incentivized both Sinn Féin and the DUP to increase their votes: the reward would be more ministries. The logical way to increase their votes was to become more moderate while assuring their core supporters that they remained their people's tribunes (Mitchell *et al.* 2009). This change is now widely recognized, but immediately after 1998 many incorrectly interpreted Sinn Féin and the DUP's growing popularity as evidence of growing extremism. Rather, the behaviour of the two parties was a clear example of Horowitz's core idea that if necessary, parties will moderate to win office, though, in this case, based on institutions that he rejects. The effective extension of the d'Hondt rule to the election of the joint premiership in 2007 gave Sinn Féin and the DUP incentives to become and remain the largest parties in their respective blocs, consolidated moderation and, as with the rest of the executive, facilitated power-sharing without requiring either party expressly to endorse the other party's nominee. This was, we believe, an appropriate institutional modification when trust was lacking and needed to be cultivated.

The most plausible counterfactual world to what transpired is fairly clear. The exclusion of republicans from a new executive would have posed major problems for the peace process, and, therefore, for political stability. This scenario would likely have produced less disarmament, less police and judicial reform and therefore more violence. Increased violence would have put tremendous pressure on the parties in a moderates-only coalition, had the moderates been prepared to form one. Why should anyone believe that in this counterfactual world the moderates would not only have cooperated, but also managed to pacify those fighting?

The d'Hondt SPA mechanism has not been the sole variable contributing to Northern Ireland's recent political stability, and we agree that it is difficult to weigh its salience. There were many other virtuous conflict-regulating changes in the Agreement: its negotiation demonstrated effective inter-governmentalism; the

British and Irish governments helped resolve many contentious issues that posed difficulties; and it was made clear to the DUP during the period leading up to the resumption of power-sharing in 2007 that the alternative was going to be something it would like even less, namely strengthened British–Irish cooperation in governing Northern Ireland (Hain 2012). But SPA rules also mattered, and complemented these changes.

Ironically, the institutional rule that proved most problematic in the early post-Agreement years owed more to centripetal than to consociational thought. Between 1998 and 2007, the FM and DFM, equal in powers, though with different titles, were elected by a concurrent majority of registered nationalists and unionists in the Assembly. This power-sharing rule was designed to ensure that one of the top two office holders would be a unionist and one would be a nationalist, but it was also meant to facilitate the election of two moderates, because hardliners were unlikely to win cross-community support. Both offices were interdependent: if either the first minister or the DFM died or resigned, both offices became vacant, an idea thought necessary to prevent a problem inherent in the use of formal centripetal rules to elect representatives from different blocs: upon a vacancy, one bloc's representatives could refuse to support someone supported by the other bloc. If the FM and DFM could not be elected or re-elected, the Agreement provided for fresh Assembly elections within six weeks. The rule was the initiative of the leading moderate parties in each bloc, the SDLP and UUP, and was included because these were the leading parties in the negotiations of 1997/1998 (O'Leary 1999). The institution of dual premiership immediately became a lightning rod for disagreement.

The fundamental problem, again, was that neither set of moderates enjoyed 'stable dominance' within their blocs. In the Assembly elections of 1998, pro-Agreement unionists won 30 seats to the 28 of unionists who were opposed, but one 'yes unionist' jumped sides, leading to an even intra-bloc balance between moderates and hardliners. The UUP was badly divided, with a prominent figure, Jeffrey Donaldson, walking out of the Agreement's negotiations, and constantly challenging his leader before he resigned with two other MLAs in December 2003. The lack of an intra-bloc balance that favoured moderates made Trimble's leadership precarious, and tempted him to employ the centripetal rules used for the election of premiers in an ultimately failed attempt to extract concessions from the British government and from nationalists. The suspension of the Agreement's institutions by the Westminster Parliament in 2000, 2001 and 2002 flowed from threatened resignations by Trimble, who calculated that it would put pressure on Sinn Féin to oblige the IRA to decommission, and on the British government to limit policing reform, which in turn would help Trimble with his opponents in the UUP and his party in its competition with the DUP.

Initially, rather than risking new Assembly elections or risking Trimble not being re-elected FM by the Assembly – a genuine possibility – the British government suspended the institutions, thereby antagonizing nationalists, including the Irish government, and setting back agreement on contentious issues for a number of years. In July 2001, Trimble did resign, forcing the SDLP's DFM

Durkan's resignation, but when the two sought office again, they failed to get elected by two unionist votes, though they had the support of over 70 per cent of the Assembly. They were rescued by the votes of members of a couple of small non-ethnic parties who re-designated themselves as 'unionists' to re-elect the dual premiers, attracting ridicule to the rules. The impasse that existed between the Assembly elections of November 2003 and May 2007 may reasonably be traced directly to the centripetal rules for electing the dual premiership (and the intra-unionist balance of power). When the DUP won a majority of the unionist bloc's seats in the 2003 Assembly elections, it had a formal veto on the election of the dual premiers, which it exercised de facto for four years. That is why the scrapping of the (centripetal) concurrent majority election rule, and its replacement by a functional equivalent to d'Hondt, was recommended for the election of the two premiers (McGarry and O'Leary 2004a, 29; 2004c). It was implemented in the St Andrews Agreement. The change facilitated the DUP's decision to enter a power-sharing pact with Sinn Féin. Its MLAs did not have to support a Sinn Féin candidate for DFM.

Conclusion: the comparative relevance of executives formed through sequential and proportional allocation rules

Northern Ireland's institutional case history over four decades suggests that coalitions constructed through sequential and proportional allocation rules have advantages over centripetal coalitions of moderate parties and over alternative forms of consociational coalition. Sequential and proportional coalitions are facilitated by an inter-bloc balance of power among rivalrous communities, or by an inter-bloc balance combined with an intra-bloc balance. These rules adjust to changes in the proportional balance of power between and within blocs, and produce incentives for hardline parties to moderate, and they have other system-maintaining qualities. They help explain why such an executive design materialized in Northern Ireland, and why it has been successful thus far.

Centripetal coalitions, in contrast, seem much less likely to be agreed in deeply divided areas, since they exclude the hardliners who are necessary for peace, and are unlikely to function as hoped for if agreed (or imposed). Centripetal coalitions appear to need moderate parties to be stably dominant within key blocs, an uncommon condition in deeply divided areas. Sequential proportional executive formation mechanisms are also an adaptable political technology. They may be formally entrenched in constitutions, temporary, or informal and temporary. Temporary use will be more satisfactory to those who insist on the value of governments that clearly alternate, but they risk the dangers associated with exclusion once the transition expires. Different divisors may be matched to the needs of different polities – d'Hondt is likely to be preferred where there are dominant large parties, Sainte-Laguë where this is not so, and the Danish rule may be considered as a way of incorporating minorities that are supported by 20 per cent or so of the population. Such flexibility increases the range of places in which this technology is likely to be attractive. The same array of rules may be usefully employed in the legislature, such as in staffing the chairs and deputy chairs of legislative committees, or, perhaps, in the appointment of judges with legislative confirmation, and in political appointments to boards.

These mechanisms are worth considering wherever agreements are needed following violent conflict, but they may also be infused into extant power-sharing agreements. A decision to opt for an SPA mechanism would address Belgium's consecutive delays in executive formation, and the executive formation problems Kenya experienced in 2008/2009. Had Fiji adopted such a mechanism in 1999, it would have stopped Prime Minister Chaudhry giving the most important portfolios to ethnic Indians, and perhaps forestalled the Fijian-led putsch in 2000 that brought down his government. Sequential proportional executives may aid change from corporate to liberal consociations, which reformers seek in Lebanon and Bosnia. Sequential proportional mechanisms, in short, may offer deeply divided places one helpful democratic conflict-regulation mechanism that should be seriously considered by negotiators and mediators. They certainly do not guarantee peace or stability, neither in Northern Ireland nor elsewhere, but no institutional mechanisms can do that.

Notes

1 The original version of this chapter was published in *Ethnopolitics* 15, no. 5.
2 Mancur Olson's hypothesis that older democracies would stagnate over time (unless they had all-encompassing or corporatist interest group arrangements, wars or charismatic breaks with the past) has not generally been vindicated (Mueller 1983; Olson 1982; Persson and Tabellini 2005, 216). Extensive econometric studies by economists have established correlations, and plausible causal linkages, between presidentialism and majoritarianism and comparatively lower public – including welfare – expenditures, but they admit that their analysis of the economic effects of constitutions has merely "scratched the surface of the policies most likely to promote economic growth" (Persson and Tabellini 2005, 278). More extensive welfare and more universal public goods, after all, may be growth-enhancing. Currently, it does not take a PhD in economics to believe that the poor growth performance of the longest established proportional and parliamentary systems in Europe likely owes most to the specific (non-fiscal) arrangements created for the Eurozone rather than to the institutions of member-states.
3 This is how Horowitz reads Lijphart's grand coalition.
4 The argument is set out at length in O'Leary (2005), and has been endorsed by Arend Lijphart in correspondence.
5 But see Brams and Kaplan (2004), O'Leary *et al.* (2005). As yet, there are no real-world examples of Brams' interesting idea that ministries should be divided according to fair division rules in which the allocation procedure would not invariably benefit the party which wins the most votes at each stage (Brams 2008; Brams and Kaplan 2004). We suspect this is because the idea is deeply embedded in democracies that the party that wins the most votes should have a consistent advantage. We therefore focus here on sequential division rules, recognizing that Brams and others have promoted reasonable alternatives which merit scholarly and policy-makers' attention.
6 On different ways of conceptualizing proportionality in relation to electoral systems see Gallagher (1991, 1992).
7 The d'Hondt divisor rule, named after the Belgian mathematician Viktor d'Hondt, was independently invented by Thomas Jefferson to allocate the number of seats in

the US House of Representatives to be held by the several states according to their respective population shares (Balinski and Peyton Young 1982).
8 Burundi has a large Hutu majority, but the Tutsi are a formerly dominant minority with strength in the military that cancels out the Hutu's demographic advantage, so it presents a sociological dual balance of power.
9 Some places have opted for grand coalitions even when they have lacked deep ethnic divisions and possessed majority parties capable of governing alone – Sweden and the UK formed 'national governments' in the face of external threats during wartime. Of 32 parliamentary systems examined by Lijphart (1999, 97–98), 22 per cent had an oversized coalition that comprised at least 80 per cent of the seats in the legislature.
10 Mitchell et al. (2009), Rabushka and Shepsle (2009 [1972]). Outflanking occurs when a hardline party successfully wins votes from a more moderate party in its bloc by accusing the latter of betraying the bloc's voters through its preparedness to compromise across bloc lines.
11 The AV is a preferential majoritarian voting system. Horowitz believes that it encourages moderation because the high threshold (50 per cent + 1) forces politicians to reach out across ethnic lines for the margin of victory, while its preferential rules encourage voters to vote across bloc lines on lower preferences.
12 Papua New Guinea has used the AV for legislative elections, but it is a highly fragmented place rather than one of the dualistic or tripolar places normally classified as deeply divided (Reilly 2001), and it was first imposed under colonial administration. Whether Fiji was deeply divided at the adoption of AV has been questioned: divisions were then cross-cutting (Fraenkel and Grofman 2004).
13 "Confronted with an interethnic centrist coalition, the strategy [extremist parties] typically pursue is to oppose the coalition from the flanks as a sellout of group interests. Nothing in AV changes this" (Horowitz 2004, 512).
14 There is a long history of the failure of 'cross-voting' schemes (Elster 2013).
15 See "Cabinet Joiners" (*The Economist*, 15 January 2015).
16 Horowitz acknowledged that the fate of Sunningdale played a key role in the decision to embrace SPA rules, but thought that all involved in the decision had misread history (Horowitz 2002, 215).
17 Calculated from www.ark.ac.uk/elections/fa73.htm.
18 The SDLP wanted troops used to break the strike, but their unionist partners wanted to negotiate with the loyalists (Wolff 2002, 6).
19 It was briefly outlined among other possibilities in Rose (1976).
20 One of Hume's closest aides, Denis Haughey, explained:

> Hume was electrified by the thought of turning off the violence and saving human life ... [But h]e was fitting that into a framework of thinking which I think could be summarised as this: the middle ground is not taking shape in the way that we [in the SDLP] hoped it would as a consequence of the Anglo-Irish Agreement, and it is not going to take shape, because of the divisive effect upon opinion being generated by the violence ... and for as long as that violence goes on we are not going to get a sufficiently strong middle ground to mount any kind of structure of power ... [However,] if we are going to switch off the violence, we have got to offer these guys [republicans] something; we have got to offer them a place in the scheme of things ... it has got to be inclusive.
> (McLoughlin 2010, 145)

21 See "Time to Tackle Agreement Flaws Because Current Rules Just d'Hondt Work." *Belfast Telegraph*, 12 December 2003.
22 Horowitz (2002, 213). AV would have had to be imposed upon the parties in 1973, since there was little chance of the SDLP accepting a majoritarian voting system, or the dominant anti-power-sharing unionists accepting anything that would have benefited their moderate opponents. As anti-power-sharing unionists were so dominant

throughout 1974 and 1975, they would have won an overwhelming majority of seats in Northern Ireland in an AV election after the first count in each district, with no need for inter-bloc transfers. Politicians, particularly from the majority bloc, would have been discouraged from reaching out across blocs in the climate of the early to mid-1970s, because of the danger that they would lose more votes in their own bloc than they would gain from the other bloc. Nor was there much hope – as evidence from preferential PR-STV elections showed – that voters would have responded positively to such inter-bloc appeals. In the Assembly elections of 1973, only an estimated 0.25 per cent of vote transfers crossed bloc lines (McAllister 1975; Coakley and Fraenkel 2010, 6). John Coakley, in a simulation of how the AV would have worked in Assembly elections between 1973 and 2007, found that its main consequence would have been to wipe out the moderate middle (the APNI) (see Coakley 2009). A study of the 50 contested local government by-elections between 1985 and 2010, which were held under AV, found that they offered no advantage to moderates. Since 31 of the 50 had either no nationalist or no unionist candidate, they demonstrated another weakness of AV in a deeply divided polity: the relative absence of the required heterogeneous constituencies (details available from authors).
23 The electoral turnout fell, however. For the 2007 and 2011 Assembly elections, it was 63 per cent and 55 per cent, respectively. This fact cannot, however, be treated as proof of electoral disenchantment with consociation: there were anti-Agreement parties and politicians running for office, and Northern Ireland's turnout was significantly higher than the turnout for elections to the Scottish Parliament and the Welsh Assembly during the same years.
24 The arrest and subsequent release of Sinn Féin President Gerry Adams in May 2014 did not lead the DUP to consider withdrawal from the executive. Indeed, Sinn Féin had reciprocated its governmental partner in advance: when a sex and expenses scandal enveloped Peter and Iris Robinson (the FM's wife, who was also an elected politician), republicans remained silent. Each dominant party has so far respected the idea that the other side must choose its own leaders.
25 D'Hondt

> provided a fig-leaf: any decision to accept an all-inclusive consociational form of government could now be explained away as the compulsory outworkings of an imposed electoral method, rather than as a decision taken voluntarily by themselves which would violate their traditional skepticism about power-sharing. Such reasoning might appear eccentric but then Unionism has always been more about maintaining appearances than many of its critics and admirers have understood.
> (Godson 2004, 339)

References

Balinski, Michael L. and H. Peyton Young. 1982. *Fair Representation: Meeting the Ideal of One Man, One Vote*. New Haven, CT: Yale University Press.

Bogaards, Matthijs. 2014. *Democracy and Social Peace in Divided Societies: Exploring Consociational Parties*. Basingstoke: Palgrave Macmillan.

Brams, Steven J. 2008. *Mathematics and Democracy: Designing Better Voting and Fair-Division Procedures*. Princeton, NJ: Princeton University Press.

Brams, Steven J. and Todd R. Kaplan. 2004. "Dividing the Indivisible: Procedures for Allocating Cabinet Ministries to Political Parties in a Parliamentary System." *Journal of Theoretical Politics* 16: 143–173.

Brams, Steven J. and D. Marc Kilgour. 2010a. "Stabilizing Power Sharing." In *Collective Decision Making*, edited by Adrian Van Deemen and Agnieszka Rusinowska, pp. 169–184. Berlin: Springer.

Brams, Steven J. and D. Marc Kilgour. 2010b. "The Instability of Power Sharing." In *Power, Freedom, and Voting*, edited by Matthew Braham and Frank Steffen, pp. 227–243. Berlin: Springer.

Cheeseman, Nic and Blessing-Miles Tendi. 2010. "Power-Sharing in Comparative Perspective: The Dynamics of 'Unity Government' in Kenya and Zimbabwe." *Journal of Modern African Studies* 48, no. 2: 203–229.

Coakley, John. 2009. "The Political Consequences of the Electoral System in Northern Ireland." *Irish Political Studies* 24, no. 3: 253–284.

Coakley, John and Jon Fraenkel. 2010. "Ethnic Conflict and Electoral Engineering: The Single Transferable Vote in Northern Ireland." Annual Conference of the Political Studies Association of Ireland, Dublin Institute of Technology.

Cunningham, Michael J. 1991. *British Government Policy in Northern Ireland, 1969–89: Its Nature and Execution*. Manchester: Manchester University Press.

Deschouwer, Kris and Philippe van Parijs. 2013. "Electoral Engineering for a Stalled Federation." In *Power-Sharing in Deeply Divided Places*, edited by Joanne McEvoy and Brendan O'Leary, pp. 112–134. Philadelphia: University of Pennsylvania Press.

Elster, Jon. 2013. *Securities against Misrule: Juries, Assemblies, Elections*. Cambridge: Cambridge University Press.

Fisk, Robert. 1975. *The Point of No Return: The Strike Which Broke the British in Ulster*. London: André Deutsch.

Fraenkel, Jon. 2003. "Electoral Engineering and the Politicisation of Ethnic Friction in Fiji." In *Can Democracy be Designed? The Politics of Institutional Choice in Conflict-Torn Societies*, edited by Sunil Bastian and Robin Luckham, pp. 220–253. London: Zed Books.

Fraenkel, Jon and Bernard Grofman. 2004. "A Neo-Downsian Model of the Alternative Vote as a Mechanism for Mitigating Ethnic Conflict in Plural Societies." *Public Choice* 121, nos. 3 and 4: 487–506.

Fraenkel, Jon and Bernard Grofman 2006a. "Does the Alternative Vote Foster Moderation in Ethnically Divided Societies? The Case of Fiji." *Comparative Political Studies* 39, no. 5: 623–651.

Fraenkel, Jon and Bernard Grofman 2006b. "The Failure of the Alternative Vote as a Tool for Ethnic Moderation in Fiji? A Rejoinder to Horowitz." *Comparative Political Studies* 39, no. 5: 663–665.

Gallagher, Michael. 1991. "Proportionality, Disproportionality and Electoral Systems." *Electoral Studies* 10, no. 1: 33–51.

Gallagher, Michael. 1992. "Comparing Proportional Representation Electoral Systems: Quotas, Thresholds, Paradoxes and Majorities." *British Journal of Political Science* 22, no. 4: 469–496.

Garry, John. 2009. "Consociationalism and Its Critics: Evidence from the Historic Northern Ireland Assembly Election 2007." *Electoral Studies* 28, no. 3: 458–466.

Garry, John. 2014. "Holding Parties Responsible at Election Time: Multi-Level, Multi-Party Government and Electoral Accountability." *Electoral Studies* 34: 78–88.

Godson, Dean. 2004. *Himself Alone: David Trimble and the Ordeal of Unionism*. London: Harper-Collins E-books.

Hain, Peter. 2012. "From Horror to Hope: Northern Ireland Breakthrough." In *Outside In*, pp. 310–353. London: Biteback.

Hanf, Theodor. 1993. *Coexistence in Wartime Lebanon: Decline of a State and Rise of a Nation*, translated by John Richardson. London: I.B. Tauris.

Hix, Simon and Bjørn Høyland, eds. 2011. *The Political System of the European Union*. Basingstoke: Palgrave Macmillan.

Horowitz, Donald. L. 2000. "Constitutional Design: An Oxymoron?" In *Designing Democratic Institutions*, edited by Ian Shapiro and Stephen Macedo, pp. 253–284. New York: New York University Press.

Horowitz, Donald. L. 2001. "The Agreement: Clear, Consociational and Risky." In *Northern Ireland and the Divided World: Post-Agreement Northern Ireland in Comparative Perspective*, edited by John McGarry, pp. 89–108. Oxford: Oxford University Press.

Horowitz, Donald. L. 2002. "Explaining the Northern Ireland Agreement: The Sources of an Unlikely Constitutional Consensus." *British Journal of Political Science* 32: 193–220.

Horowitz, Donald. L. 2004. "The Alternative Vote and Interethnic Moderation: A reply to Fraenkel and Grofman." *Public Choice* 121, nos. 3–4: 507–516.

Horowitz, Jeremy. 2009. "Power-Sharing in Kenya." Paper presented at the Workshop on Political Inclusion in Africa, American University.

Kerr, Michael. 2011. *The Destructors: The Story of Northern Ireland's Lost Peace Process*. Dublin: Irish Academic Press.

Lijphart, Arend. 1999. *Patterns of Democracy: Government Forms and Performance in Thirty-Six Countries*. New Haven, CT: Yale University Press.

Lijphart, Arend. 2008. *Thinking about Democracy: Power Sharing and Majority Rule in Theory and Practice*. New York: Routledge.

Lijphart, Arend. 2012. *Patterns of Democracy: Government Forms and Performance in Thirty-Six Countries*, 3rd edn. New Haven, CT: Yale University Press.

Loizides, Neophytos. 2009. "'Pro': An Appraisal of the Functionality of Annan V." In *Reunifying Cyprus: The Annan Plan and Beyond*, edited by Andrekos Varnava and Hubert Faustmann, pp. 82–94. London: I.B. Tauris.

Loizides, Neophytos. 2015. *Designing Peace: Cyprus and Institutional Innovations in Divided Societies*. Philadelphia: University of Pennsylvania Press.

Mattes, Michael and Burcu Savun. 2009. "Fostering Peace after Civil War: Commitment Problems and Agreement Design." *International Studies Quarterly* 53, no. 3: 737–759.

McAllister, Ian. 1975. *The 1975 Northern Ireland Convention Election*. Survey Research Centre. Occasional Paper No. 14. Strathclyde: University of Strathclyde.

McCrudden, Christopher and Brendan O'Leary. 2013. "Courts and Consociations, Or How Human Rights Courts May De-stabilize Power-Sharing Settlements." *European Journal of International Law* 24, no. 2: 477–501.

McCrudden, Christopher, John McGarry, Brendan O'Leary and Alex Schwartz. 2016. "Why Northern Ireland's Institutions Need Stability." *Government and Opposition* 51, no. 1: 30–58.

McGarry, John and Charles Graham. 1990. "Co-determination." In *The Future of Northern Ireland*, edited by John McGarry and Brendan O'Leary, pp. 155–174. Oxford: Oxford University Press.

McGarry, John and Brendan O'Leary. 2004a. "Introduction: Consociational Theory and Northern Ireland." In *The Northern Ireland Conflict: Consociational Engagements*, John McGarry and Brendan O'Leary, pp. 1–61. Oxford: Oxford University Press.

McGarry, John and Brendan O'Leary. 2004b. *The Northern Ireland Conflict: Consociational Engagements*. Oxford: Oxford University Press.

McGarry, John and Brendan O'Leary. 2004c. "Stabilising Northern Ireland's Agreement." *Political Quarterly* 75, no. 3: 213–225.

McGarry, John and Brendan O'Leary. 2006a. "Consociational Theory, Northern Ireland's Conflict, and its Agreement. Part One. What Consociationalists Can Learn from Northern Ireland." *Government and Opposition* 41, no. 1: 43–63.

McGarry, John and Brendan O'Leary. 2006b. "Consociational Theory, Northern Ireland's Conflict, and its Agreement. Part Two. What Critics of Consociation Can Learn from Northern Ireland." *Government and Opposition* 41, no. 2: 249–277.

McGarry, John and Brendan O'Leary. 2007. "Iraq's Constitution of 2005: Liberal Consociation as Political Prescription." *International Journal of Constitutional Law* 5, no. 4: 670–698.

McLoughlin, P.J. 2010. *John Hume and the Revision of Irish Nationalism*. Manchester: Manchester University Press.

Mitchell, Paul, Geoffrey Evans and Brendan O'Leary. 2009. "Extremist Outbidding in Ethnic Party Systems Is Not Inevitable: Tribune Parties in Northern Ireland." *Political Studies* 57, no. 2: 397–421.

Mueller, Dennis C. 1983. *The Political Economy of Growth*. New Haven, CT: Yale University Press.

Nordlinger, Eric A. 1972. *Conflict Regulation in Divided Societies*. Occasional Papers in International Affairs. Vol. 29. Cambridge, MA: Center for International Affairs, Harvard University.

Norris, Pippa. 2008. *Driving Democracy: Do Power-Sharing Institutions Work?* Cambridge: Cambridge University Press.

Ó Dochartaigh, Niall. 2011. "'Everyone Trying', the IRA Ceasefire 1975: A Missed Opportunity for Peace?" *Field Day Review* 7, 20 November: 51–77.

O'Duffy, Brendan. 2007. *British–Irish Relations and Northern Ireland: From Violent Politics to Conflict Regulation*. Dublin: Irish Academic Press.

O'Leary, Brendan. 1999. "The Nature of the Agreement." *Fordham Journal of International Law* 22, no. 4: 1628–1667.

O'Leary, Brendan. 2004a. "The Anglo-Irish Agreement: Folly or Statecraft?" In *The Northern Ireland Conflict: Consociational Engagements*, edited by John McGarry and Brendan O'Leary, pp. 62–96. Oxford: Oxford University Press.

O'Leary, Brendan. 2004b. "The Nature of the Agreement." In *The Northern Ireland Conflict: Consociational Engagements*, edited by John McGarry and Brendan O'Leary, pp. 260–293. Oxford: Oxford University Press.

O'Leary, Brendan. 2005. "Debating Consociational Politics: Normative and Explanatory Arguments." In *From Power-Sharing to Democracy: Post-Conflict Institutions in Ethnically Divided Societies*, edited by Sid Noel, pp. 3–43. Montreal and Kingston: McGill-Queens University Press.

O'Leary, Brendan. 2010. "Electoral Systems and the Lund Recommendations." In *Political Participation of Minorities: A Commentary on International Standards and Practice*, edited by Marc Weller and Katherine Nobbs, pp. 363–400. Oxford: Oxford University Press.

O'Leary, Brendan. 2013. "Power Sharing in Deeply Divided Places: An Advocate's Introduction." In *Power-Sharing in Deeply Divided Places*, edited by Joanne McEvoy and Brendan O'Leary, pp. 1–66. Philadelphia: University of Pennsylvania Press.

O'Leary, Brendan and Geoffrey Evans. 1997. "Northern Ireland: La Fin de Siecle, The Twilight of the Second Protestant Ascendancy and Sinn Féin's Second Coming." *Parliamentary Affairs* 50, no. 4: 672–680.

O'Leary, Brendan, Bernard Grofman and Jørgen Elklit. 2005. "Divisor Methods for Sequential Portfolio Allocation in Multi-Party Executive Bodies: Evidence from Northern Ireland and Denmark." *American Journal of Political Science* 49, no. 1: 198–211.

O'Leary, Brendan, Tom Lyne, Jim Marshall and Bob Rowthorn. 1993. *Northern Ireland: Sharing Authority*. London: Institute for Public Policy Research.

Olson, Mancur. 1982. *The Rise and Decline of Nations: Economic Growth, Stagflation, and Social Rigidities.* New Haven, CT: Yale University Press.

Persson, Torsten and Guido E. Tabellini. 2005. *The Economic Effects of Constitutions.* Cambridge, MA: MIT Press.

Powell, G. Bingham. 1982. *Contemporary Democracies: Participation, Stability, and Violence.* Cambridge, MA: Harvard University Press.

Powell, G. Bingham. 2000. *Elections as Instruments of Democracy: Majoritarian and Proportional Visions.* New Haven, CT: Yale University Press.

Rabushka, Alvin and Kenneth A. Shepsle. 2009 [1972]. *Politics in Plural Societies: A Theory of Democratic Instability.* New York: Pearson Longman.

Reilly, Ben. 2001. *Democracy in Divided Societies: Electoral Engineering for Conflict Management.* Cambridge: Cambridge University Press.

Romano, David. 2014. "Iraq's Descent into Civil War: A Constitutional Explanation." *Middle East Journal* 68, no. 4: 547–566.

Rose, Richard. 1976. *Northern Ireland: A Time of Choice.* Basingstoke: The Macmillan Press.

Taagepera, Rein and Matthew S. Shugart. 1989. *Seats and Votes: The Effects and Determinants of Electoral Systems.* New Haven, CT: Yale University Press.

Wolff, Stefan. 2002. "Introduction: From Sunningdale to Belfast, 1973–1998." In *Peace at Last? The Impact of the Good Friday Agreement on Northern Ireland*, edited by Jörg Neuheiser and Stefan Wolff, pp. 1–24. New York: Berghahn Books.

4 Consociationalism in the Brussels Capital Region

Dis-proportional representation and the accommodation of national minorities

Thibaud Bodson and Neophytos Loizides

Introduction

In this chapter, we provide a theoretically informed analysis of the Brussels power-sharing model, emphasizing its broader relevance for governing divided places. The Brussels Capital Region (BCR) provides a unique system of regional and urban governance not widely researched in consociational studies. Power-sharing arrangements in Brussels have enabled the peaceful cohabitation of the two main ethno-linguistic groups: a French-speaking majority and a Dutch-speaking minority. Well-functioning – even successful – power-sharing arrangements are rare across ethnically divided societies as implied elsewhere in this volume; hence Brussels' institutional design deserves wider academic attention.

Specifically, the BCR's relevance lies in the mechanisms implemented for the protection of the Dutch-speaking minority. Whereas the traditional literature on consociationalism stresses the importance of proportional representation for the protection of minorities, the BCR model adopts a different approach, based on over-representation of the Dutch-speaking minority, or what we call "protective dis-proportional representation." The argument presented in this chapter is that over-representation of an ethno-linguistic minority at the executive and legislative levels can be a possible instrument for stabilization, functionality and pacification in a divided society. And yet, over-representation can pose problems for the promotion of justice, fairness and democracy. In the BCR, the over-representation of the Dutch-speaking group has raised legal issues related to the rights to equal representation and non-discrimination. As this chapter demonstrates, addressing these legal concerns is crucial if the current consociational arrangements are to satisfy basic human rights standards as well as maintain stability and functionality.

To establish the context of our analysis, we begin this chapter with a brief introduction to the Belgian federal structure. We then analyze several key institutional features of the Brussels model at the Parliament and government level, which are aimed at the protection of the Dutch-speaking minority. Next, we consider the extent to which these institutional features deviate from the principle of strict proportional representation. Finally, we discuss the legal validity of the BCR protective dis-proportional representation model with regard to the rights of equality and non-discrimination.

The Belgian federal state

Belgium's federal model has been shaped by a long process of often-difficult relations between its two main language groups; the Dutch-speaking majority represents about 60 per cent of the population and is mainly concentrated in Flanders; the French-speaking minority accounts for most of the remaining 40 per cent, with the majority living in Wallonia. The small German-speaking minority counts for less than 1 per cent of the total population of the country.[1]

Belgian independence in 1831 resulted from a revolution led by the French-speaking aristocracy against the arbitrary and autocratic polity of the Dutch ruler William I, Prince of Orange. The subsequent secession of the Belgian territory from the United Kingdom of the Netherlands led to the domination of the Dutch-speaking Flemish population by the French-speaking upper class who assumed the important administrative, political, military and economic posts (de Winter 2006, 77). A cultural, linguistic and ideological rift crystallized between the communities, resulting in each having a weak understanding of the other community's patterns, and causing resentment among the Dutch-speaking population and its political elite. More recently, the economy has developed unevenly, confirming the gap between both linguistic communities: on the one hand, a flourishing economy in the north has made Flanders one of the wealthiest regions in the world; on the other hand, French-speaking Wallonia is engaged in a long-lasting process of reconversion of its moribund heavy industry.

In this context, the overlap of the Flemish people's claim for the recognition of their culture with the desire of the French-speaking Walloons to be in charge of their own economy has resulted in a shared interest in regional and community autonomy. This led to the progressive transformation of the Belgian unitary structure into a full-fledged three-tiered federal state (federal, regional and community). From 1970 onward, three regions – the Flemish, Brussels Capital and Walloon territorial regions – were created primarily to address Walloon economic concerns. Three language communities – the French, Flemish and German communities – were also established as a consequence of the Flemish desire for autonomy in cultural, educational and linguistic matters. The Belgian central government became a federal government in charge of residual competences (Deschouwer 2009, 33; Schneckener 2002, 354) (see Figure 4.1).

In Belgium's current federal structure, each region and community possesses its own parliament and government, although in Flanders the parliaments and governments of the Flemish region and the Flemish community have merged to create a single Flemish Parliament and government. Unfortunately, the country-wide establishment of new institutional structures guaranteeing substantial levels of autonomy has not eased all tensions. The two language communities continue to debate further transfers of competences from the federal level.

Thus, the historical cleavages rooted in ethno-linguistic, cultural and economic differences have been addressed by the implementation of a political structure articulated around a subtle combination of *group autonomy* (i.e., the capacity for "these groups to have authority to run their own internal affairs,

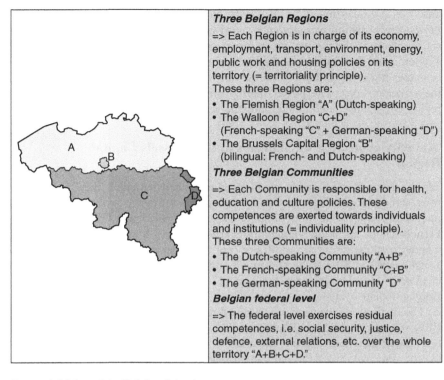

Figure 4.1 Map of the Belgian federal structure.

especially in the areas of education and culture") and *power-sharing* (i.e., "the participation of representatives of all significant communal groups in political decision making process [at the federal level], especially in the executive") (Lijphart 2004, 97). In addition, the Belgian institutional structure provides a limited system of *veto rights* for each community as well as *proportional representation* of the different groups within the main public institutions. According to Christopher McCrudden and Brendan O'Leary (2013, 7–9), the cumulative presence of these four characteristics – group autonomy, power-sharing, veto rights and proportional representation – make Belgium a consociational democracy.

The classical literature on power-sharing arrangements distinguishes *liberal* from *corporate* consociationalism. As demonstrated elsewhere in this volume, the difference between these forms lies in the way in which a society's institutions reflect its segmentation into groups. If the different groups are sociologically pre-determined, we can speak of *corporate consociations*. Alternatively, if a model leaves the democratic process to define the different coalitions and no a priori segmentation of the society into groups is provided, we can talk of *liberal consociations*.[2] The first part of the Belgian Constitution, entitled "On federal

Belgium, its components and its territory," organizes the institutional structure based on pre-determined, or *corporate*, ethno-linguistic lines. In Belgium, *corporate* segmentation was straightforward given the relatively monolithic territorial division of the population into two groups: the French-speaking group in Wallonia and the Dutch-speaking group in Flanders. This geographical distinction does not work in the BCR, however, where both groups are intermingled on the same territory. The power-sharing arrangements of this bi-ethnolinguistic region will be discussed in the following section.

Minority protection mechanisms in the Brussels Capital Region

Within the relatively sophisticated Belgian federal structure, the BCR institutions should be seen both as a constituent region of the federal system and as a microcosm of it owing to its bi-ethnic character. Specifically, the BCR's ratio of French-/Dutch-speaking populations is approximately 85 per cent to 15 per cent, whereas nationally, a ratio of 40 per cent to 60 per cent gives the advantage to Dutch speakers. This is the reason why numerous mechanisms analyzed in this chapter need to be understood as part of a broader political balance within the Belgian federal system.

The institutional protections provided to the Dutch-speaking minority in the BCR are present at both parliamentary and governmental levels. Within the BCR Parliament there are three key mechanisms intended to protect Dutch speakers: (1) the organization of the Parliament into two language groups; (2) a double-majority rule for passing certain acts; and (3) an 'alarm bell' procedure within the legislature which can be triggered when a language group feels threatened.

The organization of the Parliament into two language groups

Given the bilingual status of Brussels, on the day of regional elections voters *can decide* whether they want to vote for candidates registered on French-speaking or on Dutch-speaking lists (Coffé 2006, 100). Each single list running in the elections must be registered in one, and only one, of these two language groups. Given that citizens have a more or less acute sense of belonging to a language group, and considering that group identities may or may not be fixed, it was thought inappropriate to lock voters into a group on a permanent basis. Article 23 of the Special Act of 12 January 1989 on Brussels Institutions (the 1989 Brussels Act) specifies that members elected from Dutch-speaking lists constitute the Dutch-Speaking Group (DSG), whereas members elected from French-speaking lists constitute the French-Speaking Group (FSG) in the BCR Parliament.

The electoral process is organized under Article 20 of the 1989 Brussels Act. This provision originally implemented a two-stage system for the allocation of the regional Parliament's 75 seats. In the first stage, the electoral results of all political parties belonging to a particular language group were aggregated in order to calculate the relative weight of each group and to allocate them a certain number of seats accordingly. Once one knew how many seats each language group would receive, the second stage provided for a proportional distribution of the seats *within* both groups. The 2001 Lombard Agreements revised this system of seat allocation in two ways. The first modification was an increase in the number of parliamentary seats from 75 to 89. The second revision provided for the *automatic attribution of a fixed number of seats to each group*, i.e., 17 seats for the DSG and 72 for the FSG. The second stage in the 1989 Act remains untouched, with the electoral results determining the seat allocation *within* each language group according to the proportionality rule. This double modification strengthens the representation of the DSG within the Parliament for two different reasons. First, the automatic and fixed distribution of seats for each language group guarantees a stable representation of the Dutch-speaking minority within the BCR Parliament. Second, the 17:72 ratio of seats surpasses the real ratio of persons voting for lists belonging to the DSG/FSG. The allocation of a fixed number of seats to each language group, no matter their relative electoral weight, was intended to prevent the political erosion of the Dutch-speaking minority in Brussels, a phenomenon observed over recent elections. Finally, the changes in the 2001 Lombard Agreements enable a more *nuanced* representation of the DSG, since the larger number of seats entails a better representation of the political diversity of the Dutch-speaking community in Brussels. The new system was applied for the first time in the 2004 regional elections (Lagasse 2003, 176, 179).

A double-majority rule for passing certain acts

The second mechanism aimed at the protection of the Dutch-speaking minority occurs at the level of lawmaking. The 1989 Brussels Act provides that draft laws related to certain important matters, such as the regulation of the regional Parliament or the election and, to a certain extent, the revocation of the government, require a *double majority*, i.e., a majority in the whole Parliament plus a majority within each language group. If the proposed draft does not obtain the required majority within each language group, a second vote is held at least 30 days later; this time, for the act to be promulgated, it is only required that it is supported by one-third of the members of each language group plus a majority within the whole Parliament. The 30-day delay provides reflection time for the deputies of each language group. Overall, the double-majority rule aims at protecting the Dutch-speaking minority from laws that could be passed unilaterally by the FSG through the simple use of its majority.

An 'alarm bell' procedure within the legislature

Finally, Article 31 of the 1989 Brussels Act states that if three-quarters of the members of a language group consider that a draft law "threatens the relationship between both communities in Brussels," they can trigger an *alarm bell procedure*, suspending the legislative promulgation process and referring the issue to the BCR government for arbitration. The government must give an advisory opinion within 30 days (Uyttendaele 2011, 316). At the end of this period, the proposed law, possibly amended by the government, is again submitted to the Parliament for a vote where it can be passed by a simple majority. As in the case of the double-majority rule, the alarm bell procedure seeks to protect the Dutch-speaking minority from FSG majoritarianism. Whereas it is more significant from a symbolic point of view, the alarm bell procedure is less protective than the double-majority rule as it does not prevent the majority from eventually passing a law against the minority's interests. The alarm bell procedure has never been used so far in Brussels.[3]

In addition to the mechanisms guaranteeing the protection of the Dutch-speaking minority within the BCR Parliament, other mechanisms protect it at the level of government: (1) the election of government by Parliament; (2) a requirement for parity within government combined with a consensus rule for decision-making; and (3) the a priori determined competences exerted by the ministers.

The election of the government by Parliament

Articles 34 and 35 of the 1989 Brussels Act explain the method by which the five candidates for ministerial positions are chosen by Parliament.[4] Apart from the minister-president who is considered neutral and above the separation into language groups, two members belong to the DSG and two belong to the FSG (Coffé 2006, 101). The five candidate-ministers, including the minister-president, must be presented on a single list and supported by the majority of Parliament and a majority of deputies within each language group. Given that this common list is the result of negotiations between political parties after the elections, the success of the executive formation process is uncertain. The Belgian national government is selected in the same manner, and this has proven to be a critical weakness of the country's federal model contributing in 2010 and 2011 to a 541-days long period of government making negotiations.

In the Brussels Capital Region, the law provides a default solution when parties fail to reach agreement. Specifically, Article 35, §2 of the 1989 Brussels Act states that if parties cannot agree on a list, the minister-president of the Brussels government is elected by a majority of Parliament. To be eligible for this post, a candidate needs to collect five signatures from members of the regional Parliament. The four other government ministers are elected separately by the majority of Parliament after having been supported by a majority within the language group to which they belong. If no majority is reached within Parliament, another vote is held at least 30 days later. Since the implementation of the 2004 electoral reform this default solution has never been employed. A government or a minister may be subject to a non-confidence motion and be dismissed by Parliament, but only on the condition that this motion is constructive, i.e., Parliament presents a substitute for the dismissed government/minister. The decision must be made by the majority of the members of the language group to which the minister belongs (Art. 36 of the 1989 Brussels Act). Article 36 of the 1989 Brussels Act provides that if Parliament decides to dismiss the entire government, the decision must be made by a concurrent majority of Parliament and each language group.

A requirement for parity within government combined with a consensus rule for decision-making

The Dutch-speaking minority benefits from even stronger protection measures at governmental than at parliamentary level, inasmuch as it is allocated the same number of ministerial portfolios as the FSG.[5] Furthermore, an unwritten rule states that within the government decisions are made according to a collegial process, with dialogue and consensus used to respect and protect ethno-linguistic groups. This means that every minister has an informal veto power, including those belonging to the Dutch-speaking minority (Coffé 2006, 101). The objective of these measures is to integrate the ethno-linguistic groups and political parties, and create a climate of cooperation rather than defiance and competition (Lijphart 2004, 101).

The a priori determined competences exerted by the ministers

Finally, Article 37 of the 1989 Brussels Act defines how portfolios[6] are allocated to members of the government if an agreement on allocation is not forthcoming. If the members of the government cannot agree on the distribution of portfolios, the minister-president is the first to choose which pre-determined competences he or she wishes to exert; the two members of the FSG are able to choose their preferred competences in second and fourth position, and the two ministers from the DSG choose in third and fifth position (Lagasse 2003, 177). This allocation system, which is comparable to Northern Ireland's sequential portfolio allocation system, aims to ensure that DSG ministers are not simply assigned "empty portfolios" (McGarry and Loizides 2015).

To conclude, this description of the mechanisms guaranteeing the protection of the Dutch-speaking minority in Brussels may be analyzed in the light of the four characteristics of consociational arrangements discussed earlier, i.e., (1) the *sharing of executive and legislative powers* between the two communities; (2) the existence of *veto rights* for each community; (3) a repartition of competences enabling *community autonomy*; and (4) the use of *the proportionality principle* for the representation of the different communities. As we see in the BCR, the mechanisms guaranteeing the presence of two language groups within Parliament and the requirement for parity within government provide for the *sharing of executive and legislative powers* (1). The double-majority rule for passing certain acts in Parliament, as well as the consensus rule for decision-making within government, constitute variations of the *veto right* (2). However, the BCR model does not rely on *community autonomy*[7] (3), and as we will discuss more extensively in the following section, does not follow *proportionality* (4).

The effects of minority protection on proportional representation in Brussels

Proportional representation (PR) is traditionally considered important for divided societies as it can secure the representation of different identity groups at all levels of the political structure. For present purposes, we define PR as the representation of the people's suffrage as accurately as possible through the allocation of seats and posts at some decision level, i.e., within Parliament and in the government, according to the ratio obtained by each political party in the elections. Lijphart argues that the basic aim of PR is "to represent both majorities and minorities, and instead of over-representing or underrepresenting any parties, to translate votes into seats proportionally" (Lijphart 1984, 150). The *ratio legis* of basic PR is that, in the decision-making process, the various segments of society receive a proportional share. In that regard, PR is related to the fundamental liberal principles of equality and non-discrimination, since it entails a representation of the population where every voter is equal.

Over-representation in favour of smaller groups, as Lijphart argues, may be desirable in countries where the population is broken down into an ethnic majority and one or more ethnic minority groups (Lijphart 2004, 103). However, how much minority over-representation can be justified and endorsed by majorities is unclear in consociational theory. As we show in this section, the mechanisms of minority protections implemented at parliamentary and governmental level in the BCR deviate significantly from strict proportionality, and this arguably does not contradict but rather complements the major principles of consociationalism.

At the parliamentary level, the rule according to which each language group receives a fixed number of seats is likely to entail a significant deviation from proportionality. In the 2004 BCR elections, 62,516 people voted for lists belonging to the DSG, whereas 391,216 voted for lists belonging to the FSG. According to the 17:72 ratio of seats in the legislature, 3,677 votes were necessary to elect one candidate in the DSG and 5,433 votes for one candidate in the FSG. This deviation from proportionality amounted to a ratio of 1:0.68 in favour of the DSG.[8] In the 2009 elections this ratio was even more pronounced, with 51,818 votes cast for the DSG and 408,870 for the FSG. A candidate from a DSG list needed 3,084 votes to be elected as a deputy, whereas a candidate from a FSG list needed 5,679 votes, almost double the number. The latter resulted in a gap of 1:0.54 in favour of the DSG.[9] With a total of 460,688 votes, 88.75 per cent of the Brussels population voted for French-speaking parties and 11.25 per cent voted for Dutch-speaking parties. Simple application of a basic PR rule would have led to the allocation of 79 seats to French-speaking parties and ten seats to Dutch-speaking parties, instead of the 72:17 ratio prescribed under Article 20 of the 1989 Brussels Act. More recently, in the 2014 regional elections, the FSG lists gathered 409,048 votes whereas the DSG lists collected 53,379, amounting to 5,681 votes for each FSG seat compared to 3,139 for each DSG seat.[10]

This review of the electoral dividers over the past three elections shows that DSG voters benefit disproportionally on a constant basis, with the degree of disproportionality varying according to community turnout (see Table 4.1).

The disproportionality in legislative seats allows us to better understand the scope of the distortion entailed by the other protection mechanisms described in the previous section. Hence, the *double-majority rule* entails that nine DSG deputies out of 89 deputies in total can veto draft laws in certain matters; 13 deputies from the DSG suffice to trigger the *alarm bell procedure* and temporarily prevent the expression of the majority's will; for the election and the revocation of the BCR government, nine members of the DSG are enough to make it very difficult to form a government; when composing the cabinet, the DSG receives two or three portfolios out of the five available, and so on. Hence, the disproportionate influence exerted by a limited number of representatives from the DSG conflicts with the concept of proportionality strictly defined.

From a more normative point of view, the over-representation of a minority can be justified by the fact that minority protection mechanisms are essential for the stability of the political system and the peaceful cohabitation of different community groups. Indeed, these mechanisms aim at preventing smaller groups from abandoning their religious, cultural, ethnic or linguistic specificities, under pressure from the majority, through the simple use of democratic institutions. As Nicolas Lagasse puts it, law results from a power relationship. It is the expression of a majority at a given time. Hence, in order to protect minorities from hostile decisions taken by the majority, it is essential to create protection mechanisms and arbitration possibilities (Lagasse 2003, 218). The sustainability of a political system depends on its success in accommodating fundamental group needs, such as recognition, respect and a certain degree of autonomy (Farrell 2011, 214). In this context, any application of strict proportionality confronts minorities with two intertwined risks: first, the majority may not take the minority into consideration in its decisions, since it does not need it to rule; second, through time, partly because they are not well represented and cannot protect themselves at a decision-making level, minorities may see their identity peculiarities steadily erode.

Table 4.1 Election results in the Brussels Capital Region, 2004 to 2014

	Regional elections in BCR, 2004	Regional elections in BCR, 2009	Regional elections in BCR, 2014
Votes registered for the FSG	391,216	408,870	409,048
Votes registered for the DSG	62,516	51,818	53,379
Electoral divider FSG	391,216/72 = 5,433	408,870/72 = 5,679	409,048/72 = 5,681
Electoral divider DSG	62,516/17 = 3,677	51,818/17 = 3,084	53,379/17 = 3,139

Given these two threats, strict proportionality, generally seen as an advantageous way of introducing power-sharing mechanisms within divided societies (Lijphart 2004, 99), may be considered insufficient to accommodate identity groups' claims and to protect the minority against the "tyranny of the majority" (Guinier 1994) when the difference in group size is so uneven. Strict proportionality is thus not enough for the protection of minorities and there is a need for other minority protection mechanisms. Admittedly, providing minorities with a veto right in a proportional system might offer an alternative protection mechanism different to minority over-representation. However, minority veto rights may often be less acceptable to majorities, less effective to the cross-community implementation of decision-making compared to the BCR model and frequently conducive to perpetuating conflict.

In Brussels, the guaranteed representation of the Dutch-speaking minority at both levels – Parliament and government – and the disproportionate powers it possesses considering its real share in the total population offer it strong protection against the risk of progressive erosion (Lagasse 2003, 214, 216). Hence, we label the Brussels' model a form of 'protective dis-proportional representation' rather than simple proportionality. The word 'protective' stresses the emphasis laid on the protection of minority groups. '*Dis*-proportional representation,' in turn, underlines the *dis*-tortion of proportional representation whereby some groups are over-represented or have proportionally greater powers to the detriment of others. Protective dis-proportional representation addresses certain tensions inherent in deeply divided societies, widens inclusivity as to decision-making and implementation of laws, and, in so doing, strengthens the coexistence of the region's main ethno-linguistic groups.

Two particular elements have facilitated Brussels' institutional arrangements. The first element is political. The concessions made by the French speakers in Brussels mirror the protections they enjoy at the federal level. The second element is sociological. In Brussels the feeling of belonging to one language group or the other is complemented by a sense of regional identity. In other words, among people living in Brussels there is a widely shared sentiment of defining oneself as a Brussels citizen next to Dutch or French speaker. Keeping in mind these two elements, the successful accommodation of the BCR's two ethno-linguistic groups allows an interesting observation for consociational research: over-representation of an ethno-linguistic minority at parliamentary and governmental level may be consistent with the normalization of cross-community relations, particularly in situations where national majorities become minorities at the regional level. Notwithstanding this, the distortion of proportionality resulting in over-representation raises a set of legal questions.

The legal validity of the protective dis-proportional representation model

In distorting proportionality, the protection mechanisms that exist in the BCR raise obvious legal issues. In fact, the different voting powers of citizens depending on whether they vote for candidates on DSG or FSG lists seem to bring two sets of fundamental principles into conflict: the *principle of minority protection* and the *principles of equality and non-discrimination*. Indeed, the differential treatment of the Brussels' voters seems to be in blatant contradiction with certain basic legal rules, including Article 25 of the 1966 International Covenant on Civil and Political Rights, and Article 3 of the first additional protocol of the European Convention on Human Rights (ECHR) on the right of free and equal voting, as well as Article 14 of the ECHR and Articles 10 to 11 of the Belgium Constitution on the right to equality and non-discrimination:

Article 25 of the 1966 International Covenant on Civil and Political Rights

Every citizen shall have the right and the opportunity, without any of the distinctions mentioned in Article 2 and without unreasonable restrictions: [...]
 (b) To vote and to be elected at genuine periodic elections which shall be by universal and *equal suffrage* and shall be held by secret ballot, guaranteeing the free expression of the will of the electors [emphasis added].

Article 14 of the ECHR

The enjoyment of the rights and freedoms set forth in this Convention shall be secured *without discrimination on any ground such as sex, race, color, language, religion, political or other opinion*, national or social origin, association with a *national minority*, property, birth or other status [emphases added].

Article 10 of the Belgian Constitution

No class distinctions exist in the State. *Belgians are equal before the law*; they alone are eligible for civil and military service, but for the exceptions that can be created by a law for particular cases. Equality between women and men is guaranteed [emphasis added].

Article 11 of the Belgian Constitution

Enjoyment of the rights and freedoms recognized for Belgians must be provided without discrimination. To this end, laws and federate laws guarantee among others the *rights and freedoms of ideological and philosophical minorities* [emphasis added].

Interestingly, the distortion of proportionality resulting from the protection of the Dutch-speaking minority in Brussels has been addressed by the Belgian Constitutional Court. The Court was asked by public associations to decide whether the difference of treatment resulting from the new Article 20 of the 1989 Brussels Act, which pre-determines the number of seats to be allocated to each language group and, therefore, distorts the voting power of citizens, violates the principles of equality and non-discrimination, in conjunction with the right to free and equal voting. Applying traditional reasoning, the Court evaluated whether the differential treatment rested on *objective criteria*, had a *reasonable justification* and if the measures taken were *relevant to reach the pursued objective* (Lagasse 2003, 237).[11]

In casu, the Court judged in the 35/2003 case of 25 March 2003 that the predetermined number of seats allocated to each language group *did not violate* the principle of equality and non-discrimination. It justified its judgment by referring to the Brussels model as included in the broader Belgian institutional structure and as constituting part of a balance between the country's two main communities. Furthermore, the Court considered that the principle of free and equal voting does not per se imply that the allocation of seats should represent the number of votes exactly and noted that the electoral and institutional systems implemented in Brussels aim at protecting the Dutch-speaking minority and at preserving the bilingual nature of the BCR (Lagasse 2003, 254; Alen and Muylle 2011, 376). In several other judgments, the Court has confirmed that the principle of proportional representation can be adapted to a reasonable extent in order to guarantee the *good working of democratic institutions*.[12]

In the case of Brussels, the Court has recognized the compliance of the *protective dis-proportional representation model* with the fundamental principles of equality and non-discrimination. While this decision could inspire other divided societies engaging in constitutional designs that deviate from proportionality (e.g., Bosnia-Herzegovina) or entertaining similar approaches (e.g., Cyprus), there are obvious legal and ethical limits as to how disproportional institutions can be. Therefore, the key seems to lie in the justification and reasoning behind deviating from strict proportional representation. In the case of the BCR, a steadily decreasing ratio of people voting for DSG/FSG lists could result in a degree of disproportionality considered *unjustifiable* by the Court. While the Court did not draw a line beyond which over-representation should be considered to be in contradiction with the principles of equality and non-discrimination, this possibility must exist. Will future elections in BCR put the subtle Brussels institutional compromise at risk?

Conclusions

In this chapter we have analyzed the power-sharing arrangements in the Brussels Capital Region, a case of regional governance not widely researched in the consociational literature. The relevance of the Brussels Capital Region's model lies in the mechanisms implemented for the protection of the Dutch-speaking minority and its treatment of the proportionality principle. Moreover, the BCR model demonstrates how a complex set of formal institutional arrangements can coexist with informal practices to ensure that political elites maintain a high level of collaboration while at the same time preserving the balance of intercommunal relations. Finally, Brussels demonstrates how liberal and classic consociational elements can coexist and how a set of sophisticated and original arrangements for regional and urban governance can be justified in the constitution of a liberal democracy.

We began our analysis with a presentation of the Belgian federal structure to set the broadest framework of our examination. We turned then to a study of the institutional guarantees provided to the Dutch-speaking minority in BCR at the parliamentary and governmental levels. Minority protection mechanisms, such as segmentation of Parliament into language groups, quasi-veto rights, the double-majority rule and parity within the government were considered necessary for the accommodation of the Dutch-speaking minority in Brussels. From this study we observed how minority protection mechanisms in the BCR entail a substantial deviation from strict proportional representation. Whereas the literature on consociationalism traditionally stresses the importance of proportionality for the accommodation of divided societies (Schneckener 2002, 360; Lijphart 2004, 99), the Brussels model takes a different approach, with strict proportionality being replaced by a more sophisticated 'protective dis-proportional representation' model. This deviation has been challenged in the Belgian Constitutional Court, which ultimately decided on its legitimate and justified nature within the country's broader constitutional architecture. The concessions agreed upon by French speakers at the BCR level mirror the protection they benefit from as a minority at the federal level. The BCR model also has comparative relevance and provides important insights for post-conflict and deeply divided societies. For example, power-sharing mediations across divided societies (e.g., Cyprus, Iraq, Moldova) favouring one group at the federal level could be compensated with comparable power-sharing provisions favouring another group at the regional/municipal level. Such reciprocal arrangements would augment overall federal stability.

The study of the Brussels model presented in this chapter addresses two of the three thematic priorities raised in this book: to provide a detailed articulation of the relationship between power-sharing arrangements and the promotion of justice, fairness and democracy as well as to analyze the relationship between consociational arrangements, and stability and cooperation in divided societies. The argument proposed in this chapter was that over-representation of an ethnolinguistic minority simultaneously at parliamentary and governmental level can be a possible instrument for the enhancement of stability and peace within divided societies.

Notes

1 On 1 January 2010, out of a population of 10,839,869 inhabitants, 6,251,983 Belgian citizens lived in Flemish territory, 3,498,384 were in Wallonia (including a German-speaking minority of 75,222 inhabitants, representing 0.7 per cent of the total Belgian population) and 1,089,538 lived in the BCR. For more information, see www.belgium.be/fr/la_belgique/connaitre_le_pays/Population/.
2 For a comprehensive discussion on the distinction between liberal and corporate consociationalism, see McCulloch (2014).

3 The relatively good cooperation between the linguistic groups in Brussels makes it quite unlikely for the alarm bell procedure to be used in the near future. However, the procedure also exists at the federal level where it has been deployed twice. In 1985, the Dutch-speaking group triggered the alarm bell procedure on a question related to higher education, and in 2010 the French-speaking group launched it against the Flemish project to reform the election procedures.

4 It is noteworthy that next to the minister-president and his or her four ministers, the Brussels' government is also constituted of three state secretaries in charge of secondary competences.

5 This does not take into consideration the three States Secretaries, who necessarily include at least one member of each language group.

6 Article 37 of the Brussels Act provides:

> §1 The Government proceeds to a distribution of the tasks for the preparation and the executions of its decisions. If no consensus can be reached on that matter, the competences of the members of the Government are allocated according to the following groups:
>
> > I Economic policy, energy, tourism, and bicultural matters with a regional link;
> > II Public works and transportation policy;
> > III Employment and job training policy, local administration, financial support to local sport facilities;
> > IV Territorial planning, housing, environment, nature protection, rural renovation and water policies;
> > V Finances, budget, public functions and external relations.
>
> §2. The President of the Government chooses first one of the groups mentioned in §1. The members of the largest language group choose then in second and fourth position. The members of the smallest language group chose in third and fifth position.

(Translation by the authors)

7 As we observed earlier, the definition of competences allocated to regions within the Belgian federal structure encompassed a *territoriality principle* (see Figure 4.1). Hence, in Belgium, regions (which for the most part correspond with communities) are competent for economic, employment, transport, environmental, energy, public work and housing policies. The use of these criteria in order to establish regional competences makes the characteristic of *community autonomy* irrelevant, as the competences they dispose are disconnected from any community specificity. The competences of the communities mainly concern health, education and culture policies. These competences are based on the 'individuality principle' and are exerted on the territory of the BCR by the Dutch- and the French-speaking communities, each for the individuals and the institutions resorting to their own language (see Figure 4.1).

8 IBSA-statistics, available at: www.ibsa.irisnet.be/themes/elections/elections-1#.U2Sn44F_u1U; www.ibsa.irisnet.be/themes/elections/elections-1#.U2Sn44F_u1U; www.ibsa.irisnet.be/themes/elections/elections-1#.VKqMyGN_vTp.

9 Ibid.

10 Ibid. Another way to approach this distortion of PR is to look at the ratio of seat allocations between language groups and the proportion of people voting for Dutch-speaking or French-speaking lists. In that framework from a total of 453,432 valid votes in the 2004 elections, the ratio of votes for Dutch-/French-speaking lists amounted to 1:6.26, respectively, but the 17/72 fixed allocation of seats amounted to a 1:4.24 proportion. As noted above, the 2009 elections resulted in an even more significant distortion, as the voting ratio was 1:7.89. In the 2014 regional elections, this voting ratio was slightly lower: 1:7.66 compared to the 1:4.24 for fixed seat allocation.

11 The judgment by the Belgian Constitutional Court may be compared with the high-profile case of Sejdić and Finci vs. Bosnia and Herzegovina of 22 December 2009 by the European Court of Human Rights. In both cases, consociational arrangements were challenged under the principles of equality and non-discrimination. In the Brussels case, the contestation concerned the legality of different voting powers for voters depending on whether they voted for lists belonging to one language group or the other. The Belgian Constitutional Court judged these differences to be reasonable and justified given the Belgian institutional structure. In the Sejdić and Finci case, the object of contestation were constitutional provisions which would de facto exclude some national minorities from standing for the national Parliament or the presidency. The ECtHR judged that this exclusion was without objective and reasonable justification on a 14–3 basis. Reforms to the Bosnian presidential arrangement, however, have yet to be enacted. For a comprehensive discussion of this issue, see McCrudden and O'Leary (2013).

12 See Belgian Constitutional Court, case no. 30/2003, 26 February 2003. In this case, the Belgian Constitutional Court judged that "even for elections strictly applying the proportionality-rule, one cannot avoid the phenomenon of 'lost voices.' Each vote has a different weight with respect to the final electoral result and each candidate has different chances to be elected" (B.22.3). Furthermore, Belgian law "does not prevent the lawmaker to bring some reasonable limits to proportional representations in order to guarantee the good functioning of democratic institutions" (B.22.4) (translation by the authors). See also case no. 78/2005, 27 April 2005; Alen and Muylle (2011, 245).

References

Alen, André and Koen Muylle. 2011. *Handboek van het Belgisch staatsrecht*. Berlin: Kluwer.

Coffé, Hilde. 2006. "'The Vulnerable Institutional Complexity': The 2004 Regional Elections in Brussels." *Regional and Federal Studies* 16, no. 1: 99–107.

De Winter, Lieven. 2006. "Multi-level Party Competition and Coordination in Belgium." In *Devolution and Electoral Politics*, edited by Dan Hough and Charlie Jeffery, pp. 76–95. Manchester: Manchester University Press.

Deschouwer, Kris. 2009. "Towards a Regionalization of Statewide Electoral Trends in Decentralized States? The Cases of Belgium and Spain." In *Territorial Party Politics in Western Europe*, edited by Wilfried Swenden and Bart Maddens, pp. 31–46. Basingstoke: Palgrave Macmillan.

Farrell, David M. 2011. *Electoral Systems: A Comparative Introduction*, 2nd edn. Basingstoke: Palgrave Macmillan.

Guinier, Lani. 1994. *The Tyranny of the Majority: Fundamental Fairness in Representative Democracy*. New York: Free Press.

Lagasse, Nicolas. 2003. "Les Accords dits du Lombard." In *Les Accords du Lambermont et du Lombard. Approfondissement du fédéralisme ou erreur d'aiguillage*. Brussels: Bruylant.

Lijphart, Arend. 1984. *Democracies: Patterns of Majoritarian and Consensus Government in Twenty-one Countries*. New Haven, CT: Yale University Press.

Lijphart, Arend. 2004. "Constitutional Design for Divided Societies." *Journal of Democracy* 15, no. 2: 96–109.

Loizides, Neophytos. 2016. *Designing Peace: Cyprus and Institutional Innovations in Divided Societies*. Philadelphia: University of Pennsylvania Press.

McCrudden, Christopher and Brendan O'Leary. 2013. *Courts and Consociations: Human Rights versus Power-Sharing*. Oxford: Oxford University Press.

McCulloch, Allison. 2014. "Consociational Settlements in Deeply Divided Societies: The Liberal–Corporate Distinction." *Democratization* 21, no. 3: 501–518.

McGarry John and Neophytos Loizides. 2015. "Power-Sharing in a Re-united Cyprus: Centripetal Coalitions vs. Proportional Sequential Coalitions." *International Journal of Constitutional Law* 13, no. 4: 847–872.

Schneckener, Ulrich. 2002. "Minority Governance between Self-Rule and Shared-Rule." In *Minority Governance in Europe*, edited by Kinga Gál, pp. 349–372. ECMI/LGI Series on Ethnopolitics and Minority Issues. Budapest: Open Society Institute.

Uyttendaele, Marc. 2011. *Trente leçons de droit constitutionnel*. Brussels: Bruylant.

5 Mandatory power-sharing in coup-prone Fiji

Jon Fraenkel

Introduction

The Pacific Island state of Fiji has a troubled history of attempts to overcome ethnic strife through power-sharing arrangements. In the wake of the first military overthrow of an elected government in 1987, coup leader turned Prime Minister Sitiveni Rabuka embraced a new constitution, adopted in 1997, which provided that all parties with 10 per cent or more of seats in Parliament would be entitled to participate in cabinet. In theory, this executive power-sharing formula ensured that parties representing the country's two largest communities – indigenous Fijians and Fiji Indians (in 1996, 52 per cent and 44 per cent, respectively[1]) – would cooperate in government. In practice, when in government, each of the two largest parties – one based in each community – sought to exclude the other from cabinet, and the matter was brought repeatedly before the country's law courts. Judicial intervention proved far from straightforward, and public squabbles over cabinet entitlements dominated the political agenda in 2003/2004 to such an extent that the multi-party cabinet rules themselves became the principal focus of inter-ethnic antagonism.

Nevertheless, after Fiji's third election under the new arrangements in April 2006, there occurred a brief but promising experiment combining indigenous and Fiji Indian politicians in cabinet. Even the military commander, Frank Bainimarama, saluted "the evolution of this great and new concept of power sharing at the executive level of government" and called for "total support to the Multi-party cabinet from each and every member of the Republic of Fiji Military Forces" (*Mataivalu News* July/August 2006, 3; *Fiji Times*, 28 July 2006). Unfortunately, only five months later, he would rescind that commitment and overthrow the multi-party government, leading to an extended period of military rule.

This chapter argues that while the broad objective of facilitating cross-ethnic power-sharing was the best available response to the country's history of inter-ethnic strife, Fiji's power-sharing arrangements nonetheless suffered from serious defects. First, some of the institutions worked at cross-purposes. The provisions regarding mandatory power-sharing at the executive level, for example, sat awkwardly alongside the majoritarian electoral system and the Westminster rules regarding selection of prime minister. Second, the arrangements left too wide a scope for judicial interpretation regarding both senate and cabinet entitlements. The courts at first adopted a severe interpretation of the requirement that the prime minister include qualifying parties in cabinet, but judges eventually assumed powers to greatly weaken those constraints by allowing the prime minister to appoint unaffiliated independent MPs and senators as ministers outside the power-sharing formula. Negotiations on government formation, in accordance with the new laws, failed after both the 1999 and 2001 elections. Between 2002 and 2004, court deliberations were either gamed for political purposes or, where rulings were honoured, they entailed only token portfolios with minimal responsibilities. The more robust experiment after the 2006 polls was undermined because the leader of one of the major parties preferred to join the cabinet that emerged following the December military coup, and because the military wanted to pursue an integrationist strategy of suppressing ethnic parties.

Two of the most prominent thinkers on constitutional design in divided societies, Arend Lijphart and Donald Horowitz, both get the Fiji power-sharing story wrong. Both sought initially to lay claim to the Fiji case as confirming their views in the broader debate about whether 'consociational' (Lijphart) or 'centripetalist' (Horowitz) approaches were better suited to countries like South Africa, Bosnia-Herzegovina and Northern Ireland.[2] Fiji was the only one of these countries to accept Horowitz's centripetalist advice and to adopt the alternative vote (AV) system (Fraenkel and Grofman 2006; Fraenkel 2001). This chapter focuses largely on the fate of the 10 per cent executive power-sharing formula.

Both Horowitz and Lijphart attributed an exaggerated role to power-sharing institutions in shaping the government established after the 1999 election. Horowitz initially claimed Fiji as a triumph for centripetalism. He did, however, worry that the continued heavy use of racially reserved seats had "watered down" AV's vote-pooling incentives and that the belated addition of the power-sharing formula had left Fiji with a "hybrid" system (Horowitz 2000, 267; Horowitz 2004, 256). The effect of the power-sharing rules, he argued, was "subtly to undercut" the AV system's vote-pooling influences and the resulting government was thus not a strong test of the potential of preferential electoral systems to encourage robust pre-election coalitions "because post-election coalitions are not based on compromise necessary to lure voters across ethnic boundaries" (Horowitz 2002a, 27; 2002b, 209; 2000, 268). Similarly, Lijphart claimed that "the alternative vote played a very small part in bringing about the Fijian power-sharing government in 1999" and suggested that "the much more important factor" was the executive power-sharing formula (Lijphart 2002, 49).

As this chapter shows, those verdicts cannot be sustained through careful empirical analysis of the Fiji experience simply because the power-sharing rules were, for the most part, not honoured after the elections of 1999 or 2001. Contrary to Lijphart, the government that emerged after 1999 was much more the result of the AV rules than the power-sharing formula. The largest indigenous party was excluded despite qualifying under the 10 per cent rule, a development that encouraged the ethnic Fijian disquiet that erupted in a coup exactly a year after the 1999 election. Of the three Fijian parties included by the victorious Fiji Labour Party (FLP) in the 1999/2000 cabinet, two did not qualify under the 10 per cent rule. All three, however, had exchanged preferences with the FLP, and thus delivered to that party an absolute majority in Parliament.[3] All three also experienced internal schisms over 1999/2000, and dissidents from all three figured prominently among the coup-makers that overthrew the FLP-led government in the coup of 19 May 2000.[4] Vote-pooling arrangements had dramatically failed to deliver either a robust pre- or post-election 'coalition of conviction.'

For consociational theorists, Fiji is significant not because power-sharing provisions shaped the cabinets of 1999 to 2000 or 2001 to 2006, but because it illustrates the danger that *mandatory* power-sharing arrangements may draw the law courts into partisan decisions about cabinet representation and that judges may not necessarily handle these issues well. No other ethnically divided country in the world, so far as I am aware, has witnessed such extensive litigation about cabinet entitlements under mandatory rules as Fiji. Consociational theorists are often agnostic about whether power-sharing political settlements need be *mandatory* or conventional. Some, including Lijphart, define as 'consociational' (or power-sharing) any 'grand coalition' that proportionally represents a country's ethnic or linguistic groups even when its composition is unconstrained by law (as in post-war India) (Lijphart 2002, 41–42, 42n, 46–47; Lijphart 1996). Yet, for most polities with a history of bitter inter-ethnic conflict, the choice is usually between a legal constraint on cabinet composition (whether constitutional or not) or leaving government formation to voluntary processes, which may result in the exclusion of minority groups.[5] For these reasons, Fiji's history of court deliberation on cabinet composition provides an important test case as regards the working of mandatory power-sharing rules in a deeply divided society.

Shaping a bicommunal polity

The Fiji Islands group is located to the northeast of Australia in the southwestern Pacific Ocean, and was populated only around 3,500 years ago as Lapita navigators spread eastward through Melanesia. The country became a British Crown colony in 1874. As in Guyana, Trinidad and Mauritius, indentured labourers were brought in large numbers from the Indian subcontinent to work on sugar cane plantations. The indigenous Fijian population, then in chronic decline as a result of exposure to hitherto unfamiliar infectious diseases, was mostly confined to traditional rural villages under customary chiefs. Alienation of native lands was declared unlawful by the incoming colonial administration, but ex-indentured Indians were permitted to lease land either from the Crown or from native owners.[6] In response to pressures from the Government of India, indentured migration was halted in 1916. The sugar industry was reorganized in the 1920s and 1930s. Former plantations were broken up and smaller plots leased to Indian farmers, who were no longer under indenture contracts. That pattern of landholding still prevails today.

Fiji has a long history of communal voting arrangements. In the 1920s, the British authorities rejected Indian demands for a 'common roll.' European members had selected their own representatives since 1903. From 1904 until 1963, ethnic Fijian members were nominated (without election) by the indigenous Great Council of Chiefs (thereby encouraging some enduring ethnic Fijian ambivalence towards democratic ideals) (Sukuna 1983). In 1929, race-based electoral rolls were introduced for Indian members of the Legislative Council, triggering a protracted campaign against colonial discrimination. By the mid-1940s, the Fiji Indian population slightly exceeded the indigenous population. Although despised by Fiji Indian politicians, racially reserved seats came to be seen by colonial authorities, by white residents and by the chiefs as critical for the 'protection' of the indigenous community. The call for a 'common roll' was dismissed by many ethnic Fijian and European politicians as a method of securing Indian dominance of the legislature. In preparation for self-government a brief power-sharing cabinet was introduced in the late 1960s, bringing together leading indigenous Fijian chief Ratu Sir Kamisese Mara, Fiji Indian leader A.D. Patel and prominent European Sir John Falvey, who shared portfolios with colonial officials (Norton 2004, 165; Norton 2002, 147; Lal 1992, 191).

Fiji obtained independence in 1970 under Ratu Mara's leadership, and his Alliance Party dominated government over the next 17 years. In theory, Mara's Alliance rested on a 'three-legged stool,' underpinned by separate 'Fijian,' 'Indian' and 'General electors'' associations.[7] In practice, the Alliance never won a single Indian communal seat. Fiji Indians voted instead mostly for the National Federation Party (NFP). A two-party, bicommunal polarization between the Alliance and NFP characterized all of Fiji's elections during the 1970s and early 1980s, though with various splinter parties emerging and fading away from one election to the next.[8]

Twice, the Alliance's grip on government was broken by adverse election results. On the first occasion, a narrow and unexpected election defeat for the Alliance in April 1977 triggered a constitutional crisis. The Governor-General controversially responded by re-installing Ratu Mara at the head of a minority government, pending fresh elections in September, which the Alliance won.[9] On the second occasion, the newly formed Fiji Labour Party (FLP), with a multi-ethnic leadership but a largely Fiji Indian voting base, coalesced with the NFP, and narrowly won the April 1987 election. One month later, the 95 per cent indigenous Royal Fiji Military Forces seized power.[10] Efforts at a negotiated settlement included deliberations towards a power-sharing administration (the 'Deuba Accord') (Scarr 2008, 336), but these were frustrated by a reassertion of military authority in September 1987 (often misleadingly called a 'second coup'). In the wake of the 1987 crises, a new 1990 constitution entrenched 'Fijian paramountcy,' reserving the positions of president and prime minister for ethnic Fijians and imposing an electoral law that provided solely for communal electorates (entailing 37 seats for indigenous Fijians, 27 for Fiji Indians).

Despite this institutionalization of indigenous Fijian dominance, elections in 1992 and 1994 unexpectedly encouraged inter-ethnic alliances between former coup leader turned Prime Minister Sitiveni Rabuka's *Soqososo ni Vakavulewa ni Taukei* (SVT), and the two mainly Fiji Indian-backed parties (the NFP and FLP). The 1990 Constitution had, fortuitously, been agreed to be an 'interim' arrangement, one that needed to be revisited within seven years. As a result, Fiji was soon to embark upon a remarkable home-grown experiment in constitutional design.

The multi-party cabinet rules

Fiji's 1997 Constitution was an ambitious attempt to end the deep polarization left by the 1987 coup. It entailed a political settlement between Rabuka's mainly indigenous Fijian-backed SVT and the NFP led by Jai Ram Reddy and the FLP led by Mahendra Chaudhry. A Constitutional Review Commission (CRC) was established in 1995, chaired by former New Zealand Governor General Sir Paul Reeves. The CRC widely canvassed issues of institutional design in divided societies, and consulted with both Horowitz and Lijphart. They ultimately came down in favour of Horowitz's centripetalist approach. Consequently, the CRC recommended an AV electoral system as a means for encouraging the emergence of multi-ethnic coalitions (Reeves *et al.* 1996; Horowitz 1997).

In its final version, the constitution established a 71-member Parliament, with 46 communal seats (23 Fijian, 19 Indian, 3 general and 1 Rotuman) and 25 'open' or 'common roll' constituencies. The AV system was to be used for both communal and open elections, but with a split-format ballot paper giving voters an option of endorsing party tickets (similar to that used for multi-member elections to the Australian Senate). Citizens could either complete ballots 'below the line' by ranking candidates in order of preference or they could tick in favour of a party 'above the line.' Ticks above the line endorsed party-specified preferences, a provision the CRC had thought necessary both to simplify the voting process and because greater party control over transfers of ballots would supposedly strengthen party incentives to strike accommodative deals with each other (in line with Horowitz's recommendations). Around 92 to 95 per cent of ballots were completed 'above the line,' thereby granting party officials extraordinary control over outcomes in critical marginal constituencies.[11]

The CRC took seriously Lijphart's favoured consociational proposals, but was heavily influenced by contemporary events in South Africa. The commissioners visited South Africa, where mandatory power-sharing arrangements had been introduced as part of the 1994 interim constitution. By the time of that visit, however, it was clear that South Africa was on the verge of abandoning its power-sharing laws, after De Klerk's National Party departed Nelson Mandela's national unity cabinet in May 1996 (Koelble and Reynolds 1996; Strand 2001). The CRC concluded that such arrangements were "fraught" with difficulty (Lal 1998, 93). The parliamentary committee tasked with deliberating on the CRC's report thought differently. It announced its intention to "go further" in the direction of ensuring multi-ethnic government by embracing a mandatory power-sharing deal (Parliament of Fiji 1997). It suggested that all parties with over

4 per cent of the seats in the House should be invited by the prime minister to join cabinet. This was later amended by Parliament without debate, lifting the threshold to 10 per cent. The 10 per cent provision was expected to ensure that Rabuka's SVT and Reddy's NFP would share power, possibly also with the smaller third coalition ally, the United General Party.

The critical section of the 1997 Constitution provided that the prime minister "must establish a multi-party Cabinet" able to "fairly represent the parties represented in the House of Representatives":

> In establishing the Cabinet, the Prime Minister must invite all parties whose membership in the House of Representatives comprises at least 10 per cent of the total membership of the House to be represented in proportion to their numbers in the House.
>
> Republic of Fiji 1998, S99 (5)

A critical issue in the later court deliberations was whether "their numbers in the House" referred to the qualifying 10 per cent + parties, or to the total 71 members. Judicial reasoning about the allocation of cabinet portfolios was to become closely linked to that regarding the type of 'proportionality' required in the upper house, the Senate.

Proportional representation of the lower house in cabinet was to be, oddly, mirrored by proportional representation of the opposition nominees in the Senate (a house of review without powers to initiate legislation[12]). As under the British-bequeathed 1970 Constitution, appointment to the Senate gave a powerful constitutional role to the *Bose Levu Vakaturaga* (Great Council of Chiefs), which advised the president on 14 of the Senate's 32 members.[13] The prime minister would nominate nine senators (without constraint). The remaining eight senators were to be nominated by the "Leader of the Opposition," and these needed to "comprise such number of nominees of those parties as is proportionate to the size of the membership of those parties in the House of Representatives" (Republic of Fiji 1998, S64 (2)). While Cabinet would be constrained to proportionally represent all the larger parties inside Parliament, the opposition's nominees to the Senate needed to proportionally represent all parties except that of the prime minister. Disputes over entitlements to the leader of the opposition's eight Senate posts subsequently became a perennial source of inter- and intra-party friction.

I now turn to examining how these laws influenced the formation of governments following elections in 1999, 2001 and 2006.

The 1999 election and the 2000 coup

At the first elections under the new constitutional arrangements, in May 1999, the Fiji Labour Party unexpectedly emerged with 37 seats in the 71-member *Bose Lawa* (lower house). The 1999 election had been widely expected to return a Rabuka-led government, with former Leader of the Opposition Jai Ram Reddy assuming the post of deputy prime minister. Yet the SVT won only eight seats, ten short of the 18 constituencies where it held a first-count lead. The opposition parties used the new preferential voting system to punish the incumbent government, and, in critical marginal contests, transferred ballots to the FLP rather than to the SVT. It was the AV electoral system that was decisive in determining the 1999 outcome, not the mandatory power-sharing provision.

In the Fiji Indian communal constituencies, the FLP had a relatively evenly spread 65.5 per cent of the vote. The FLP thus won all 19 of these. The party also captured 18 open constituencies. This left the NFP without a single seat in Parliament. In total, the FLP won 24 constituencies from first-count victories that relied on Fiji Indian votes, and 13 open constituencies where it drew on transfers of ballots from three indigenous-backed opposition parties (Fraenkel 2000b, 2001; Fraenkel and Grofman 2006; Lal 1999). The contest for the indigenous Fijian vote was more fractionalized, and resulted in the incumbent SVT winning only five Fijian and three open seats. The decisive difference from the previous election in 1994 was the 20 per cent share secured by the ethno-nationalist outbidder party, the *Veitokani ni Lewenivanua ni Vakarisito* (VLV – Christian Democratic Alliance), which attacked Rabuka's compromises on the constitution and called for a "Christian state."[14]

With its main architects soundly defeated, the chances of survival for the 1997 political settlement were immediately poor. While the FLP had been involved in deliberations on the new constitution, it had fought the 1999 election on bread-and-butter issues (one campaign slogan was "The constitution won't put food in your mouths"). Mahendra Chaudhry, the FLP leader, was a former trade unionist who saw ethnic politics as a smokescreen disguising more fundamental issues of social class. In the broader FLP tradition, indigenous Fijian expressions of concern about land-leasing issues, affirmative action policies for businesses and the civil service and other constitutional protections were seen by the FLP leader as reflecting the standpoint of the eastern chiefly elite, not that of the ethnic Fijian 'commoners.' Conversely, the Fijian parties regularly accused Chaudhry and the FLP of trampling on indigenous sensibilities.

Following the election, the FLP held an absolute majority, holding 37 of the 71 seats (52.1 per cent). Given the unexpectedly large scale of his victory, Chaudhry assumed the prime ministerial portfolio, the first politician of Indian descent ever to do so in Fiji. The FLP's pre-election plans to select instead an indigenous Fijian leader, Dr Tupeni Baba, were shelved (Field *et al.* 2005, 56–58). With an eye to the potential security risk, Chaudhry cautiously drew MPs into cabinet from all three of the FLP's formal or informal Fijian coalition allies, whether or not they were entitled to participate under the multi-party cabinet law (i.e., the laws were *not* the critical determining influence). With 11 seats (15.5 per cent), the Fijian Association Party (FAP) qualified for inclusion under the 10 per cent rule, but the Party of National Unity (PANU) did not (4 seats or 5.6 per cent). Nor did the VLV (3 seats or 4.2 per cent). The Fijian ethno-nationalist VLV had not joined the FLP's pre-election coalition, but it had transferred its party-controlled preference ballots to the FLP over the SVT in key marginal contests, strategizing that so doing enhanced the prospects of toppling its arch-rival. Importantly, the VLV had close links with indigenous president, Ratu Sir Kamisese Mara. The president's daughter, Adi Koila Mara, was 1 of its 3 MPs, and she too was brought into an 18-member cabinet.

The four parties of the 'People's Coalition' together held 55 of the 71 seats; yet its dominant member, the FLP, had obtained a mere 1.9 per cent of the indigenous Fijian first-preference vote. Its overall majority had depended on transfers of ballots from the FAP, PANU and the VLV, but these had been transferred in accordance with preferences indicated by party officials rather than by the voters themselves. In the aftermath of the election, there were public protests by Fijian ethno-nationalists and early schisms within the coalition, but President Mara backed the new government (Keith-Reid 1999). Over the following months, all three of the FLP's allied Fijian parties (the FAP, PANU and the VLV) experienced splits. So too did the FLP itself, with indigenous members criticizing Chaudhry's leadership. However, they were discouraged from crossing the floor by a provision in the 1997 Constitution that entailed forfeit of seats in the event of expulsion from a party.[15] Rabuka, the defeated prime minister and 1987 coup leader, resigned his seat and the SVT leadership and took up the chair of the Great Council of Chiefs.

Under the multi-party cabinet provision, the SVT was entitled to an invitation to participate in cabinet. It remained the largest Fijian party in terms of vote share (38 per cent of the first-preference indigenous communal vote, as compared with 18.2 per cent for the FAP, 19.4 per cent for the VLV and 9.5 per cent for PANU), but not in terms of seat shares, having lost out as a result of the new electoral rules. In the immediate aftermath of the election, Chaudhry issued the legally required invitation to the SVT to join the cabinet. Bristling from its election defeat, the SVT responded by setting conditions on participation, including demands for four ministerial portfolios, for three of the nine prime ministerial nominations to the Senate and that all of the Rabuka government's diplomatic and state-owned enterprise appointees be allowed to complete their terms of office (cited in Supreme Court 1999, 21–22). On 20 May 1999, Chaudhry rejected these conditions. His decision to do so was later upheld by the Supreme Court (Supreme Court 1999). The SVT's new leader, Ratu Inoke Kubuabola, was sworn in as leader of the opposition. Fiji was to pay a heavy price for this initial failure to forge a multi-ethnic cabinet.

Chaudhry's government lasted exactly a year. On the first anniversary of its term in office, it was overthrown in a so-called 'civilian coup.' The putsch was fronted by businessman George Speight, but had the backing of the military's crack regiment, the Counter-Revolutionary Warfare Squadron (Fraenkel 2000a; Lal 2000a, 2000b). The SVT and other indigenous leaders had used their time on the opposition benches to galvanize Fijian disquiet and unite the ethnic Fijian parties, including backbenchers from among the FLP's coalition partners, against the government. When Speight and his allies stormed Fiji's Parliament, on 19 May 2000, several of these MPs had foreknowledge of what to expect, including FAP MP Timoci Silatolu, who was nominally part of the governing coalition, but who became Speight's right-hand man. Hundreds of indigenous Fijians entered the parliamentary complex and camped out inside. Disturbances occurred across the country, including the ransacking of the properties of Fiji Indian farmers in the Muaniweni and Dawasamu regions of Tailevu Province (close to Speight's home village).

The president, Ratu Mara, declared a state of emergency, but was then himself pushed out of office in a counter-coup by the Republic of Fiji Military Forces. On 29 May, the military assumed executive authority and the 1997 Constitution was abrogated (although the courts were later to reverse this). Speight nevertheless retained control of Parliament and its grounds, and held Chaudhry and his cabinet hostage for 56 days. The military threw a loose cordon around the Veiuto parliamentary complex, and initiated negotiations. Speight and his allies eventually agreed to release the hostages and to depart the parliamentary complex. He and his indigenous supporters relocated to the Kalabu Fijian School in peri-urban Suva, and refused to surrender their weapons. In July, military patience snapped. Speight was arrested along with hundreds of his supporters. The schism between the military and the ethno-nationalist supporters of the 2000 coup would later intensify, and by 2006 it came to overshadow polarization between the predominantly indigenous- and Fiji Indian-backed political parties.

Earlier, in July 2000, the military had relinquished executive authority to an all-indigenous Fijian civilian interim government led by former banker and Senator Laisenia Qarase. The courts were allowed to deliberate on the legality of that administration (Williams 2001, 73–94; Hatchard and Ogowewo 2003). First in November 2000 and then again in March 2001, courts ruled that the Qarase government had no legal standing. The March Court of Appeal judgment (the 'Chandrika Prasad' case) (Court of Appeals 2001) restored the 1997 Constitution, together with its multi-party cabinet and electoral provisions. Options moving forward included: (1) an unlikely restoration of the Chaudhry government; (2) a reconvening of the 1999 Parliament to select a new prime minister; or (3) fresh elections. The possibility that Parliament might be reconvened and a new prime minister selected triggered a split in the FLP that threatened Chaudhry's leadership. To avoid that challenge, Chaudhry himself formally advised the president to dissolve Parliament. Fiji thus went back to the polls under the terms of the reinstated 1997 Constitution, resulting in a second test of its electoral and power-sharing arrangements.

The 2001 election

The 2001 election delivered a much more polarized outcome than that in 1999. Caretaker Prime Minister Laisenia Qarase founded a new party, the *Soqosoqo Duavata ni Lewenivanua* (SDL), aimed at replacing the much diminished SVT as the mainstream ethnic Fijian Party. It obtained close to 50 per cent of the indigenous vote, and 32 of the 71 seats. In the contest for the Indian communal vote, the FLP lifted its vote share from 65.5 per cent in 1999 to 74.9 per cent and overall it gained 27 seats.[16] The 25 open constituencies were split mainly between the FLP and SDL. Another new party, the Conservative Alliance *Matanitu Vanua* (CAMV), obtained 20.2 per cent of the ethnic Fijian communal vote and six seats, including one secured by incarcerated 2000 putsch leader George Speight.[17] A 'Moderates Forum,' comprising several smaller parties that had come together expecting to be advantaged by the preferential voting rules, was soundly defeated. Its ballots were mostly transferred to one or other of the larger communally identified parties.[18]

Critically, the SDL – although it was the largest party – did not have an overall majority, thereby complicating the coalition arrangements. To obtain a working majority, Qarase forged a coalition with the CAMV, one member of the breakaway New Labour Unity Party and two independents, though none of these parties had reached the 10 per cent threshold for cabinet seats. With the FLP the only party to meet the 10 per cent rule, Qarase extended the constitutionally required invitation to Chaudhry to participate in cabinet, but noted that he had "already formed a coalition with like-minded parties and individuals based on consensus and voluntary agreement" (Qarase to Chaudhry, 10 September 2001, reproduced as an annex to Court of Appeal 2002). A new 20-minister cabinet was formed comprising 16 SDL MPs and four coalition allies (*Wansolwara Online* 2001).

This action was found to be unconstitutional, first by the Court of Appeal (2002) and then twice by the Supreme Court (2003, 2004). The courts ruled that not only was the FLP entitled to positions in cabinet; it was also entitled – as the sole party other than that of the prime minister with more than 10 per cent of seats – to all of the leader of the opposition's nominees for the Senate. A critical issue for the courts was whether the FLP's 28 seats entitled it to 39 per cent of cabinet portfolios, with the denominator being membership of the house (28/71), or 47 per cent, with the denominator being the total seats held only by qualifying parties (28/50). The court's ruling in favour of the latter formula drew upon its earlier deliberations regarding the distribution of the leader of the opposition's Senate appointments, which were clearly to be awarded as a share of those held only by qualifying parties. In response to the 2003 Supreme Court decision, Qarase offered Chaudhry 14 token portfolios with minimal responsibilities in an inflated 36-member cabinet. Chaudhry took the matter back to court, hoping to use court declarations of illegality to break up the ruling coalition.

In its 2004 judgment, the Supreme Court upheld the need for proportional distribution of cabinet portfolios between the FLP and the SDL (entailing 47 per cent for the FLP), but now allowed for "Independents or Senate members, provided they do not belong to any of the parties represented in the House of Representatives" to enter cabinet independently of the power-sharing formula (Supreme Court 2004 S.114). This ruling did not follow any explicit legal provision, but earned its consistency solely from the fact that the constitution was silent about the implications of the inclusion of unaffiliated MPs in cabinet. Qarase responded by offering the FLP 14 seats in a 30-member cabinet, but making clear his intention to also appoint additional independents and senators (*Fiji Sun*, 23 July 2004). By now a new election was approaching in 2006, and public opinion was tiring of the multi-party cabinet controversies. In November 2004, Chaudhry formally rejected the prime minister's invitation to join the cabinet and became leader of the opposition.

By 2004, a new controversy was brewing as the confrontation between the military commander, Frank Bainimarama, and the Qarase government moved to centre-stage. Bainimarama had opposed the 2000 coup but had installed Qarase as prime minister in July of that year. For Qarase, the hung Parliament in the wake of the 2001 election had encouraged the coalition with the CAMV, which included George Speight. For Bainimarama, the 2000 coup crisis had destabilized the Republic of Fiji Military Forces, and restoring stability required the suppression of those associated with the CAMV, particularly in Speight's home area of northern Tailevu and on the island of Vanua Levu. Personal animosity between Qarase and Bainimarama intensified between 2002 and 2004, and was conducted through several high-profile media spats (Fraenkel and Firth 2009). In January 2004, Bainimarama had a showdown with the chief executive of the Ministry of Home Affairs, and in the same month purged five senior military officers (Radio New Zealand International, 19 January 2004; *Fiji Sun*, 21 January 2004). Tension briefly abated after the commander had his contract renewed (*Fiji Sun*, 30 January 2004; Radio New Zealand International, 1 February 2004), but flared up again in mid-2005, during controversies around the Qarase government's Reconciliation, Tolerance and Unity Bill. Bainimarama called the Bill, which potentially entailed an amnesty for the 2000 coup perpetrators, a product of "warped and corrupt minds" and said that it was aimed at "ethnic cleansing of the Indian race" (Fiji Times, 12 July 2005). On the second reading of the Bill in June, with the public gallery of Parliament packed with military officers in full uniform, FLP MPs staged a walk-out (Bhim 2007, 129). In January 2006, the commander openly stated in the media that the military was planning a coup (*Fiji Times*, 9 January 2006; *Fiji Sun*, 10 January 2006). Shortly thereafter, on national television, FLP President Jokapeci Koroi said she would welcome the military removing the SDL from office (*Daily Post*, 13 January 2006; Lal 2006, 255). Both the FLP and the military commander, however, hoped that the forthcoming election might bring about a change in government.

The 2006 election

The 2006 election was a showdown between the heavily indigenous-backed SDL and the predominantly Indian-backed FLP. The military openly campaigned against the SDL government in Fijian villages, but Qarase's party had significantly strengthened and broadened its support among ethnic Fijians since 2001, particularly in western Viti Levu. The SDL acquired 80.6 per cent of the indigenous Fijian communal vote while the FLP captured 81.5 per cent of the Fiji Indian vote. These two parties also divided the 25 open seats between themselves: 13 for the SDL and 12 for the FLP. Overall, including the communal seats, the SDL had 36 MPs, which enabled the party to cross the threshold needed for a majority in the 71-member Parliament. The FLP had 31 MPs.[20] The AV system was of much less significance than in either 1999 or 2001 because nearly all the key contests were two-party battles with one or other party passing the 50 per cent threshold at the first count. Preferences marked on the ballot papers therefore never came into play.

Despite this highly polarized outcome, Fiji was to embark on a widely supported power-sharing experiment that lasted from May to December 2006. In the wake of the polls, re-elected Prime Minister Qarase announced his intention to form a multi-party cabinet, to include the FLP. At first, seven portfolios were offered, and FLP leader Mahendra Chaudhry was invited to submit 12 names for consideration for substantial portfolios, including: agriculture; commerce and industry; energy and mineral resources; environment; health; labour and industrial relations; and local government. There would also be ten SDL ministers but, in conformity with the 2004 Supreme Court judgment, Qarase made clear that he would appoint the two independents and several Senators outside the multi-party cabinet formula. The FLP caucus was split on how to respond, with Chaudhry opposed to joining cabinet but a majority in the party leadership favouring participation. The FLP therefore officially accepted, but Chaudhry insisted that the 'ground rules' for deliberations be settled first, and claimed an entitlement to eight portfolios rather than seven. He also said he would not himself serve in cabinet.

Qarase responded by lifting the offer to nine FLP portfolios in what was to be a 24-member cabinet, but declined Chaudhry's other conditions. The president swore in the SDL and other ministers on 23 May, thereby offering a de facto ultimatum. One day later, nine FLP MPs took up their portfolios. With the multi-party cabinet thus forged, Chaudhry sought unsuccessfully to become leader of the opposition. He insisted that FLP ministers be bound by party policies, and to vote in Parliament along party lines. Qarase demanded that FLP ministers be bound by collective responsibility and cabinet confidentiality.

The fate of the multi-party cabinet became inextricably linked with the buildup to the 2006 coup. Soon after the election, the military commander resumed his public attacks on the Qarase government. A failed attempt to replace him as head of the RFMF in October only stiffened Bainimarama's resolve. The 2007 budget was put before Parliament in November, and included provision for a 2.5 per cent increase in value-added tax (VAT). Chaudhry and his FLP allies opposed the VAT increase, but most of the FLP ministers wanted to sustain the power-sharing arrangement. Chaudhry insisted that they vote along party lines while Qarase demanded that they support government policy. Qarase ultimately relented, and indicated that the FLP ministers would be allowed to abstain.

Five of the nine FLP ministers in the power-sharing cabinet opposed the budget. Four, including Krishna Dutt and Poseci Bune, absented themselves. On 2 December, Dutt and Bune – who were identified as Chaudhry's key opponents – were formally expelled from the FLP. Three days later, Bainimarama seized power, effectively ending Fiji's short-lived experiment with power-sharing democracy. Initially, the coup was claimed to be a minor 'clean-up campaign' against corruption, but it soon became clear that the military had assumed control for the long haul. The Court of Appeal eventually deliberated on the legality of the post-coup interim government in April 2009 and found (as it had in 2001) that this was illegal. Hopes that this might trigger a similar return to elective democracy were quickly dashed. The next day, the 1997 Constitution was abrogated. When a new constitution was drawn up in 2013, the mandatory power-sharing provisions and the alternative vote electoral system had vanished.[21]

Discussion

The short-lived May to December 2006 multi-party cabinet experiment was the first occasion since independence that the leaders of the two largest parties – one representing the ethnic Fijians, the other indigenous Fijians – had joined together in cabinet. Although ultimately destroyed by the military coup, the arrangement was under pressure beforehand. The expulsion of Dutt and Bune would in all probability have led to their losing their seats in Parliament.[22] It sent a clear message to other FLP ministers that they had to toe the party line. From the moment Chaudhry had refused to join his colleagues in cabinet immediately after the 2006 election, it was clear – as then Vice-President Ratu Joni Madraiwiwi put it – that the FLP leader was placing himself "in a strategic position to destroy the multiparty cabinet" (Ratu Joni Madraiwiwi, Speech to the Fiji Institute of Accountants, cited in Pareti and Fraenkel 2007, 101).

Chaudhry joined the interim cabinet installed one month after the military coup, and assumed the portfolios for finance, sugar reform, public enterprise and national planning. The sternest resistance to the 2006 coup was in mid-2007, when teachers and nurses went on strike against 5 per cent pay cuts imposed by the military-backed interim government. They were defeated largely because Chaudhry used his labour movement connections to split the trade union movement (Fraenkel 2008, 454–55). Ultimately, the FLP leader paid a heavy price for this alliance with the military commander. Pushed out of the interim cabinet (nominally 'resigning') in August 2008, Chaudhry switched allegiances and soon thereafter became a vociferous critic of the Bainimarama government. Yet when democratic elections resumed in September 2014, his FLP secured just 2.4 per cent of the national vote. The vast majority of Fiji Indians, who had once supported the FLP, gave their backing instead to Bainimarama's new FijiFirst Party, propelling the military commander into the position of democratically elected prime minister. A key component of Bainimarama's election message was that he had legitimately overthrown a 'racist' and 'illegal' government. This was a reference to the 2001 to 2006 Qarase government, not the short-lived power-sharing administration of May to June 2006. For propaganda purposes, with an increasingly heavily censored media, that brief experiment in power-sharing democracy was to be airbrushed out of national-level discussion of Fiji's history.

Was Fiji's power-sharing arrangement doomed to failure from the start? Difficulties were to be anticipated. After all, the law was put in place precisely because multi-ethnic government had not arisen spontaneously. By comparison, power-sharing arrangements in Africa are regularly fraught with difficulties (Cheeseman and Tendi 2010). Where such arrangements have survived, as in Northern Ireland under the Good Friday Agreement or in Bosnia-Herzegovina under the Dayton Peace Accord, external enforcers have often played a critical enforcement role (McGarry and O'Leary 2006, 52–54; Guelke 2012). The great strength of the Fiji arrangements was that they were brokered locally, with minimal outside assistance, and effectively entailed a compact between leaders of the two major communities. The critical tragedy, from the outset in 1999, was that those leaders failed to gain sufficient support for their historic compromise in either the indigenous Fijian or Fiji Indian communities. Were the difficulties subsequently encountered the product of inherent flaws in power-sharing arrangements, or were these a result of contingent and avoidable circumstances?

Fiji's experiment suggests several implications for power-sharing theory and practice. First, Fiji's arrangements highlight the risk that mandatory executive power-sharing rules may entail extensive court deliberations, and that judges from majoritarian jurisdictions may be ill-equipped to handle such cases.[23] Fiji's institutions were poorly formulated and, in several respects, inconsistent. The 'Compact' in the 1997 Constitution spoke of voluntary coalitions, though this conflicted with the belatedly introduced mandatory power-sharing provisions. The 1995/1996 Constitutional Review Commission had suggested limiting cabinet size to 15, but the 1997 Constitution left no such constraint, paving the way for the bloated cabinets Qarase offered to accommodate court rulings. What was meant by cabinet 'proportionality' was not spelled out clearly in the 1997 Constitution, and so judges drew upon provisions regulating the leader of the opposition's Senate nominees. These ambiguities left too great a scope for judicial interpretation, and as a result these issues had to be considered again and again in the law courts. The courts initially adopted a restrictive interpretation, requiring invitations to participate in cabinet in proportion to the total only of the qualifying parties rather than the House of Representatives as a whole, but then freed the prime minister from that restraint by allowing additional independents and non-affiliated Senators to enter cabinet outside the power-sharing formula.

A second conclusion from Fiji's experiment is that hybrid combinations of majoritarian and power-sharing arrangements do not work well. The 1997 Constitution required the appointment of a prime minister who "in the President's opinion" was able to "form a government that has the confidence of the House of Representatives" (Republic of Fiji 1998, S. 98). Only after securing the majority necessary to become head of government, a process that often requires agreement on the distribution of portfolios, was the prime minister required to reconfigure the governing coalition so as to incorporate other qualifying parties. Pressures were predictably most intense in 2001 to 2006 when the party of the prime minister did not have a majority on the floor of Parliament. Stronger power-sharing rules require a more thorough overhaul of Westminster procedures for appointing governments. In neighbouring New Caledonia, which also has a mandatory power-sharing law, cabinet is selected reflecting the proportions of qualifying parties in the territorial assembly *before* the choice of the president. In Northern Ireland, the first minister is nominated by the largest party in the Assembly and the deputy first minister is nominated by the largest party in the largest 'designation' ('unionist,' 'nationalist' or 'other') other than that of the first minister (St. Andrews Agreement 2006). Other portfolios are then allocated to parties using the d'Hondt formula (O'Leary et al. 2005). Fiji's arrangements were less well crafted, reflecting their belated addition into a largely Westminster-based constitution.

The majoritarian electoral arrangements likewise worked to the detriment of the power-sharing formula. While the SVT would have likely lost the 1999 election under any other electoral arrangement, the scale of its defeat was magnified by the use of the AV system. With either a first-past-the-post or a proportional representation system, it would likely have achieved at least double the number of seats. The SVT had been the party of government, and it remained the mainstream Fijian party going into the election. Its 1999 defeat ultimately entailed its demise. Ahead of the next election, a new Fijian party would emerge that was not committed to the 1997 constitutional compromise. Equally damagingly, the use of AV wiped out the National Federation Party, despite its having a sizeable share of the 1999 Fiji Indian vote (32 per cent). As a result, there was left a mono-ethnic opposition in Parliament and a government widely perceived to represent Fiji Indian interests. At the 2001 elections, the disproportionality in electoral outcomes worked against the small but still significant Moderates Forum parties as well as against the parties with most support in western Viti Levu. By 2006, Fiji had become so polarized, with only two substantial ethnically based parties, that AV had little impact upon outcomes and the election was reasonably proportional in outcomes. It was a mismatch to have a proportional representation system for cabinet, but a non-PR system for general elections.

Conventional criticisms of power-sharing institutions centre on the absence of an effective opposition, and the risk that cabinet deliberation will result in "political chaos, deadlock and strife, and weak government" (Horowitz 2000, 257; Lal 2003). When the Bainimarama government initiated deliberations on its preferred post-2006 coup institutional arrangements through its National Council for Building a Better Fiji, it commissioned a report by an overseas consultant, Richard Herr from the University of Tasmania, which called for "the elimination of constitutional provisions that mandate executive power-sharing." The report reviewed 'Westminster' and 'Washington' forms of government, but showed no familiarity with power-sharing administrations elsewhere in the world or even with the controversies surrounding Fiji's pre-2006 coup multi-party cabinet experiment. Power-sharing arrangements were rejected simply because they were thought to undermine "the coherence of the Westminster model" and to "compromis[e] collective responsibility" and "accountability" (Herr 2008).

Under the May to December 2006 multi-party cabinet, the formal opposition was reduced to only two United People's Party MPs, though in practice Chaudhry's decision to remain outside government ensured a continuing confrontationist tenor in the country's parliamentary politics, as did the brewing military revolt. In Fiji, 36 years of post-independence government opposition politics had not facilitated careful scrutiny of government legislation. Instead it more usually entailed the implementation of policies irrespective of opposition resistance. By contrast, the

May to December Parliament referred the three most controversial parts of the SDL's policy agenda – the Reconciliation, Tolerance and Unity Bill, the Qoliqoli Bill and the Indigenous Land Claims Tribunal Bill – to parliamentary subcommittees, involving the FLP MPs. This enhanced the incentives for compromise, even if the experiment was cut short before one could assess its longer run efficacy.[24] For countries where political parties tend to be organized along ethnic lines, 'winner-takes-all' parliamentary arrangements do not ensure either constructive opposition or careful scrutiny of government policy. In Fiji's case, even the idea of having a 'leader of the opposition' was a residue from the originally anticipated majoritarian style of decision-making.

The risk of deadlock under the power-sharing arrangements was evident in the case of the SDL's planned VAT increase as part of the 2007 budget. Under Fiji's arrangements, there was no minority or mutual veto (on the consociational pattern of Northern Ireland, Bosnia or New Caledonia), so the power-sharing arrangements did not necessarily prevent the majority from forcing its agenda, except plausibly in response to a desire to avoid the potential breakup of the multi-party cabinet. The post-2006 coup interim government ditched the planned VAT increase immediately after the coup, only to later reintroduce it in the 2012 budget once the full impact of the coup on government finances became apparent. The criticism that power-sharing cabinets render governments ineffective implies that, free from that constraint, governments would follow a more constructive course, but this is rarely accurate. Some degree of constitutionally inbuilt restraint concerning decisions on the most ethnically divisive issues may be indispensable in a country with a history of divisions like those in Fiji.

Poorly devised legal provisions may plausibly explain some of the difficulties between 1999 and 2006, but they cannot account for the failure of the May to December 2006 power-sharing experiment. Nor do these explain why the earlier efforts to form a multi-party cabinet were unsuccessful. The initial failure in 1999 was linked to the SVT's shock at the scale of its election defeat. It was exacerbated by the use of AV, but was also encouraged by Chaudhry's dismissal of the salience of ethnic compromise and insistence on the primacy of class. In 1999, Chaudhry was also reluctant to include ministers from the government he had just ousted, particularly since many of these had been implicated in the 1987 coup. The People's Coalition cabinet reflected the weak coalition delivered by the AV system, rather than a government shaped by the multi-party cabinet rules. The power-sharing provisions therefore did not "subtly undercut" the AV system, as Horowitz claimed, but nor did the AV system "play a very small part" in the 1999 outcome, as Lijphart believed. Hence, the 1999 election was a much more important test of AV's potential to deliver cross-ethnic conciliation and moderation than either author recognized at the time.

Following the 2001 election, Chaudhry's 'acceptance' of Qarase's invitation was due to pressures within his own party, but the 2001 to 2004 multi-party cabinet court controversies soon became a method both for seeking to break up the SDL–CAMV coalition and for casting into doubt the legitimacy of the government.[25] For the largely indigenous government, despite the discomfort of repeated declarations of its own illegality, the court controversies kept ethnic polarization at the forefront of Fiji's politics and emphasized the need for 'Fijian unity' in the face of a threatened return of the FLP to government. At no stage between 2001 and 2004 were compromises publicly offered by either party leader, for example, to exchange raw numerical cabinet entitlements for favoured portfolios or concessions on policy issues. Compromise seemed unnecessary over an issue that was to be settled solely by recourse to the law courts. Both Qarase and Chaudhry were politicians who were firmly entrenched in their own communal camps, and both proved unable to articulate any broader national vision. Instead of fostering compromise, the power-sharing provisions in the constitution had become the principal focus of inter-ethnic antagonism.

Finally, the central dilemma confronting mandatory power-sharing arrangements is that they are normally introduced because conflicting parties are not disposed to reach voluntary agreements. Yet they ultimately require some voluntary cooperation in order to deliver on their objectives. The legal apparatus can potentially force the parties to sit together inside something called a 'cabinet,' but it cannot require those so assembled to initiate compromise on ethnically divisive issues. Nor does this necessarily ensure that executive government is conducted in accordance with the decisions of that 'cabinet,' particularly in states where the rule of law is contested. If politicians do voluntarily commence cooperation, there is also the risk that hostile communal electorates will punish them for so doing. In bicommunal settings with power-sharing cabinets, the minority party runs the risk of being seen as a powerless actor and thus losing popular support. The key challenge for the short-lived 2006 multi-party cabinet experiment was to secure real influence for the minority party, and to enable its leaders to achieve Fiji Indian backing for the new arrangements. Whether it could have achieved this in the absence of the December 2006 military coup is now impossible to know.

Notes

1 Proportions subsequently shifted, due largely to Fiji Indian out-migration. At the 2007 census, ethnic Fijians formed 56.8 per cent of the population, whereas Fiji Indians accounted for 37.5 per cent (Fiji Bureau of Statistics, 2017).
2 Consociationalist approaches entail executive-level power-sharing, proportional representation both as regards legislative elections and civil service appointments, forms of devolved authority and/or federalism and vetoes for minorities. Centripetalist approaches entail preferential voting systems, particularly with a high threshold for victory (such as the Australian-style alternative vote system) and/or presidential distribution requirements, as in Nigeria, Kenya and Indonesia.
3 As I examine later, Fiji's AV system had a party ticket option that allowed party officials control over the transfer of ballots if voters ticked 'above the line,' as the overwhelming majority did.
4 For details of these internal rebellions, see Fraenkel (2000a).
5 Lijphart writes:

> [I]nformal rules generally work better because they are more flexible – but perhaps also because they reflect a higher level of trust among groups and group

120 J. Fraenkel

> leaders. When sufficient mutual trust is lacking and inter-group relations are highly contentious, there is probably no alternative to formal constitutional and legal rules to govern power-sharing and autonomy in deeply divided societies.
>
> (Lijphart 2002, 54)

6 Around 5 per cent of the total land area alienated prior to 1874 was later recognized as freehold. Much of this was in fertile coastal and riverine areas. Further land alienation was briefly allowed under Governor Everard im Thurn between 1905 and 1908.
7 General electors were those other than Fijian or Indian (including European, part-European, Chinese and, since 1990, 'other Pacific Islanders').
8 An exception to the predominantly two-party contest was the September 1977 polls, when the NFP vote was split between 'dove' and 'flower' factions.
9 For detail on the 1977 crisis, see Scarr (2008, 230–233) and Lal (1992, 243–245).
10 The acronym survived the post-coup name change to Republic of Fiji Military Forces (Henceforth RFMF).
11 Fiji Elections Office estimate, personal communication, 1999.
12 The Senate could delay ordinary bills and suggest non-binding amendments to legislation, but it had no powers of veto except concerning bills on land and Fijian or Rotuman affairs (Republic of Fiji 1998, S. 47, S. 185).
13 Another Senator was appointed by the president on the advice of the Council of Rotuma (Republic of Fiji 1998. S. 64 (1)).
14 This call was not one likely to endear the party to the 44 per cent Fiji Indian community, the vast majority of who are either Hindu or Muslim.
15 In the run-up to the 2001 election, two prominent indigenous FLP members, Tupeni Baba and Kenneth Zinck, broke away to form the New Labour Unity Party.
16 This was lifted to 28 after the Court of Disputed Returns overturned the result for Nadi Open in August 2002, leading to the solitary NFP MP Prem Singh losing his seat (Supreme Court 2002). That decision was based on a mistaken reading of the Electoral Act (see Fraenkel 2002), as the Supreme Court unanimously later found, although two of its three judges declined to reverse the decision on the grounds that the court lacked jurisdiction (Supreme Court 2002).
17 Speight later lost his seat after missing three consecutive sittings of Parliament. His brother won the resulting by-election.
18 In total, the Moderates Forum parties won four seats, but three of these were the three 'general communal' constituencies, allocated to 'other' communities (Europeans, part-Europeans, Chinese and 'other Pacific Islanders') i.e., those where neither indigenous Fijians nor Fiji Indians cast ballots. The last, Nadi Open, was obtained by the NFP drawing largely upon Fiji Indian votes, but that result was overturned following a court decision, and the seat was instead awarded to the FLP.
19 Qarase to Chaudhry, 10 September 2001, reproduced as an annex to Court of Appeal, Chaudhry vs. Qarase, President and Attorney General, Civil Action No. 282 of 2001, Misc 1/2001, 15 February 2002.
20 The remaining four contests were fought for the 'General voter' communal seats and the seat for the island of Rotuma, i.e., contests where neither ethnic Fijian nor Fiji Indian voters cast ballots.
21 Subsequent developments, including the 2013 Constitution and the 2014 election, are not covered in this chapter, since they are irrelevant to consideration of either the mandatory power-sharing rules or the AV system. For an analysis of the 2013 Constitution, see Citizens' Constitutional Forum 2013. For the 2013 Constitution itself, see Republic of Fiji 2013. On the 2014 election under open-list proportional representation, see Larson (2014) and Fraenkel (2015a, 2015b).
22 The 1997 Constitution (S. 71 (1), (h)) provided that the "place of a member of the House of Representatives becomes vacant if the member [...] is expelled from the political party for which he or she was a candidate at the time he or she was last

elected" as long as the "expulsion was in accordance with rules of the party relating to party discipline."
23 Many of the judges sitting on the bench for the multi-party cabinet cases came from Australia or New Zealand.
24 Drafts of these three bills were discussed in cabinet, and put before Parliament on 8 August, which decided to refer them to committee (see Green 2009, 11, 19n).
25 As a result of the multi-party cabinet controversies, the Commonwealth Ministerial Action Group kept Fiji on its agenda until early 2004 (see Commonwealth 2001).

References

Bhim, Mosmi. 2007. "The Impact of the Reconciliation, Tolerance and Unity Bill on the 2006 Election." In *From Election to Coup in Fiji: The 2006 Campaign and its Aftermath*, edited by Jon Fraenkel and Stewart Firth, pp. 111–143. Canberra: ANU E-Press.

Cheeseman, Nic and Blessing-Miles Tendi. 2010. "Power-Sharing in Comparative Perspective: The Dynamics of 'Unity Government' in Kenya and Zimbabwe." *Journal of Modern African Studies* 48, no. 2: 203–229.

Citizens' Constitutional Forum. 2013. "An Analysis: 2013 Fiji Government Constitution." Available at www.cr.org/downloads/CCF_analysis_FijiGovtConstitution2013.pdf.

Commonwealth. 2001. "Commonwealth Secretary-General's Special Envoy to return to Fiji Islands," 19 September, available at: www.thecommonwealth.org/press/31555/34582/34872/commonwealth_secretary_general_s_special_e.htm.

Court of Appeal. 2001. Republic of Fiji and Attorney-General v. Chandrika Prasad, Civil Appeal No ABU0078/2000S, 1 March.

Court of Appeal. 2002. Chaudhry v. Qarase, President and Attorney General, Civil Action No 282 of 2001, Misc 1/2001, 15 February.

Daily Post. Daily Newspaper, Suva.

Field, Michael, Tupeni Baba and Unaisi Nabobo-Baba. 2005. *Speight of Violence: Inside Fiji's 2000 Coup.* Auckland: Reid Publishing.

Fiji Bureau of Statistics. 2017. www.statsfiji.gov.fj/.

Fiji Sun. Daily Newspaper, Suva. Available at: http://fijisun.comfj/.

Fiji Times. Daily Newspaper, Suva. Available at: http://fijitimes.com.

Fraenkel, Jon. 2000a. "The Clash of Dynasties and the Rise of Demagogues; Fiji's Tauri Vakaukauwa of May 2000." *Journal of Pacific History* 35, no. 3: 295–308.

Fraenkel, Jon. 2000b. "The Triumph of the Non-Idealist Intellectuals? An Investigation of Fiji's 1999 Election Results." *Australian Journal of Politics and History* 46, no. 1: 86–109.

Fraenkel, Jon. 2001. "The Alternative Vote System in Fiji; Electoral Engineering or Ballot-Rigging?" *Commonwealth and Comparative Politics* 39, no. 2: 1–31.

Fraenkel, Jon. 2008. "Fiji: Melanesia in Review." *The Contemporary Pacific* 20, no. 2: 454–455.

Fraenkel, Jon. 2015a. "An Analysis of Provincial, Urban and Ethnic Loyalties in Fiji's 2014 Election." *Journal of Pacific History* 50, no. 1: 38–53.

Fraenkel, Jon. 2015b. "The Remorseless Power of Incumbency in Fiji's September 2014 Election." *The Round Table* 104, no. 2: 151–164.

Fraenkel, Jon and Stewart Firth. 2009. "The Fiji Military and Ethnonationalism: Analyzing the Paradox." In *The 2006 Military Takeover in Fiji: A Coup to End all Coups?*, edited by Jon Fraenkel, Stewart Firth and Brij V. Lal, pp. 117–138. Canberra: ANU E-Press.

Fraenkel, Jon and Bernard Grofman. 2006. "Does the Alternative Vote Foster Moderation in Ethnically Divided Societies? The Case of Fiji." *Comparative Political Studies* 39, no. 5: 623–651.

Green, Michael. 2009. "Fiji's Short-lived Experiment in Executive Power-Sharing, May–December 2006." State, Society & Governance in Melanesia, Discussion Paper No. 2.

Guelke, Adrian. 2012. "The Potency of External Conflict Management." In *Conflict Management in Divided Societies: Theories and Practice*, edited by Stefan Wolff and Christalla Yakinthou, pp. 249–262. London: Routledge.

Hatchard, John and Tunde Ogowewo. 2003. *Tackling the Unconstitutional Overthrow of Democracies: Emerging Trends in the Commonwealth*. London: Commonwealth Secretariat.

Herr, Richard. 2008. "The Political Architecture of Democracy: Power-Sharing Options for Fiji." In *National Council for Building a Better Fiji, Joint Report on Electoral Reform*.

High Court. 2002. Krishna Prasad v. Rupeni Nacewa, Walter Rigamoto and Prem Singh, High Court at Lautoka, Judgment, 8 February.

Horowitz, Donald L. 1997. "Encouraging Electoral Accommodation in Divided Societies." In *Electoral Systems in Divided Societies: The Fiji Constitutional Review*, edited by Brij V. Lal and Peter Larmour, pp. 2–37. Canberra: ANU Press.

Horowitz, Donald L. 2000. "Constitutional Design: An Oxymoron?" In *Designing Democratic Institutions*, edited by Ian Shapiro and Stephen Macedo, pp. 253–284. *Nomos* XLII. New York: New York University Press.

Horowitz, Donald L. 2002a. "Constitutional Design: Proposals Versus Process." In *The Architecture of Democracy: Constitutional Design, Conflict Management and Democracy*, edited by Andrew Reynolds, pp. 15–36. Oxford: Oxford University Press.

Horowitz, Donald L. 2002b. "Domesticating Foreign Ideas in the Adoption of New Institutions: Evidence from Fiji and Indonesia." In *Sovereignty under Challenge: How Governments Respond*, edited by John Montgomery and Nathan Glazer, pp. 197–220. New Brunswick, NJ: Transaction Publishers.

Horowitz, Donald L. 2004. "Some Realism about Constitutional Engineering." In *Facing Ethnic Conflicts: Towards a New Realism*, edited by Andreas Wimmer *et al.*, pp. 245–257. Lanham, MD: Rowman and Littlefield.

Keith-Reid, R. 1999. "Chaudhry: The Man in the Hot Seat." *Fiji Business Magazine*, June.

Koelble, Thomas and Andrew Reynolds. 1996. "Power-Sharing in the New South Africa." *Politics and Society* 24, no. 3: 221–236.

Lal, Brij V. 1992. *Broken Waves: A History of the Pacific Islands in the Twentieth Century*. Honolulu: University of Hawaii Press.

Lal, Brij V. 1998. *Another Way: The Politics of Constitutional Reform in Post-Coup Fiji*. Canberra: NCDS/Asia Pacific Press.

Lal, Brij V. 1999. "A Time to Change – The Fiji General Elections of 1999." Regime Change and Regime Maintenance in Asia and the Pacific, Discussion Paper No. 23. Canberra: ANU.

Lal, Brij V. 2000a. "Madness in May: George Speight and the Unmaking of Modern Fiji." In *Fiji Before the Storm – Elections and the Politics of Development*, edited by Brij V. Lal, pp. 175–194. Canberra: Asia Pacific Press.

Lal, Brij V. 2000b. "'Chiefs and Thieves and Other People Besides': The Making of George Speight's Coup." *Journal of Pacific History* 35, no. 5: 281–293.

Lal, Brij V. 2006. *Islands of Turmoil: Elections and Politics in Fiji*. Canberra: Asia-Pacific Press.

Lal, Victor. 2003. "Fiji's Mandatory Power-Sharing and Electoral System Need a Complete Overhaul." *Pacific Islands Report*, 23 July.
Larson, Erik. 2014. "Fiji's 2014 Parliamentary Election." *Electoral Studies* 36, no. 1: 235–239.
Lijphart, Arend. 1996. "The Puzzle of Indian Democracy: A Consociational Interpretation." *American Political Science Review* 90, no. 2: 258–268.
Lijphart, Arend. 2002. "The Wave of Power-Sharing Democracy." In *The Architecture of Democracy: Constitutional Design, Conflict Management and Democracy*, edited by Andrew Reynolds, pp. 37–54. Oxford: Oxford University Press.
Maitaivalu News, Republic of Fiji Military Forces, newsletter.
McGarry, John and Brendan O'Leary. 2006. "Consociational Theory, Northern Ireland's Conflict, and its Agreement. Part 1: What Consociationalists can Learn from Northern Ireland." *Government and Opposition* 41, no. 1: 43–63.
Norton, Robert. 2002. "Accommodating Indigenous Privilege; Britain's Dilemma in Decolonising Fiji." *Journal of Pacific History* 37, no. 2: 133–156.
Norton, Robert. 2004. "Seldom a Transition with such Aplomb: From Confrontation to Conciliation on Fiji's Path to Independence." *Journal of Pacific History* 39, no. 2: 163–184.
O'Leary, Brendan, Bernard Grofman and Jørgen Elklit. 2005. "Divisor Methods for Sequential Portfolio Allocation in Multi-Party Executive Bodies: Evidence from Northern Ireland and Denmark." *American Journal of Political Science* 49, no. 1: 198–211.
Pareti, Samisoni and Jon Fraenkel. 2007. "The Strategic Impasse: Mahendra Chaudhry and the Fiji Labour Party." In *From Election to Coup in Fiji: The 2006 Campaign and its Aftermath*, edited by Jon Fraenkel and Stewart Firth, pp. 89–103. Canberra: ANU E-Press.
Parliament of Fiji. 1997. Report of the Joint Parliamentary Select Committee on the Report of the Fiji Constitutional Review Commission, Parliamentary Paper No. 17.
Radio New Zealand International, Radio Station, Wellington, New Zealand. Available at: http://radionz.co.nz/international.
Ratu Sir Lala Sukuna. 1983. *Fiji: The Three-Legged Stool: Selected Writings of Ratu Sir Lala Sukuna*. London: Macmillan.
Reeves, Paul, Tomasi Vakatora and Brij V. Lal, eds. 1996. "The Fiji Islands: Towards a United Future." Parliamentary Paper No. 34. Suva: Report of the Fiji Constitutional Review Commission.
Republic of Fiji. 1998. Constitution of the Republic of the Fiji Islands, Suva.
Republic of Fiji. 2013. Constitution of the Republic of Fiji. Suva.
Scarr, Deryck. 2008. *Tuimacilai: A Life of Ratu Sir Kamisese Mara*. Crawford House.
Strand, Per. 2001. "Finalizing the South African Constitution: The Politics of the Constituent Assembly." *Politikon* 28, no. 1: 47–63.
Supreme Court. 1999. President of the Republic of Fiji Islands v. Inoke Kubuabola, Mahendra Chaudhry and Adi Kuini Speed, FJSC 8, Miscellaneous Case No 1 of 1999.
Supreme Court. 2002. Prem Singh v. Krishna Prasad, Rupeni Nacewa and Walter Rigamoto, CBV0001.2002S, Judgment, 18 July.
Supreme Court. 2004. Opinion of the Supreme Court in the Matter of Section 123 of the Constitution Amendment Act 1997 and in the Matter of a Reference by the President for an Opinion in Questions as to the effect of Section 99 of the Constitution, Miscellaneous Case No 1 of 2003, Judgment, 9 July.
Williams, George. 2001. "The Case that Stopped a Coup: The Rule of Law and Constitutionalism in Fiji." *Oxford University Commonwealth Law Journal* 1, no. 1: 73–94.

6 Ethnic power-sharing coalitions and democratization

Nils-Christian Bormann

Introduction[1]

Almost 40 years ago, Arend Lijphart famously remarked that for ethnically divided societies "the realistic choice is not between the British normative model of democracy and the consociational model, but between consociational democracy and no democracy at all" (Lijphart 1977, 238). Central to Lijphart's theory is a grand coalition of political leaders from different ethnic groups, who share executive power with the aim of avoiding civil wars. Thus, in contrast to the ideal-typical Westminster democracy, which entails bare-majority governments based on winner-takes-it-all electoral rules and confrontational government–opposition interactions (Lijphart 1999, 2), power-sharing democracy emphasizes consensus and shared decision-making. Critiques of Lijphart's claims abound,[2] but they do not always dispute the value of power-sharing governments for stability in ethnically divided societies. Recent research considers executive power-sharing as one of the central ingredients of negotiated settlements to end civil wars (e.g., Mattes and Savun 2009) and ethnic inclusion into the executive strongly reduces the risk of the onset of civil war (Cederman et al. 2013). Others find positive associations between power-sharing institutions such as proportional representation and the quality of democracy (Norris 2008), or between power-sharing arrangements in negotiated settlements following civil wars and higher chances of democratization in post-conflict states (Hartzell and Hoddie 2015). Even one of Lijphart's fiercest critics, Donald Horowitz, concludes that "the only escape from regimes of ethnic inclusion and exclusion lies in coalition arrangements" (Horowitz 2000, 440). In sum, there is considerable agreement that executive power-sharing is conducive to peaceful relations in ethnically divided societies, and that this stability furthers the chances of democratic rule to emerge and survive.

Yet outside the consociational literature there is a healthy skepticism about the chances of the success of democracy in multi-ethnic polities that goes back to Mill's 1861 essay "Considerations on Representative Government" (Mill 1958 [1861]; Dahl and Tufte 1973). Scholars of ethnic politics usually point to ethnic outbidding and inter-group violence as significant threats to the viability of democracy in ethnically divided states (Horowitz 1993; Rabushka and Shepsle

2008). In contrast, Lijphart advances the view that democracy is possible and can survive if political leaders form grand coalitions that bridge ethnic differences. His optimistic claim has been criticized, in part because grand coalitions inhibit government change and thereby constrain elite responsiveness to citizens (see, e.g., Lustick 1997; Rothchild and Roeder 2005). Indeed, several quantitative studies indicate that ethnic diversity is a hindrance to democratization, in particular when a country has a predominantly Muslim population. These studies commonly rely on aggregated socio-structural fractionalization or polarization indices, and do not consider the interactions of political leaders (Powell 1982, 44–46; Barro 1999; Norris 2008).[3]

Curiously, Lijphart's concern with the relationship of ethnic power-sharing and democracy receives little attention in comparative studies of democratization,[4] which usually fall into either structural or situational approaches. Structuralists generally highlight socio-economic factors such as income levels and economic inequality. In 1959, Seymour Martin Lipset first advanced the thesis that rising levels of development make the masses demand democracy, and equip them with the resources to obtain it (Lipset 1959; Inglehart and Welzel 2005; Epstein *et al.* 2006; Kennedy 2010). More recently, political economists emphasize the power of history. In their accounts, institutional legacies from different colonial strategies determine the long-time economic and political regime trajectory of states (Acemoglu and Robinson 2006; Boix 2003; Boix and Stokes 2003). Elites feature more prominently in these studies due to their ability to veto democratization when it threatens to entail progressive taxation. When the threat of taxation is low, in particular when economic inequality is at the right level, elites allow democratic reforms to occur. According to Boix and Acemoglu's and Robinson's models, elite behaviour is a function of macro-economic forces. Thus, in structural theories, elite behaviour is usually a function of economic development and institutions but rarely an independent explanation of democratization.

Contrary to most structural approaches, proponents of situational theories put more emphasis on the actions of political elites during transition periods. In this tradition, mass demands for democratization based on structural changes are insufficient for bringing about democracy. Transition periods occur spontaneously, for example, during international waves (Huntington 1991; Gleditsch and Ward 2006) or even entirely at random (Przeworski *et al.* 2000). Political elites can veto democratization independent of exogenous factors. Scholars who advance situational accounts suggest that the success of transitions depends on an agreement between moderates and hardliners inside the regime (O'Donnell *et al.* 1986; Przeworski 1992). Political elites take centre-stage in these approaches but only during transition periods. However, the ethnic identity of leaders and their access to power hardly play any role in either structural or situational approaches.

Whereas scholars of democratization only pay attention to elite behaviour during transition periods, students of authoritarian regimes emphasize power-sharing between a dictator and the ruling coalition as a crucial mechanism of regime stability (Gandhi and Przeworski 2007; Svolik 2009). The central hypothesis in this literature states that dictatorships survive longer when the ruler can credibly commit future cooperation with other elites via institutions such as parliaments or political parties (Geddes 2003; Magaloni 2008; Boix and Svolik 2013). In other words, elite cooperation in authoritarian regimes decreases the likelihood of democratization. This diagnosis contradicts Lijphart's (1977, 238) claim that elite power-sharing is central to the emergence and survival of democracy in ethnically divided societies. This contradiction constitutes the main research puzzle of my contribution.

To provide an answer to this puzzle, my theoretical argument explores the variation of multi-ethnic polities through the ethnic make-up of the executive. It explores two dimensions of government coalitions: their ethnic representativeness and their ethnic diversity. By representativeness I refer to the proportion of the population that share their ethnic identity with political leaders in the government. Here I use the terms 'ethnic majority regime' and 'ethnic minority regime' to reflect the level of representativeness. By diversity I mean the share of ethnically distinct leaders included in the government; that is, the regime itself can be either multi-ethnic or mono-ethnic. The two dimensions correlate to some extent, since more included ethnic groups imply both higher degrees of representativeness and diversity, but not greatly so. For example, Bashar al-Assad's regime in multi-ethnic Syria is unrepresentative, since elites in the executive share their ethnic identity with only about 12 per cent of the population. It is also not diverse, since the central government positions are held exclusively by Alawites. Ghana's government, on the other hand, has usually represented a large share of the population and most of the country's ethnic groups. Governments can be mono-ethnic but representative, such as Turkey prior to its democratic transition in 1983, or they can be unrepresentative but diverse, such as pre-partition Pakistan, which featured a coalition between Punjabi, Pashtun and Mohajir elites but excluded Bengalis, Sindhis, Hindus and Baluchis. In total, Pakistan's excluded groups accounted for more than 60 per cent of the population.

The implications for democratization are twofold: first, with respect to the representativeness of the government, democratization would imply the certain end to the rule of Assad's minority government, but Ghana's encompassing power-sharing coalition has been able to embrace democracy without risking its access to power. Yet, most authoritarian elites certainly prefer authoritarian rule to democratic rule even if they were to win future majority elections. Thus, second, the ethnic diversity of the government is crucial. In an ethnically homogeneous coalition, the dictator, who has the most to lose from democratization, is more likely to enjoy the loyalty and support of other members from his or her own group, and is better able to resist democratization pressures. Whereas some elites may want to initiate democratic reforms, they have more leeway from the dictator when they do not share the dictator's ethnic identity. In a multi-ethnic coalition, diverse elites can leave the coalition and consequently threaten the survival of the regime. More diverse coalitions are thus more likely to democratize than less diverse coalitions.

In order to test my propositions, I draw on the Ethnic Power Relations (EPR) dataset that provides information on the power access of elites from politically relevant ethnic groups in over 150 states between 1946 and 2009 (Cederman *et al.* 2010, 2013). I construct my power-sharing variables from data on the ethnic composition of executives in authoritarian regimes. Using two different measurements of democratic transitions and a new estimator that captures international diffusion effects, my empirical analyses reveal that authoritarian regimes governed by ethnic majority coalitions have the highest probability of democratization. In contrast, single-group minority regimes are most likely to remain autocratic as predicted by my theory.

This study bridges structural and situational theories of democratization by linking government and opposition ethnic elites to their non-elite group members. Structural characteristics of country-level ethnic diversity such as a country's fractionalization measure obviously impact upon what government coalitions are possible and how much support any elite would receive under sincere ethnic voting. However, structural indicators neither determine coalition membership nor impact directly upon the interactions of elites within power-sharing coalitions. Thus, this study offers a far more specific assessment of multi-ethnicity and democratization. It also adds empirical flesh to the often homogeneous and amorphous portrayal of political elites in studies of democratization. Whereas situational models often distinguish between hard-liners and reformers and assume that this role is fixed (O'Donnell and Schmitter 1986; Przeworski 1992), structural approaches generally assume that elites are adverse to democratization when it threatens their economic well-being (Boix 2003; Acemoglu and Robinson 2006). In this study, elites' position depends on the amount of support elites in government enjoy from their ethnic groups and the diversity of this support basis. When the ethnic composition of the government changes so do the chances of democratization.

Ethnic power-sharing and democratization

Before outlining my argument in detail, I define key concepts, in particular ethnic groups, their leaders and the autocracy–democracy distinction. Ethnic groups are defined in the Weberian tradition as "cultural communities based on a common belief in putative descent" whose members share linguistic, religious or racial identity markers (Weber 1978). Following Henry Hale, ethnic differences are not meaningful in themselves but because ethnic identity markers reduce uncertainty they often become aligned with the pursuit of political goals by elites (Hale 2008). Put differently, political elites, the individuals who have potential access to state power and vie for societal support to improve their own influence, regularly appeal to their co-ethnics because they find it easier to form political coalitions along ethnic lines. However, their co-ethnics do not follow them naturally; support is often contingent upon elites providing material incentives such as patronage benefits to them.

I distinguish democratic and authoritarian regimes by the extent to which they balance the power between elites and the masses. To be precise, political elites in dictatorships are less dependent on mass support because they do not face competitive elections. However, they are not completely independent from societal backing because the risk of violent removal from office looms over authoritarian rule (cf. Bueno de Mesquita *et al.* 2003). I therefore define democratization as a shift of power from elites to masses through the introduction of meaningful institutional rules that allow the masses to influence the composition of the government.[5] This definition touches on a debate in consociational theory about the accountability of elites in a grand coalition. Where power-sharing arrangements guarantee certain elites government positions independent of electoral results as, for example, in Bosnia-Herzegovina or Lebanon, democratic accountability is difficult if not impossible to attain (e.g., Jarstad 2008). However, I embrace John McGarry and Brendan O'Leary's (2007) "liberal" interpretation of power-sharing, which promotes ethnic coalitions as voluntary rather than constitutionally forced agreements. Even in the latter case, intra-ethnic competition may lead to meaningful democratic procedures that are easily distinguishable from authoritarian arrangements, which display no meaningful competition for the vote between different elites. Again, this does not mean that authoritarian elites do not require social support but this support is not contested in effective elections.

To evaluate the prospect of democratization in multi-ethnic dictatorships, I consider two theoretical dimensions that characterize all regimes, their representativeness and their diversity. In terms of representativeness, where the government represents less than half of the country's population, I denote these cases as 'ethnic minority regimes.' I denote cases where ethnic elites are associated with more than 50 per cent of the population as 'ethnic majority regimes.' When elites are surprised by mass demands for democracy, as in the situational account of democratization, they fear losing power. This fear increases proportionally with the amount of influence that is at stake. If the current ruling elites represent only a very small part of the population, they strongly resist change. Ethnic minority regimes simply have no chance of winning future elections held under majority rule. In order to secure their rule against a numerically superior opposition, ethnic minority governments such as Assad's Syria or Saddam Hussein's Iraq respond to popular demands for democratization with brutal oppression tactics. As a result, the prospect of governing in a more inclusive post-transition coalition is small for incumbent elites of minority governments, regardless of their ethnic diversity.[6] Instead, legal prosecution and possibly even the death sentence await the likes of Hussein or Idi Amin.

In contrast, the cost–benefit calculations of government elites who represent a majority of the population are different. Already, Samuel Huntington (1968) and Dankwart Rustow (1970) argued that a shared consensus among national leaders is a precondition for successful democratization because future long-term exclusion under majority rule becomes less likely. More recently, Dan Slater (2012) articulates this argument for East and Southeast Asian states where he and his collaborators describe the "strong-state democratization" mechanism. In brief, autocratic incumbents with whom a majority of the population identifies ethnically, as, for example, in Taiwan, Singapore or Malaysia, value long-term access to office and respond positively to popular pressure for democracy among their own constituency in order to "concede to thrive" (see also Slater and Wong 2013). In terms of costs and benefits, elites in these regimes prefer to give up some of the financial advantages of unchecked authoritarian rule to the risk of being overthrown in a democratic revolution. I summarize this argument in my first hypothesis.

H1 *Democratization is more likely to occur in ethnic majority regimes than under ethnic minority rule*

Thus far, I have focused on the link between elites and masses qua ethnicity. This link depends in substantial part on the relationship among political elites. Put differently, the degree of ethnic representativeness of authoritarian governments is a function of the degree of national integration and the ethnic diversity of the government. National integration – that is, the degree of ethnic homogeneity within the entire population – is a long-term process (Weber 1976), which is difficult to manipulate under the contemporary international minority protection regime (Jenne 2007). Increasing the diversity of the regime – that is, including political elites from ethnically distinct groups into the governing coalition – increases its size by bringing in additional supporters. The second part of my argument suggests that multi-ethnic regimes should be more likely to democratize than would mono-ethnic governments.

Why should mono-ethnic regimes differ from their multi-ethnic counterparts? Why, for example, should Malaysia be more likely to democratize than Singapore? Where ethnic coalitions rule the state, the likelihood of democratization should be higher because the dictator, who has the most to lose through a democratic transition, is weaker relative to ethnically diverse ruling coalitions than vis-à-vis ethnically homogeneous allies. At the same time, I argue that authoritarian elites are not as strongly opposed to democratization as is often assumed in the literature – under certain circumstances they might even favour it.

First, the power differential between the dictator and the ruling coalition is more balanced in multi-ethnic ruling coalitions. The threat of exit from the ruling coalition is much stronger for elites who build on an independent power base such as a distinct ethnic group. In other words, multi-ethnic coalitions are more likely to break apart than mono-ethnic ones (Horowitz 2000, 369–379; Bormann 2014, 109–114). As coalition breakdown correlates highly with the likelihood of coups d'état and other irregular regime changes (Bormann 2014, 110), elites in multi-ethnic coalitions have far more bargaining power vis-à-vis the dictator than do elites who come from the same ethnic identity as the dictator. Although ethnic groups may encompass divisions along party lines (e.g., McLauchlin and Pearlman 2012), it is usually easier to manipulate organizational differences than ethnic ones. The dictator has more leeway in dealing with rival elites in very homogeneous regimes, such as the monarchies in the Middle East and North Africa, or other family-run dictatorships, such as Singapore or the Dominican Republic.

Second, the limits imposed upon the dictator's power by independent power bases of multi-ethnic elites have significant repercussions for the likelihood of democratization. Members of the authoritarian ruling coalition have reason to opt for democratic institutions, despite a relative loss of influence towards the masses (Boix 2003; Acemoglu and Robinson 2006). I argue that the motives of elites who favour democracy over dictatorship lie, first, in the relative power gains vis-à-vis the dictator and, second, in reducing the personal risks they face under authoritarian rule. With respect to the former motive, Svolik (2009, 478) articulates the standard assumption about the average dictator who has the "ability and desire to acquire more power at the expense of the ruling coalition" (see also Driscoll 2012). As a result of the power-seeking behaviour of the dictator, authoritarian elites face very high personal risks (cf. Bueno de Mesquita *et al.* 2003). Losing control of the government in democracies entails moving to the opposition benches. Losing power in dictatorships has far worse consequences, including public humiliation, imprisonment, physical harm and loss of property and life. Consequently, authoritarian elites generally prefer democratic rules that effectively constrain the power of any one person and which reduce their personal risks relative to authoritarian arbitrariness. Elites in multi-ethnic regimes then have both the motive and the ability to effectively contain the dictator and to introduce democratic institutions.[7] I thus agree with Lijphart's prediction, though not with the underlying institutional motivational mechanisms leading to democratization, in my second hypothesis.

H2 *Democratization is more likely to occur under multi-ethnic governing coalitions than under mono-ethnic rule*

Scholars of authoritarian politics have also identified the threats to elites in dictatorships – the power-seeking behaviour of the dictator and the high stakes for elites – but their answer is not democratization but authoritarian parties and legislatures that credibly guarantee power-sharing between the dictator and other elites (Gandhi and Przeworski 2007; Magaloni 2008; Boix and Svolik 2013). Credible power-sharing through these institutions then prolongs the survival of these regimes. While I tend to agree with the general thrust of these arguments, I believe they are limited on two counts. First, institutions such as parties and legislatures are obviously a step towards democracy already. Daniela Donno (2013), for example, argues that competitive authoritarian regimes are particularly likely to democratize. Second, legislatures in autocracies may not be very successful in balancing the dictator, as Joseph Wright and Abel Escriba-Folch (2012) point out. Others highlight that the effectiveness of party-based regimes in managing conflicts among elites depends on the context in which they were founded (Smith 2005; Slater 2010; Levitsky and Way 2012). Given these shortcomings, I reiterate that democratic institutions offer far better protection for political elites from violent prosecution than do authoritarian ones.

Table 6.1 summarizes my argument by linking the representativeness and diversity of ethnic coalitions in authoritarian regimes to the likelihood of democratization. Of the four possible regimes, mono-ethnic minority governments should have the smallest probability of democratization, whereas

Table 6.1 Theoretical link between ethnic representativeness and diversity, and the likelihood of democratization

Diversity	Representativeness	
	Minority support	Majority support
Mono-ethnic	Small	Medium
Multi-ethnic	Medium	High

multi-ethnic majority coalitions should have the largest likelihood of democratization. The other two coalition types fall in between these two extremes.

Four observations are in order. First, ethnic heterogeneity is not a curse that prevents states from democratizing but it does influence the likelihood of democratization through the ethnic composition of the executive. Second, dictatorships are more likely to democratize when incumbent regimes represent a majority of the population. Third, the more diverse the elite coalition, the more sizeable it is, and the more influential ruling elites are vis-à-vis the dictator, so that they can push through democratic reforms against the resistance of the dictator. Fourth, a priori, my argument does not attribute more weight to the diversity or the representativeness dimension of ethnic representativeness in government. Whether one of these dimensions dominates the other is an empirical question that is not easy to answer because a more diverse ethnic coalition usually implies a more representative regime as well.

Case selection and key variables

In order to test my hypotheses, I investigate the probability of democratization in all autocratic regimes after 1945 where political actors claim to act on behalf of multiple ethnic groups. As Geddes and colleagues (2013) note, the sample of non-democracies is not equivalent to the sample of authoritarian regimes. To reduce the risk that my conclusions are simply a function of the underlying sample of dictatorships or the definition of democracy, I rely on two definitions of authoritarian regimes and democratization. First, I employ the Polity IV dataset and code democratization whenever a state reaches a democracy score higher than 5 (Jaggers and Gurr 1995; Marshall *et al.* 2011). A second set of analyses uses the data by Geddes *et al.* (2014) (GWF). In contrast to the more complex Polity IV coding of democratization, GWF use a minimalist definition of democracy and exclude "provisional governments and warlordism" from their sample of authoritarian regimes. Democratization occurs when a state holds competitive and fair elections in which at least 10 per cent of the total population is eligible to vote, and the government is able take power without interference by outside forces (Geddes *et al.* 2013). In total, my data include 85 Polity IV transitions and 100 democratization events in the GWF data between 1946 and 2009. Table 6.2 lists all transition cases from the two datasets.

Table 6.2 Democratic transitions in the Polity IV and GWF sample, 1946 to 2009

Country	Polity IV transitions	GWF transitions
Albania	2002	1991
Argentina	1973, 1983	1946, 1973, 1983
Azerbaijan		1992
Bangladesh	1991	1990, 2008
Benin	1991	1970, 1990
Bolivia	1982	1979, 1982
Brazil	1985	1985
Bulgaria	1990	1990
Burundi	2005	1993, 2003
Central African Republic		1993
Chile	1964, 1989	1989
Colombia	1957	1958
Republic of Congo		1991
Costa Rica		1949
Croatia	2000	
Cyprus	1968	
Czechoslovakia	1990	1989
Ecuador	1979	1947, 1966, 1979
El Salvador	1984	1994
Fiji	1999, 2004	
France	1946, 1969	
Georgia	2004	2003
Ghana	1979, 2001	1969, 1979, 2000
Greece	1975	1974
Guatemala	1996	1995
Guinea-Bissau	2005	1999, 2003
Guyana	1992	
Honduras	1982, 1989	1956, 1981
Hungary	1990	1990
Indonesia	1999	1999
Italy	1947	
Kenya	2002	2002
Laos	1957	1962
Liberia	2006	2003
Madagascar	1992	1993
Malawi	1994, 2004	1994
Malaysia	2008	
Mali	1992	1991
Mauritania		2007
Mexico	1997	2000
Moldova	1993	
Mongolia	1992	1993
Myanmar		1960
Nepal	1999, 2006	1991, 2006
Nicaragua	1990	1990
Niger	1992, 2004	1991, 1999
Nigeria	1979	1979, 1999
Pakistan	1956, 1973, 1988	1971, 1988, 2008
Panama	1989	1951, 1955, 1989
Paraguay	1992	1993

Country	Polity IV transitions	GWF transitions
Peru	1980, 2001	1956, 1963, 1980, 2000
Philippines	1987	1986
Poland	1991	1989
Romania	1996	1989
Russian Federation	2000	
Senegal	2000	2000
Serbia and Montenegro	2000	2000
Sierra Leone	2007	1996
South Africa	1992	1994
Spain	1978	1976
Sri Lanka	2001, 2006	1994
Sudan	1965, 1986	1964, 1986
Syria	1954	1947, 1954
Taiwan	1992	2000
Thailand	1992	1973, 1988, 1992, 2007
Togo		1963
Turkey	1946, 1960, 1973, 1983	1950, 1961, 1983
Ukraine	1994	
Zambia	1991, 2008	1991

My empirical analysis relies on the Ethnic Power Relations dataset (EPR-ETH) to code the main explanatory variables (Cederman *et al.* 2010, 2013). EPR-ETH includes information on the access of elites to government power in all states in which ethnicity is a politically relevant cleavage. Put differently, whenever national elites make political claims on behalf of ethnic groups or the state actively discriminates against a subset of ethnic groups, ethnicity is coded as relevant.[8] This is the case in over 150 independent states after 1946, including the vast majority of authoritarian regimes.[9]

I rely on three different operationalizations that describe the ethnic diversity and representativeness of governments. First, the share of the population that is represented by elites in the state executive, such as the military junta, the communist executive committee or at the royal court, signifies the representativeness of the government. Second, the number of distinct ethnic groups in the coalition, measured as the count of included groups in the EPR data, captures the diversity of the government.[10] Third, four dummies combine these two dimensions by distinguishing single-group and coalition governments as well as their minority and majority status. Ethnic coalitions enjoy majority support when their members constitute more than 50 per cent of the ethnically relevant population.

In order to avoid attributing cases of democratization to post-transition ethnic coalitions, a process known as reverse causality, I lag all four coalition indicators. Since the EPR data already measure the ethnic composition of the government at the beginning of each calendar year, my approach only measures coalitions which have been in power at least one year prior to any transition. As a result, my analysis should even be immune to small measurement error in the timing of transitions. This conservative strategy weakens my results. I discuss reverse causality in greater detail in the robustness section below.

As shown above, the literature on democratization focuses primarily on structural country-level characteristics. To account for these confounding influences my analyses include a number of controls and variables. GDP per capita and economic growth proxy modernization effects are lagged by one and two years, respectively. Higher economic development is expected to increase the chances of both democratization and democratic survival. High growth is likely to stabilize existing regimes. To account for collective action problems that may delay democratization, all analyses include an ethnic fractionalization index and a logged population variable. The fractionalization index is calculated from the groups included in the EPR-ETH data. All other socio-economic indicators are taken from Hunziker and Bormann (2013).

Structuralists, such as Acemoglu and Robinson (2006), stress the importance of historical legacies in bringing about and maintaining democracy. As a rough proxy for the various mechanisms, I include a count of past democratic transitions calculated from the Polity IV and GWF datasets. In addition, all models include a count of years since the establishment of the authoritarian regime, or 1946; that is, the first year in the dataset to control for temporal dependence.[11] Situational explanations of democratization suggest that transitions in neighbouring states vastly increase the likelihood of democracy. All analyses of democratization therefore include a spatial lag of the dependent variable within a 750-kilometre radius around the state 'at risk' of democratization. I calculate these variables with the help of the CShapes dataset devised by Weidmann et al. (2010).

Empirical tests

In order to test my hypotheses, I rely on a new quasi-maximum likelihood Logit estimator that models the contemporaneous diffusion effect of binary outcomes such as democratization. In this Spatial Logit model, the diffusion effect is bounded between −1 and 1. A correlation of .5 indicates substantial neighbourhood influence.[12] Regular Logit models would assume that democratic transitions in neighbouring countries during the same year would each be causing the other independently. In other words, they would overestimate the impact of interdependent wave effects. In contrast, my Spatial Logit estimator takes into account that neighbourhood democratic transitions during the same year are dependent on one another. As a result, it does not overstate the effect of regional diffusion.

Table 6.3 presents four models that assess Hypotheses 1 and 2 on the basis of the Polity IV sample. Model 1 tests whether the ethnic representativeness of the government influences the probability of democratic transitions (H1). Model 2 assesses the diversity hypothesis by estimating the effect of the log of the number of groups represented in the executive on democratization (H2). Model 3 combines representativeness and diversity measures in three dummy indicators that represent various government constellations. Finally, Model 4 combines the representativeness and size variables. The first two models thus constitute independent tests of the representative and diversity mechanisms. The third model explicitly combines the two indicators into the three dummy variables. Specifically, it highlights the difference to mono-ethnic minority regimes, the base category, which should have the smallest probability of democratization according to my theory. Model 4, in contrast, pits the representativeness and the diversity variables against one another to see if one of them carries more weight in predicting democratization.

Across all four models, the coalition indicators exhibit a positive correlation with democratization, and the estimated effects are statistically significant. Both of my hypotheses are supported by the strong positive correlation of the representativeness and diversity indicators in Models 1 and 2. In Model 3, which takes minority mono-ethnic regimes such as Syria as its baseline, the majority coalition indicator exhibits the strongest relationship with democratization as measured by the Polity IV data. Although mono-ethnic majority governments and minority coalitions have a positive impact upon democratization relative to the baseline, they are statistically insignificant at conventional levels. In other words, states with multiple politically relevant ethnic groups have the best chance to democratize when governed by an encompassing coalition government. Model 4 sheds some light on the relative importance of the two main mechanisms. While both estimated effects of the representativeness and the diversity indicators decrease substantially, the representativeness indicator remains stronger and more precise. In contrast, the diversity effect is only significant at the 0.1 level.

The control variables exhibit mixed effects. Higher economic development is more likely to lead to democratization but is statistically insignificant during the period under study here, as shown by Adam Przeworski *et al.* (2000). As expected, economic growth stabilizes dictatorships and prevents regime change. States with larger populations are more likely to democratize and significantly so in Models 2 and 4. One explanation for this result could be that smaller states can be more easily controlled and monitored by a dictator and other ruling elites. Protest against the regime is therefore easier to subdue. In line with earlier writings by Robert Dahl (1971) and G. Bingham Powell (1982), a higher degree of ethnic fractionalization reduces the likelihood of democratization but only reaches the 5 per cent level of significance in Model 2 (see also Przeworski *et al.* 2000). As soon as a measure for the representativeness of the government is included, the estimated effect of fractionalization is far weaker and becomes statistically insignificant. The reason for this may be that it is easier to form exclusive minority regimes in states where the opposition is fractionalized. Finally, past transitions and neighbourhood effects show a robust and positive effect on the likelihood of democratization. In particular, the diffusion effect is sizeable. Both a state's own previous experiences with democracy and neighbourhood effects increase the demand for more democracy.

The GWF dataset employs an alternative definition of democratization and includes a slightly different set of cases than do the Polity IV data. Next to

136 N.-C. Bormann

Table 6.3 Polity IV democratization and ethnic power-sharing, 1946 to 2009

	(1)	(2)	(3)	(4)
Representativeness	1.761** (0.546)			1.253* (0.596)
Diversity – log (count)		0.803** (0.251)		0.492 (0.291)
Minority, multi-ethnic government			0.979 (0.874)	
Majority, multi-ethnic government			1.205** (0.428)	
Majority, mono-ethnic government			0.789 (0.430)	
Ln (GDP p.c.)	0.187 (0.215)	0.247 (0.218)	0.217 (0.223)	0.173 (0.207)
GDP growth	−4.248*** (1.200)	−4.059*** (1.207)	−4.160** (1.307)	−4.274*** (1.266)
Log (population)	0.325 (0.168)	0.400* (0.177)	0.274 (0.171)	0.360* (0.163)
Ethnic fractionalization	−0.004 (0.501)	−1.627** (0.551)	−0.929 (0.602)	−0.767 (0.675)
Past transitions	1.311*** (0.368)	1.271*** (0.363)	1.283*** (0.361)	1.292*** (0.358)
Regime years	0.002 (0.002)	0.003 (0.002)	0.002 (0.002)	0.003 (0.002)
Neighbour, democratic transition	0.488*** (0.086)	0.509*** (0.090)	0.462*** (0.093)	0.526*** (0.086)
Constant	−6.638*** (1.517)	−5.575*** (1.493)	−5.521*** (1.447)	−6.209*** (1.425)
N	3,997	3,997	3,997	3,997
	−356.613	−358.090	−356.699	−356.405
AIC	731.227	734.180	735.397	732.811

Notes
* = $p < 0.05$; ** = $p < 0.01$; *** = $p < 0.001$.
Standard errors in parentheses.

offering a useful robustness check, it adds information on authoritarian institutions. The literature on authoritarian regimes argues that power-sharing institutions such as political parties increase regime stability by inducing power-sharing between a dictator and members of the ruling coalition (Gandhi and Przeworski 2007; Magaloni 2008; Boix and Svolik 2013). These studies thus predict that power-sharing coalitions decrease the likelihood of democratization, and challenge the predictive power of my diversity hypothesis.

Table 6.4 presents the results of four models that include three authoritarian regime type variables, but otherwise do not differ from Models 1 to 4. Adding information on authoritarian institutions does not cast any doubt on the positive evaluations of my hypotheses: the diversity and representativeness effects of authoritarian governments continue to exert a positive and statistically significant effect on the probability of democratization.

The one difference in Table 6.3 is that Model 8 attributes more explanatory power and certainty to the diversity rather than the representativeness effect. However, I hesitate to attribute too much emphasis on the different results in Models 4 and 8 because an additional group in the government by definition implies a higher representativeness score. It is probably safe to say that the two variables act in combination, since this is also supported by the estimated effect of majority coalitions in Model 7.[13] This conclusion is also in line with Slater's "strong-state democratization" thesis, which holds that large and inclusive ethnic coalitions are likely to concede to popular demands for democratization in order to thrive under democratic rule (Slater 2012; Slater and Wong 2013).

The GWF models also assess authoritarian institutional accounts of regime stability. Compared to monarchies, only military rule significantly increases the probability of democratization in all four models as expected by the authoritarian power-sharing literature (Geddes 2003; Wright and Escriba-Folch 2012). Party rule has a positive but non-significant effect on the chances of democratization. However, parties do stabilize authoritarian regimes compared to less institutionalized personalistic and military rules.[14] Nonetheless, this result questions the interpretation of authoritarian parties as power-sharing institutions. Not only do actual power-sharing measures influence the likelihood of democratization positively, but party-based regimes do not differ significantly from the highly exclusive monarchies that are predominantly located in the Middle East (Vogt *et al.* 2016). An alternative interpretation is that political parties in authoritarian regimes are an indicator of regime strength through mechanisms that are different from power-sharing, such as information and patronage flows.

The estimates of the remaining control variables differ only slightly from the Polity IV sample. The population variable and past transitions cease to be significantly related to democratization while older autocratic regimes are more likely to democratize compared to the results in Table 6.3. In alternative robustness tests, I assess various additional control variables such as the level of inequality, ongoing and past violence, and regional dummies as well as alternative specifications of my main explanatory variables[15] (see Table 6.4).

Alternative explanations: reverse causality

An important objection to the statistical results presented above is the possibility of reverse causality. Put differently, democratization actually causes elite coalitions rather than the other way around. Although I lag all my explanatory variables, reverse causality is still possible. This concern is particularly important because existing theories predict exactly that democracy makes coalition government more likely. Horowitz represents the common understanding, as he holds that democratic elections force ethnic elites to coalesce with leaders of other

Table 6.4 GWF democratization and ethnic power-sharing, 1946 to 2009

	(5)	(6)	(7)	(8)
Representativeness	1.235*			0.482
	(0.498)			(0.526)
Diversity – log (count)		0.980***		0.869**
		(0.258)		(0.292)
Minority, multi-ethnic government			0.859	
			(0.630)	
Majority, multi-ethnic government			0.957*	
			(0.406)	
Majority, mono-ethnic government			0.720	
			(0.402)	
Party dictatorship	0.764	0.385	0.824	0.380
	(0.836)	(0.739)	(0.766)	(0.772)
Personalist dictatorship	1.571	1.329	1.639*	1.318
	(0.849)	(0.745)	(0.781)	(0.769)
Military dictatorship	2.825**	2.566***	2.896***	2.575**
	(0.867)	(0.756)	(0.796)	(0.783)
Ln (GDP p.c.)	0.245	0.356	0.289	0.303
	(0.267)	(0.256)	(0.277)	(0.255)
GDP growth	−3.523*	−3.344*	−3.463*	−3.464*
	(1.471)	(1.448)	(1.465)	(1.453)
Log (population)	0.061	0.190	0.009	0.187
	(0.198)	(0.188)	(0.211)	(0.197)
Ethnic fractionalization	0.247	−1.625*	−0.185	−1.326
	(0.520)	(0.641)	(0.662)	(0.738)
Past transitions	0.584	0.609	0.552	0.584
	(0.321)	(0.318)	(0.325)	(0.322)
Regime years	0.017*	0.016*	0.018*	0.016*
	(0.007)	(0.007)	(0.007)	(0.007)
Neighbourhood, democratic transition	0.264**	0.318***	0.271**	0.325***
	(0.098)	(0.096)	(0.103)	(0.095)
Constant	−6.981***	−6.320***	−6.350**	−6.553***
	(2.064)	(1.779)	(2.112)	(1.777)
N	3,561	3,561	3,561	3,561
	−325.885	−321.515	−325.679	−321.462
AIC	675.770	667.030	679.358	668.924

Notes
* = p <0.05; ** = p <0.01; *** = p <0.001.
Standard errors in parentheses.

ethnic groups (Horowitz 2000, 433). Lars-Erik Cederman and colleagues ostensibly support this assertion when they make the following observation: "Just as the degree of democracy has increased over the last couple of decades, a similar improving trend can be detected in terms of the power access of ethnic groups" (Cederman *et al.* 2013, 215). In the following I will argue that reverse causality does not account for the results I presented above, and that instead, my theoretical argument – that majority, multi-ethnic coalitions are more likely to lead to democratization – does.

More specifically, there are two possibilities by which democratization may be the cause of ethnic coalitions rather than the other way around. On the one hand, democratic institutions may indeed be more effective in bringing about ethnic coalitions than authoritarian institutions, and democratization processes may begin before established datasets code a successful democratization. On the other hand, ethnic elites may anticipate future democratic change and form larger elite coalitions in order to resist it, or to survive early elections.

Regarding the first possibility, Cederman and colleagues (2013, 221) reach the conclusion that "democracy does not immunize countries against [ethnic] discrimination of large parts of the population." In the EPR data, ethnic discrimination categorically excludes ethnic power-sharing. While their statement does not imply that democracy has no effect on ethnic power-sharing, it questions a strong direct causal effect. Similarly, I do not find a positive correlation between the *level* of democracy in the Polity IV data, and the degree of representativeness or diversity. In addition, lagging episodes of democratization and estimating their effect on government representativeness or diversity do not reveal a statistically significant relationship. To the contrary, the median age of majority coalitions in the Polity IV sample is ten years and it even climbs to 12 years in the GWF data.[16] In other words, ethnic coalitions have governed for some time before democratization sets in. These empirical patterns strongly contradict the first possibility of reverse causality, which identifies extended democratization periods as the cause of ethnic coalitions.

The alternative possibility of reverse causation states that elites form coalitions in anticipation of democratic demands because they want to resist democratization. If it were correct, larger coalitions should reduce the risk of democratization. My analyses have shown that this is clearly not the case. Elites may also form coalitions prior to democratization in order to survive later elections. This motive and its empirical implications are more difficult to detect, but the distribution of coalition ages once more reduces its plausibility. In addition, two more points make it an unlikely explanation of the observed patterns. First, excluded elites may not want to board a sinking ship and would rather side with the opposition. Second, my theoretical argument builds on Slater's "strong-state democratization" thesis, which he develops by using a careful qualitative analysis of historical cases (Slater 2012; Slater and Wong 2013). In Malaysia, for example, Slater and his co-authors identify a long-living and tight-knit multi-ethnic elite coalition as the originator of democratization. The convergence of qualitative and quantitative results increases my confidence in the theoretical account put forward above.

Model predictions

One strategy to assess the usefulness of a statistical model is to evaluate its ability to make useful statements on real-world cases. This section presents a list of successful predictions and near misses, and discusses the contribution of the key variables, the population share represented in the government and the number of included groups, to those results.

Table 6.5 lists the top five predictive successes and failures from Model 8.[17] Model fit statistics such as the Akaike Information Criterion report a better performance of the GWF models over the Polity IV models, and the continuous variables of representativeness and diversity do better than the coalition dummies. According to the model, the median probability of democratization irrespective of the covariates is about 4 per cent in a country year. The predicted probabilities (PP) in Table 6.5 are far larger than the median, indicating an accurate identification of democratization events. Put differently, since democratization is a rare event, chances of 30 to 50 per cent of democratization for one year are very high, particularly when they compound over a number of years.

Out of the successes, three of the five cases are power-sharing examples. In Pakistan, Ghana and Thailand, the government consisted of representatives of more than one group. Argentina and Panama are examples of representative nation-states that exclude smaller minorities. They also point to the fact that multiple factors explain democratization, including historical contingencies and economic growth. Returning to the three power-sharing successes, only Ghana is governed by a grand coalition, while Pakistan and Thailand excluded some ethnic minorities at the time of their transitions. Some of these excluded minorities, such as the Malay Muslims in Thailand and the Baluchis in Pakistan, have rebelled against the state following democratization, which demonstrates that democracy may be the form of government for the majority of a country's inhabitants but that it does not guarantee peaceful relationships among all societal groups.

Table 6.5 GWF model predictions: successes and failures

Country	Year	PP	Population share	Incl. groups
Successes				
Argentina	1983	0.48	0.99	1
Pakistan	2008	0.42	0.79	3
Panama	2008	0.39	0.80	1
Ghana	1979	0.37	1	5
Thailand	1973	0.35	0.96	2
Failures				
Argentina	1982	0.49	0.98	1
Ghana	1976	0.49	1	5
Syria	1952	0.47	1	5
Pakistan	2002	0.42	0.79	3
Nigeria	1976	0.41	0.99	5

Turning to the failed predictions, all five cases are good misses, as they identify regimes that made the transition to democracy within a short time after the prediction here. Argentina transitioned in 1983, Ghana in 1979, Syria in 1954 and Nigeria experienced a short stint of democracy in 1979. Ghana and Nigeria also exemplify cases of neighbourhood diffusion. In Pakistan, the time between the failed 2002 prediction and the eventual transition in 2008 is larger than in the other two cases but at least the two power-sharing variables remain the same. In this case, other variables missing from the model such as the mobilization of Pakistan's lawyers following the dismissal of the country's chief justice offer a better account for the timing of the transition. These contextual factors are difficult to model. Overall, though, it is reassuring to learn that the model seems to correctly identify cases that are close to democratization and that the power-sharing variables are more often than not in line with the hypotheses.

Conclusion

About four decades ago, Lijphart (1977, 238) asserted that the only chance for democracy to take root and sustain itself in plural societies was the accommodation of ethnic elites in coalition governments. In this study, I combine Lijphart's argument with new research on authoritarian power-sharing, and apply them to the literature of democratization. Specifically, I employ a large-N approach that tests whether or not ethnic power-sharing coalitions improve the probability of democratization. The statistical results show that ethnically more diverse and more representative elite coalitions increase the likelihood of democratic transitions. These results complement consociational theory in two ways. On the one hand, they do show that ethnic power-sharing is conducive for democratic rule to emerge in multi-ethnic states. On the other, they reinforce research on authoritarian politics by demonstrating that ethnic power-sharing is a key element of many dictatorships, and thus commonly occurs outside democratic regimes. In other words, this study vindicates Lijphart's optimism of ethnic elite coalitions' benefits for democracy, although for different reasons. Ethnic coalitions often precede the emergence of consociational institutions and frequently exist prior to the transition to democracy. This study thus questions the institutional underpinnings of consociational theory (cf. Bormann 2014).

It also questions the behavioural assumptions made by Lijphart. Rather than attributing ethnic coalitions to elites who care for the greater good and exhibit "constructive statesmanship" (Lijphart 2002, 44), my theory posits that democratization is the outcome of conflict between the dictator and political elites from other ethnic groups. Although my statistical results do not allow me to explicitly pinpoint the theoretical mechanism I advance above, they shed doubt on elites' benevolence. If political leaders would often opt for the greater good, the constellations of ethnic power should make no difference. Yet exactly those regimes that have the most to lose from democratization – that is, minority regimes – tend to avoid it. The fact that existing qualitative studies discuss a similar mechanism in different geographic settings (Slater

2012; Slater and Wong 2013) increases my confidence that the theoretical interpretation of this study enjoys some validity.

The findings of this study also run counter to existing expectations of other literature on democratization and authoritarianism. Democratization scholars who propose structuralist models usually highlight the general aversion of elites to any type of democratic reform, and students of authoritarian politics generally point to the regime-stabilizing effect of so-called power-sharing institutions. My theoretical argument differs from existing writings in one key assumption: I claim that authoritarian ruling elites who are not the dictator actually prefer democracy to dictatorship because of the high stakes of the political game in authoritarian regimes that can result in the dispossession of personal property, physical harm or even death. In particular, I suggest two mechanisms that link ethnic power-sharing to an increased probability of democratization. On the one hand, authoritarian regimes that represent a majority of the population through ethnic linkages embrace popular pressures for democratization because they want to be on the right side of history, and continue to govern in the future. In the long run popular pressures for democratization can endanger their power position, and remove them from office. On the other hand, elites may push for democratic reform themselves because it levels the imbalance between the ruling elites and the dictator. It therefore decreases the dangerous risks political elites face when losing office in 'brutish' authoritarian systems.

To my knowledge, the analysis in this study is the first that explores what Daniel Ziblatt refers to as the "the coalitional underpinnings of democratic reform" from the vantage point of ethnic cleavages (Ziblatt 2006, 326). By considering the representation of politically relevant ethnic groups in the executive of authoritarian regimes, it goes beyond purely structural indices of ethnic diversity as well as mechanic links between so-called power-sharing institutions and presumed elite behaviour. By considering more dynamic measures of coalition make-up, it bridges situational and structural approaches to the study of democratization. The question, however, is how far ethnicity is representative of other cleavages such as class or ideology that play a crucial role in transition processes (Collier 1999). Are inclusive ethnic coalitions also inclusive class coalitions, or do the distinct cleavages cross-cut each other? If the answer to this question affirms the latter perspective, then the interaction among different cleavage dimensions may mask very important dynamics not considered in this study. Until we have better data on the importance of cleavages other than ethnicity, the actual influence of coalition politics on the stability of authoritarian regimes hangs in the balance.

Notes

1 I would like to thank Lars-Erik Cederman, Allison McCulloch, Brendan O'Leary and Manuel Vogt for their very helpful comments.
2 Andeweg (2000), Bogaards (2000) and Horowitz (2002) provide encompassing reviews of the most common critiques.
3 Studies that identify Muslim majority populations as a key obstacle to democratization include Fish (2002) and Teorell et al. (2010).

4 The major exception is work by Slater (2009) published in the *American Journal of Sociology*.
5 This influence may be indirect, as in parliamentary systems, or direct, as in presidential regimes.
6 Recall that ethnic minority governments may consist of coalitions between leaders from different ethnic groups as in the Central African Republic (1983–1993), the Democratic Republic of Congo (1969–2009), Ivory Coast (1995–2000), Pakistan (1949–1971), the Republic of Congo (1965–1969, 1978–1979, 1986–1991, 1999–2009), Sudan (2007–2009) and Uganda (1972–1973).
7 Note the similarity to the transition literature's distinction between reformers and hardliners (Przeworski 1992) where the dictator and his co-ethnics are hardliners while ruling elites from other ethnic groups make up the reformist camp. My argument also extends to cases where the preferences of some group elites tend towards autocratic rule and preferences of elites from another group are reformist as long as the latter have the ability to put pressure on the hardliners through the threat of exit.
8 Discrimination can be both negative and positive. The USA, for example, changed its treatment of African Americans on the national level with the Voting Rights Act from negative to positive discrimination.
9 Most states where ethnicity does not play a role may be found in Western and Northern Europe. An authoritarian exception in which EPR does not consider ethnicity to be a politically meaningful cleavage is Somalia.
10 Because the coalition argument sets in once the government expands from one to two groups and the exit threat loses importance the more groups are represented in the coalition, I log the diversity indicators.
11 It is common to model these regime years as second- (Wright and Escriba-Folch 2012, 296) or third-order polynomials (Carter and Signorino 2010) but in these analyses higher order polynomials do not improve model fit significantly according to likelihood ratio tests. Semi-parametric estimates of the functional form of temporal dependence also reveal an approximately linear function form.
12 The model is part of a larger project that attempts to model various types of endogeneity for binary dependent outcomes. See Wucherpfennig *et al.* (2014).
13 An F-test of joint significance clearly warrants the inclusion of both variables in Models 4 and 8.
14 Wald-tests reveal statistically significant differences.
15 The results are available from the author upon request.
16 The first quantile is at 3 and 7.5 years, respectively.
17 Some country years appeared multiple times in the top five. In these cases I only chose the most likely case from one country and moved down the list until five unique country cases were reached.

References

Acemoglu, Daron and James A. Robinson. 2006. *Economic Origins of Dictatorship and Democracy*. Cambridge: Cambridge University Press.

Acemoglu, Daron, Simon Johnson and James A. Robinson. 2001. "The Colonial Origins of Comparative Development: An Empirical Investigation." *American Economic Review* 91, no. 5: 1369–1401.

Andeweg, Rudy B. 2000. "Consociational Democracy." *Annual Review of Political Science* 3, no. 1: 509–536.

Barro, Robert J. 1999. "Determinants of Democracy." *Journal of Political Economy* 107, no. 6: 158–183.

Bogaards, Matthijs. 2000. "The Uneasy Relationship between Empirical and Normative Types in Consociational Theory." *Journal of Theoretical Politics* 12, no. 4: 395–423.

Boix, Carles. 2003. *Democracy and Redistribution*. New York: Cambridge University Press.

Boix, Carles and Susan C. Stokes. 2003. "Endogenous Democratization." *World Politics* 55, no. 4: 517–549.

Boix, Carles and Milan W. Svolik. 2013. "The Foundations of Limited Authoritarian Government: Institutions and Power-Sharing in Dictatorships." *Journal of Politics* 75, no. 2: 300–316.

Bormann, Nils-Christian. 2014. *The Causes and Consequences of Ethnic Power-Sharing*. PhD thesis. ETH Zürich.

Bueno de Mesquita, Bruce, Alastair Smith, Randolph M. Siverson and James D. Morrow. 2003. *The Logic of Political Survival*. Boston, MA: MIT Press.

Carter, David B. and Curtis S. Signorino. 2010. "Back to the Future: Modeling Time Dependence in Binary Data." *Political Analysis* 18, no. 3: 271–292.

Cederman, Lars-Erik, Kristian S. Gleditsch and Halvard Buhaug. 2013. *Inequality, Grievances, and Civil War*. New York: Cambridge University Press.

Cederman, Lars-Erik, Andreas Wimmer and Brian Min. 2010. "Why Do Ethnic Groups Rebel? New Data and Analysis." *World Politics* 62, no. 1: 87–119.

Collier, Ruth Berins. 1999. *Paths Toward Democracy: The Working Class and Elites in Western Europe and South America*. Cambridge: Cambridge University Press.

Dahl, Robert A. 1971. *Polyarchy: Participation and Opposition*. New Haven, CT: Yale University Press.

Dahl, Robert A. and Edward R. Tufte. 1973. *Size and Democracy*. Stanford, CA: Stanford University Press.

Donno, Daniela. 2013. "Elections and Democratization in Authoritarian Regimes." *American Journal of Political Science* 57, no. 3: 706–716.

Driscoll, Jesse. 2012. "Commitment Problems or Bidding Wars? Rebel Fragmentation as Peace Building." *Journal of Conflict Resolution* 56, no. 1: 118–149.

Epstein, David L., Robert Bates, Jack Goldstone, Ida Kristensen and Sharyn O'Halloran. 2006. "Democratic Transitions." *American Journal of Political Science* 50, no. 3: 551–569.

Fish, M. Steven. 2002. "Islam and Authoritarianism." *World Politics* 55, no. 1: 4–37.

Gandhi, Jennifer and Adam Przeworski. 2007. "Authoritarian Institutions and the Survival of Autocrats." *Comparative Political Studies* 40, no. 11: 1279–1301.

Geddes, Barbara. 2003. *Paradigms and Sand Castles: Theory Building and Research Design in Comparative Politics*. Ann Arbor, MI: University of Michigan Press.

Geddes, Barbara, Joseph Wright and Erica Frantz. 2013. "New Data on Autocratic Breakdown and Regime Transitions." Technical Report. Pennsylvania State University. Available at http://dictators.la.psu.edu/.

Geddes, Barbara, Joseph Wright and Erica Frantz. 2014. "Autocratic Breakdown and Regime Transitions: A New Dataset." *Perspectives on Politics* 12, no. 2: 313–331.

Gleditsch, Kristian Skrede and Michael D. Ward. 2006. "Diffusion and the International Context of Democratization." *International Organization* 60, no. 4: 911–933.

Hale, Henry E. 2008. *The Foundations of Ethnic Politics: Separatism of States and Nations in Eurasia and the World*. Cambridge: Cambridge University Press.

Hartzell, Caroline A and Matthew Hoddie. 2015. "The Art of the Possible: Power Sharing and Post-Civil War Democracy." *World Politics* 67, no. 1: 37–71.

Horowitz, Donald L. 1993. "Democracy in Divided Societies." *Journal of Democracy* 4, no. 4: 18–38.

Horowitz, Donald L. 2000. *Ethnic Groups in Conflict*. 2nd edn. Berkeley: University of California Press.

Horowitz, Donald L. 2002. "Constitutional Design: Proposals versus Processes." In *The Architecture of Democracy: Constitutional Design, Conflict Management, and Democracy*, edited by Andrew Reynolds, pp. 15–36. Oxford: Oxford University Press.

Huntington, Samuel P. 1968. *Political Order in Changing Societies*. New Haven, CT: Yale University Press.

Huntington, Samuel P. 1991. *The Third Wave: Democratization in the Late Twentieth Century*. Norman, OK: University of Oklahoma Press.

Hunziker, Philipp and Nils-Christian Bormann. 2013. "Size and Wealth in the International System: Population and GDP Per Capita Data for Political Science." Typescript: ETH Zurich.

Inglehart, Ronald and Christian Welzel. 2005. *Modernization, Cultural Change, and Democracy: The Human Development Sequence*. Cambridge: Cambridge University Press.

Jaggers, Keith and Ted Robert Gurr. 1995. "Tracking Democracy's Third Wave with the Polity III Data." *Journal of Peace Research* 32, no. 4: 469–482.

Jarstad, Anna K. 2008. "Dilemmas of War-to-Democracy Transitions: Theories and Concepts." In *From War to Democracy: Dilemmas of Peacebuilding*, edited by Anna K. Jarstad and Timothy D. Sisk, pp. 17–36. Cambridge: Cambridge University Press.

Jenne, Erin K. 2007. *Ethnic Bargaining: The Paradox of Minority Empowerment*. Ithaca, NY: Cornell University Press.

Kennedy, Ryan. 2010. "The Contradiction of Modernization: A Conditional Model of Endogenous Democratization." *Journal of Politics* 72, no. 3: 785–798.

Levitsky, Steven R. and Lucan A. Way. 2012. "Beyond Patronage: Violent Struggle, Ruling Party Cohesion, and Authoritarian Durability." *Perspectives on Politics* 10, no. 4: 869–889.

Lijphart, Arend. 1977. *Democracy in Plural Societies: A Comparative Exploration*. New Haven, CT: Yale University Press.

Lijphart, Arend. 1999. *Patterns of Democracy: Government Forms and Practices in 36 Countries*. 2nd edn. New Haven, CT: Yale University Press.

Lijphart, Arend. 2002. "The Wave of Power-Sharing Democracy." In *The Architecture of Democracy: Constitutional Design, Conflict Management, and Democracy*, edited by Andrew Reynolds, pp. 37–54. Oxford: Oxford University Press.

Lipset, Seymour Martin. 1959. "Some Social Requisites of Democracy: Economic Development and Political Legitimacy." *American Political Science Review* 53: 69–105.

Lustick, Ian S. 1997. "Lijphart, Lakatos, and Consociationalism." *World Politics* 50, no. 1: 88–117.

Magaloni, Beatrix. 2008. "Credible Power-Sharing and the Longevity of Authoritarian Rule." *Comparative Political Studies* 41, nos 4–5: 715–741.

Marshall, Monty G., Keith Jaggers and Ted Robert Gurr. 2011. *The Polity IV Project – Political Regime Characteristics and Transitions, 1800–2010*. Technical Report Center for Systemic Peace. Available at www.systemicpeace.org/polity/polity4.htm.

Mattes, Michaela and Burcu Savun. 2009. "Fostering Peace after Civil War: Commitment Problems and Agreement Design." *International Studies Quarterly* 53, no. 3: 737–759.

McLauchlin, Theodore and Wendy Pearlman. 2012. "Out-Group Conflict, In-Group Unity? Exploring the Effect of Repression on Intramovement Cooperation." *Journal of Conflict Resolution* 56, no. 1: 41–66.

Mill, John Stuart. 1958 [1861]. *Considerations on Representative Government.* New York: Liberal Arts Press.
Norris, Pippa. 2008. *Driving Democracy.* Cambridge: Cambridge University Press.
O'Donnell, Guillermo, Philippe C. Schmitter and Laurence Whitehead. 1986. *Transitions from Authoritarian Rule.* Baltimore, MD: Johns Hopkins University Press.
Powell, G. Bingham. 1982. *Contemporary Democracies: Participation, Stability, and Violence.* Cambridge, MA: Harvard University Press.
Przeworski, Adam. 1992. "Games of Transition." In *Issues in Democratic Consolidation*, edited by Scott Mainwaring, pp. 105–152. Notre Dame, IN: University of Notre Dame Press.
Przeworski, Adam, Michael E Alvarez, Jose A. Cheibub and Fernando Limongi. 2000. *Democracy and Development: Political Institutions and Well-Being in the World, 1950–1990.* Cambridge: Cambridge University Press.
Rabushka, Alvin and Kenneth A. Shepsle. 2008. *Politics in Plural Societies: A Theory of Democratic Instability.* Harlow, UK: Pearson.
Reynolds, Andrew. 2011. *Designing Democracy in a Dangerous World.* Oxford: Oxford University Press.
Rothchild, Donald and Philip G. Roeder. 2005. "Power Sharing as an Impediment to Peace and Democracy." In *Sustainable Peace: Power and Democracy after Civil Wars*, edited by Philip G. Roeder and Donald Rothchild, pp. 29–50. Ithaca, NY: Cornell University Press.
Rustow, Dankwart A. 1970. "Transitions to Democracy: Toward a Dynamic Model." *Comparative Politics* 2, no. 3: 337–363.
Slater, Dan. 2009. "Revolutions, Crackdowns, and Quiescence: Communal Elites and Democratic Mobilization in Southeast Asia." *American Journal of Sociology* 115, no. 1: 203–254
Slater, Dan. 2010. *Ordering Power: Contentious Politics and Authoritarian Leviathans in Southeast Asia.* Cambridge: Cambridge University Press.
Slater, Dan. 2012. "Strong-State Democratization in Malaysia and Singapore." *Journal of Democracy* 23, no. 2: 19–33.
Slater, Dan and Joseph Wong. 2013. "The Strength to Concede: Ruling Parties and Democratization in Developmental Asia." *Perspectives on Politics* 11, no. 3: 717–733.
Smith, Benjamin. 2005. "Life of the Party: The Origins of Regime Breakdown and Persistence under Single-Party Rule." *World Politics* 57, no. 3: 421–451.
Svolik, Milan W. 2009. "Power Sharing and Leadership Dynamics in Authoritarian Regimes." *American Journal of Political Science* 53, no. 2: 477–494.
Teorell, Jan, Marcus Samanni, Nicholas Charron, Soren Holmberg and Bo Rothstein. 2010. "The Quality of Government Dataset." University of Gothenburg: The Quality of Government Institute. Available at www.qog.pol.gu.se.
Vogt, Manuel, Nils-Christian Bormann, and Lars-Erik Cederman. 2016. "Democracy, Ethnic Exclusion, and Civil Conflict: The Arab Spring Revolutions from a Global Comparative Perspective." In *Peace and Conflict*, edited by David A. Backer, Jonathan Wilkenfeld and Paul K. Huth, pp. 57–66. London: Routledge.
Weber, Eugene. 1976. *Peasants into Frenchmen: The Modernization of Rural France, 1870–1914.* Redwood City, CA: Stanford University Press.
Wilkenfeld and Paul K. Huth, pp. 57–66. London: Routledge. Weber, Max. 1978. *Economy and Society.* Los Angeles: University of California Press.
Weidmann, Nils B., Doreen Kuse and Kristian S. Gleditsch. 2010. "The Geography of the International System: The CShapes Dataset." *International Interactions* 36, no. 1: 86–106.

Wright, Joseph and Abel Escriba-Folch. 2012. "Authoritarian Institutions and Regime Survival: Transitions to Democracy and Subsequent Dictatorship." *British Journal of Political Science* 42, no. 2: 283–309.

Wucherpfennig, Julian, Aya Kachi and Nils-Christian Bormann. 2014. "Estimating Interdependence across Space, Time and Outcomes in Binary Choice Models." Paper Prepared for Presentation at the 2014 General Conference of the European Political Science Association, Edinburgh, 19–21 June.

Ziblatt, Daniel. 2006. "How Did Europe Democratize?" *World Politics* 58, no. 2: 311–338.

7 Lebanon
How civil war transformed consociationalism

Matthijs Bogaards

Introduction[1]

Consociationalism is most closely associated with the work of Dutch political scientist Arend Lijphart. The concept was first used to explain democracy and political stability in the Netherlands, a country characterized for much of the early part of the twentieth century by religious and ideological divisions. Almost immediately the empirical scope was extended to Austria, Belgium and Switzerland, all peaceful, prosperous, industrialized countries in Western Europe with consolidated democracies (Lijphart 1968, 1969, 1977).[2] Although the boundaries of the consociational universe are not entirely clear, Lebanon (1943–1975, 1989–), South Africa (1994–1996), Bosnia-Herzegovina (1995–), Northern Ireland (1998–) and Burundi (2005–) have all been claimed and analyzed as cases of contemporary consociationalism.[3] All of the countries that turned consociational following the end of the Cold War did so after going through a civil war. This raises the question, paraphrasing John McGarry and Brendan O'Leary (2009): what is different about consociationalism "after the deaths of thousands"?

Strangely, even though Rupert Taylor (2009, 7, 9) notices a "major regeneration of the consociational research programme" and a "new wave" of consociations involving "conflicted societies moving from war to peace," so far the special challenges of consociationalism following civil war have not received due attention in the rich consociational literature. This is problematic for at least three reasons. Empirically, we want to know whether the institutions and behavioural patterns that characterize consociationalism work in the same way when consociationalism is established not to avoid conflict, but after violent ethnic conflict has broken out and cleavages have turned into battle lines. Theoretically, we need to know how much analytical leverage consociational concepts such as the 'self-negating prediction' have in post-conflict societies, and also whether consociational theory's 'favourable factors' have as much purchase in such societies as in those that have not experienced violence. Normatively, we need to know whether the recommendation that consociation be "engineered" (Lijphart 1977) also holds for countries coming out of a civil war and, if so, what the process of adoption and the nature of the institutions should be.

There are good reasons to think that civil war makes a difference. First, the starting positions are in stark contrast: maintaining peace and stabilizing democracy versus restoring peace and (re)democratization. Second, the favourable factors for consociationalism: socio-cultural and socio-economic background conditions versus the factors that help end civil war and prevent its recurrence. Third, consociational agreements following war originate from peace agreements rather than from elite agreements. Fourth, instead of informal understandings, post-war institutional choices are usually based on written guarantees. Fifth, the internal players following conflict include armies, rebel groups and militias, not only political parties. Sixth, external and international players were largely absent from the accounts of peaceful consociations, but occupy centre-stage in the resolution of civil war and its aftermath. Finally, and likewise, the military and other security forces are of little concern in classic consociations, but of major significance following civil war.

This chapter examines the way that civil war has transformed consociationalism in Lebanon, the only country to adopt consociationalism twice: before and after its civil war.[4] At both times, all four consociational principles of a grand coalition, proportionality, segmental autonomy and mutual veto were present (Lijphart 1977, 148–149; Fakhoury Mühlbacher 2009, 77, 327). The case of Lebanon therefore allows for a more systematic investigation of the impact of widespread political violence upon consociational power-sharing. Thus far, most accounts of consociationalism in Lebanon emphasize continuity rather than change and comprehensive comparisons over time are rare. The analysis presented here demonstrates that the civil war transformed consociationalism in Lebanon in seven key respects.

Consociationalism following civil war

Thinking about the ways in which consociationalism following civil war is different, it is helpful to structure the discussion along seven dimensions: the stakes, favourable factors, incentives, institutions, domestic actors, external actors and the military. No doubt other differences can be identified, but these seven dimensions go to the heart of consociational power-sharing, capture the most important variables in consociational theory, and allow for sufficient empirical nuance.

First, the stakes. In consociational theory, the adoption of the four principles of a grand coalition, proportionality, mutual veto and segmental autonomy is the outcome of a deliberate decision by elites to change their style of behaviour from competition to collaboration. In what Lijphart calls a self-negating prediction, "elites cooperate in spite of the segmental differences dividing them because to do otherwise would mean to call forth the prophesied consequences of the plural character of the society" (Lijphart 1977, 100). In the classic consociational democracies, these consequences did not normally entail fear of the outbreak of a civil war, although the early consociational literature was preoccupied with political stability. Belgium may fall apart if and when its elaborate consociational institutions finally fail, but even if this happens, civil war is not on the horizon. The stakes are and were much higher in a place like Lebanon where a failure to reach a settlement means continued violence. Following civil war, the best that one can hope for is to avoid the recurrence of violence and it is the memory of civil war caused by the failure of political elites to settle their differences peacefully that informs the search for consociational solutions.

Second, there is a whole range of favourable factors that are believed to help create and maintain a consociational democracy (Bogaards 1998). Some of these factors seem relevant to post-conflict politics (for example, the demographic balance between the various groups), but there is a need to go beyond these classic variables and to include variables from research on conflict onset, duration and termination (see Bogaards 2013). The factors that facilitate a consociational solution to civil war are likely to differ from the factors that ease the reform of a political system into a consociational direction.

Third, looking at incentives, Donald Horowitz (2002) and Ian Shapiro (2003) have focused attention on the 'adoption' question. Horowitz (2002, 20) argues that the "consociational approach is motivationally inadequate," since it relies on statesmanship and on the ability of leaders to make self-negating predictions. In his own work, Horowitz examines the incentive structure of ethnic elites and how this can be influenced through political engineering. Indeed, Horowitz (2008, 1237) sees protracted civil war as "one of the circumstances that can produce sufficient weakness to induce acceptance of a consociational constitution." If a majority group is weakened and minority rebels are only prepared to lay down their arms in exchange for guarantees, then consociational solutions have a better chance of being accepted, even more so as there is likely to be international pressure to reach an agreement (Horowitz 2008, 1238–1239). Paradoxically, following Horowitz, who is no fan of consociations, it should be easier to adopt them following civil war than in times of peace.

Fourth, moving from incentives to institutional practice, is there anything particular about consociational institutions adopted after civil war? Different from the informal "politics of accommodation" in the Netherlands (Lijphart 1975), consociational features in the contemporary cases tend to be written down in peace agreements and subsequently codified and constitutionalized.[5] The emergence of consociationalism following civil war has also coincided with the introduction of a distinction between 'liberal' and 'corporate' consociations in the literature. According to McGarry and O'Leary (2007, 675), a corporate consociation relies on "predetermination" and "accommodates groups according to ascriptive criteria, such as ethnicity or religion, on the assumption that group identities are fixed and that groups are both internally homogeneous and externally bounded." In contrast, a liberal or "self-determined" consociation "rewards whatever salient political identities emerge in democratic elections, whether these are based on ethnic or religious groups, or on subgroup or trans-group identities" (McGarry and O'Leary 2007, 675). The new constitution of Iraq and the new dispensation in Northern Ireland are said to conform to McGarry and O'Leary's favoured liberal consociation, whereas Lebanon approximates more closely the corporate type of consociation.[6]

Allison McCulloch (2014a, 507) observes how the new consociational democracies of Bosnia-Herzegovina, Burundi, Lebanon and Northern Ireland all adopted corporate consociationalism, although Northern Ireland also has elements of liberal consociationalism. McCulloch explains the correlation between civil war and corporate consociationalism as stemming from the understandable desire of parties coming out of civil war for hard guarantees. The rigidity of corporate consociations makes them difficult to reform from the inside. Already under the French mandate the Maronites enjoyed a privileged position. They were over-represented in Parliament, controlled the presidential executive, and occupied the most important positions in the security sector. Inflexible institutions prevented a correction of the sectarian imbalance when demographics changed.

Fifth, the elites of classic consociational democracies are the leaders of the main political parties, in which each party represents a particular community or segment. The elites in post-war consociationalism may also be party politicians, but many of them will not have got to the bargaining table and into Parliament and public office through elections alone. Among the new political elite we find former rebels, warlords, heads of militias and generals. No leading Dutch or Swiss politician was ever accused of having being involved with terrorism or of having been implicated in war crimes, but such accusations are common in Northern Ireland, Bosnia-Herzegovina, Burundi and Lebanon.

Sixth, in contrast with the classic cases, post-war consociationalism is not left to politicians, and nor are domestic elites necessarily in the driving seat. Indeed, one encounters frequent criticism in new settlements of decisions being made elsewhere: the role of the USA and the European Union in Bosnia-Herzegovina, South Africa leading the peace process in Burundi, and the crucial role of Dublin and London in the Belfast Agreement. Partly as a consequence, many contemporary cases of consociationalism following civil war exhibit what may be called 'compromised sovereignty.'

Finally, the recent literature on post-conflict societies has paid ample attention to issues of security, including decommissioning, disarmament and rehabilitation. Caroline Hartzell and Matthew Hoddie (2007) list military power-sharing as one of four types of power-sharing, next to political, economic and territorial. While the first three types of power-sharing may all be found in the consociational literature, with a clear emphasis on political and territorial power-sharing, references to military power-sharing are conspicuous by their absence. This has changed with the emergence of consociationalism following civil war.[7]

The case of Lebanon

The previous section presented seven reasons to believe that consociationalism following civil war differs from consociations in countries that have not experienced war.[8] This chapter seeks to advance our knowledge of consociationalism following civil war by examining one particular case, Lebanon, the only country to adopt consociationalism twice: in 1943 and in 1989. The National Pact of 1943 provided the foundation for independence and formed the culmination of consociational practices going back to the nineteenth century. The Ta'if Agreement of 1989 concluded a civil war that had been raging since 1975. Although it is common to read that "The Ta'if Agreement was National Pact Mark II" (Tonge 2014, 97) or that "little had changed" (Clark and Zahar 2015, 5), this chapter argues that such a view overlooks important differences, which are revealed through a systematic comparison of the stakes, favourable factors, process, institutions, domestic actors, external actors and the role of the military in pre- and post-civil war Lebanon. Table 7.1 provides an overview of the differences between the 1943 National Pact and the 1989 Ta'if Agreement. It casts immediate doubt over assertions such as that "Ta'if in theory *restores* a consociational sectarian order" (Hudson 1997, 117, emphasis in original).[9] In what follows, the chapter explains how the civil war has transformed consociationalism in Lebanon.

The stakes

According to Michael Kerr (2005, 114), "the agreement, which later became known as the National Pact, was primarily a device to achieve independence." Kerr (2005, 125) in fact plays down its importance, emphasizing political continuity and criticizing what he calls "the myth of the Pact." The Pact was concluded in the middle of the Second World War, at a time when Lebanon was occupied by the British and by the French free forces. The National Pact fixed the ratio of Christian to Muslim seats in Parliament at 6:5, reserved the presidency for Maronites, the position of prime minister for a Sunni Muslim and the position of speaker of Parliament for a Shia Muslim. The Ta'if Agreement reduced the power of the president and created a balance between Christians and

Table 7.1 Consociationalism in Lebanon from the National Pact to the Ta'if Agreement

	1943	*1989*
Stakes	Independence	Peace
Favourable factors	Tradition of elite accommodation, no majority segment, small population size	End of Cold War Civil war stalemate
Process	Elite agreement	Peace agreement
Institutions	Unwritten pact	Constitutional amendments
Domestic actors	Politicians	Politicians, militia leaders
External actors	France, United Kingdom	Saudi Arabia, Algeria, Morocco, Syria
Military	–	Disarmament of most militias

Muslims in Parliament, still over-representing the Christians, whose numbers have declined, and under-representing the Shia (McCulloch 2014b, 87–88). Superficially, then, the differences between the 1943 National Pact that paved the way for independence and the 1989 Ta'if Agreement that helped end a civil war, though fighting would continue into 1990, are in the details.

This view, however, ignores that the stakes were not merely different, but that there was a trade-off between them. Peace came at the price of sovereignty. As is discussed below in the section on external actors, the appendix to the Ta'if Accord legitimated Syria's role in Lebanese politics for a transitory period (Zahar 2002). Post-civil war Lebanon was not a sovereign state and qualifies at best as a democracy with reserved domains, one of the four types in Wolfgang Merkel's typology of "defective democracies" (Bogaards 2009). The formal and informal limits to the decision-making power of democratically elected Lebanese have led some to classify Lebanon as a "semi-authoritarian regime" up until the Syrian departure in 2005 (Fakhoury Mühlbacher 2009, 427). At the very least, the lack of sovereignty reduced the quality of Lebanese democracy.

To appreciate how Lebanon won peace but lost independence and compromised its democracy in the process of reinstating consociationalism, it is helpful to make a comparison with the Netherlands. The so-called 'pacification' of 1917 in Holland is seen as the starting point of consociational democracy (Lijphart 1975). It was a package deal among the main political parties, which each represented an ideology, class and religion. The agreement served three purposes at once: it demonstrated that the country, despite internal divisions, was united, thereby protecting its sovereignty and independence as a neutral state during the First World War, and it marked the final push towards mass politics with its extension of suffrage. In other words, Dutch consociationalism combined peace, sovereignty and democracy, whereas the Lebanese Ta'if Accord forced the country into a painful trade-off, giving up some of its pre-war independence and democracy in return for a Syrian-enforced peace.

Favourable factors

Lijphart (1985, 120) lists four favourable factors for consociational democracy in Lebanon: the absence of a majority segment, its small population size, a tradition of accommodation and segments of equal size. The first three factors are rated as very favourable, the last one as merely favourable. The only factor viewed as very unfavourable is 'external threats,' because foreign policy and Lebanon's position in the Arab world divide instead of unite the various Lebanese communities.[10] Or, more precisely, international divisions tend to map onto internal divisions, thereby reinforcing them. Overall, Lijphart gives Lebanon a score of two, thus viewing the background conditions for consociational democracy in Lebanon as moderately favourable.[11] In fact, Lebanon scores higher than Belgium. According to Lijphart (1977, 154), "it is primarily due to Lebanon's increasingly unfavorable international environment – combined with the internal flaw of consociational rigidity – that the 1975 breakdown of the democratic regime must be attributed." This judgment hints at the decisive role of one (un)favourable factor: the international context and whether it stimulates national unity or instead deepens divisions. In Lebanon, the latter has always been the case, with the brief exception of the period surrounding the National Pact and independence. Surveying the literature, one notes that the favourable factors for consociational democracy are hardly ever invoked to explain the Ta'if Accord or the second coming of consociationalism in Lebanon (see, e.g., Fakhoury Mühlbacher 2009). The only exception is the frequently heard observation that Lebanon is a country of minorities (Lijphart 1985, 120; Hanf 1993). The fact that no sect can govern by itself has necessitated restraint and promoted great skill in the art of alliance formation.

The favourable factors have always been contested in the consociational literature, either because of their number and nature or because of their theoretical status (Bogaards 1998). The case of Lebanon shows another deficit: whether consociationalism is adopted following civil war is not merely due to the decisions of domestic elites and background variables; it crucially depends on processes and factors that are the staple of international relations and peace and conflict studies, not comparative politics. The Ta'if Accord coincided with the end of the Cold War, which made it easier for the USA to allow Syria a role in Lebanon. The first Gulf War strengthened Syria's hand as a useful ally in the buildup of an international coalition against Saddam Hussein following Iraq's invasion of Kuwait. The peace agreement came after the civil war had exhausted itself. As the Lebanese say: "no victor and no vanquished" (Rosiny 2015, 490). The quantitative literature on civil war termination routinely works with independent variables such as war duration, intensity and the notion of stalemate (see Bogaards 2013). Such factors have been absent from the consociational literature, but it would seem that much could be gained from supplementing the favourable factors for consociational democracy with the factors that contribute to civil war termination if one wants to understand consociationalism following civil war.

Process

The elite pact of 1943 was a "gentleman's agreement" between the most senior politicians of the time: President Bishara al-Khoury, a Maronite, and Prime Minister Riyad al-Sulh, a Sunni (Abul-Husn 1998). The peace agreement of 1989 was officially negotiated among the surviving members of the last duly elected Lebanese Parliament, convening in a mountain city that hosts the royal family of Saudi Arabia during the hot summers. In that sense, the peace agreement was "the product of the elected officials who were not, in most cases, belligerents in the war" (Norton 1991, 461). Hanf (1993, 583) calls Ta'if "the hour of the foxes" as against the lions or militia leaders. This assessment, though, should be qualified, foreshadowing the discussion of the changing nature of domestic actors and the increasing role of foreign powers below. First, in the peace negotiations preceding the Ta'if Agreement, such as in Lausanne and

Geneva in 1983/1984, militia leaders increasingly replaced traditional elites (Faris 1994). Second, the sections of the agreement in the appendix having to do with Syria's role in Lebanon could not be amended by the deputies meeting in Ta'if, since they "were the outcome of international and regional negotiations primarily between Syria and the members of the Arab Tripartite Committee" (Salam 2003, 41). This troika of Saudi Arabia, Algeria and Morocco had been formed by the Arab League in 1989. Based on interviews with participants, Theodor Hanf (1993, 589) describes the proceedings in Ta'if as follows:

> Before the conclave the troika had discussed the paragraphs [dealing with the question of military and political relations between Lebanon and Syria] word for word with the Syrian government. Where opinions had differed, the Syrian view had ultimately prevailed. The foreign ministers of the troika assured the deputies that they were not in a position to achieve more.

Whereas the National Pact of 1943 was a voluntary agreement to consolidate consociational practices by the leaders of the country's two main sects, the Ta'if Accord is seen as "imposed consociationalism" (Kerr 2005).

Institutions

According to Lijphart (1977, 149), "on the whole, consociational democracy in Lebanon must be judged to have performed satisfactorily for more than thirty years. Its main weakness was the inflexible institutionalization of consociational principles." This is a standard account. Consociationalism in Lebanon broke down because the Maronites invested in "political institutions which ensured their dominance, but at the price of institutional inflexibility and exclusiveness" (Crighton and Mac Iver 1991, 138). The political system was thus ill-prepared to deal with the mobilization of, especially, the Shia community that followed the modernization of society (Farah 1975). Likewise, Michael Hudson (1988, 231, emphasis in original; see also Hudson 1976) notes how "increasingly, the uneasy (elite) agreement on the key question of the *distribution* of power among sects within the elite cartel came to be challenged both on the elite and mass levels." Because the stagnant distribution of political offices over time diverged ever more from changing demographic patterns, Yiftachel Oren (1992, 323–324) even sees Lebanon changing from a classic consociational democracy into a control regime, in which social peace is maintained not through accommodation but through the hegemony of one group and the suppression of others.[12]

Overall, "the reforms agreed to in Taif altered both the powers of the most important organs of state and, implicitly, the division of power between the communities" (Hanf 1993, 587). The constitutional amendments of 1990 made the prime minister head of the government, reducing the powers of the president. The speaker of the Chamber of Deputies saw the length of his tenure increase from one year to the full term of Parliament and was to play a key role in the nomination of the prime minister. The Ta'if Agreement propagated the idea of cabinet government, envisioning the Council of Ministers as a collective body. Cabinet decisions were to be taken "by mutual agreement" and decisions on "issues of vital concern" were to require a two-thirds majority. The list of "vital issues" was quite long. Moreover, if it loses more than one-third of its ministers, the whole government is deemed to have resigned. The Ta'if Accord thus corrected the concentration of power in a one-person executive under the 1943 agreement into a collective executive that functioned "in accordance with the principles of consociation" (Hanf 1993, 587). This is not how the political system worked in practice however. Instead, a "troika" emerged of the president, prime minister and speaker, who bypassed the cabinet if they agreed and relied on Syria if they did not agree (Khazen 2003, 72). There is one thing the National Pact and the amended constitution have in common: neither assigned offices to communities, but it was understood that, as before, top-level jobs would be distributed according to sectarian affiliation and that the president would be a Maronite, the prime minister a Sunni and the speaker of Parliament a Shia.

The assassination of former Prime Minister Rafik Hariri in 2005 triggered the massive protests against Syria's presence in Lebanon that led to its withdrawal the same year. These protests and the countermovement were organized in the form of two coalitions, named after the date of their main demonstrations, namely 8 March versus 14 March. These coalitions themselves were formed in 2004 in reaction to UN Security Council Resolution 1559, which, among others, called upon all remaining foreign forces to withdraw from Lebanon and the disbanding and disarmament of all militias.[13] The resolution was embraced by those critical of Syria whereas Syria's friends and especially Hezbollah, whose power and even existence was directly threatened, were opposed. This is another illustration of the profound impact of decisions taken elsewhere on Lebanese politics.

Domestic actors

When we examine the actors involved in the National Pact and the Ta'if Agreement, we notice a striking change in the cast. Augustus Norton (1991, 467) describes the first government formed following the civil war as "a government of militias." Many warlords entered Parliament unelected, being appointed to vacant seats and profiting from the increased size of Parliament. According to Rola El-Husseini (2012, 121), the post-war elite in Lebanon "is largely made up of warlords, rich entrepreneurs from the Lebanese diaspora, Syria's clients, and notables who have retained or regained political influence." Survey research shows how perceptions of influence of various elites have changed over time (Hanf 2003, 212). In 1975, traditional elites or *zu'ama* were seen as the most powerful group, five times more powerful than the next most influential group, namely religious leaders. With the advent of the civil war, party leaders, "in effect the militia leaders" (ibid.), became the most powerful group, four times as influential as the second placed group, the merchants. Following the end of the civil war, traditional leaders are seen as having regained some of their influence and the influence of party leaders has declined substantially, although it is still much higher than before the civil war. Taken together, officials of the state (ministers and military officers) are now the most influential group. Of course, this group includes many party leaders and former militia leaders. For example, the first minister in charge of the new Ministry of Displaced was Walid Jumblatt, a former militia leader (Ghosn and Khoury 2011, 393). The speaker of Parliament since 1992 is Nabih Berri, long-time leader of the Amal militia and party.

Hudson (1997, 109) refers to civil war Lebanon as the "Militia Republic." Anne Marie Baylouny (2014, 333) prefers to use the term "armed political parties," observing how four of these "established complex political and economic institutions and administrative structures within defined territorial enclaves under their control, de facto mini-states or cantons" (see also Bieber 2000, 275). Samir Khalaf (2002, 251) writes about "a war system" and Georges Corm (1994) uses the term "militia system" to stress the common aims and tactics of the various communal militias. Corm estimates that "over a fifteen-year period, Lebanese militias accrued some US$30 billion to $40 billion in armaments, supplies, and money from domestic and foreign sources" (p. 218) and views the militias as "genuine partners in crime" (p. 220).[14] Early in the war, the militias consolidated their territorial strongholds and made little sustained effort to gain ground afterward. For Tony Badran (2009, 55), the "most significant recurring lesson was that regardless of military capabilities, militias were not really able to take over and/or hold positions in hostile territory, outside its [sic] direct area of influence." Most violence was directed at civilians, who were terrorized through sniping, kidnapping and blind shelling (Corm 1994, 215). Much of the fighting was intra-communal. Khalaf (2002, 234) notes how "internecine violence and factional turf wars became bloodier and more rampant" as the war went one. Corm criticizes the Ta'if Accord for rewarding the "champions of communal violence" (p. 228). Farid El Khazen (2003, 61) wryly notes how the inclusion of militia leaders in the political process "led to the institutionalization of the war system in the postwar political order."

External actors

Externally, the former colonial powers of France and Britain have been replaced by regional powers. The international dimension has always been the key to an understanding of Lebanese politics right from the start, when the country was carved out of greater Syria. Brenda Seaver (2000, 271), stressing the contribution of international factors in the failure of consociationalism in Lebanon, even claims that it is more important for Lebanon's future to find a solution to the Palestinian problem than to get the institutions right.

In 1991 Lebanon signed the "Treaty of Brotherhood, Cooperation and Coordination with Syria," and thereby "effectively conceded a permanent place in Lebanese political and security arrangements to Syria, whose troops remained in Lebanon until 2005" (Tonge 2014, 103). Marie-Joëlle Zahar (2009, 294) notes that "from 1991 until 2005, the behavior of Syria and its Lebanese political allies was not bound by the rules of the game negotiated at Taif. Instead, these rules were twisted and discarded in the name of political expediency." Since Syria had occupied large parts of Lebanon for most of the duration of the civil war, the Ta'if Agreement in practice merely confirmed the loss of Lebanese sovereignty. Hanna Ziadeh (2006, 172) uses the phrase "sovereignty impeded nation-state." The Lebanese state did not regain full control of its territory following the Syrian withdrawal in 2005, because "Hezbollah's governance of the south of the country provides a state-within-a state" (Tonge 2014, 112). It should be added that Israel occupied the south of Lebanon from 1985 to 2000 and continues to hold disputed territories on its border. Thus, while the National Pact of 1943 helped establish Lebanese sovereignty, the appendix of the Ta'if Agreement and its partisan and partial implementation resulted in a loss of sovereignty.

A neat distinction between domestic and external actors in Lebanon is not always possible. For example, the Sunni Islamic Association (al-Jama'ah al'Islamiyya) had ties to the Muslim Brotherhood in Egypt and Syria. Its militia, al-Mujahidin, fought in the Lebanese civil war. The Shia Hezbollah (Party of God) has its origins in Iraq but rose to prominence following the Iranian revolution, and receives guidance and support from Iran (Hamzeh and Dekmejian 1993). Eyal Zisser (2009, 157) even describes Hezbollah as "the handiwork of Tehran, if not simply its instrument." While this statement may exaggerate the influence of this particular external actor, there is no doubt that the role of external actors in post-war Lebanon has greatly increased compared to the pre-war period. As in other cases of consociationalism following civil war, it is impossible to view domestic politics in Lebanon as self-contained.

The military

This leads us to the final difference between pre- and post-civil war consociationalism: the role of military power. From a consociational viewpoint, the extension of the principle of proportionality to the armed forces and security sector is only logical. Oren Barak (2012) points to the need for adequate representation of all communities in the army and its officer corps, something that was lacking in Lebanon before the civil war. However, Lebanon's problems are more serious than descriptive representation. One of the militias, Hezbollah, is still active and more powerful than ever, having "the most impressive non-state army in the world" (Worrall 2013, 242).

Hezbollah rose to prominence as the leading organization in what is known as the 'Islamic Resistance' against the Israeli occupation of southern Lebanon, which lasted until 2000. Eitan Azani (2013, 902) views Hezbollah as a "hybrid terrorist organization," combining military resistance, social welfare and political activity. It also provoked the devastating Israeli invasion of July 2006. Four months later, Amal and Hezbollah ministers resigned from the government, demanding a government of national unity. In May 2008, fighting broke out after the rump cabinet acted against Hezbollah, leading the party/militia to flex its military muscle and occupy parts of Beirut. Talks between the main parties in Doha, Qatar resulted in an agreement that led to the appointment of a new president by Parliament, a government of national unity with enough opposition members to allow them to halt decisions over matters of vital concern to them, and a return to the electoral law of 1960 (Corstange 2010). The result is a further entrenchment of sectarian divisions instead of a gradual softening, as promised in the Ta'if Agreement.[15] It still took five months to form the government of national unity, which lasted slightly more than a year. Since then, attempts have been made to form another government of national unity, but it is indicative of the continuing stalemate in Lebanese politics that the parliamentary elections of 2014 were postponed until 2017, since Parliament could not agree on a new president and a new electoral law (see Geukjian 2014). Lebanon's Hezbollah is fighting in Syria's internationalized civil war and the massive influx of Syrian refugees has strained the capacity of the Lebanese state and society (Fakhoury 2014, 517–518).

Conclusion

Stephan Rosiny (2015, 486, emphasis added) sees the Ta'if agreement as "a transitory power-sharing arrangement under which consociational guarantees *should* have gradually been replaced by centripetal and, finally, integrationist patterns of inter-communal cooperation." The key word here is "should," because it has been difficult to implement centripetal institutions or to make progress with the abolition of confessionalism. As John Nagle (2015) explains, the Christian minorities in particular insist on "entrenching ethnicity" as they are bound to lose from the kind of reforms foreseen in the Ta'if Agreement. In Tamirace Fakhoury Mühlbacher's (2009, 453) apt phrase, Lebanon therefore seems "condemned to the consociational wheel of fortune."

Understandably, there is a tendency in the consociational literature to focus on the similarities between pre- and post-civil war Lebanon. Some accounts even come close to ignoring the civil war in the analysis, skipping directly from pre-war consociationalism to post-war consociationalism.[16] The seeming inevitability and inescapability of consociationalism for a divided country like Lebanon has led to an emphasis on continuity. This chapter has tried to show that superficial similarities between the communal power-sharing arrangements of pre- and post-civil war Lebanon should not blind us to the important differences. These were discussed under seven headings: the stakes, favourable factors, incentives, political institutions, domestic actors, external actors and the military. On closer scrutiny, post-civil war consociationalism in Lebanon turned out to be very different from the First Republic: former militia leaders joined party politicians in ruling the country, Syria occupied large parts of Lebanon and held sway, Hezbollah formed a state-within-a-state, and the provisions of the formal Ta'if Accord of 1989 have proved far easier to circumvent than the unwritten National Pact of 1943. Peace was restored at the price of democracy and sovereignty.

There is a widespread feeling, documented by survey research, that the beneficiaries of the Ta'if Accord are the Sunni (Ghosn and Khoury 2011, 389). The

Shia continue to press for more political power and although Syria's influence waned after 2005 and even more so after it succumbed to its own civil war, the role of Iran has increased as the main inspiration and supporter of Hezbollah (Worrall 2013; DeVore and Stähli 2015). Hezbollah "was not present at Taif" and the organization was "strongly critical of the accord [...] particularly the corporate consociational allocation of offices" (Hamdan 2013, 45). The strongest advocate for a deconfessionalization of Lebanese politics at the moment is Hezbollah which, together with Amal, stands to gain from the adoption of an electoral system of proportional representation and, as the largest minority, the Shia would stand a good chance of delivering the prime minister, an office that is currently unattainable to them (Rabil 2011). This also puts the international community in a bind. Peter Seeberg (2009, 95) notes the paradox that EU democracy promotion in Lebanon may strengthen Hezbollah, whose military wing was included in the EU list of terrorist organizations in 2013.[17]

It is easy to think that Lebanon's predicament is somehow unique, as a plural country wedged on the border of Europe and the Middle East, in a highly volatile region and wide open to the vagaries of international politics. Certainly, almost all of the many studies on Lebanon are of the single case study type. Even the consociational literature, despite Lijphart's comparative pioneering work, is largely organized by country. For that reason, scholars have failed to notice the striking resemblance between Lebanon and other recent cases of consociationalism following civil war. For example, complaints about foreign meddling and loss of sovereignty would surely resound in Bosnia-Herzegovina. Bitter remarks about the political role of former militias would echo in Burundi. Cynical comments about the incompetence of local politicians who have to be bailed out by outsiders would resonate on the streets of Belfast. Colombians living in the 1960s would have known all too well what it is like to have the perpetrators of violence sharing power. On the other hand, the Cypriots could remind the Lebanese that the only thing worse than having some kind of consociationalism after civil war is not having a common political system at all. What this goes to show is that consociationalism following civil war is different and that we need to come to terms with this, empirically, normatively and theoretically.

The empirical lessons of the Lebanese case study have been highlighted above. The theoretical lesson is that consociational concepts such as the "self-negating prediction" and the favourable factors for its adoption and success are not much help in explaining or predicting actors' decisions to end the fighting and participate in a consociational regime. In Lebanon, the changing international environment and the military stalemate enabled a consociational solution to the civil war. In this respect, the consociational literature has much to learn from peace and conflict studies. Normatively, the case of Lebanon brings to the fore the tension between consociationalism as a short-term solution to civil war and a long-term problem for political and social integration. In Lebanon as well as in other regimes following civil war, including possibly Syria (Rosiny 2013), the search is for some kind of "biodegradable consociationalism," like the magic stitches that help heal a wound and then dissolve by themselves. That search continues.

Notes

1 The clarity and accuracy of the argument were greatly improved thanks to the excellent comments from the editors and Stephan Rosiny. Any remaining issues are solely the responsibility of the author.
2 Not that this was always so. Austria experienced political violence in the 1930s in the context of Austrofascism. Switzerland experienced a civil war in 1847 between Catholic, conservative cantons and the confederation. The number of casualties in both cases, though, does not compare to the bloodshed in the cases listed below.
3 South Africa following apartheid is covered in Bogaards (2014), which analyzes the extent of consociationalism in the interim constitution, the permanent constitution and the ANC as a 'consociational party.'
4 Northern Ireland experimented with consociationalism in the Sunningdale Agreement of the early 1970s, long before the Good Friday Agreement of 1998 (see Reilly 2001). However, owing to the brevity of this experience, the status of Northern Ireland as part of the United Kingdom, and the fact that political violence pre-dates the first attempts at consociationalism in Northern Ireland, only Lebanon offers a proper before-and-after picture.
5 The constitutionalization of consociationalism is not limited to countries coming out of a civil war, as the federalization of Belgium shows.
6 For a critical analysis of Iraq as a liberal consociation, see Bogaards (forthcoming).
7 The literature on Northern Ireland has brought the importance of policing to the fore (McGarry and O'Leary 1999).
8 In my current book project, I examine seven cases of consociationalism following civil war (Bosnia-Herzegovina, Burundi, Colombia, Kosovo, Lebanon, Macedonia and Northern Ireland) and two cases of consociationalism prior to civil war (Cyprus and Lebanon) to find out what is different about these experiences.
9 Abul-Husn (1998, 119–123) likewise talks about consociationalism being restored. Messarra (1986, 138–139) takes the theme of continuity to its extreme, describing the civil war as "barbarian consociationalism" (*consociation sauvage*) or a "pre-consociation," a prelude to the implementation of the four consociational principles.
10 Indeed, the political crisis of 1958, which was resolved through American military intervention, was about Lebanon's international relations, not its domestic politics (Hudson 1976).
11 For a more pessimistic assessment, see Dekmejian (1978).
12 The interesting questions of how an unwritten pact can lead to rigidity and whether informal institutions may be more difficult to change than formal ones will be explored in a separate paper.
13 See www.un.org/press/en/2004/sc8181.doc.htm.
14 Lebanon's economy did surprisingly well following the collapse of the state in the second half of the 1970s, and Kurtulus (2012, 1293) even argues that the general welfare of Lebanese citizens improved during the first seven years of the civil war. This is attributed to the marginal role of the state, emigration, remittances and job opportunities provided by the militias.
15 Salamey and Tabar (2008, 253) even write about a "degenerate consociational model in Lebanon."
16 Fakhoury Mühlbacher's (2009) otherwise comprehensive book has 477 pages, but includes no chapter on the civil war. Instead, the analysis jumps from consociationalism in pre-war Lebanon (ch. 2) to post-war Lebanon, the Ta'if Accord and the Second Republic (ch. 3).
17 See www.consilium.europa.eu/en/policies/fight-against-terrorism/terrorist-list.

References

Abul-Husn, Latif. 1998. *The Lebanese Conflict: Looking Inward*. Boulder, CO: Lynne Rienner.

Azani, Eitan. 2013. "The Hybrid Terrorist Organization: Hezbollah as a Case Study." *Studies in Conflict and Terrorism* 36, no. 11: 899–916.

Badran, Tony. 2009. "Lebanon's Militia Wars." In *Lebanon: Liberation, Conflict, and Crisis*, edited by Barry Lubin, pp. 35–61. Basingstoke: Palgrave Macmillan.

Barak, Oren. 2012. "Representation and Stability in Postwar Lebanon." *Representation* 48, no. 3: 321–333.

Baylouny, Anne Marie. 2014. "Born Violent: Armed Political Parties and Non-State Governance in Lebanon's Civil War." *Small Wars and Insurgencies* 25, no. 2: 329–353.

Bieber, Florian. 2000. "Bosnia-Herzegovina and Lebanon: Historical Lessons of Two Multireligious States." *Third World Quarterly* 21, no. 2: 269–281.

Bogaards, Matthijs. 1998. "The Favorable Factors for Consociational Democracy: A Review." *European Journal of Political Research* 33, no. 4: 475–496.

Bogaards, Matthijs. 2000. "The Uneasy Relationship between Empirical and Normative Types in Consociational Theory." *Journal of Theoretical Politics* 12, no. 4: 395–424.

Bogaards, Matthijs. 2009. "How to Classify Hybrid Regimes? Defective Democracy and Electoral Authoritarianism." *Democratization* 16, no. 2: 399–423.

Bogaards, Matthijs. 2013. "The Choice for Proportional Representation: Electoral System Design in Peace Agreements." *Civil Wars* 15, no. S1: 71–87.

Bogaards, Matthijs. 2014. *Democracy and Social Peace in Divided Societies: Exploring Consociational Parties*. Basingstoke: Palgrave Macmillan.

Bogaards, Matthijs. Forthcoming. "Iraq's Constitution of 2005: Three Problems, Four Misconceptions, Some Suggestions." In *Power Sharing and Power Relations*, edited by Andreas Mehler and Caroline Hartzell.

Clark, Janine and Marie-Joëlle Zahar. 2015. "Critical Junctures and Missed Opportunities: The Case of Lebanon's Cedar Revolution." *Ethnopolitics* 14, no. 1: 1–18.

Corm, Georges. 1994. "The War System: Militia Hegemony and Reestablishment of the State." In *Peace for Lebanon? From War to Reconstruction*, edited by Deirdre Collings, pp. 215–230. Boulder, CO: Lynne Rienner.

Corstange, Daniel. 2010. "The Parliamentary Election in Lebanon, June 2009." *Electoral Studies* 29, no. 2: 285–289.

Crigthon, Elizabeth and Martha Abele Mac Iver. 1991. "The Evolution of Protracted Ethnic Conflict: Group Dominance and Political Underdevelopment in Northern Ireland and Lebanon." *Comparative Politics* 23, no. 2: 127–142.

Dekmejian, Richard. 1978. "Consociational Democracy in Crisis." *Comparative Politics* 10, no. 2: 251–265.

DeVore, Marc and Armin Stähli. 2015. "Explaining Hezbollah's Effectiveness: Internal and External Determinants of the Rise of Violent Non-State Actors." *Terrorism and Political Violence* 27, no. 2: 331–357.

El-Husseini, Rola. 2012. *Elite Politics in Postwar Lebanon*. Syracuse, NY: Syracuse University Press.

El Khazen, Farid. 2003. "The Postwar Political Process: Authoritarianism by Diffusion." In *Lebanon in Limbo: Postwar Society and State in an Uncertain Regional Environment*, edited by Theodor Hanf and Nawaf Salam, pp. 53–74. Baden-Baden: Nomos.

Fakhoury Mühlbacher, Tamirace. 2009. *Democracy and Power-Sharing in Stormy Weather: The Case of Lebanon*. Wiesbaden: Verlag für Sozialwissenschaften.

Fakhoury, Tamirace. 2014. "Do Power-Sharing Systems Behave Differently amid Regional Uprisings? Lebanon in the Arab Protest Wave." *Middle East Journal* 68, no. 4: 505–520.
Farah, Tawfic. 1975. *Aspects of Modernization and Consociationalism: Lebanon as an Exploratory Test Case*. Lincoln, NE: Middle East Research Group.
Faris, Hani. 1994. "The Failure of Peacemaking in Lebanon, 1975–1989." In *Peace for Lebanon? From War to Reconstruction*, edited by Deirdre Collings, pp. 17–30. Boulder, CO: Lynne Rienner.
Geukjian, Ohannes. 2014. "Political Instability and Conflict after the Syrian Withdrawal from Lebanon." *Middle East Journal* 68, no. 4: 521–545.
Ghosn, Faten and Amal Khoury. 2011. "Lebanon after the Civil War: Peace or the Illusion of Peace?" *Middle East Journal* 65, no. 3: 381–397.
Hamdan, Amal. 2013. "The Limits of Corporate Consociation: Taif and the Crisis of Power-Sharing in Lebanon since 2005." In *Lebanon: After the Cedar Revolution*, edited by Are Knudsen and Michael Kerr, pp. 39–59. Oxford: Oxford University Press.
Hamzeh, Nizar and Hrair Dekmejian. 1993. "The Islamic Spectrum of Lebanese Politics." *Journal of South Asian and Middle Eastern Studies* 16, no. 3: 25–42.
Hanf, Theodor. 1993. *Coexistence in Wartime Lebanon: Decline of a State and Rise of a Nation*. London: I.B. Tauris.
Hanf, Theodor. 2003. "The Sceptical Nation: Opinions and Attitudes Twelve Years after the End of the War." In *Lebanon in Limbo: Postwar Society and State in an Uncertain Regional Environment*, edited by Theodor Hanf and Nawaf Salam, pp. 197–228. Baden-Baden: Nomos.
Hartzell, Caroline and Matthew Hoddie. 2007. *Crafting Peace: Power-Sharing Institutions and the Negotiated Settlements of Civil Wars*. University Park: Pennsylvania State University Press.
Horowitz, Donald L. 2002. "Constitutional Design: Proposals versus Processes." In *The Architecture of Democracy: Constitutional Design, Conflict Management, and Democracy*, edited by Andrew Reynolds, pp. 15–36. Oxford: Oxford University Press.
Horowitz, Donald L. 2008. "Conciliatory Institutions and Constitutional Processes in Post-Conflict States." *William and Mary Law Review* 49, no. 4: 1213–1248.
Hudson, Michael. 1976. "The Lebanese Crisis: The Limits of Consociational Democracy." *Journal of Palestine Studies* 5, nos 3–4: 109–122.
Hudson, Michael. 1988. "The Problem of Authoritative Power in Lebanese Politics: Why Consociationalism Failed." In *Lebanon: A History of Conflict and Consensus*, edited by Nadim Shehadi and Dana Haffar Mills, pp. 224–239. London: I.B. Tauris.
Hudson, Michael. 1997. "Trying Again: Power-Sharing in Post-Civil War Lebanon." *International Negotiation* 2, no. 1: 103–122.
Kerr, Michael. 2005. *Imposing Power-Sharing: Conflict and Coexistence in Northern Ireland and Lebanon*. Dublin: Irish Academic Press.
Khalaf, Samir. 2002. *Civil and Uncivil Violence in Lebanon: A History of the Internationalization of Communal Conflict*. New York: Columbia University Press.
Kurtulus, Ersun. 2012. "Exploring the Paradoxical Consequences of State Collapse: The Cases of Somalia 1991–2006 and Lebanon 1975–1982." *Third World Quarterly* 33, no. 7: 1285–1303.
Lijphart, Arend. 1968. "Typologies of Democratic Systems." *Comparative Political Studies* 1, no. 1: 3–44.
Lijphart, Arend. 1969. "Consociational Democracy." *World Politics* 21, no. 2: 207–225.
Lijphart, Arend. 1975. *The Politics of Accommodation: Pluralism and Democracy in the Netherlands*. 2nd rev. edn. Berkeley: University of California Press.

Lijphart, Arend. 1977. *Democracy in Plural Societies: A Comparative Exploration.* New Haven, CT: Yale University Press.
McCulloch, Allison. 2014a. "Consociational Settlements in Deeply Divided Societies: The Liberal–Corporate Distinction." *Democratization* 21, no. 3: 501–518.
McCulloch, Allison. 2014b. *Power-Sharing and Political Stability in Deeply Divided Societies.* London: Routledge.
McGarry, John and Brendan O'Leary. 1999. *Policing Northern Ireland: Proposals for a New Start.* Belfast: Blackstaff Press.
McGarry, John and Brendan O'Leary. 2007. "Iraq's Constitution of 2005: Liberal Consociation as Political Prescription." *International Journal on Constitutional Law* 5, no. 4: 670–698.
McGarry, John and Brendan O'Leary. 2009. "Power Shared After the Deaths of Thousands." In *Consociational Theory: McGarry and O'Leary and the Northern Ireland Conflict*, edited by Rupert Taylor, pp. 15–84. London: Routledge.
Messarra, Antoine Nasri. 1986. "Les Chances de Survie du Système Consociatif Libanais: D'une Consociation Sauvage à un Modèle Consociatif Rationalisé." In *La Sociét de Concordance: Approche Comparative*, edited by Theodor Hanf, pp. 105–154. Beyrouth: Université Libanaise.
Nagle, John. 2015. "Between Entrenchment, Reform and Transformation: Ethnicity and Lebanon's Consociational Democracy." *Democratization*, 23, no. 7: 1144–1161
Norton, Augustus. 1991. "Lebanon after Ta'if: Is the Civil War Over?" *Middle East Journal* 45, no. 3: 457–473.
Oren, Yiftachel. 1992. "The State, Ethnic Relations and Democratic Stability: Lebanon, Cyprus and Israel." *GeoJournal* 28, no. 3: 319–332.
Rabil, Robert. 2011. *Religion, National Identity, and Confessional Politics in Lebanon: The Challenge of Islamism.* Basingstoke: Palgrave Macmillan.
Reilly, Benjamin. 2001. *Democracy in Divided Societies: Electoral Engineering for Conflict Management.* Cambridge: Cambridge University Press.
Rosiny, Stephan. 2013. "Power Sharing in Syria: Lessons from Lebanon's Taif Experience." *Middle East Policy* 20, no. 3: 41–55.
Rosiny, Stephan. 2015. "A Quarter Century of 'Transitory Power-Sharing': Lebanon's Unfulfilled Ta'if Agreement of 1989 Revisited." *Civil Wars* 17, no. 4: 485–502.
Salam, Nawaf. 2003. "Taif Revisited." In *Lebanon in Limbo: Postwar Society and State in an Uncertain Regional Environment*, edited by Theodor Hanf and Nawaf Salam, pp. 39–51. Baden-Baden: Nomos.
Salamey, Imad and Paul Tabar. 2008. "Consociational Democracy and Urban Sustainability: Transforming the Confessional Divides in Beirut." *Ethnopolitics* 7, nos 2–3: 239–263.
Seaver, Brenda. 2000. "The Regional Sources of Power-Sharing Failure: The Case of Lebanon." *Political Science Quarterly* 115, no. 2: 247–271.
Seeberg, Peter. 2009. "The EU as a Realist Actor in Normative Clothes: EU Democracy Promotion in Lebanon and the European Neighourhood Policy." *Democratization* 16, no. 1: 81–99.
Shapiro, Ian. 2003. *The State of Democratic Theory.* Princeton, NJ: Princeton University Press.
Taylor, Rupert. 2009. "Introduction: The Promise of Consociational Theory." In *Consociational Theory: McGarry and O'Leary and the Northern Ireland Conflict*, edited by Rupert Taylor, pp. 1–11. London: Routledge.
Tonge, Jonathan. 2014. *Comparative Peace Processes.* Cambridge: Polity Press.

Worrall, James. 2013. "Reading Booth in Beirut: Is Hizbollah an Emancipatory Actor?" *Studies in Conflict & Terrorism* 36, no. 3: 235–254.
Zahar, Marie Joëlle. 2002. "Peace by Unconventional Means: Lebanon's Ta'if Agreement." In *Ending Civil Wars: The Implementation of Peace Agreements*, edited by Stephen Stedman, Daniel Rothchild and Elizabeth Cousens, pp. 566–597. Boulder, CO: Lynne Rienner.
Zahar, Marie Joëlle. 2009. "Liberal Interventions, Illiberal Outcomes: The United Nations, Western Power and Lebanon." In *New Perspectives on Liberal Peacebuilding*, edited by Edward Newman, Roland Paris and Oliver Richmond, pp. 292–315. Tokyo: United Nations University Press.
Ziadeh, Hanna. 2006. *Sectarianism and Intercommunal Nation-Building in Lebanon*. London: Hurst & Company.
Zisser, Eyal. 2009. "Hizballah in Lebanon: Between Tehran and Beirut, Between the Struggle with Israel, and the Struggle for Lebanon." In *Lebanon: Liberation, Conflict, and Crisis*, edited by in Barry Lubin, pp. 155–176. Basingstoke: Palgrave Macmillan.

8 Power-sharing in Burundi
An enduring miracle?

Stef Vandeginste

Introduction

On 28 August 2000, after approximately two years of international (initially Tanzanian, later South African) peace mediation, a Peace and Reconciliation Agreement for Burundi was signed in Arusha (Tanzania). Sixteen years later, this chapter reflects on the backbone of the Arusha Agreement which decisively shaped Burundi's twenty-first-century political institutions. More than anywhere else on the African continent, power-sharing played a central role in Burundi's political transition serving the dual purpose of war termination and creating more inclusive political governance.

Before introducing the use, merits and limitations of power-sharing as a conflict resolution and state transformation mechanism in Burundi, two paradoxes of the Arusha Agreement are worth noting from the outset. First, at the time when the Arusha Agreement was signed, it was greeted with major skepticism by both policy-makers as well as academic Burundi watchers (Reyntjens 2001). References to the other Arusha peace agreement – for neighbouring Rwanda, signed one year before the 1994 genocide – and how that one was treated as an insignificant piece of paper by its signatories were rife. Given the doubts about its durability at the time of its signature, the current status of Burundi's Arusha Agreement, which is systematically referred to as its roadmap to peace, is quite remarkable. Second, unlike most other peace agreements, the Arusha Agreement had almost no short-term effect yet produced considerable longer term effects. In the short term, it failed to put an end to the civil war because the two main rebel movements did not sign the Agreement. In fact, it was not until December 2008 that the last rebel movement agreed to lay down arms. In the meantime, however, the constitutional blueprint laid down in the Arusha Agreement had been adopted by referendum and a new constitution – with detailed and complex power-sharing provisions that were copied from the Agreement – was proclaimed on 18 March 2005. Burundi is thus one of the few countries that experienced both a major peace agreement and far-reaching constitutional reform in close temporal association (Mehler 2013, 24).

For an analysis of the Burundian case, this chapter draws upon two strands of the scientific literature. On the one hand, I use insights from studies of power-sharing from a war termination perspective. On the other, I use the scholarly research that looks at power-sharing from the perspective of political institution-building in deeply divided societies. These two aspects are interconnected, as Timothy Sisk demonstrates when pointing at two puzzling knowledge gaps that remain about the use of power-sharing for durable conflict resolution (Sisk 2013). Under what conditions do elites find it in their interests to share power with adversaries? How may war-ending elite-negotiated pacts evolve into more enduring social contracts? Sisk suggests that more contingent- and context-specific knowledge is needed to answer those questions. It is my hope that an analysis of the Burundi situation can shed light that is of wider relevance beyond the case addressed here. As this chapter demonstrates, the context-specific contingencies require a *longue durée* perspective, which is often overlooked in the scholarly literature on power-sharing. One of the important historical aspects this chapter addresses is Burundi's tradition of single-party rule and how this impacts upon the functioning of its contemporary power-sharing institutions.

The structure of the chapter is as follows. First, it presents a state-of-the-art picture of power-sharing in Burundi, with particular attention to how evolutions in the political landscape have eroded one dimension of power-sharing without however, at this point, fundamentally undermining it. Throughout the 2015 electoral crisis, occasioned by President Pierre Nkurunziza's ambitions for a third term, the continuation of Arusha-style power-sharing was one of the major stakes. The next sections look at the 'miracle' – an event that is not explicable by natural or scientific laws, according to the Oxford Dictionary – of the adoption and survival of power-sharing in Burundi. Finally, it looks at a number of historically rooted factors that help explain the dynamics of power-sharing in Burundi over the past 15 years: ethnic power-sharing in combination with single-party rule, state centralism, militarism and neo-patrimonialism.

Power-sharing in Burundi: a state of the art

A post-colonial history marked by large-scale ethno-political violence

After acceding to independence in 1962, Burundi became the scene of more than three decades of authoritarian one-party rule and a failed transition towards democracy (1988–1993), which unleashed a civil war that – as stated in the Arusha Agreement – was "fundamentally political with extremely important ethnic dimensions" (Article 4). It was fundamentally political because, above all, it was driven by a struggle among political elites for control over the state and its resources. This also remains the essence of non-violent (or rather, despite worrisome recent trends, much less violent) political competition in Burundi today. At the same time, the struggle was highly ethnic. Although the applicability of the notion of ethnicity has sometimes been disputed in the context of Burundi – its main identity groups Hutu (estimated around 85 per cent), Tutsi (14 per cent) and Twa (1 per cent) (CIA World Factbook 2014) sharing the same territory, language and religion – the ethnic nature of the conflict stands beyond doubt.

168 S. Vandeginste

The civil war opposed a government and army dominated by members of the Tutsi demographic minority against two Hutu-dominated rebel movements. Ethnically motivated persecution and massacres were rife. Ethnic massacres of Hutu by the army in 1972 and of Tutsi by Hutu militants in 1993 have been characterized as genocide in some UN reports (although this qualification was not the result of any international judicial inquiry). The latter wave of killings was sparked by the assassination, on 21 October 1993 after only 100 days in office, of Melchior Ndadaye (FRODEBU party – Front for Democracy in Burundi), the first democratically elected Hutu president.

Multi-dimensional power-sharing

Unlike the situation in neighbouring Rwanda, Burundi's civil war came to an end through a negotiated settlement, not through military victory. This modality of its transition from conflict to peace continues to dominate several aspects of Burundi's post-conflict institutional set-up. The peace agreements for Burundi – the Arusha Agreement of 2000 supplemented by the 2003 Global Ceasefire Agreement with the largely Hutu rebel movement CNDD-FDD (National Council for the Defense of Democracy – Forces for the Defense of Democracy, originally an armed dissident group of FRODEBU members) and the 2006 Comprehensive Ceasefire Agreement with Palipehutu-FNL (Party for the Liberation of the Hutu People – National Liberation Forces) – included a complex and multi-dimensional power-sharing arrangement.[1] The dimensions of this arrangement are summarized in Table 8.1.

Of the four 'classical' – political, military, territorial and economic – dimensions of power-sharing (Hartzell and Hoddie 2007), Burundi does not have any territorial power-sharing nor any non-territorial form of segmental autonomy. Because of the specific features of its ethnic divisions, which are not based on separate territorial communities, territorial power-sharing or other forms of self-government were never on the table of the peace negotiations. It would therefore be hard to draw conclusions from the case of Burundi for the use of territorial power-sharing and its impact on the success or failure of negotiated peace settlements (Hartmann 2013; Zanker *et al*. 2015). Furthermore, except for one provision, neither the peace agreements nor the constitution explicitly provides for economic power-sharing. However, it is important to note that the beneficiaries of political and military power-sharing automatically also benefit economically

Table 8.1 Power-sharing dimensions in Burundi

Power-sharing dimensions	Political power-sharing	Military power-sharing
Ethnic	D1	D2
Between (former) political opponents	D3	D4

and financially from their guaranteed share of political and military power. In Burundi, prosperity, wealth and social status are hard to imagine without (at least partial) control over the political and military institutions of the central state (Ndikumana 2005). This implicit economic dimension of power-sharing is made explicit in one constitutional provision which states that state-owned companies will be administered in accordance with the ethnic quotas that are also used for the ethnic cohabitation within the National Assembly and government: 60 per cent Hutu and 40 per cent Tutsi (Article 143 of the Constitution of 18 March 2005).

In addition to combining a political and military dimension, Burundi's negotiated transition also fuses ethnic and non-ethnic power-sharing. On the one hand, as presented in more detail below, power-sharing entails a complex set of quota-based provisions guaranteeing ethnic cohabitation in the state's political and military institutions. This has led some observers to consider Burundi to be the most consociational polity in Africa (Lemarchand 2007). On the other hand, power-sharing in Burundi amounts to a 'classical' pact between (former) adversarial elites, with incumbent and insurgent leaders agreeing to lay down arms and share the cake. While these two dimensions overlap to some extent – which is not surprising in a country where political and ethnic competition largely coincided for several decades – it is important to note that the overlap between the ethnic and the non-ethnic dimension is far from complete. For instance, political parties and their electoral lists are legally required to be multi-ethnic. This has two important consequences, as will be discussed in further detail below. One is that Burundi has not been caught in the trap of ethnocracy (Howard 2012). The other is that although power-sharing in Burundi has, over recent years, been under considerable pressure in its non-ethnic dimension, this has – thus far – not undermined the stability of ethnic power-sharing. Before analyzing these recent developments, I will now briefly introduce the four dimensions of power-sharing in Burundi that are outlined in Table 8.1 in more detail.

A closer look at Burundi's power-sharing dimensions

Ethnic power-sharing at the level of political institutions (D1) is constitutionally engineered through a system of guaranteed representation of ethnic segments in the National Assembly, the Senate and the Commune Councils, as well as the Council of Ministers, the presidency (with two vice-presidents from different ethnic groups) and local commune administrators. This is achieved on the basis of ethnic quotas and, in the case of elected bodies the composition of which is not in accordance with the constitutional quotas, cooptation of additional members. Owing to the overwhelming demographic majority of Hutu (85 per cent), proportionality is not strictly applied but, rather, is combined with an over-representation of the Tutsi (14 per cent) and Twa (1 per cent) minorities. Guaranteed representation of Tutsi ranges from one-third (communal administrators) to 40 per cent (the Council of Ministers and the National Assembly) to 50 per cent (the Senate). In combination with qualified majority requirements (either two-thirds or three-quarters) that apply to the enactment of legislation and to other powers of the legislature (e.g., the election of members of the national electoral commission), this grants a de facto veto right to Tutsi Members of Parliament.[2]

Military ethnic power-sharing (D2) is also codified in the 2005 Constitution. For a period to be determined by the Senate, no more than 50 per cent of the national defence and security forces (the army, the police and the intelligence service) may belong to one ethnic group. In addition, the government minister in charge of the armed forces cannot be from the same ethnic group as the minister in charge of the police. The Senate – itself composed on the basis of Hutu/Tutsi parity and a guaranteed co-opted representation of the Twa minority – is charged with monitoring the implementation of these constitutional quota requirements. The implementation of these provisions has, quite remarkably, not given rise to any serious controversy over the past decade. In the case of elected assemblies, ethnicity of candidates is stated on the electoral lists. In the absence of ethnic identity cards or other formal registration of ethnicity of Burundian citizens, military ethnic power-sharing quotas are applied through stated self-identification (and peer control).

Political power-sharing between former opponents (D3) was a crucial aspect of the Arusha Agreement, of the 2003 Global Ceasefire Agreement and, to a lesser extent – due to the by then significantly weakened position of Palipehutu-FNL (International Crisis Group 2007) – of the 2006 Comprehensive Ceasefire Agreement. The Arusha Agreement was signed by a coalition of predominantly Hutu parties – the 'G7' – led by FRODEBU and a coalition of predominantly Tutsi parties – the 'G10' – led by former single party UPRONA (Unity and National Progress), as well as by the National Assembly (dominated by FRODEBU) and the government (dominated by UPRONA). The Agreement provided for a broad-based transitional government of national unity, originally for 36 months, in which between 50 and 60 per cent of the ministerial portfolios were allocated to the G7 group of predominantly Hutu parties, the other ministries going to UPRONA and other G10 parties. For the post-transition period as well, a coalition government model was put forward (and codified in the 2005 Constitution), with each party obtaining 5 per cent of the votes at the legislative elections being entitled to a proportionate number of ministerial positions. This 'grand coalition' arrangement was even extended to the presidency, with the two vice-presidents representing different political parties (as well as ethnic groups). Unless in the (at that time unlikely) event of a new predominantly Tutsi party becoming more successful, this was essentially and above all a political life-insurance policy for the UPRONA party. No matter how poor its electoral performance, UPRONA was assured of positions at the level of the vice-presidency and in government, assuming that it obtained 5 per cent of the votes cast (which was, given the result of the 1993 elections, a very realistic threshold). Through the General Ceasefire Agreement of November 2003, the CNDD-FDD obtained, for the remainder of the transition leading up to the 2005 general elections, a considerable number of positions (four ministers in government, 15 Members of

Parliament, three provincial governors, two ambassadors, 30 local government administrators and 20 per cent of state-owned companies). Following the 2005 elections (which were generally perceived as free and fair), CNDD-FDD became the most powerful political party. It reinforced its position in the 2010 elections, which were largely boycotted by the political opposition and which constituted a first blow to this political (D3) dimension of Burundi's power-sharing (Vandeginste 2011). I return to more recent developments in this dimension below.

Military power-sharing between former opponents (D4) was laid down as a general principle in the Arusha Agreement which stated that combatants of political movements were to be included in the restructured army and police force. This dimension was the most crucial aspect of the 2003 and, again to a lesser extent, the 2006 peace agreements. A Forces Technical Agreement Protocol of the 2003 peace agreement spelled out in detail the military power-sharing in the new defence and security forces, with 60 per cent of positions remaining in the hands of the government forces and 40 per cent taken up by CNDD-FDD. From a historical perspective, the transformation of Burundi's security forces on the basis of power-sharing was highly remarkable. For decades after independence, they had been the strong arm of successive Tutsi-dominated UPRONA governments. Furthermore, they were considered to be the 'life insurance' of Tutsi civilians, the importance of which became all the more clear following the genocide against Tutsi in neighbouring Rwanda in 1994. In addition, the army was also responsible for the assassination of Hutu President Ndadaye (FRODEBU) in October 1993 – which Sullivan (2005) accurately described as the use of its (military) veto right by Tutsi elites – the event that gave rise to the establishment of the CNDD-FDD. In light of all these historical antecedents and given the extreme cruelty of Burundi's civil war, restructuring the defence and security forces on the basis of power-sharing – between Tutsi and Hutu and between incumbents and insurgents – seemed extremely unrealistic at the time of the peace negotiations process. Nevertheless, this turned out to be an essential and durable cornerstone of Burundi's transition to peace. Before addressing this 'miraculous' adoption and survival of power-sharing in Burundi, this chapter examines the current state of power-sharing in Burundi as of early 2016.

Recent developments

First of all, it is worth recalling that power-sharing in Burundi – in all four dimensions – has not remained a rhetorical commitment but has been implemented for more than a decade now. Nevertheless, doubts have arisen as to whether power-sharing in Burundi will stand the test of time much longer, leading some observers to announce a "bye-bye to Arusha" (International Crisis Group 2012). It is clear indeed that Burundi's power-sharing arrangement has been under pressure due to of a number of recent developments. This section briefly addresses the gradual erosion of one of the pillars (D3) of power-sharing following the disputed 2010 general elections. Next, the chapter addresses the prospects for power-sharing in Burundi in light of the government's 2014 failed attempt at amending the constitution. Finally, it examines the increasing pressure on Burundi's power-sharing arrangement as a result of the turbulent and violent 2015 electoral process.

Political power-sharing between the former enemies, CNDD-FDD and UPRONA, went remarkably well until the 2010 general elections. As explained in more detail elsewhere, the 2010 elections constituted a significant blow to power-sharing in Burundi (Vandeginste 2011). The 2005 to 2010 coalition government's dominant party CNDD-FDD led by President Nkurunziza won an overwhelming victory at these elections which, after a first round of disputed local elections, were boycotted by most of the opposition parties (but not by UPRONA). CNDD-FDD obtained 81 per cent of the votes at the National Assembly elections and a three-quarters majority in the Senate. Following the withdrawal of other presidential candidates, Nkurunziza was re-elected with 91 per cent of the votes cast in direct presidential elections. This allowed CNDD-FDD to extend its control over most of the state apparatus. However, much to the frustration of some of its militants, the party was constitutionally required to share power in a coalition government despite its electoral triumph. UPRONA, which obtained 11 per cent of the votes in the National Assembly elections, obtained the first vice-presidency and three out of 20 ministerial posts. Contradicting the optimism of Pippa Norris (2009) about the democratizing effect of power-sharing elections, the 2010 Burundi elections strengthened autocratization rather than democratization (Lindberg 2009). Domestic and international watchdogs subsequently denounced the shrinking of political space and, in particular, increasing restrictions on the functioning of civil society, media and opposition parties (Amnesty International 2014). As it managed to do with other opposition parties, CNDD-FDD has been extremely efficient in exacerbating and exploiting internal divisions within UPRONA. As the result of a carefully orchestrated judicial saga, which came to an end in February 2014, UPRONA is now split into two wings. The current legally registered and recognized UPRONA is a CNDD-FDD-friendly dissident wing, which is not recognized by most of the historical party leadership that signed the Arusha Agreement in 2000. The other wing includes most of the UPRONA Members of Parliament elected in 2010 and presumably has more support from the traditional UPRONA electorate, but the Minister of Interior (CNDD-FDD) has refused its registration as a political party (see, in more detail, Vandeginste 2014b). In other words, although, formally speaking, Burundi still had a coalition government, in reality it became a CNDD-FDD single-party government in disguise. This erosion of the third pillar (D3) of power-sharing in Burundi has, however, thus far not undermined ethnic (political and/or military) power-sharing. Nevertheless, this development may well be the first step in a longer term CNDD-FDD controlled process of putting an end to Arusha-style power-sharing. It is reminiscent of the concern expressed by Tutsi negotiators at the time of the Arusha peace negotiations. They (unsuccessfully) requested that only those parties truly representing the mainstream Tutsi community – rather than seemingly ethnically diverse but in reality Hutu-controlled parties – should be allowed to send Tutsi to Parliament.

In November 2013, without any prior consultation or even public announcement, the Burundian government initiated a constitutional amendment process. The initial secrecy of this initiative fuelled a public perception and fear that this was a unilateral CNDD-FDD attempt at doing away with the Arusha Agreement. Others viewed it as an attempt to circumvent presidential term limits, signaling President Nkurunziza's intention to run for a third term in 2015. During the parliamentary debate on the new constitutional draft, however, government officials merely referred to certain constitutional implications of Burundi's integration into the East African Community and to the need to 'simplify' certain complexities of Burundi's legislative process. At no point was it stated that time had come to end the power-sharing arrangements agreed upon in Arusha. Yet, in the bill submitted to Parliament, two proposed amendments did affect power-sharing. First, it was proposed that the two vice-presidents be replaced by one – more ceremonial than provided for in the Arusha Agreement – vice-president (of another ethnic group and political party than the president) and a prime minister. Second, it was proposed that Parliament enact legislation with a simple majority instead of a two-thirds majority, which de facto annulled the Tutsi veto. Considerable national and diplomatic pressure was exerted on Burundi's Members of Parliament in order to safeguard the Arusha Agreement. For an amendment of the constitution, a majority of two-thirds (in the Senate) and four-fifths (in the National Assembly) is required. Against all odds, and because nearly all UPRONA MPs no longer supported the coalition government after the party split referred to above, the proposal was rejected in Parliament by one vote in March 2014. In reaction, President Nkurunziza announced that the constitutional amendment would likely be reinitiated following the 2015 elections, either through Parliament or through a popular referendum.

The 2015 general elections constituted one of the most turbulent episodes in Burundi's post-colonial history. They were marked by unprecedented mass demonstrations and severe political violence in the capital city Bujumbura. A general climate of fear led tens of thousands of citizens to cross the border into neighbouring countries. A failed coup d'état attempt was staged against President Nkurunziza on 13 May 2015 by an Arusha-style coalition of dissident army generals, including both former CNDD-FDD rebellion leaders (led by Hutu General Godefroid Niyombare) and former Tutsi government army generals. After some initial hesitation, most 'real' opposition parties (but not the formally registered UPRONA) boycotted the polls. Most international organizations, including the African Union and the European Union, withdrew their observation missions. Above all, major controversy arose around President Nkurunziza's third-term ambitions (Vandeginste 2015). This even caused an internal split within Nkurunziza's own party, and several CNDD-FDD dignitaries, including Second Vice-President Gervais Rufyikiri, joined the forces opposing Nkurunziza's third term and went into exile in Rwanda and Belgium. Although the local, legislative and presidential polls were delayed for about one month as a result of the security situation and logistical difficulties and in response to international calls, the Nkurunziza government went ahead with the elections. Nkurunziza was inaugurated on 20 August 2015 for a third term. While this is a blatant violation of the Arusha Agreement, the Constitutional Court – shortly before the coup attempt – ruled that a third term was permitted under the Constitution.[3] Nkurunziza's third term has therefore become largely associated with a perceived desire, on behalf of the hardliners within CNDD-FDD, to fully renege on Arusha. In his inaugural speech, Nkurunziza somewhat enigmatically stated, without entering into more detail, that he would mobilize everyone to respect the constitution, the Arusha Agreement and the other peace agreements but that he would correct certain 'irregularities' they contain. Although Nkurunziza appointed a council of ministers which respects the ethnic quota power-sharing requirements, this did not calm the situation. Close advisors of the president were assassinated, opposition members arrested and tortured while the army chief of staff narrowly escaped an assassination attempt. Tensions within the Burundian government army forces increased considerably during and after the elections. While the implementation of the Arusha Agreement reduced ethnic tensions and limited violence, it is undeniable that the post-election crisis poses the risk of reactivating the old ethnic divide, including within Burundi's armed forces. How Arusha dealt with the army has been crucial to stability in Burundi, as I explain in more detail below. Pro-government websites have increasingly framed the demonstrations and the violence in 'old' Hutu versus Tutsi terms. A new movement was created by the opposition in exile, including prominent CNDD-FDD defectors. Quite tellingly, it calls itself the National Council for the Respect of the Arusha Agreement and the Rule of Law (CNARED, *Conseil National pour le respect de l'Accord d'Arusha et l'Etat de droit au Burundi*). On 28 August 2015, on the occasion of the fifteenth anniversary of the Arusha Agreement, UN Secretary-General Ban-Ki moon stated that "Never has the spirit of Arusha been as sorely tested as in the past five months" (UN 2015). As of early 2016, predicting the future of power-sharing in Burundi has become more uncertain than ever since the signature of the Arusha Agreement.

The miraculous adoption of power-sharing?

After describing the state of power-sharing in Burundi, I now turn to what Donald Horowitz (2014) refers to as the "adoption problem." What are the factors that explain why Burundi adopted power-sharing, unlike several other ethnic conflict-ridden societies that could theoretically also benefit from introducing consociational or other accommodating institutions? Can scientific laws explain the introduction of power-sharing in Burundi or did it require some kind of divine intervention?

Lijphart's favourable conditions

One of Arend Lijphart's major contributions to our understanding of democracy and its institutions was his identification and refining of conditions that are favourable (or unfavourable) for introducing consociational power-sharing.

Other scholars have also addressed this crucial question, some of them challenging Lijphart's initial insights (e.g., Bogaards 1998; Schneckener 2002). It is clear that at the time of the Arusha peace negotiations, several presumably favourable conditions were absent in Burundi: there was a demographic majority segment (Hutu); the size of the ethnic segments was very unequal; there was no common external threat; despite the political relevance of regional divisions, there were no significant cross-cutting cleavages softening the ethnic identity divide; there was no geographical concentration of segments and there was no tradition of inter-ethnic accommodation and compromise. Others factors were favourable: the small number of ethnic segments, the small population size and the overarching loyalty to the one Burundian nation. On balance, these favourable domestic factors do not explain the introduction of power-sharing in Burundi. Let us therefore take a look at two other factors that have recently gained more attention in the literature: elite choices and the role of external actors. Both of these are particularly relevant in the context of internationally mediated peace negotiations between segmental elites, a context that is notably different from the one that Lijphart studied in his earlier work.

Elite behaviour

Horowitz (2014, 8) refers to asymmetric preferences as one of the obstacles to introducing ethnic power-sharing. In Burundi, this means that elites representing the large Hutu majority are likely to oppose consociational power-sharing and to prefer bare majority rule, while elites representing the Tutsi minority are likely to want a consociation. Horowitz argues that a consociational regime can therefore be adopted only when the majority is momentarily weak. This was indeed the case in Burundi in the late 1990s. FRODEBU's 1993 electoral victory had de facto been annulled through violence, in particular the assassination of President Ndadaye and other officials in October 1993 and a creeping coup d'état (Reyntjens 2009), which to a large extent restored UPRONA rule, with President Pierre Buyoya (Tutsi) returning to power in July 1996. This levelled the demographically unequal playing field and turned power-sharing into a potentially interesting option for both segmental elites, both of which also realized that military victory was close to impossible. But, as the literature indicates, more is needed for elites to engage in cooperative power-sharing behaviour.

Trust has been studied extensively as a driving factor for the introduction and functioning of power-sharing in multi-ethnic societies (see, e.g., Karmis and Rocher 2012) and there is a general scholarly recognition of its importance. In the 1990s, Burundi was characterized by a very low degree of trust at all levels of society, including among political elites. Nic Cheeseman (2011, 343) rightly characterizes the 1994 situation in Burundi as a case of "politics of distrust." The deliberate undermining of earlier attempts at inter-ethnic political accommodation, the extreme level of ethnic violence and the regional context, in particular the 1994 genocide in Rwanda, quite understandably had a devastating impact upon inter-ethnic trust. Nevertheless, power-sharing was accepted by those mutually distrustful elites. Two factors are helpful in shedding light on this puzzle. First, in line with peace negotiation theory about the ripeness of conflicts for resolution (Zartman 1989), Burundi's segmental elites found themselves deadlocked in a mutually hurting stalemate. Both parties had come to realize that negotiating a way-out might produce a non-zero-sum outcome. This perception had partly come about as a result of international sanctions imposed following the July 1996 coup d'état by Burundi's neighbours and of the reduction in aid volumes by Burundi's international partner countries and institutions. Second, the power-sharing arrangement negotiated in Arusha was not completely new to the parties around the table. While international actors played an important role in putting it on the agenda (see below), Burundi had experienced a decade of trial and error with ethnic power-sharing (Vandeginste 2009; Reyntjens 2015). The (limited) successes and (major) failures of these earlier experiences constituted an important learning process for the negotiating parties in Arusha, almost all of whom were politicians who had played an active part in the earlier trial-and-error process. Compared to earlier attempts, the power-sharing negotiated at Arusha was much more complex: there were more quotas, more minority guarantees, more timing modalities, more oversight mechanisms, etc. In summary, and a lesson to be learned from the Burundian case, the Arusha talks and the subsequent steps taken in the peace process managed to engineer mutually acceptable fear-reducing institutions, which in essence compensated for the lack of trust among the parties.

International engagement with Burundi

In addition to these domestic factors, a strong and lasting international involvement with the conflict in Burundi has important explanatory value. Between early 1998 and August 2000, the Arusha peace negotiations process was led by two mediators: initially former President Nyerere of Tanzania and, after his death, former President Mandela of South Africa. In particular Mandela's moral authority came close to the 'divine' intervention required for the miracle of power-sharing in Burundi to become reality. In short, while Nyerere – and Tanzania's lead in imposing regional sanctions upon Burundi – created the situation that gave rise to the mutually hurting stalemate, Mandela – and South Africa's experience with post-apartheid power-sharing – was instrumental in forcing the negotiating parties to accept a power-sharing way out. Inspired by South Africa's legacy and at some points heavily criticized by Tutsi negotiators for considering Hutu as victims of Burundi-style apartheid, Mandela viewed both the causes of the Burundian conflict and the solution in highly ethnic terms (Bentley and Southall 2005, 75). While finding inspiration in the South African case, Mandela was flexible enough not to merely copy-paste the South African model. Several power-sharing modalities, both for the interim and the post-transition period including Mandela's suggestion for a revolving presidency between Hutu and Tutsi, were put on the table until Mandela reached what he considered to be a 'sufficient consensus.' Despite important reservations (in particular from Tutsi hardliners, who had a proven spoiler capacity) and significant skepticism regarding the effectiveness of the deal (in particular because the two main Hutu rebel movements were not involved), Mandela pushed through and even arranged a last-minute flight for US President Bill Clinton to attend the signing ceremony so as to step up the pressure and to make it virtually impossible for Burundi's negotiating parties to reject the deal. As discussed in the following section, international engagement did not end with the signature of the agreement. An Implementation Monitoring Committee (IMC) was established to supervise and coordinate the implementation of the agreement during a transitional period (initially 36 months). The IMC was chaired by a representative of the United Nations and included representatives of the Organization of African Unity and the Regional Peace Initiative for Burundi. While this confirms Andreas Mehler's (2013) finding that norm-diffusing external actors play an important role in the adoption of power-sharing-based constitutional reforms in divided societies, it does not in itself explain the durability of power-sharing in Burundi, which this chapter addresses next.

The miraculous survival of power-sharing?

Doubts have been expressed concerning the added value and the durability of formal power-sharing institutions that are established in the context of largely externally driven negotiation processes, in particular on the African continent. According to Ian Spears, formal inclusion through power-sharing generally proves to be short-lived in countries characterized by weak, dysfunctional or non-existent states. In his view, Burundi is the exception that proves the rule that peace in Africa continues to revolve around issues of resources and patronage rather than institutions (Spears 2013, 49). The impact of neo-patrimonial politics upon power-sharing in Burundi is referred to below and is indeed key to understanding recent dynamics. At the same time, the contribution of the re-engineering of formal political and military institutions to a decade of peace and stability in Burundi stands beyond doubt. This begs the question why, in the particular (and, according to Spears, exceptional) case of Burundi, formal power-sharing has so far survived. Here again, several factors are relevant.

First, unlike in other cases (including South Africa) where power-sharing is deliberately meant to be transitional, Burundi's peace agreements did not contain any sunset clause. Quite to the contrary, as described above, all dimensions of power-sharing were 'written in stone' in a post-transition constitution that can only be altered with a four-fifths majority in Parliament. Aware of their weak electoral base, Tutsi signatories would never have accepted sunset clauses.

Second, power-sharing has been criticized by several scholars for creating perverse incentives. It is said to reward non-institutional and violent political competition and, as a result, provide inspiration to conflict entrepreneurs and politicians who may conclude that there is always a way to negotiate their way to power (LeVan 2011; Tull and Mehler 2005). Given the antecedents Burundi experienced, there was reason to fear that Arusha might not be the last power-sharing deal. When, after the local elections of May 2010, the opposition boycotted the remainder of the 2010 general elections, this was certainly part of their strategy. Recent history (Burundi in 1993, but also Kenya and Zimbabwe in 2008 and 2009) had taught the opposition that an electoral defeat could be negotiated away. However, history also indicates that the use of armed violence is an essential precondition for successfully implementing this strategy. Largely caught by surprise and faced with international approval of the local election process, Burundi's opposition parties – also struggling with a considerable lack of internal cohesion – did not use violence, did not jeopardize peace and failed to renegotiate the 2010 electoral results. However, the aftermath of the 2015 'failed' elections may well promote another round of – violence leading to another round of – power-sharing negotiations. As of early 2016, it is unclear who exactly would be the parties at the negotiations table. However, opposition leaders in exile informally share the view that such power-sharing negotiations between incumbents and opponents – a division which no longer coincides with the pre-Arusha ethnic fault lines – may well be necessary to safeguard the ethnic power-sharing agreed at Arusha and to put a halt to the gradual erosion of Arusha which the Nkurunziza regime set in motion following the 2010 elections.[4] In other words and quite paradoxically, in their view, 'some' violence may well be needed to bring the Nkurunziza regime to the negotiations table and to safeguard Arusha-style peace and stability in the longer run. In January 2016, two rebel movements – one of them led by the May 2015 coup leader General Niyombare – announced an armed struggle to topple the Nkurunziza government.

Third, the architects of power-sharing cleverly designed an electoral system that smoothly matches the compromise reached at Arusha and even fosters a process of socialization with the practice of ethnic power-sharing. This intelligent design may best be illustrated by referring to the electoral lists used in National Assembly elections. The Electoral Code provides for a system of blocked lists, with candidates ranked in a fixed order and voters indicating a party (rather than an individual candidate) of their preference. Of every three candidates on the electoral list, one must be of another ethnic group than the other two. In practice, this means that predominantly Hutu parties (like CNDD-FDD) have one Tutsi candidate ranked in second or third position on the electoral list, and vice versa for predominantly Tutsi parties (like UPRONA). This has two important effects. First, the outcome of the elections is very likely to be more or less in line with the 60 per cent Hutu/40 per cent Tutsi quota imposed by the constitution. Corrections are carried out through co-optation by the Electoral Commission: in addition to the 100 elected MPs, 15 were coopted in 2005, six in 2010 and 21 in 2015.[5] Second, this system adds an important centripetal dimension to ethnic power-sharing in Burundi. Parties need to attract candidates and voters across the ethnic divide and party officials are automatically involved in inter-ethnic exchange and dialogue. This illustrates the importance of harmonic electoral rules for the sustainability of constitutional power-sharing arrangements. Although, as discussed, the 2010 elections had very serious negative consequences for one 'political' pillar (D3) of power-sharing and for political pluralism more generally, ethnic power-sharing (D4) has survived the electoral earthquake thus far. We can however not exclude, as Horowitz suggests, that over time, when the Hutu majority regains its full strength, it no longer sees any interest in maintaining consociation.

Fourth, Burundi confirms the correlation which Hartzell and Hoddie (2007) found between the successful use of power-sharing and the presence of an international peacekeeping operation (see also Walter 2002). The sustained international presence in Burundi has had a military as well as a political dimension. An African Union operation (MIAB) was launched in February 2003 while peace negotiations with the CNDD-FDD rebel movement were ongoing. It was replaced by a UN peacekeeping operation (ONUB) in June 2004. The last troops of the South African peacekeeping contingent left Burundi in December 2009. This military operation went hand in hand with an important political presence to monitor and ensure the implementation of the peace accords. Each year, up until December 2014, the presence of a UN political office in Burundi (BINUB, later BNUB) was extended by the UN Security Council, be it with an increasingly more limited mandate. Burundi was also placed on the UN Peacebuilding Commission's (PBC) agenda in June 2006 and, as of early 2016, a Burundi specific configuration of the PBC under Swiss chairmanship continues to monitor and support the peace and statebuilding process. For more than a decade now, the implementation of the power-sharing arrangements in the Arusha Agreement and subsequent peace agreements has stood at the heart of the mandate of the international peacekeeping and peacebuilding presence in Burundi. To potential spoilers of the peace process it has been consistently made clear that there was no alternative to the settlement agreed at Arusha, a message that resonated less clearly with the gradual retreat of international actors on the ground.

What most national and international observers welcome as sustainable power-sharing may be perceived by some (in particular Hutu) political actors as a problem of immobilism (Horowitz 2014, 11). Some CNDD-FDD members, albeit in small numbers yet gaining strength following the 2015 internal party split, have indeed suggested that there is need for a renegotiation and a loosening of the consociational dispensation. Without requesting an end to consociation, national and international public opinion has been tested (for instance, through messages on government-friendly websites) as to whether it would not be more democratic to adopt 'pure' proportionality instead of proportionality combined with the minority over-representation that Burundi currently applies. The practical consequences of this seemingly more democratic proposal (i.e., reducing the 40 or 50 per cent guaranteed stake for Tutsi to 15 per cent) would be far-reaching and would fundamentally undermine the meaning of ethnic power-sharing in Burundi. Other not yet widely shared opinions have been voiced arguing that Burundi is now no longer ethnically divided (which is correct for the time being in that the main current political cleavages are not ethnic) and that Burundian citizens and their political representation no longer need to be organized along ethnic categories. To make this argument, some CNDD-FDD members find inspiration in the approach Rwanda adopted following the genocide. In Rwanda, ethnicity was officially banned and ethnic divisions 'wished away' through a policy based on integration (rather than accommodation), unity and Rwandan citizenship (Vandeginste 2014a). Such an approach is however in reality rarely devoid of ethnic content and may well amount to a secularized version of the dominant group's rule (McCrudden and O'Leary 2013, 131). This is surely, and quite understandably, how the Tutsi minority in Burundi would perceive such a reform.

The dynamics of power-sharing in Burundi seen from a political *longue durée* perspective

Much of our scholarly thinking around power-sharing and, more generally, about conflict to peace processes in particular countries is event-centred. From a research perspective, in particular for the purpose of comparative case study research, it is understandable to isolate certain transformative developments and periods in the history of a certain state and society. It allows us to code research objects and thus scientifically manage the chaos of transition processes. Two decades of research on Burundi have taught me that there are certain inherent limitations and dangers in that approach. Even the most foundational or sovereign moments, such as the signing of the Arusha Agreement when fundamental rules and institutions were renegotiated, need to be understood as part of a historical continuum. A longer term perspective in the study of even recent or contemporary history is extremely helpful in understanding certain peculiarities of the context-driven development of power-sharing. As explained above, the introduction of power-sharing deeply affected Burundian politics, but, at the same time, Burundian politics deeply affected how its power-sharing 'model' took shape. Even after constitutional earthquakes, deep-rooted political structures are quite stubborn and evolve slowly. Long-standing attitudes, beliefs and orientations concerning the exercise of political authority are essential keys to understanding the reality of power-sharing in Burundi today.

Although this would require more in-depth analysis, there are four aspects of Burundi's 'political culture' (a contested notion which I use here in general terms) that can be connected with the specific dynamics of power-sharing there, and which can help us understand its adoption and maintenance. These aspects are: a tradition of single-party rule, state centralism, militarism and neo-patrimonialism. Taken together, these also help explain why introducing institutions that are commonly used in power-sharing *democracies* did not make Burundi more democratic.[6] Power-sharing stabilized Burundi's state institutions and brought peace, but it would be erroneous to assume that, with the signing of the peace accords and the adoption of a new constitution, deep-rooted governance problems have automatically disappeared.

Ethnic power-sharing and single-party rule

The overwhelming victory of CNDD-FDD in the 2010 elections as well as the erosion of one of the four pillars of power-sharing in Burundi described above

(D3) have produced quasi single-party rule. As the run-up to the 2015 general elections clearly reveals, CNDD-FDD control over the entire state apparatus is such that the distinction between party and state has become a legal fiction rather than an empirical reality. This is strikingly reminiscent of the role played by the former single party UPRONA under the first republic. Under the Constitution of 11 July 1974, "The Party determines the general political orientation of the Nation and inspires the action taken by the State. It controls the Government and the judiciary" (Art. 19); "The Party reflects the profound aspirations of the people. It educates and supports them; it guides them in the realization of its aspirations" (Art. 20, my translation). While it is unthinkable that these provisions could be part of Burundi's constitutional law today, they are a remarkably accurate description of CNDD-FDD's current role in politics and society. The 2015 elections further consolidated CNDD-FDD hegemony but at the same time incumbent President Nkurunziza's third-term ambitions have caused an unexpected internal split within CNDD-FDD. Quite paradoxically, Nkurunziza's ambitions and the resulting turbulence have made the return to stable single-party rule less likely than would have been the case if CNDD-FDD had nominated another presidential candidate. A major difference between the primarily mono-ethnic (Tutsi) UPRONA in the 1970s and the CNDD-FDD today, however, is the multi-ethnic nature of the party leadership and its elected officials. As of early 2015, one-third of its MPs, half of its Senators, four (out of 15) of the party's government ministers and three (out of 14) of its provincial governors were Tutsi. This suggests that CNDD-FDD is a consociational party, i.e., a party that accommodates ethnic segmentation within its own party structures (Bogaards 2014). Further research would be needed to draw firmer conclusions on this particular subject. Yet, two things stand out clearly. First, CNDD-FDD continues to be perceived as a predominantly Hutu party (a notion which is also implicitly referred to in Article 124 of the constitution which requests that the two vice-presidents of the Republic belong to parties with an ethnically different profile). This is due to obvious historical reasons. When it comes to the army in particular, officers continue to be referred to as 'former government army' (ex-FAB, i.e., Tutsi) or 'former rebel movement' (ex-FDD, i.e., Hutu). Also at the level of the party's infamous Imbonerakure youth wing, there is – at the very least and in the absence of scientific research on this – a perception of Hutu dominance. Second, the consociational appearance of the party is, at least in part, the consequence of the sophisticated, centripetal electoral quota requirements referred to above, the ethnically mixed electoral lists in particular. This has certainly had a moderating effect on the behaviour of the party leadership. But this does not mean that the Tutsi constituency perceives CNDD-FDD Tutsi as authentic representatives of the Tutsi, and certainly not as authentic as the members of a 'real' Tutsi party. In any case, while CNDD-FDD dominance over the state is in line with decades of UPRONA single-party rule, the ethnic power-sharing dimension within the party seems new. On closer inspection, however, there is also an important historical antecedent for this apparent novelty.

In 1988, following the army's ruthless suppression of a Hutu uprising in the north of the country, President Buyoya launched a process of political liberation which, in his own words, "inaugurated a policy of power-sharing" in Burundi (Buyoya 1998, 82). Buyoya created a commission in charge of studying the question of national unity and established a government of national unity, led by a Hutu prime minister and composed of an equal number of Hutu and Tutsi. Burundi's first and informal experiment with ethnic power-sharing was not linked to constitutional reform, nor to international mediation or multi-party democracy. It was only after the end of the Cold War that Buyoya also embarked upon democratization, a process that collapsed in October 1993. As of early 2016, Pierre Buyoya is the African Union High Representative for Mali and the Sahel. Behind the scenes, he also remains influential in Burundian politics and – until he spoke out publicly against Nkurunzira's third term – was on good terms with his former enemy. Buyoya's model of ethnic power-sharing under a single party regime undoubtedly continues to provide inspiration to the current regime in Bujumbura. From a historical perspective, the case could be made that it is more home-grown and indigenous than multi-party consociationalism.

This begs another interesting counterfactual question. When negotiating power-sharing in Arusha, some Tutsi representatives proposed that only Tutsi parties should send Tutsi MPs to Parliament, arguing that Tutsi MPs who belong to predominantly Hutu parties are unlikely to defend Tutsi interests. This proposal was rejected. Leaving aside other aspects (including the more centrifugal nature of that kind of dispensation), it is worth asking whether, if that proposal had been adopted, multi-partyism would have fared better.

State centralism

Several authors have warned that, because local-level dynamics are not taken into account, national elite power-sharing bargains risk having no effect at the local level (see, e.g., on neighbouring Democratic Republic of the Congo, Autesserre 2010). Other scholars have found that territorial power-sharing – a dimension which is absent in Burundi – offers the surest way to secure peace (Jarstad and Nilsson 2008). In light of these scholarly insights, it may seem a paradox that, although local-level elites did not play a role in its design or implementation, the power-sharing deal concluded at the national political and military level had an immediate and lasting effect all over Burundi (Simons et al. 2013). Apart from the small size of Burundi's territory, a long-standing tradition of an increasingly centralized pyramidal hierarchy characterizing the exercise of political authority is an important explanatory factor.

Burundi is not a colonial artefact. The kingdom of Burundi, the borders of which correspond roughly to the current ones, was founded towards the end of the seventeenth century (Vansina 1972). According to Thomas Laely, throughout pre-colonial times, monarchical central power was responsible for the functional integration and remarkable cohesiveness of ethnic relations (Laely 1997, 699). In colonial times, the political administration became increasingly centralized and hierarchical (Lemarchand 1966, 432). Despite the apparent rupture that came with the replacement of the monarchy by the republic shortly after Burundi won independence, there was in reality a high degree of continuity between the concept of the traditional monarch and the presidential head of state. In his analysis of the 2014 pre-electoral situation, Christian Thibon (2014) refers repeatedly to Burundi's ongoing "monarchical political culture." In line with these historical roots, national elite consensus has also easily trickled down to the local level because there are no local elites or, more correctly, because local elites are political elites only if they are at the same time national elites. Vice versa, national elites who spend most of their time in the capital city Bujumbura are at the same time also closely connected to their province and commune of origin, and publicly identify themselves as such. Provincial electoral circumscriptions – notably different from Rwanda's one national circumscription (Stroh 2010) – also encourage the maintenance of local networks by national political elites.

Militarism

It may come as a surprise that ethnic power-sharing in Burundi has not collapsed despite the undermining of its political, non-ethnic dimension (D3). The most reasonable explanation seems to be that military rather than political power-sharing was the key variable in Burundi's transition from conflict to peace. As long as military power-sharing holds out – i.e., the defence and security forces do not fall apart into their old constituent parts (the former government forces and the former rebel movements) – power-sharing should survive the political quarrels among civilian, non-military political forces. This, again, is in line with an age-old tradition that military force and political authority inevitably go hand in hand. More accurately, recent history has taught Burundians that there cannot be political authority without military force. For Hutu, the main lesson to be drawn from President Ndadaye's assassination in October 1993 is that a successful accession to political power – even if it is legitimized by the ballot box – is not possible without military force. Lasting approximately three months, Ndadaye was the first Burundian president who was a civilian. A decade after his assassination, CNDD-FDD successfully negotiated its accession to power on the basis of its military nuisance capacity. It is doubtful whether civil–military relations have fundamentally changed since the return of peace to Burundi, despite the constitutionally anchored principle of civilian supremacy over military affairs. It is widely known that real power rests with a group of generals – some of them wearing civilian clothes – around President Nkurunziza. The 2015 internal CNDD-FDD crisis has clearly demonstrated that the military wing rules the party. Not coincidentally, following the 2015 elections, President Nkurunziza's newly appointed senior advisors on civilian affairs are all high-ranking military. Devon Curtis (2013) argues that despite their rhetorical adherence to liberal governance, international peacebuilders have contributed to an order where violence, coercion and militarism remain central.

Neo-patrimonialism

Underneath the surface of constitutional and other reforms of state structures, politics in Burundi is highly determined by a lack of separation between the public and private spheres and by informal networks and relationships in which state resources serve the interests of competing 'patron' elite groups and their 'client' support groups. Here as well, there is a historical continuity between the post-conflict polity and the traditional patronage system which structured societal relations from the king down to the peasant. Viewed from this perspective, power-sharing was a successful conflict resolution tool insofar as it was a non-zero-sum solution that catered to elite interests. It was therefore a rational politico-economic decision for elites on both sides of the ethnic and political divide to accept the internationally proposed power-sharing compromise and the aid carrot that came with it. According to Peter Uvin and Leanne Bayer (2013, 272), what is being rebuilt in Burundi is a neo-patrimonial power structure that replicates the pre-war order, be it with additional elites that control power and resources for their own benefit. Seen from this perspective, the success of power-sharing in Burundi must be understood first and foremost as a function of its ability to reshuffle the stakes of competing political elites in Burundi's neo-patrimonial political marketplace in a way that these elites are willing to abide by (De Waal 2009). This offers a particularly relevant perspective from which to explain the sustainability of military power-sharing in Burundi. At the time of writing, more than 5,400 Burundian troops participate in the AU peacekeeping mission in Somalia (AMISOM). Burundi started deploying a contingent in Somalia in December 2007. Drawn from the new national defence force, these peacekeepers include both Hutu and Tutsi, former government soldiers as well as former rebel fighters. In addition to its beneficial effects in terms of professionalization and socialization with inter-ethnic collaboration (Samii 2013), Burundi's military presence in Somalia also offers major financial benefits to the individual soldiers taking part in AMISOM, the Burundian state and the elites with access to state resources.

Conclusion

Burundi is a fascinating case for the study of the relationship between power-sharing and conflict resolution and political transition in Africa. This chapter addresses what, at first sight, seems to be the miracle of adoption and survival of Burundi's multi-dimensional power-sharing arrangement. On closer inspection, however, there are several domestic and international factors which, taken together, explain the 'success' of power-sharing in Burundi. In general, the Burundi case shows that the institutional engineering of ethnic peace through power-sharing is possible, even in situations of fragile statehood, in particular when there is sustained international involvement and when certain long-standing and 'stubborn' historical political features can be accommodated under the new institutional dispensation.

The prospects for power-sharing in Burundi are mixed. On the one hand, military power-sharing has thus far proven to be resilient, and there has been significant collaboration and socialization between both political and military elites. Important centripetal elements were built into the institutions, showing that centripetalism and consociationalism can complement each other. Furthermore, power-sharing has strongly mitigated ethnic grievances, the main source of violent mass mobilization. On the other hand, the introduction of power-sharing institutions has not produced democratic post-conflict governance. Burundi illustrates the necessary but difficult match between power-sharing and elections. Elections have seen Burundi shift towards more authoritarian de facto single-party rule. While this has so far not had any negative impact upon ethnic power-sharing, renewed premature attempts to revise the current constitutional framework and move away from the Arusha Agreement may have such an impact. The violent dynamics and the unstable outcome of the 2015 elections have fuelled the fear that power-sharing in Burundi faces an uncertain future.

Notes

1 These peace agreements are available in full version on the website *Law, Power and Peace in Burundi*: www.uantwerpen.be/burundi (Section Paix-Peace).
2 More details on these highly complex and typically consociational institutional arrangements and how they are put into practice – which, it is worth stressing, they have been over the past decade – may be found in my earlier publications (Vandeginste 2009, 2014).
3 The Court ruled that, contrary to the Arusha Agreement which imposed a strict two-term limit, the constitution permitted a third term for the first post-transition president because he was indirectly elected by Members of Parliament. While the Arusha Agreement provided for an exceptional indirect modality of the first post-transition presidential elections, the constitution was worded somewhat ambiguously. This enabled the Court to rule that the exception not only applied to the *modality* of the presidential elections but also concerned the application of the term limit to the first post-transition presidency (Vandeginste 2015).
4 Confidential conversations with the author.
5 Co-optation is done by the Electoral Commission in a fairly autonomous way (with a possibility to appeal its decisions before the Constitutional Court, as has happened in a limited number of cases in 2010 and 2015). All parties obtaining a score above the electoral threshold obtain an equal (i.e., not proportional) number of additional representatives in the Assembly. Co-opted members are non-elected candidates ranked below the elected candidates of the same party in different regional circumscriptions, selected so as to enable the 'correction' of the electoral results in terms of ethnic and gender representation.
6 Burundi's Freedom House Index score for 2000 was 6 (1 is the best score, 7 is the worst score). Burundi moved up to a 'partly free' status in 2006 with a score of 4 (5 for civil liberties, 3 for political rights). Between 2007 and 2015, its score moved down to 5.5 (6 for political rights and 5 for civil liberties).

References

Amnesty International. 2014. *Burundi: Locked Down: A Shrinking of Political Space*. London.
Autesserre, Séverine. 2010. *The Trouble with the Congo. Local Violence and the Failure of International Peacebuilding*. Cambridge: Cambridge University Press.

Bentley, Kristina and Roger Southall. 2005. *An African Peace Process: Mandela, South Africa and Burundi*. Cape Town: HSRC Press.
Bogaards, Matthijs. 1998. "The Favourable Factors for Consociational Democracy: A Review." *European Journal of Political Research* 33, no. 4: 475–496.
Bogaards, Matthijs. 2014. *Democracy and Social Peace in Divided Societies: Exploring Consociational Parties*. Basingstoke: Palgrave Macmillan.
Buyoya, Pierre. 1998. *Mission possible: construire une paix durable au Burundi*. Paris: L'Harmattan.
Cheeseman, Nic. 2011. "The Internal Dynamics of Power-Sharing in Africa." *Democratization* 18, no. 2: 336–365.
CIA World Factbook. 2014. Available at www.cia.gov/library/Publications/the-world-factbook/geos/by.html.
Curtis, Devon. 2013. "The International Peacebuilding Paradox: Power Sharing and Post-Conflict Governance in Burundi." *African Affairs* 112, no. 446: 72–91.
De Waal, Alex. 2009. "Mission without End? Peacekeeping in the African Political Marketplace." *International Affairs* 85, no. 1: 99–213.
Hartmann, Christof. 2013. "Territorial Power Sharing and the Regulation of Conflict in Africa." *Civil Wars* 15, S1: 123–143.
Hartzell, Caroline and Matthew Hoddie. 2007. *Crafting Peace. Power-Sharing Institutions and the Negotiated Settlement of Civil Wars*. University Park: Pennsylvania State University Press.
Horowitz, Donald L. 2014. "Ethnic Power Sharing: Three Big Problems." *Journal of Democracy* 25, no. 2: 5–20.
Howard, Lise Morjé. 2012. "The Ethnocracy Trap." *Journal of Democracy* 23, no. 4: 155–169.
International Crisis Group. 2007. *Burundi: Finalising Peace with the FNL*. Brussels.
International Crisis Group. 2012. *Burundi: Bye-bye Arusha?* Brussels.
Jarstad, Anna and Désirée Nilsson. 2008. "From Words to Deeds: the Implementation of Power-Sharing Pacts in Peace Accords." *Conflict Management and Peace Science* 25, no. 3: 206–223.
Karmis, Dimitrios and François Rocher, eds. 2012. *La Dynamique Confiance/Méfiance dans les Démocraties Multinationale: Le Canada sous l'Angle Comparatif*. Ville de Québec: Presses de l'Université de Laval.
Laely, Thomas. 1997. "Peasants, Local Communities and Central Power in Burundi." *Journal of Modern African Studies* 35, no. 4: 695–716.
Lemarchand, René. 1966. "Social Change and Political Modernisation in Burundi." *Journal of Modern African Studies* 4, no. 4: 401–433.
Lemarchand, René. 2007. "Consociationalism and Power Sharing in Africa: Rwanda, Burundi and the Democratic Republic of the Congo." *African Affairs* 106, no. 422: 1–20.
LeVan, Carl. 2011. "Power Sharing and Inclusive Politics in Africa's Uncertain Democracies." *Governance* 24, no. 1: 31–53.
Lindberg, Staffan. 2009. *Democratization by Elections. A New Mode of Transition*. Baltimore, MD: Johns Hopkins University Press.
McCrudden, Christopher and Brendan O'Leary. 2013. *Courts and Consociations. Human Rights versus Power-Sharing*. Oxford: Oxford University Press.
Mehler, Andreas. 2013. "Consociationalism for Weaklings, Autocracy for Muscle Men? Determinants of Constitutional Reform in Divided Societies." *Civil Wars* 15, S1: 21–43.

Ndikumana, Léonce. 2005. "Distributional Conflict, the State and Peace Building in Burundi." *The Round Table: The Commonwealth Journal of International Affairs* 94, no. 381: 413–427.

Norris, Pippa. 2009. "All Elections Are Not the Same. Why Power-Sharing Elections Strengthen Democratization." In *Democratization by Elections: A New Mode of Transition*, edited by Staffan Lindberg, pp. 148–175. Baltimore, MD: Johns Hopkins University Press.

Reyntjens, Filip. 2001. "Chronique Politique au Rwanda et au Burundi." In *L'Afrique des Grands Lacs. Annuaire 2000–2001*, edited by Stefaan Marysse and Filip Reyntjens, pp. 53–74. Paris: L'Harmattan.

Reyntjens, Filip. 2009. *The Great African War: Congo and Regional Geopolitics*. Cambridge: Cambridge University Press.

Reyntjens, Filip. 2015. "Burundi: Institutionalizing Ethnicity to Bridge the Ethnic Divide." In *Constitutions and Conflict Management in Africa: Preventing Civil War through Institutional Design*, edited by Alan Kuperman, pp. 27–50. Philadelphia: University of Pennsylvania Press.

Samii, Cyrus. 2013. "Perils or Promise of Ethnic Integration? Evidence from a Hard Case in Burundi." *American Political Science Review* 107, no. 3: 558–573.

Schneckener, Ulrich. 2002. "Making Power-Sharing Work: Lessons from Successes and Failures in Ethnic Conflict Regulation." *Journal of Peace Research* 39, no. 2: 203–228.

Simons, Claudia, Franzisca Zanker, Andreas Mehler and Denis Tull. 2013. "Power-Sharing in Africa's War Zones: How Important is the Local Level? *Journal of Modern African Studies* 51, no. 4: 681–706.

Sisk, Timothy. 2013. "Power-Sharing in Civil War: Puzzles of Peacemaking and Peacebuilding." *Civil Wars* 15, S1: 7–20.

Stroh, Alexander. 2010. "Electoral Rules of the Authoritarian Game: Undemocratic Effects of Proportional Representation in Rwanda." *Journal of Eastern African Studies* 4, no. 1: 1–19.

Sullivan, Daniel. 2005. The Missing Pillars: A Look at the Failure of Peace in Burundi through the Lens of Arend Lijphart's Theory of Consociational Democracy." *Journal of Modern African Studies* 43, no. 1: 75–95.

Thibon, Christian. 2014. *Les Élections de 2015 au Burundi: Enjeux, Inquiétudes, Espoirs et Inconnu(e)s*. Nairobi: Observatoire des Grands Lacs en Afrique.

Tull, Dennis and Andreas Mehler. 2005. "The Hidden Costs of Power-Sharing: Reproducing Insurgent Violence in Africa." *African Affairs* 104, no. 416: 375–398.

UN Secretary-General. 2015. Statement Attributable to the Spokesperson for the Secretary-General on Burundi. New York, 28 August. Available at www.un.org/sg/statements/index.asp?nid=8937.

Uvin, Peter and Leanne Bayer. 2013. "The Political Economy of Statebuilding in Burundi." In *Political Economy of Statebuilding: Power after Peace*, edited by Mats Berdal and Dominik Zaum, pp. 263–276. London: Routledge.

Vandeginste, Stef. 2009. "Power-Sharing, Conflict and Transition in Burundi: Twenty Years of Trial and Error." *Africa Spectrum* 44, no. 3: 63–86.

Vandeginste, Stef. 2011. "Power-Sharing as a Fragile Safety Valve in Times of Electoral Turmoil: The Costs and Benefits of Burundi's 2010 Elections." *Journal of Modern African Studies* 49, no. 2: 315–335.

Vandeginste Stef. 2014a. "Governing Ethnicity after Genocide: Ethnic Amnesia in Rwanda versus Ethnic Power-Sharing in Burundi." *Journal of Eastern African Studies* 8, no. 2: 263–277.

Vandeginste, Stef. 2014b, "Chronique Politique du Burundi 2013–2014." In *L'Afrique des Grands Lacs. Annuaire 2013–2014*, edited by Filip Reyntjens, pp. 13–36. Paris: L'Harmattan.

Vandeginste, Stef. 2015. "Burundi's Electoral Crisis – Back to Power-Sharing Politics as Usual?" *African Affairs* 114, no. 457: 624–636.

Vansina, Jan. 1972. *La Légende du Passé: Traditions Orales du Burundi*. Tervuren: MRAC.

Walter, Barbara. 2002. *Committing to Peace: The Successful Settlement of Civil Wars*. Princeton, NJ: Princeton University Press.

Zanker, Francisca, Claudia Simons and Andreas Mehler. 2015. "Power, Peace and Space in Africa: Revisiting Territorial Power-Sharing." *African Affairs* 114, no. 454: 72–91.

Zartman, I. William. 1989. *Ripe for Resolution: Conflict and Intervention in Africa*. Oxford: Oxford University Press.

9 Mostar as microcosm
Power-sharing in post-war Bosnia

Sumantra Bose

Twenty years after the Dayton Peace Agreement (DPA) ended the Bosnian war, the future of Bosnia-Herzegovina (BiH) as a joint state of three antagonistic peoples is still uncertain, if not precarious. The hope that cooperation and integration would prevail over time has not materialized. To explain why, this chapter focuses on the city of Mostar in Herzegovina (southern BiH), one of BiH's five largest urban centres, and the chequered history of internationally engineered power-sharing there from the mid-1990s through 2015.

Mostar is an important case study for assessing the governability of power-sharing in post-war BiH because it reflects, in microcosm, its larger Bosnian context. Once a showcase of Titoist Yugoslavia's (1945–1991) ideology of *bratstvo i jedinstvo* (brotherhood and unity), given the city's mix of Croats, Muslims (now Bosniaks) and Serbs, Mostar came to symbolize the ethnic cleansing and population exchanges at the heart of the 1992 to 1995 conflict. A particularly brutal war within the Bosnian war broke out between Croat and Bosniak forces in 1993, the defining moment of which was the destruction of the iconic sixteenth-century *Stari Most* (Old Bridge), which spanned the Neretva River and connected the eastern and western parts of Mostar. The city is also the most (in)famous example of post-war BiH's fractured and polarized condition. Consequently, it has been viewed by the international community as a key test case of whether cooperation, leading to integration and reconciliation, can work in BiH. The protracted international engagement with Mostar represents the travails of the international community's statebuilding project in BiH. At the same time, Mostar also reveals how the 'macro' issues of inter-group relations, and particularly the troubled nature of the Federation of Bosnia and Herzegovina (FBiH), have impacted at the grassroots level. My account of Mostar draws upon field research conducted on numerous visits between 1998 and 2014.

Croat–Bosniak hostilities were ended by the Washington Agreement of March 1994, the terms of which were folded into the Dayton Peace Agreement in November 1995. The bedrock of the Dayton settlement is territorial self-rule for BiH's ethno-national communities – Bosniaks, Bosnian Serbs and Bosnian Croats. The country consists of two 'Entities': the largely self-governing Republika Srpska (RS) and the Bosniak–Croat Federation of Bosnia and Herzegovina (FBiH), which divide BiH's land area almost equally.[1] While the RS is unitary and relatively centralized, the FBiH consists of ten cantons to which most governance is devolved. Five cantons have very large Bosniak majorities, and three have very large Croat majorities. Of the other two, Central Bosnia canton has a sizeable Bosniak majority and a substantial Croat minority, and the Herzegovina-Neretva canton, centred on the city of Mostar, has a slim Croat majority and a very substantial Bosniak minority. These two cantons – areas of fierce Bosniak–Croat fighting during the Bosnian war – were given special power-sharing regimes by the DPA due to their mixed populations, with some governance devolved further from the cantonal to the municipal level.

Public opinion in BiH on fundamental issues of statehood and its form is still sharply polarized two decades after the war's end. A state-wide survey conducted in 2010 revealed that 68 per cent of Bosniaks but only 16 per cent of Bosnian Croats and 5 per cent of Bosnian Serbs believed that BiH "should be a centralized state without Entities and cantons." The same survey, done by PULS-Ipsos, reported that 59 per cent of the FBiH's residents believed that the Bosniak–Croat Entity should be abolished. In the RS, conversely, loyalty to the Entity is very strong, but without any sense of allegiance to the BiH joint state. A PRISM Research survey conducted in 2013 reported that 59 per cent of RS Serbs want the RS to be a fully independent state, 11 per cent want the RS to merge with Serbia and 17 per cent are content with their Entity's 'state-within-a-state' status within BiH.

The Dayton structure of diffused and layered sovereignty fits into one of the four pillars of the consociational model – namely segmental autonomy. The DPA also established institutions with very limited competencies at the common-state (BiH) and FBiH levels. These operate on the basis of the other three pillars of consociation: government by grand coalition at the centre, strict proportionality (often parity) in the allocation of public offices, and veto powers for the representatives of the three groups if a "vital interest" of their community is at risk (Bose 2002, 60–89). Three attributes of the DPA deserve highlighting. First, the Dayton settlement was not only internally but also *externally* confederal. The two Entities were expressly permitted to develop cooperative relationships with neighbouring states and Bosnians are entitled to hold citizenship of other countries (for example, numerous BiH Croats have Republic of Croatia passports).

Second, the DPA tried to balance recognition of ethno-national rights and autonomy with a guarantee of individual human rights: the right of return for refugees and internally displaced persons (IDPs) to their pre-war homes. The war, the driving logic of which was the creation of mono-ethnic territories through mass expulsions, displaced more than half of BiH's 4.4 million people – 1.3 million became refugees and over 1 million were internally displaced. Promotion of 'minority returns' – where expellees return to their original homes in a place now dominated by another ethno-national community – became a top objective of the post-war international supervisory regime of BiH. While some 467,000 minority returnees were recorded across BiH by 2010 as per UNHCR figures, including about 170,000 Bosniaks to the RS – where perhaps 20,000 Bosniaks remained at the end of the war, down from over 500,000 at the beginning of the conflict – this scale of minority return has not restored the pre-war multinational mosaic. The vast majority of BiH's people live today in areas solidly, and often overwhelmingly, populated by their own ethno-national community. The RS is about 85 per cent Serb, while Serbs may be found only as a negligible minority in the territories of the FBiH.

Third, post-war BiH became a laboratory of international peacebuilding and state-making intervention. The apex body was the Peace Implementation Council (PIC), a consortium of 55 governments and international organizations. The top international official on the ground in BiH was (and is) the High Representative (HR), heading up an Office of the High Representative (OHR) with headquarters in Sarajevo and several regional offices, such as OHR-South in Mostar. After 1997, when the PIC significantly enhanced the HR's powers of intervention, the HR functioned as a quasi vice-regal authority for a decade. Meanwhile, a North Atlantic Treaty Organization (NATO)-led peacekeeping force (60,000-strong at its peak in 1996) ensured security, a United Nations mission (UNMiBH) monitored and reformed policing through an International Police Task Force (IPTF) up until 2002, the Organization for Security and Cooperation in Europe (OSCE) organized the early post-war elections, the UNHCR oversaw refugee and IDP returns, and the World Bank, the United States Agency for International Development (USAID) and the International Monetary Fund (IMF) provided reconstruction assistance and expertise. For the first decade after the DPA, BiH had strong characteristics of an international protectorate-cum-trusteeship. The gradual drawdown of international resources and engagement has meant that international involvement has progressively declined to negligible levels over the second post-Dayton decade. In what follows, I detail two distinct periods in Mostar's local power-sharing tribulations and the various international attempts to facilitate power-sharing between the city's Croats and Bosniaks. Before I describe those efforts, an overview of how Mostar has changed – and not changed – over the past two decades would be helpful.

In the early post-war years, Mostar was a very tense and visibly 'abnormal' place. Up until about 2000, very few citizens of either part ever ventured across the de facto dividing line – the frozen frontline of the 1993/1994 armed conflict – running through the city centre. No significant returns of displaced Bosniaks to the city's western (Croat) side occurred until 2001. Two currencies were used in the two parts of the divided city (Croatia's *kuna* on the western side) until 1998, when the BiH Central Bank, under international supervision, introduced the KM (convertible mark) as the single currency for the whole of BiH, gradually overcoming initial opposition in both Serb and Croat areas. Moreover, the threat of violence hung like a pall over the city in the immediate post-war period. In one incident in 1997, one man was killed and some 20 others injured when Bosniaks, trying to pay their respects to kin buried in the wartime Liska Street cemetery located on the Croat side of the city only a few hundred yards from the former frontline, were attacked by a crowd of Croats, consisting of civilians as well as both plain-clothes and uniformed West Mostar police. The last major eruption of violence in Mostar was in the spring of 2001 when there was rioting in West

Mostar during a campaign led by the HDZ-BiH – the dominant political party among BiH's Croats and the sister organization of Croatia's HDZ (Croatian Democratic Union) – against the international supervisors of BiH. The rioting was triggered by an international crackdown on illicit BiH Croat ('Herceg-Bosna') institutions but was rooted in a deeper opposition to the FBiH framework of power-sharing with the Bosniaks.

By 2000, the KM ruled on both sides of the city, as it did across all of BiH, and crossing the 'border' between the two sectors across the former city-centre frontline had ceased to be very dangerous, but citizens still rarely visit the 'other side.' The rebuilt Old Bridge, inaugurated in 2004 at the original's site on the Neretva River as part of a World Bank-UNESCO project, has in recent years become the focal point of a renewal of tourism in Mostar's historic, Ottoman-era *Stari Grad* (Old Town). But the division of Mostar into effectively two cities – a larger, more populous and mostly Croat-populated sector across most of the sprawling west bank, and a smaller and poorer Bosniak sector on the east bank and a slice of the west bank abutting the Neretva – is still entrenched.

In 2009, the think-tank International Crisis Group observed that:

> [O]n the surface, much has been accomplished [through international intervention in Mostar]. The firefighters, emergency services, water utility and large public companies that handle everything from sanitation to road and park maintenance have all been consolidated into single city-wide entities. But the unity is paper-thin. Where duplication once meant two institutions offering the same service to different parts of Mostar, it now means one institution with all key functions doubled and extensive ethnic separation.

The water utility, while run by an "ostensibly unified public company," remained divided: "Every administrative department duplicates this parallel structure, with two incumbents in each post" (International Crisis Group 2009, 11–12). The same applies to the school system. In 2000 a Croat high school named after a Herzegovinian Franciscan priest opened in a repaired section of the *Gimnazija* (the pre-war elite high school) building on the former frontline in the city centre. After Bosniaks objected, OHR-South mediated an agreement which led to the establishment of a Bosniak-run high school – named after Aleksa Šantić (1868–1924), the Serb poet from Mostar, whose name the pre-war institution carried – on the same premises following further reconstruction of the damaged building. The 'two-schools-under-one-roof' phenomenon may be found in some other places in post-war BiH, mostly in towns where relatively significant minority returns have occurred.

Up until mid-2000, Mostar had two entirely separate police forces. After much effort by the UNMiBH and the IPTF, a semblance of an integrated police structure was created. But as a confidential UNMiBH report noted after integration:

> The Bosniak side [still] reports to the Bosniak deputy interior minister [of Herzegovina-Neretva canton] and the Croat side to the Croat minister. [...]

All sections of the ministry have the position of deputy filled by [a member of] the other ethnic group. This creates parallel chains of command.

Joint patrols of one Croat and one Bosniak officer were instituted, yet officers continued to be paid from nominally merged but actually separate budgets in the cantonal Interior Ministry (MUP), with Croat officers paid much more than their Bosniak counterparts. When I asked an UNMiBH official to explain, I was told: "Earlier, they were like accounts in two different banks. Now they are like two different accounts in the same bank."

There are instances where even façade integration has not been possible. Electricity is still a divided service, with the Croat and Bosniak sectors of Mostar receiving their supply separately from different companies that exploit the Neretva's hydro-electric capacity. Likewise, two universities operate in Mostar: the University of Mostar on the west side and the University Džemal Bijedić (the name of the city's pre-war university, named after a prominent Bosniak politician of socialist Yugoslavia who hailed from Mostar) on the east side. Social and cultural life is equally segregated. The diving competition from the reconstructed Old Bridge held every summer is an all-Bosniak event, and Croats congregate at a performance and exhibition centre located on the *Rondo*, a circular junction of six streets in west Mostar.

Visual markers make sure that the divide is etched into the city's skyline. A row-like line of slender minarets of *dzamije* (mosques), mostly built after the war, rise from the streets of the Bosniak west-bank enclave just east of the *Bulevar* (Boulevard), the former frontline. On the other side, a few hundred yards into a street leading west from the Boulevard, stands an imposing Catholic (Franciscan)[2] church with a literally towering spire, whose height (350 feet) dwarfs the line of minarets across the road. The church is a repaired version of a nineteenth-century original, but the monumental bell tower dates to the early 2000s. A gigantic steel-and-concrete cross sits on Mount Hum overlooking the city, from where Bosnian Croat forces shelled and fired on Bosniak-held parts of Mostar during the war. The cross, installed in 2000 ostensibly to commemorate the 2,000th anniversary of Christ's birth, is visible from almost all parts of the city but towers especially conspicuously over the Bosniak sector; its precise location may have been chosen to ensure this. In short, Mostar's condition of soft partition 20 years after the war mirrors that of BiH as a whole.

Local politics in a divided city

Mostar was the first place in BiH to come under an international peacebuilding regime. A European Union Administration of Mostar (EUAM) was established in July 1994, 16 months before the DPA ended the Bosnian war, and lasted up until January 1997. The EUAM's brief was then taken over by a consortium of international agencies (OSCE, UN-IPTF, UNHCR, etc.) with the OHR operating as the coordinator of the joint enterprise. Mostar was viewed by the international community as vital to shoring up the FBiH *and* to the statebuilding agenda for

BiH as a whole. The goal was to reintegrate and eventually reunify Mostar, and fostering power-sharing between the political leaderships of west Mostar and east Mostar was crucial. As part of this effort, the EUAM brokered an Interim Statute of Mostar in 1996, which divided the city into six municipalities, three each in the Croat and Bosniak sectors. The statute also established a "Central Zone" in the ruined city centre, to be administered by a power-sharing city government. The EUAM then organized local elections in Mostar in June 1996, with NATO-led peacekeeping troops providing security. Mostar thus piloted elections in post-war BiH, prior to the first elections to constitute common-state, Entity and cantonal (in the FBiH) institutions in September 1996.

The 1996 Mostar election saw a participation rate of nearly 55 per cent, including many refugee ballots cast in polling centres outside BiH. The Bosniak nationalist Party of Democratic Action (SDA) polled 49 per cent and the Croat HDZ-BiH 46 per cent; a non-nationalist list, which included the Social Democratic Party (SDP-BiH, the former communists), polled only 3 per cent. Twenty years on, party politics remains substantially the same in Mostar. The SDA and the HDZ-BiH are still the dominant parties, although their dominance is no longer as pronounced. The SDP has limited support in the Bosniak part of the city, and smaller Bosniak parties have a minor presence. On the Croat side, the HDZ-BiH has some competition from its splinter group formed in 2006, the HDZ-1990, and smaller Croat parties have also made their presence felt intermittently (notably in the local elections of 2008).

A divided city council, 1996 to 2004

The seats in the 37-member city council elected in 1996 were divided prior to the election on a national quota basis: there were to be 16 Bosniaks, 16 Croats and five 'Others' (namely Serbs). The results gave the SDA list a majority, 21 members including five Serbs, while the HDZ-BiH gained 16 seats. The city council was paralysed from birth. The HDZ-BiH boycotted it until well into 1997, agreeing eventually to token participation on condition that the mayor would be a Croat (with a Bosniak deputy mayor). During the deadlock, there were evictions from their apartments at gunpoint of scores of Bosniak families still living on the western side and the infamous Liska Street incident, described above, also occurred during this time. When the OSCE organized BiH-wide local elections in September 1997, the results in Mostar were substantially unchanged. Safet Oručević, the SDA deputy mayor, became mayor and HDZ-BiH's Ivan Prskalo became deputy mayor.

The city council (and executive) alternated between anaemic and comatose as post-war Mostar evolved in some ways while retaining its fundamental condition of a deeply divided and polarized city. Meanwhile the Central Zone, intended by Mostar's international overseers to serve as a core and a focal point for the city's reintegration, gradually evolved from a ruined 'no man's land' into a buffer zone between the two distinct parts of Mostar. By 2003 the more or less phantom city government had a new Bosniak SDA mayor, Hamdija Jahić, and a new Croat

HDZ-BiH deputy mayor, Ljubo Bešlić. The International Crisis Group (2003, 3) observed:

> The city government – comprising the mayor, deputy mayor and department heads – has not met in formal session for eight months, although it is supposed to meet every week. The city council has been similarly moribund although it is required by the Interim Statute to meet at least every two months. What is most striking is that no one appears to regard this as odd.

The 1996 Interim Statute's major innovation was to create six 'city municipalities' (which I will refer to as 'municipalities') in Mostar, three each in the Croat and Bosniak parts of the city. The municipalities created in the Bosniak sector were Mostar Stari Grad (Old Town), Mostar North and Mostar Southeast. In the Croat sector, they were Mostar Southwest, Mostar West and Mostar South. Each of these six municipalities directly elected its own council (25 members) and each had its own executive headed by a mayor and a deputy mayor. The size of the city council was reduced from 37 to 30 members, of whom ten had to be Croats, ten Bosniaks and ten 'Others' (Serbs), to reflect the city's pre-war ethno-national mix.[3] Eighteen of these 30 city council members were directly elected from the six municipalities (three from each), and 12 in a city-wide competition. Thus almost all Mostarians, barring the small population of the Central Zone, marked three ballots in local elections after 1996: one for their municipal council, one for the three city council members elected from their municipality and one for the city-wide competition. The Central Zone's residents had only one ballot, for the city-wide competition to elect 12 of the 30 members of the city council.

Of the six municipalities, the most populous were Mostar Southwest on the Croat side and Mostar-Stari Grad on the Bosniak side. Mostar West, in the Croat sector, also had a sizeable population, while the other three – Mostar South on the Croat side and Mostar North and Mostar Southeast on the Bosniak side – consisted of less populous suburbs and villages around the city's periphery. Thus the architecture of the city's government was two-layered, with the city council (and executive, headed by the city mayor and deputy mayor) on top of the six municipal councils, each with its own executive headed by the municipality mayor and deputy mayor. Croat hardliners disliked the division of the city's Croat sector into three municipalities. Nonetheless, this was the structure of the city's administration until the local elections of autumn 2004, which took place under a revised framework and procedures specified in a new city statute proclaimed by BiH's international high representative in January 2004.

Power-sharing mechanisms were built into the sub-city, municipal layer of government by the 1996 statute. Thus the three Croat-majority municipalities would each have Croat mayors but Bosniak deputy mayors, and the latter would have charge of returns by refugees and IDPs to the municipality. The same applied, in reverse, to the three Bosniak-majority municipalities (Bosniak mayors and Croat deputy mayors). Moreover, Article 56 of the 1996 Statute specified the ethno-national composition of each of the six 25-member municipal councils. In five of the six municipal councils, no ethno-national group would have a majority (>50 per cent) of the members. Thus the overwhelmingly Croat-populated Mostar Southwest municipality could have a maximum of 12 Croats on its 25-member council, along with six Bosniaks and seven 'Others.' The overwhelmingly Bosniak-populated Stari Grad municipality could likewise have a maximum of 12 Bosniaks on its 25-member council, along with four Croats and nine 'Others.' This formula of dividing seats was based on Mostar's pre-war demographic mix. In only one of the six municipalities, namely sparsely populated and outlying Mostar Southeast, could one ethno-national group have a majority on the council (19 Bosniaks along with three Croats and three 'Others').

The stipulations regarding the ethno-national composition of the city council and the six municipal councils were supplemented by a complex procedure of allocating seats remaining *after* the ethno-national quotas had been filled through the Sainte-Laguë method (a PR-based formula). This additional procedure was designed to favour parties with mixed, multinational candidate lists (see Bose (2002, 120–121) for details).

All this engineering failed to produce the desired effects of cooperation and reintegration. In July 1998 I found out that Marko Rožić, Croat deputy mayor of the Stari Grad municipality since the local elections of September 1997, had not attended his office in the Bosniak enclave of the west bank even once in ten months. In June 1998 Mustafa Skoro, Bosniak deputy mayor of Mostar Southwest since September 1997, started repairing his damaged house located in that municipality. The first night after the repairs began, an empty Bosniak house next to his was firebombed and gutted. Bosniak returns to Mostar Southwest picked up modestly only in 2001 after Wolfgang Petritsch, the international High Representative in BiH from 1999 to 2002, dismissed the hardline Croat mayor of Mostar Southwest in late 1999 along with the head of the municipality's housing department. But 18 years later, this populous area continues to be the core of the emphatically Croat sector of Mostar.

The failure of international designs in Mostar has parallels at higher levels. Under reforms to the Entity constitutions enacted under international supervision in 2002 the RS has two vice-presidents, a Croat and a Bosniak, in addition to the (Serb) president and up to half of the ministers in the RS government are non-Serbs, mostly Bosniaks. The three ethno-national communities have equal representation in the (weak) upper chamber of the RS National Assembly, the Entity's legislature. But this has not changed the character and functioning of the RS as an emphatically *Serb* proto-state. The main reason is that even after minority returns the population of the RS is only about 15 per cent Bosniak (and Croats are negligible), just as the populations of the two parts of Mostar remain largely Croat and very largely Bosniak, respectively. In September 2003 Vjekoslav Kordić, Croat mayor of the suburban Mostar South municipality, admitted that he met with the three mayors of the Bosniak-majority municipalities "only for formal meetings with international officials meant for 'photographing, smiling and getting donations' " (International Crisis Group 2003, 3).

The system of allocating seats on the city council and the municipal councils devised by the international community to favour parties with mixed, multinational candidate lists did not work due to another key constraint: the absence of any parties with cross-ethnic support in Mostar (as in BiH as a whole). In local elections in April 2000, the HDZ-BiH won the majority of seats on all of the three municipal councils in the city's Croat sector. In Mostar Southwest, where Croats were entitled to fill only 12 of the 25 seats, the HDZ-BiH secured 15 seats by strategically nominating several candidates from the remnant Serb community on its list. In Mostar West, another populous inner-city municipality, Croats were entitled to fill only ten of the 25 seats but the HDZ-BiH won 15 seats using the same strategy. In the outlying and less populated Mostar South municipality Croats were entitled to fill 12 of the 25 seats but the HDZ-BiH list won 19 seats, including at least three Bosniaks in addition to several Serbs. Likewise, in all three Bosniak-majority municipalities the SDA-led list won majorities by using the same method of nominating remnant Serbs, although the SDA is a purely Bosniak party and Bosniaks were entitled to fill only 12 of the 25 seats in Stari Grad and 11 of the 25 seats in Mostar North.

In mid-2002 Petritsch finished his three-year term as High Representative. His successor was Paddy Ashdown, a British political figure who served as HR for three and half years, until early 2006. Petritsch noted in 2003 that "during the first one and a half years" of his three-year term he extensively used his decree powers to enact decisions, impose legislation and fire intransigent (elected) Bosnian officeholders of all three communities. However, he then developed doubts about the authoritarian, interventionist approach and tried to popularize the notion of "local ownership" (*samoodgovornost*) of the peacebuilding and state-making process during the second half of his term (interview cited in Bose 2005, 322). But Ashdown resolutely pursued a muscular approach. In 2003 he publicly identified Mostar's reintegration and unification as one of his top priorities and at the start of 2004 declared that he was poised to take action to make it "a modern European city" and rid BiH of "a running sore that can poison the whole body politic of the country" (quoted in International Crisis Group 2009, 3).

By this time, a politically crucial demographic shift had taken place in Mostar. The vote shares of the SDA and the HDZ-BiH in the early post-war elections in the city (June 1996, September 1997) suggested roughly equal Croat and Bosniak populations, plus a tiny minority of Serbs on both sides. When the voter register for BiH-wide general elections in October 2002 to constitute common-state, Entity and cantonal institutions was published, however, it showed that of 65,148 registered voters in the six municipalities and the Central Zone, as many as 45,802 (70 per cent) were residents of the three largely Croat municipalities. Even after considering Bosniak returnees to these municipalities and the Serbs, this suggested that Croats were now a clear majority – possibly approaching as much as 60 per cent – in Mostar. In 2008, this was still largely so. Of the 88,629 registered voters in the six former municipalities – abolished by Ashdown's 2004 city statute but retained as electoral units; see below – 53,917 (61 per cent) were in the largely Croat sector, mostly in Mostar

Southwest (29,522) and Mostar West (17,406). The other 39 per cent (34,712) were in the largely Bosniak sector, well over half (18,977) in Stari Grad. These figures indicate an overall Croat majority. The shift may be due to two factors: more Croats have settled in and around Mostar in the post-war period, mostly from the rural Herzegovinian hinterlands and perhaps central Bosnia, while the Bosniak sector has undergone depopulation, probably because of the lack of employment opportunities. The demographic shift to the advantage of the Croats changed the dynamics of Mostar's politics, and the stances and priorities of its Croat and Bosniak leaders.

Two commissions were formed in Mostar during 2003 at Ashdown's initiative to devise a blueprint for reforming the city's political structure. The first consisted of nine members (three Bosniaks, three Croats and three Serbs) chosen by the Bosniak mayor and Croat deputy mayor from among names submitted by seven political parties. The SDA and HDZ-BiH viewpoints dominated. This commission disintegrated amid acute disagreement and walkouts and resignations by Bosniak representatives. The HDZ-BiH espoused a single city government with its constitutive and operational principles reflecting population proportions, i.e., the Croat majority. It argued that this was the norm in other cities and municipalities of BiH. The SDA rejected this and insisted on parity representation. The SDA was also very keen to preserve the constituent municipalities of the city as statutory bodies with their own elected institutions and budgets.

The divide was revealing. Bosniak politicians and public opinion have always favoured a less parity-based and more majoritarian FBiH, where they outnumber Croats by three to one, as well as a unitary and more centralized state of BiH, where they are probably close to a majority (50 per cent) of the population, outnumbering Serbs by about 1.5:1 and Croats by over 3:1. In Mostar, the SDA stance mirrored the insistence of the Croats on strict parity in the FBiH *and* that of the Bosnian Serbs on the autonomy of the RS, and was based on the same spectre – exaggerated or not – of discrimination, second-class status and worse.

After the commission collapsed, Ashdown appointed a second Commission for Reforming the City of Mostar in September 2003, this time with an international chairman, a German. The Commission was given a three-month deadline until mid-December, and predictably failed. In mid-January 2004 Ashdown told the west Mostar daily *Dnevni List*: "I will solve Mostar." On 28 January 2004, using his sweeping HR decree authority, he proclaimed a new city statute, to come into effect on 15 March 2004. Its preamble noted in passing that "the parties involved in the Commission failed to reach a consensus on two outstanding issues" (OHR 2004a). In fact these were *the* two issues: the constitutive and operational principles of a reconfigured city government and the question of the constituent municipalities. Ashdown simultaneously published a "letter to the citizens of Mostar," decorated with a 'Mostar: Jedan Grad' (Mostar: One City) logo, which asked them to "please make sure [that] your voice is heard by your politicians" (OHR 2004b). This was an example of one of the two doctrinal fallacies of international strategy in post-war BiH: the false distinction between 'good' citizens and 'bad' politicians, overlooking the fact that the clout of the politicians derives from their public support. The other was the search for non-nationalists, almost non-existent in BiH's politics, which consumed and wasted much international energy in the first post-war decade.

One city? Mostar, 2004 to 2015

The 2004 Mostar statute of 58 articles promulgated by Ashdown was based on an implicit philosophy of 'One City, One Government, One Legislature, One Executive.' The statute abolished the six constituent municipalities (and the Central Zone), asserting in the preamble that the municipalities had been "used [...] to create parallel institutions and divide the City." Instead, "the City of Mostar shall be one unit of local self-government." The territories of the abolished municipalities were converted into "six (6) City areas," which would serve as "electoral constituencies" for the purpose of electing 18 of 35 members of a single City Council, three from each area. The other 17 members of the City Council would be elected in a parallel ballot from "the City as one electoral constituency." This dual electoral system was a carry-over from the existing practice, except that the municipalities would no longer exist as autonomous bodies and the number of members of the city council elected in the city-wide ballot increased from 12 (of 30) to 17 (of 35). The statute stipulated a minimum of four and a maximum of 15 City Council members from each "Constituent People" – in effect, this meant that Croats and Bosniaks could have no more than 15 members each on the 35-member Council and Serbs were guaranteed four members (one seat was reserved for 'Others'). The City Council would operate by majority vote except for certain important matters, including amendments to the statute, adoption of the "single and unified" City budget and removal of the mayor, which required a two-thirds majority.

The statute also abolished the de facto co-mayoralty of the city; although described as 'mayor' and 'deputy mayor,' the Croat and Bosniak (or Bosniak and Croat) incumbents of those posts were regarded for practical purposes as co-mayors of the city. Instead, one "Mayor shall represent the City" as "the bearer of the executive authority." Implicitly, the mayor would be a City Council member belonging to the single largest political party on the Council. The single "City Administration" would establish "branch offices [...] in the City areas [the former municipalities] for the sole purpose of delivering [...] services to the citizens within their own neighborhoods." The only other concession made to devolved governance in the city was that the three City Council members elected from each "City Area" could form a "Committee" for their area – thus six such committees – but with a threadbare remit.

This statute was not only a radical departure from the 1996 statute; it also inverted the BiH Election Law's original provisions regarding Mostar. The BiH Election Law was passed by the common-state Parliament in August 2001, by majority vote in its House of Representatives and unanimous vote in its House of Peoples. The Law's Article 14.10 (later deleted) stated that Mostar's City

Council would be indirectly elected by the 150 directly elected members of the six municipal councils and would, in turn, elect its speaker and the city mayor (Bose 2002, 240–241). The 1996 city statute tried to balance devolution with (re)integration and the 2001 Election Law sought to create a bottom-up structure for the city's governance. The statute imposed by Ashdown aimed to create a centralized, top-down structure with embedded power-sharing.

In July 2004 the replica of the Old Bridge across the Neretva was inaugurated in a grand ceremony after three years of construction. The jamboree was covered live by leading international broadcast media and featured on the front pages of newspapers across the world the following day. The reaction in the Croat sector of Mostar ranged from studied indifference to surly hostility. But even in the overwhelmingly Bosniak Stari Grad, skepticism prevailed:

> Local Bosniaks poured scorn on the international obsession with the bridge's alleged wider meaning, such as that voiced by the international community's high representative Paddy Ashdown, who said that the bridge is a cornerstone of Bosnia's reconstruction as a multi-ethnic society. [And] Bosnia could, according to Ashdown, become a bridge between Islamic countries and Europe, helping the two worlds overcome misguided views of each other. [...] "That may be too much reconciliation for one bridge," said a local Bosniak.
>
> (Transitions Online 2004)

In October 2004 local elections were held in Mostar, on the basis of the new city statute, as part of local elections across BiH. The HDZ-BiH emerged as the single largest party, with 14 seats on the 35-member City Council, and the SDA was the second largest party. The impression of stability, and of acquiescence in Mostar to the new statute, was however an illusion. The City Council and administration were minimally functional only because the SDA and the HDZ-BiH already had a shaky cooperation agreement at the higher level of FBiH and BiH institutions. As a by-product of this agreement the two parties entered into a pact regarding Mostar, whereby the HDZ-BiH's Ljubo Bešlić became Mostar's mayor on the understanding that the SDA's candidate would take over as mayor following the next local elections in October 2008.

Croats perceived the 2004 statute as denying the reality of a Croat-majority city, and particularly disliked its limitation of Croat membership of the City Council to 15 of 35, as well as the two-thirds majority requirement on key issues. Both communities – but especially Mostar's Bosniaks, now in thoroughly defensive mode – disliked the abolition of the constituent municipalities. Meanwhile, Ashdown's statute was challenged in the Constitutional Court of FBiH, which upheld the statute on technical grounds in March 2007. In its submission to the FBiH Constitutional Court the Mostar City Council elected in October 2004 noted:

> The former city municipalities lost the status of units of local self-government even though they were opposed to this, and [we] recommend

that if part of the [statute] decision of the High Representative for Bosnia & Hercegovina is found to be unconstitutional, that the Court then rule the whole package of changes by which the municipalities were abolished as units of local self-government to be unconstitutional.

(International Crisis Group 2009, 8)

The tenuous regime established by the 2004 statute unravelled completely following the October 2008 local elections. In Mostar, the Croat vote was badly split for the first time among three parties: the HDZ-BiH, its breakaway faction HDZ-1990 (formed in 2006) and the People's Party-Progress Through Work (NS-RzB), a small party controlled by the Lijanović business family of western Herzegovina. Remarkably, the NS-RzB performed on par with the HDZ-BiH in Mostar in October 2008. The HDZ-BiH and the NS-RzB won seven seats each on the City Council, and the HDZ-1990 won three. Thus, although the three Croat parties totalled 17 seats on the Council, one short of a majority, the HDZ-BiH's tally halved, from 14 seats in 2004. The SDA, with firm support among Bosniaks, won 12 seats and displaced the HDZ-BiH as the single largest party on the City Council. The maverick NS-RzB's success was probably due to disapproval among Croat voters of the rift between the mainstream and breakaway HDZ parties. Under the 2004 pact between the SDA and the HDZ-BiH, the SDA was supposed to get the mayoralty of Mostar for four years from October 2008. The outcome reinforced the SDA's case, since it was the single largest party in both seats and votes: 20,242 votes to HDZ-BiH's 16,258.

The HDZ-BiH however refused to support the SDA's Suad Hasandedić, "widely viewed as a decent and honest politician" (International Crisis Group 2009, 9) among both Bosniaks and Croats, for the mayoralty and insisted that its man Bešlić serve a second four-year term. The complex reasons for the *volte-face* illustrate the problems of functional power-sharing at different institutional levels in BiH.

At the city level this was a venting of the seething resentment, in the HDZ-BiH and among Croats generally, of the 2004 statute's perceived denial of the Croat-majority demography of contemporary Mostar. But the Mostar crisis was also a fall-out from festering 'macro' issues. Most BiH Croats dislike, and many detest, the forced cohabitation with the Bosniaks in the FBiH imposed upon them since the mid-1990s. They would like the asymmetry of the Dayton structure to be corrected and a unitary Croat territorial Entity on the RS model, i.e., a BiH of 'three nations, three Entities' instead of 'three nations, two Entities.' That is rejected by Bosniaks, not because Bosniaks have any attachment to the FBiH but simply to frustrate the Croats. BiH's Croats also have a litany of specific complaints about the FBiH. The accumulation of 'micro' and 'macro' grievances rooted in the dysfunctionality of the FBiH caused the crisis that enveloped Mostar in 2009.

The SDA retaliated against the HDZ-BiH's 'betrayal' by blocking the re-election of Bešlić as mayor. It did so by exploiting an arcane element of the procedure for the election of the mayor by the City Council as specified in the 2004 statute. Between October 2008 and December 2009 there were *17* sessions of the City Council which failed to elect a mayor. By spring 2009 the city institutions of Mostar were paralysed. In addition to no mayor, there was no city budget, because its adoption required a two-thirds City Council majority and the SDA on its own comprised over one-third of the members (12 of 35). From April 2009, the City of Mostar stopped paying its employees. In June and July these employees – including the firefighting unit – went on strike.

On 29 July 2009 the OHR – now headed by Valentin Inzko, an Austrian – issued a "Decision Extending the Temporary Financing of the City of Mostar for the Period from 1 April 2009 to 30 September 2009." The decree "deplor[ed] that as a result of the conduct of the elected city councillors and the parties they represent, the Mayor of the City of Mostar has not yet been elected" (OHR 2009a). On 30 October 2009 the HR issued another "Decision. [...] Ordering Election of the City Mayor of the City of Mostar to be Held." This decree, "deploring that more than one year has passed since the Local Elections were held and the Mostar City Council constituted and the City Mayor of the City of Mostar has yet to be elected," noted that "the City of Mostar has yet to adopt a budget for 2009 and the failure of the City Council of the City of Mostar to elect a Mayor has prevented such adoption, undermining the functionality of the City institutions." It further noted that "none of the sixteen attempts to elect the City Mayor of Mostar through the application of an open ballot in the last year has been successful" (OHR 2009b).

The 2004 statute specified that the election of the mayor be held by secret ballot of the City Council members. On 29 January 2009 the City Council had voted by 31 to 4 to hold the election by open ballot instead; the overwhelming majority strongly suggests a tacit cross-party and cross-ethnic collusion in paralysing the city government. The 30 October 2009 HR decree "repealed" that City Council vote and ordered the city mayor to be elected by secret ballot within 30 days. When this failed to break the logjam – there was one further 'unsuccessful' City Council session to elect the mayor – the HR issued a "Decision Enacting Amendment to the Statute of the City of Mostar" on 14 December 2009. This decree slightly amended the mayoral election procedure to render the SDA's stonewalling ineffective and ordered the mayoral election to be held within three days. The decree also empowered the mayor, once elected, "to proclaim the budget" within three days without the two-thirds majority required by the 2004 statute (OHR 2009c). Three days after this intervention, the HDZ-BiH's Bešlić was elected as mayor and the budget subsequently proclaimed.

The 2009 events rendered the 2004 statute and the structure of city government it established *kaput* (broken). But the *coup de grace* was yet to be delivered. That came when in judgments in mid-2011 and early 2012 on suits filed challenging the 2004 statute, the Constitutional Court of BiH, the apex constitutional court of the common state, ruled the statute unconstitutional on two grounds: the electoral constituencies into which the six abolished municipalities had been converted each elected the same number (three) of city councillors despite being grossly different in population size[4] (which Croats claim discriminates against their more populous sector of the city); and the statute was discriminatory to the (small) population of the abolished 1996 to 2004 Central Zone, which was not made an electoral constituency in 2004 and whose residents could therefore only vote in the city-wide competition, unlike other citizens.

Ashdown's 2004 "Decision Enacting the Statute of the City of Mostar" stated that "the Statute shall be in force on an interim basis until adopted by the City Council of the City of Mostar in due form, without amendments and with no conditions attached." Since neither of the city councils elected subsequently, in late 2004 and late 2008, ever adopted the statute, it remained an interim statute (like the explicitly named 'Interim Statute' of 1996). Once the BiH constitutional court effectively annulled the statute in 2011/2012, the only way it could be revived was by amending it as per the court's judgments. However, before an amendment process could even commence, the City Council needed to first adopt the statute, which it nearly unanimously declined to do (and then, any amendments would require a two-thirds majority to pass). Moreover, any amendments would also need to be approved by the bicameral BiH common-state Parliament, as the process would involve amending the state-wide Election Law. In the months leading up to the October 2012 state-wide local elections, HR Inzko issued a flurry of statements – part exhortation, part plea – to Mostar and BiH lawmakers to act. These appeals were ineffectual and Mostar was the only place in BiH where local elections did not take place in autumn 2012.

Post-2012, Mostar entered "a politically absurd netherworld with no legitimate local government in place" (Moore 2013, 66). The city was as polarized as ever, with Croats calling for majority rule with power-sharing provisions and Bosniaks calling for a solution approximating the 1996 Interim Statute. This situation is not as calamitous as it might sound. In October 2013, a Mostar Croat politician said: "Mostar hasn't had a city council [for a year] [...] and does it show? No." As a think-tank report noted in July 2014, "life goes on" in the city and "Mostar's mayor continues in office" (International Crisis Group 2015, 19), albeit *sans* any city-wide democratic mandate or popular legitimacy. But the shiny new City Hall completed in 2012 on the Boulevard in the city centre – on the Croat side of the former frontline, overlooking the Bosniak sector – stands forlorn and deserted, a monument to the failure of a power-sharing framework devised and dictated by international intervention.

Mostar, Bosnia and power-sharing: some conclusions

In July 2015 HR Inzko published an op-ed in the Banja Luka newspaper *Nezavisne Novine* on the occasion of the approaching twentieth anniversary of the Dayton agreement. He wrote that "most [...] would agree that many of the reforms undertaken [...] in the first ten years after the war [...] were impressive" and that "during the first ten years [...] the Dayton framework allowed the country to make progress" (OHR 2015). This was a tacit admission that the second decade had been different. Indeed, the first decade looks in retrospect almost like a golden period of peacebuilding compared to the second, when BiH stalled and stagnated and the international community seemed helpless and adrift. The sorry saga of Mostar is a prime example.

Yet this trajectory is also counter-intuitive. Things should have got easier and better over time, not the reverse. After making the valid distinction between the very difficult and challenging but promising first decade and the lost, wasted second decade, the international HR's commentary lapsed into blaming BiH's politicians. There was no trace of critical reflection on the international community's role.

As I studied BiH closely during the first post-war decade (Bose 2002, 2005, 2007), I am aware both of the scale of the challenge which the ruined, fractured country represented and of the positive developments enabled even then by international involvement. The former frontlines became porous after a few years and several hundred thousand displaced people were able to return to their original areas. The minimal wherewithal of shared statehood was put in place, such as the single BiH currency from 1998 and the State Border Service, staffed by members of all three ethno-national groups, which has controlled BiH land and air entry and exit points since 2000. The state-wide Election Law of 2001 enabled BiH's admission to the Council of Europe. In 2004/2005 a milestone was reached when defence was brought under the common state and an umbrella BiH army (currently 15,000 personnel) was created. BiH continued to suffer very high levels of unemployment and emigration, especially among younger and educated people, but this is neither unique in the region nor in transitional post-war contexts more generally.[5]

In *Bosnia after Dayton* I argued that "encouragement of cooperation across the dividing lines, not 'integration,' represents the most effective way forward for this fractured society" and as an international strategy, "a clearly defined but relatively modest set of goals may in the end leave the least divisive and most usable legacy for Bosnians themselves, in cooperation with other former Yugoslavs, to build on in the future" (Bose 2002, 138, 272). But the 'integrative' approach continued to dominate international thinking and strategy. An exemplar is Ashdown's 2004 Mostar statute, whose legacy is Mostar's re-emergence since 2009 as *the* symbol of division and polarization in post-war BiH. This was accompanied by equally ill-judged attempts by BiH's international supervisors to force 'integration' at the 'macro' level. In 2005, during Ashdown's term, BiH's international officialdom began a push for "a comprehensive police reform" (International Crisis Group 2014, 24) that would take policing away from Entity jurisdiction in the RS and cantonal jurisdiction in the FBiH, and create a 'national' BiH police force operating under the common state. This was made a condition for the EU to sign a Stabilization and Association Agreement (SAA) with BiH. There was no convincing justification for this. Policing across BiH had slowly improved in the post-war years, including in minority-returnee areas of the RS, particularly due to UNMiBH-IPTF efforts through 2002. Moreover, policing is normally in the jurisdiction of sub-state units of government in federations and other decentralized states. The international manoeuvres were fiercely resisted, especially by the RS, and fizzled out in 2007. The EU eventually concluded a SAA with BiH in mid-2015. One matter which BiH's politicians and public largely agree upon across ethno-national fault lines is the desirability of EU membership (even in the EU's currently troubled situation). As a politician belonging to Milorad Dodik's ruling party in the RS noted in mid-2013: "It is in the RS's interest to be in the EU and that can only be through [the common state of] Bosnia & Hercegovina" (International Crisis Group 2014, 23).[6] Instead of being strategically used, this card was squandered in the misguided quest for 'integration.'

In *Bosnia after Dayton*, I noted that "a pattern has emerged [of] [...] a series of ding-dong battles between the heavy guns of the IC [international community] elite and the lethal snipers among the local elites" and that "the international predicament [...] is perhaps best described by a paradoxical phrase: power and powerlessness" (2002, 7, 9). The later battles over Mostar illustrate this. But to compound the follies of BiH's own international officialdom, the European Court of Human Rights (ECHR) entered the picture in December 2009, coinciding with the collapse in Mostar of the dispensation imposed in 2004 by Ashdown.

In 2006 two BiH citizens, Dervo Sejdić and Jakob Finci, of Roma and Jewish backgrounds, respectively (both tiny minorities in BiH), had complained to the ECHR that the BiH Constitution discriminated against them because only Bosniaks, Serbs and Croats can stand for election to the three-member BiH common-state presidency or become members of the BiH Parliament's indirectly elected House of Peoples. At the end of 2009, the ECHR ruled in their favour by a strong majority vote; its judgment said that those elements of the BiH Constitution did violate the prohibitions on discrimination of the European Convention on Human Rights. One of the dissenting judges wrote that the Sejdić and Finci representations "may appear to be the simplest the Court has had to deal with to date but they may well be, concurrently, among the more insidious" (McCrudden and O'Leary 2013, 479).

In 2008, the three-member BiH state presidency made a presentation to Brussels wishing to formally apply for their country's membership of the EU. The BiH Constitution had to be amended in line with the ECHR's judgment on the Sejdić-Finci case – a practically Herculean and politically infeasible objective – before the EU would consider an application for membership. In 2014, the constitutional reform condition was dropped by the EU after five years and a so-called 'initiative' of the UK and German governments regarding BiH, focused on economic reforms, started to be bandied about instead in late 2014 and early 2015. The belated climb-down and reset was initiated by an intervention in March 2014 by Vesna Pusić, the Social Democratic foreign minister of Croatia (which became an EU member-state in July 2013) that BiH's EU prospects should not be held hostage to constitutional reform conditions.[7] But by 2015 the EU and the 'international community' elements still engaged with BiH were floundering in a Bosnian labyrinth of their own making, and the EU was preoccupied with coping with its own crises. BiH's application to join the EU was eventually accepted by Brussels in early 2016.

Tragically ironic, the international statebuilders paid no attention to the kind of constitutional reform BiH *did* need once a degree of post-war stabilization had been achieved, as it had by 2003 with porous internal borders and sizeable minority returns. In January 2004, the think-tank European Stability Initiative presented a proposal to revise the institutional architecture of the BiH state established by the DPA, with the objective of ensuring BiH's future as a viable federal state. The proposal correctly identified the FBiH as the most dysfunctional as well as unnecessary layer of the political structure. Thus it proposed:

> to progressively abolish the [Bosniak–Croat] Federation, and with it [...] the Entities [...] [to create a] simplified, three-layered federal state – the ten cantons of the current Federation, Republika Srpska, and the Brčko District [...] turning BiH into a normal, European federal system with central, regional and municipal governments.
>
> (European Stability Initiative 2004)

This was a timely proposal, and at once innovative and feasible. It simply necessitated doing away with the FBiH layer of the multi-tiered state structure and, of course, the FBiH was (and is) disliked by Bosniaks and despised by Croats, and regarded as redundant by both. Then the 12 already autonomous units of BiH which remained – the RS, the ten Federation cantons and the Brčko District – would become constituent cantons of the reconfigured federal state in a symmetric arrangement, with the RS the territorially largest and most populous canton. A cantonized BiH on these lines made a lot of sense, and still does. It did not involve any redrawing of internal borders (a Pandora's Box), left the RS undisturbed except for the semantic change from a self-governing 'entity' to a self-governing 'canton,' and at one stroke removed the most unworkable element of the Dayton architecture: the FBiH. As a Sarajevo-based international official noted in 2012: "If we solve the Federation, we solve the state" (International Crisis Group 2014, 18). The municipalities throughout the country would operate as before, and the RS would continue to participate in the limited central (common-state) institutions operated on consociational principles. So would the other cantons – five with very large Bosniak majorities, three with very large Croat majorities and three mixed cantons: Central Bosnia with a Bosniak majority and substantial Croat minority, Herzegovina-Neretva with a Croat majority but very substantial Bosniak minority, and the Brčko District, whose 93,000 residents are about 43 per cent Serb, 27 per cent Croat, 27 per cent Bosniak and 3 per cent 'Other' from estimates based on the October 2013 census.[8]

As the International Crisis Group noted (2014, 40), when "launched [...] in 2004" the proposal had "broad support among leaders of all three [ethnonational] communities."[9] BiH's international officialdom showed no interest. Even as the proposal was being launched in Sarajevo in January 2004, HR Ashdown was finalizing his fiat for the reunification of Mostar. Over the next two years, until the end of Ashdown's tenure in January 2006, the OHR in

Sarajevo concentrated on creating a plethora of phantom common-state ministries and agencies (International Crisis Group 2014, 27–29).

The BiH state of three peoples is precarious for two fundamental reasons. First, the disagreement over the legitimacy of BiH as a sovereign state which led to war in 1992 is still very sharp. As I have noted elsewhere, inverting Clausewitz, post-1995 politics in BiH has substantially been the continuation of the war by other means (Bose 2002, 6). Second, the war left a legacy of deep distrust between the communities that strongly persists, acutely so in locales such as Mostar.

Nonetheless, there is one element of the power-sharing architecture of the post-Dayton state which is workable. This is the empirical diffusion of sovereignty to ethno-national territories born of the war. An example at the 'macro' level is the RS, and an example at the 'micro' level is the structure of self-rule established for the two parts of Mostar by the DPA's "Mostar Annex" and the city's 1996 Interim Statute. In both cases, the bedrock (self-rule) was topped by a superstructure of shared institutions constituted and operated on consociational principles – at the common-state and city levels, respectively. BiH Serbs, a minority in the state-wide context, see the RS's juridical and empirical autonomy as the *sine qua non* of their (grudging) participation in the BiH state. Mostar's Bosniaks, a minority in the city-wide context, want the provisions of the 1996 city statute which gave self-rule status and powers to their part of the city to be restored. The international overseers' attempts to integrate the state, and the city, by eliminating or undermining ethno-national territorial autonomy and replacing it with a centralized form of power-sharing have *not* worked.

A related characteristic of the international approach in post-war BiH has reinforced polarization. International officials constantly emphasized the building of the Bosnian state, and pursued policies of integration and centralization that usually backfired, while ignoring the transnational nature of the Dayton settlement I noted at the outset of this chapter: that it is both internally and *externally* confederal and seeks to encourage open borders and cooperative ties between BiH and its neighbouring states. The international statebuilders' focus on the domestic dimension, and that too with the 'integrative' mindset dominant, was music to the ears of most Bosniaks – though in practice it never went far enough to satisfy them – but anathema to most BiH Serbs and BiH Croats, who believed that the international purpose was to lock them into a state whose legitimacy they dispute. A wiser international strategy would have stressed the DPA's transnational dimension, and encouraged BiH's Serbs and Croats to see the state of BiH – a demographic and cultural microcosm of the former Yugoslavia – not as a prison but as a bridge connecting them to Serbia and Croatia.

There was a saying in the region – "without Bosnia there is no Yugoslavia, and without Yugoslavia there is no Bosnia" – which still holds in the post-Yugoslav era. It has been rightly argued that the way to cope with self-determination disputes that spill across frontiers is "to make a virtue of porous borders and intertwined economies and cultures" by fostering "cross-border economic development and political cooperation" (Talbott 2000). Up until 1992,

Mostar was oriented towards Split, the city on Croatia's southern Dalmatian coast, Tuzla in northeastern Bosnia towards Belgrade, and Banja Luka, the RS capital in the northwest, towards Croatia's capital Zagreb. Had this been factored into the international statebuilding strategy in BiH, it would have helped ease – though not erase – the bitter divides within the country.

In November 1997 Momčilo Krajišnik, then serving as the first Serb member (1996–1998) of the three-member BiH state presidency, said:

> Whether Bosnia will disintegrate completely or whether it becomes stronger depends [...] on economic laws and future circumstances. But that is not something for the current generation. [...] What our children and grandchildren choose to do is up to them.
>
> (Bose 2002, 149)[10]

Twenty years after the end of the Bosnian war, it could be that this convicted war criminal spoke presciently.

Notes

1 According to a BiH-wide census conducted in autumn 2013 – the first since the last Yugoslav-era census of 1991 – BiH has about 3.8 million people, 63 per cent of whom live in the Federation and 35 per cent in the RS; the remaining 2 per cent live in northeast Bosnia's Brčko District, which is governed separately from the Entities but belongs jointly to both. The census is anticipated to show that the ethno-national composition of BiH is approximately 48 per cent Bosniaks, 33 per cent Serbs and 15 per cent Croats (*Dnevni Avaz*, cited in Parliamentary Research Blog 2014). At the outbreak of the Bosnian war in April 1992, BiH's population of 4.4 million was about 45 per cent Bosniak, 35 per cent Serb and 18 per cent Croat.
2 The Franciscan order has been active in BiH since the medieval era and is a very important part of the history of Croats in BiH.
3 In 1992, the vast majority of Mostar's 25,000 to 30,000 Serbs had been expelled from or had fled the city, and very few returned.
4 The two least populous electoral constituencies (former municipalities) on the two sides of Mostar each had fewer than 7,000 voters in 2008. By contrast, the most populous Bosniak-majority electoral constituency, Stari Grad, had nearly 19,000 voters and the most populous Croat-majority one, Mostar Southwest, had almost 30,000 voters.
5 A 2004 BiH-wide survey showed that 62 per cent of BiH residents aged under 30 wanted to emigrate; in 2012 an identical survey revealed a figure of 81 per cent (Balkan Insight 2013).
6 That Serbia is making steady progress towards EU membership through a pragmatic approach, especially on Kosovo, is a major influence on attitudes in RS.
7 On the unfairness of the EU stance towards BiH on the Sejdić-Finci issue, citing examples from long-standing EU states such as Belgium and more recent entrants such as (south) Cyprus, see European Stability Initiative (2013).
8 There would in fact be a non-contentious case for merging the territorially smallest and least populous canton – the Podrinje canton centred on the eastern Bosnia town of Goražde – into the adjacent Sarajevo canton. The Podrinje canton had 25,000 people according to the October 2013 census, overwhelmingly Bosniaks. The contiguous Sarajevo canton had 438,000, largely Bosniaks. Then a federal BiH of 11 cantons would consist of (1) the RS, (2) four very largely Bosniak cantons centred on the cities of

Sarajevo, Tuzla, Zenica and Bihać, (3) three very largely Croat cantons (western Herzegovina, western Bosnia, known as Canton 10, and Posavina on BiH's northeast border with Croatia) and (4) three mixed cantons – Herzegovina-Neretva (centred on Mostar), Central Bosnia and Brčko District – each with power-sharing regimes.
9 Only one sizeable party, the exclusively Bosniak 'Party of Bosnia and Hercegovina' (SBiH) led by Haris Silajdžić, was opposed owing to the SBiH's commitment to the abolition of the RS and the establishment of a unitary and centralized Bosnian state.
10 Krajišnik was the speaker of the BiH Parliament when, in October 1991, the Parliament passed a resolution on BiH's sovereignty by majority (Bosniak + Croat) vote amid outraged opposition from Serb deputies. The Serbs then withdrew from the BiH Parliament, formed their own Parliament, and began preparing for war. Krajišnik was a member of the apex Bosnian Serb political leadership during the war. In 2000 he was arrested at his home outside Sarajevo by international peacekeeping troops and taken to The Hague to stand trial at the ICTY, where he was sentenced in 2006 to 27 years for complicity in crimes against humanity, reduced on appeal in 2009 to 20 years. In 2013 he was released upon completion of two-thirds of his custodial sentence and returned to a hero's welcome in the RS.

References

Balkan Insight. 2010. "Most Young Bosnians Would Emigrate 'Tomorrow', Survey Says." 7 January.
Bose, Sumantra. 2002. *Bosnia after Dayton: Nationalist Partition and International Intervention.* New York: Oxford University Press.
Bose, Sumantra. 2005. "The Bosnian State a Decade after Dayton." *International Peacekeeping* 12, no. 3: 322–335.
Bose, Sumantra. 2007. *Contested Lands: Israel-Palestine, Kashmir, Bosnia, Cyprus, and Sri Lanka.* Cambridge, MA, and London: Harvard University Press.
European Parliamentary Research Blog. 2014. Bosnia 2013 Census. Available at https://epthinktank.eu/2014/01/27/bosnia-2013-census/.
European Stability Initiative. 2004. *Making Federalism Work: A Radical Proposal for Practical Reform.* Berlin: Brussels and Sarajevo.
European Stability Initiative. 2013. *Lost in the Bosnian Labyrinth: Why the Sejdić-Finci case should not Block an EU application.* Berlin, Brussels and Istanbul.
International Crisis Group. 2003. *Building Bridges in Mostar.* Sarajevo and Brussels.
International Crisis Group. 2009. *Bosnia: A Test of Political Maturity in Mostar.* Sarajevo and Brussels.
International Crisis Group. 2014. *Bosnia's Future.* Sarajevo and Brussels.
McCrudden, Christopher and Brendan O'Leary. 2013. "Courts and Consociations, or How Human Rights Courts May Destabilize Power-Sharing Settlements." *European Journal of International Law* 24, no. 2: 477–501.
Moore, Adam. 2013. *Peacebuilding in Practice: Local Experience in Two Bosnian Towns.* Ithaca, NY, and London: Cornell University Press.
Office of the High Representative. 2004a. "Decision Enacting the Statute of the City of Mostar." Sarajevo, 28 January.
Office of the High Representative. 2004b. "High Representative's Letter to the Citizens of Mostar." Sarajevo, 28 January.
Office of the High Representative. 2009a. "Decision Extending the Temporary Financing of the City of Mostar for the Period from 1 April 2009 to 30 September 2009." Sarajevo, 29 July.

Office of the High Representative. 2009b. "Decision Repealing the Conclusion of the City Council of the City of Mostar No. 01–02–10/09 of 29 January 2009 and Ordering Election of the City Mayor of the City of Mostar to be Held." Sarajevo, 30 October.

Office of the High Representative. 2009c. "Decision Enacting Amendment to the Statute of the City of Mostar." Sarajevo, 14 December.

Office of the High Representative. 2015. "Op-ed by the High Representative on the 20th Anniversary of the DPA." Sarajevo, 29 July.

Talbott, Strobe. 2000. "Self-Determination in an Interdependent World." *Foreign Policy* 118: 155–157.

Transitions Online. 2004. "Mostar: The Bridge over the Neretva." 26 July.

10 Power-sharing and the pursuit of good governance
Evidence from Northern Ireland

Joanne McEvoy

Introduction

In deeply divided societies transitioning to stable democracy, new political institutions are faced with the challenge of providing good governance for all citizens. This challenge is particularly pertinent for power-sharing systems whereby representatives of a previously marginalized group are now included in government. In a lively research field, debate continues on the potential benefits and limitations of establishing power-sharing in war-torn territories. Some scholars are skeptical of the potential of power-sharing, especially the consociational variant, to facilitate sustainable peace over time (Taylor 2009; Pospieszna and Schneider 2013; Sisk 2013). Other scholars argue that power-sharing institutions can promote inter-group cooperation and political stability (Hartzell and Hoddie 2003, 2007; O'Leary 2013; McCrudden *et al.* 2016; McCulloch 2014a; McEvoy 2015). But beyond this wider analysis of the impact of power-sharing upon political stability, inter-group cooperation and the pursuit of sustainable peace, we do not know much about whether and how power-sharing systems deliver for citizens in the form of good or effective governance.

Power-sharing theory is relatively silent on the concepts of governance and good governance. Going back to Arend Lijphart, consociational theory assumes that political elites in a grand coalition will cooperate despite their differences and mutual mistrust, owing to a self-negating prophecy (Lijphart 1977, 100). Since segmental/ethnic elites are incentivized to take their places in a cross-communal coalition, consociational theory assumes that they will get on with the business of governing. Theorizing on what makes power-sharing 'work,' scholarly discussions usually pertain to institutional options ranging from electoral design to executive formation procedures, the use of mutual veto rights and segmental autonomy as well as the broader institutional choice between liberal and corporate consociation (McCulloch 2014b). There is considerably less, if any, focus on whether and how power-sharing can help deliver good governance in the post-conflict environment. Arguably, however, the realization of good governance will be important for political stability. If power-sharing governments are unable to provide sufficient levels of good governance, the whole post-agreement edifice will likely be at stake. This chapter explores the relationship between power-sharing and the pursuit of good governance in Northern Ireland. As power-sharing democracy is founded on cross-community government, the chapter seeks to better understand the dynamics of governance in a complex, often fragile setting where the contending groups are in the process of rebuilding community relations.

The concepts of governance and good governance have been subject to considerable debate among academics and policy-makers (see Fukuyama 2013; Gisselquist 2014; Rotberg 2014). Put simply, governance is understood as "the exercise of political power to manage a community's affairs" (Gisselquist 2014, 515; see also Weiss 2000). At a minimum, there is a shared acceptance that good governance requires effective service delivery; that is, governance as performance. Robert Rotberg writes that governance should be understood as "a bundle of deliverables that citizens expect, crave or demand" (2007, 153). Good governance is the provision of several important public goods: the provision of security; the rule of law; the right to political participation; the capacity to pursue economic opportunity; and service provision in terms of healthcare, education and other public services (Rotberg 2014, 515). While measuring good governance is far from a straightforward task (Gisselquist 2014), I draw from Rotberg's work (2007, 2014) to suggest that an evaluation of how a state or government performs on behalf of citizens means identifying policy outcomes. As in majoritarian democracy, good governance in power-sharing systems means performance in service delivery or the provision of 'abundant political goods' for all citizens. I suggest that given the considerable challenges in transitioning from violent conflict to power-sharing democracy, the provision of security and effective security governance is essential to achieving good governance. This chapter pays particular attention to the improved security situation in Northern Ireland (arising from decommissioning, demilitarization and police reform) as evidence of improved security governance, despite the presence of ongoing security challenges. I argue further that clear policy formulation and implementation is crucial to good governance. The chapter explores the ways in which power-sharing in Northern Ireland has impacted upon the ability to formulate and implement policy. It is clear that post-Agreement governance has been replete with challenges, inter-party disagreements, policy stalemates and political crises. In seeking to explain the nature of these difficulties, the chapter arrives at a 'mixed record' assessment: notwithstanding the many challenges, the political institutions in Northern Ireland have stabilized over time and parties appear intent upon maintaining power-sharing.

It is worth noting the rationale for power-sharing in Northern Ireland. Following 30 years of violent conflict, the Good Friday Agreement (GFA) of 1998 established a new set of political institutions with power-sharing government between nationalists and unionists at its core. With internal power-sharing as well as institutions reflecting relations between Northern Ireland and the Republic of Ireland, and between the UK and Ireland, the Agreement provided a compromise to the competing self-determination claims. Existing literature explains why the political parties supported the GFA (Aughey 2001; McIntyre 2001; McEvoy 2015; O'Leary

2001). For nationalists, the GFA contained features for which the moderate nationalist Social Democratic and Labour Party (SDLP) had long campaigned: internal power-sharing plus an 'Irish dimension,' achieved through the creation of the North–South Ministerial Council. For the Ulster Unionist Party (UUP), the Agreement was about cementing Northern Ireland's constitutional position within the UK and ending the violence carried out by the Provisional Irish Republican Army (IRA). Northern Ireland would remain within the UK (based on the consent principle whereby a change to the region's constitutional status would occur only with majority support of the people of Northern Ireland). A significant departure in the Agreement lies in its emphasis on inclusivity. For the first time, republicans, led by Sinn Féin, were prepared to support a peace settlement that did not secure their primary aim of Irish unity. Sinn Féin leaders, including party President Gerry Adams, sought to sell the deal to the republican base by claiming that the new political arrangements would provide an alternative, transitional means to realize a united Ireland while also improving rights on behalf of the nationalist/republican community (Adams 2003, 367–368).

Power-sharing between the two main communities had been a key policy proposal for some time, going back as far as British government papers in the early 1970s which informed the Sunningdale communiqué of 1973 (McEvoy 2015, 39–60). The GFA was novel given the inclusion of several important institutional features, notably the use of the d'Hondt procedure for executive formation (sequential portfolio allocation) and cross-community voting procedures in the assembly (see McGarry and O'Leary, Chapter 3, this volume). Overall, the GFA is a consociational settlement with Lijphart's four features of consociationalism all evident in the Agreement: cross-community executive power-sharing; proportionality; mutual vetoes; and segmental autonomy, albeit the latter to a lesser extent. Scholarly debate continues on whether and how the consociational features have facilitated effective, stable power-sharing in Northern Ireland. I have argued elsewhere that the fully inclusive nature of the GFA was important for the establishment and maintenance of the new political arrangements and arguably helped these institutions 'stick' despite the ongoing challenges (McEvoy 2015, 211). In recent years, there has been considerable discussion about whether the time is right to revise the consociational structures. It may be too early to do so. As Christopher McCrudden and colleagues point out, there is important "accumulated wisdom" regarding the operation of the power-sharing institutions and though Northern Ireland has achieved a great deal under the Agreement, "its progress remains fragile" (McCrudden *et al.* 2016, 54). Given this fragility, it is an opportune time to assess whether power-sharing in Northern Ireland has delivered for its citizens.

Providing improved security governance

Improved security and ongoing security challenges

A balanced appreciation of security governance in Northern Ireland requires a review of the levels of security established since the Good Friday Agreement

(GFA) of 1998 and an assessment of the security sector reforms achieved. On the levels of security since the Agreement, the overall situation has dramatically improved. The numbers of security-related deaths, bombings and shooting incidents have all considerably reduced over time.[1] For example, at the height of the Troubles, there were 470 security-related deaths in 1974 compared to 55 such deaths in 1998, the year the GFA was adopted; since 2004 the number of security-related deaths has consistently remained in single figures annually (Police Service of Northern Ireland 2015). Security-related incidents (including bombings and shootings) have also been much reduced over time: there were 3,208 shooting incidents in 1974, 211 in 1998 and 73 in 2014.[2] With regard to the post-Agreement levels of security, Northern Ireland is undoubtedly a much better place than it was in the 1990s, 1980s and the 1970s. The nature of paramilitary violence, occurring at considerably lower levels, has shifted to intra-group violence in the form of punishment beatings and assaults within both the loyalist and republican communities, with dissident republicans responsible for targeting both the security services and civilians within their own community (Hayes and McAllister 2013, 211–212; McGarry and O'Leary 2009; Morisson and Horgan 2016).

Despite the much improved security situation, challenges remain, most notably in relation to the increase in dissident republican violence since 2007 (see International Monitoring Commission 2010). In recent years, Northern Ireland has witnessed a sustained period of low-level dissident republican activity (see Horgan and Morrison 2011; Morisson and Horgan 2016; Frampton 2012; Frenett and Smith 2012; Whiting 2015). Multiple groupings have been responsible for the violence, particularly the Real IRA (RIRA), the Continuity IRA (CIRA) and Óglaigh na hÉireann (ONH). These groups reject the Agreement and believe in the utility of armed conflict to achieve a united Ireland. Martyn Frampton (2012) points to the process of republican fragmentation that has occurred since the GFA. To explain the increase of dissident republican violence in recent years, he highlights the move on the part of Sinn Féin in late 2006 and early 2007 to support the PSNI and the requirement, pushed by the International Monitoring Commission (IMC), for the Provisional IRA to confirm that it had disbanded its operational structures (Frampton 2012, 231). Frampton suggests that these developments, unpalatable for some republicans, were compounded by Martin McGuinness acting as deputy First Minister alongside the Democratic Union Party's Ian Paisley as First Minister, with misgivings further cemented by Sinn Féin's disappointing electoral performance in the Irish Republic. Since 2009, dissident republicans have been linked to the murders of a prison officer, two police constables and two soldiers.[3] These groups have also been blamed for the murders of several republicans as well as numerous bombings and shooting incidents, hoax alerts and punishment beatings in republican areas (Morisson and Horgan 2016).

Despite posing a very real threat, it is clear that the dissident republican groups are not likely to operate at a similar level to the IRA during the conflict. Not denying the serious nature of the threat, the IMC reported that "in terms of weapons, money, personnel and support the present dissident campaign in no way matches the range and tempo of the IRA campaign of the Troubles" (IMC 2010, 6). The IMC's final report tells of a mixed record on the security front whereby dissident republicans have displayed "classic signs of insurgent terrorism" but "quite unlike the 'Troubles' in its intensity or, we believe, its potential" (IMC 2011, 13). While it is highly unlikely that dissident republicans would be able to bring Northern Ireland back to pre-ceasefire levels of violence, the aim of these groups, however, is to continue to destabilize Northern Ireland with ongoing targeting of the PSNI and other security personnel. In a speech to the UK House of Commons in February 2015, Secretary of State for Northern Ireland Theresa Villiers warned that "a number of small, disparate but dangerous groupings of dissident republican terrorists continue with their attempts to undermine Northern Ireland's democratic institutions through the use of violence" (Villiers 2015). She stated that the threat to Northern Ireland remained "severe" given that these groups "retain lethal intent" and called for ongoing vigilance on the part of the security forces and the general public. A recent assessment of paramilitary activity commissioned by Villiers states that all of the paramilitary groups operating during the conflict "remain a feature of life" in the region with the most serious threat posed by dissident republicans whereby "at any given time, a terrorist attack is highly likely" (Independent Report 2015, 1). Paramilitary groups continue to "cause serious harm to the communities within which they are embedded and undermine support for policing." More positively, however, the report suggests that the leaders of paramilitary groups (excluding dissident republicans) "are committed to peaceful means to achieve their political objectives" (Independent Report 2015, 2).

Decommissioning and demilitarization

The security situation in Northern Ireland has changed dramatically following the decommissioning of paramilitary weapons on the part of republican and loyalist groups. The GFA states that the parties "reaffirm their commitment to the total disarmament of all paramilitary organisations," confirm their intention to work with the Independent International Commission on Decommissioning (IICD) and to achieve full decommissioning within two years (Agreement 1998, 25). As Bill Rolston (2007, 269) notes, the "minimalism" of the statement deferring decommissioning to a later date was difficult for unionists to accept, leading Ulster Unionist leader David Trimble to delay executive formation for 18 months. With IRA decommissioning not secured despite unionist insistence, the ongoing stalemate dominated political debate and led to acrimonious inter-party relations leading to several suspensions, with the final suspension of the first mandate assembly in autumn 2002 amid allegations of an IRA spy ring at Stormont. Seeking to explain the intractability of the decommissioning issue, Kirsten Schulze and M.L.R. Smith (2000, 82–83) point to the tactical and strategic reasoning of the paramilitary groups, with paramilitaries fearing that any handing over of weapons would equal surrender. They note that the IRA's historical legacy was that it was not defeated, having fought the security forces into a stalemate, and that the organization had a tradition of not surrendering arms (Schulze and Smith 2000, 93). Loyalist paramilitaries were also reluctant to decommission, having positioned their use of violence as defence of the Protestant population and as a means to counter any threat of Irish unification. For loyalists, disarmament would have signalled their surrender to the IRA (Schulze and Smith 2000, 93). On the part of republicans, Richards (2001, 79–82) notes that the post-9/11 international strategic environment, the election of George W. Bush as US President and the arrest of three suspected IRA men for training FARC rebels in Colombia put sufficient international pressure on the group to put weapons beyond use. It is also likely that Sinn Féin's electoral success in 2001, eclipsing the SDLP as the largest nationalist party in Northern Ireland, helped persuade the IRA to embark on disarmament, in order to reap potential gains through electoral competition. Following talks with the political parties, the British government agreed to change the deadline for decommissioning from May 2000 to June 2001. The IRA responded by signalling willingness to "initiate a process" whereby it would put its weapons beyond use in the context of a "political process with the potential to remove the causes of the conflict and in which Irish Republicans and Unionists can as equals pursue our respective objectives peacefully" (cited in Schulze and Smith 2000, 78). The IRA then agreed to have its arms dumps inspected by the IICD on three occasions over 2000 and 2001, with the Commission reporting on the "substantial amount of military material" that remained secure and that the IRA had honoured its commitments (IICD 2001). From October 2001, the IRA began a series of decommissioning acts, completing the process of total decommissioning in August 2005. At the end of July 2005 the IRA had "formally ordered an end to the armed campaign" on the basis that there now existed "an alternative way" to bring about Irish unity, instructing all units to dump arms and signalling commitment to work with the IICD to complete the decommissioning process (BBC News Online, 28 July 2005). In September 2005, the IICD confirmed that the decommissioning observed and verified "represent the totality of the IRA's arsenal" and that the IRA had met its commitment to put all weapons beyond use (IICD 2005). In turn, the Loyalist Volunteer Force (LVF) announced that it would stand down its operations. In May 2007, the Ulster Volunteer Force (UVF) and the Red Hand Commando (RHC) announced the end of their violent campaign, followed in November of that same year with the Ulster Defence Association (UDA) announcing it was standing down "with all military intelligence destroyed and as a consequence of this all weaponry will be put beyond use" (UDA 2007). Over the course of 2009 and 2010, decommissioning took place by the UVF/RHC, the UDA on the loyalist side as well as the Irish National Liberation Army and the Official IRA (IICD 2009, 2010).

In addition to progress on decommissioning, the Agreement and its power-sharing structures also facilitated considerable security normalization or state demilitarization. Over the course of the conflict, Northern Ireland had witnessed a significant level of militarization on the part of the British state. At the height of the Troubles in 1972, the British government deployed 43,000 troops in Northern Ireland, a figure reduced to 13,500 by 2000 (Smyth 2004, 545). In the context of army cutbacks, the British government more recently committed to reducing troop levels to 2,000 in 2016 (*Belfast Telegraph*, 6 March 2013). Whereas decommissioning obligations as set out in the Agreement were intended to reassure republicans, demilitarization was ostensibly meant to encourage republicans. The Agreement obliged the British government to help return Northern Ireland to normal security arrangements (Agreement 1998, 25). State demilitarization gathered pace in response to IRA decommissioning. Over time, important progress included the reduction in the number of British army troops, the demilitarization of police stations, the removal of army watch towers, the enactment of replacement counter-terrorism legislation and an end to the regular role of military personnel in law enforcement (IMC 2011, 16). There was also an increased use of jury trials instead of non-jury trials, and the Maze and Crumlin Road prisons closed. As is discussed below, security normalization took a significant step towards inter-party agreement on the devolution of policing and justice powers in 2010.

Policing and justice reforms

The pursuit of good governance in post-conflict power-sharing systems will arguably not be feasible without considerable security sector reform. With the political institutions in Northern Ireland established on an inclusive basis, there was an impetus that policing structures would also secure widespread community support. Policing is a deeply contentious issue in Northern Ireland, with the two communities holding disparate views on the legitimacy of the police force. The existing police force, the Royal Ulster Constabulary (RUC) (with a 92 per cent Protestant workforce), was viewed by the minority Catholic population as wholly biased, intent on maintaining Protestant/unionist control. For unionists, however, the RUC had made huge sacrifices in fighting a war against militant republicanism. Consequently, police reform was to be a central element of the implementation of the Agreement, which heralded "a new beginning to policing in Northern Ireland with a police service capable of attracting and sustaining support from the community as a whole" (Agreement 1998, 26–27). The Agreement also states that, subject to the implementation of the relevant reforms, the British government would move to devolve policing and justice powers to the Northern Ireland Assembly. The details of police reform became the remit of an independent commission, chaired by the former governor of Hong Kong, Chris Patten. The Patten Report made 175 recommendations, including a new name for the police force (renamed the Police Service of Northern Ireland (PSNI)); a new badge and insignia, and a reduction in the size of the force. It also proposed the recruitment of equal numbers of Protestant and Catholic qualified candidates to increase the proportion of Catholic officers from 8 to 30 per cent in ten years (Independent Commission on Policing for Northern Ireland 1999).[4]

Unsurprisingly, the implementation of police reform was a particularly contentious issue that heightened inter-party divisions over the implementation of the Agreement. Unionists felt the proposed reforms went too far and nationalists maintained they did not go far enough to secure support from the Catholic population. In May 2000, the Labour government introduced the Police (Northern Ireland) Bill in the House of Commons at Westminster, met by fierce criticism from the SDLP and Sinn Féin that the legislation did not fulfil the recommendations set out in the Patten Report. The SDLP moved to accept the British government's additional police reforms in August 2001 and agreed to nominate representatives to the Policing Board and to support the new police force, the PSNI (SDLP 2001). Sinn Féin continued to be highly critical of police reform, claiming that the British government's response was to "gut the [Patten] Report and to squander the opportunity for a new beginning to policing" (Sinn Féin 2001). In the years following the suspension of power-sharing in 2002 (2002–2007), the party began to indicate that it might be prepared to consider supporting the PSNI following the restoration of devolution, including the devolution of policing and justice powers to the Assembly. In an effort to achieve agreement between the two largest parties, talks convened at St Andrews in 2006 were largely concerned with, on the one hand, securing Sinn Féin support for the PSNI and, on the other, the Democratic Unionist Party's willingness to share power with republicans. Following the party's indication that it would be prepared to carry out the St Andrews proposals to bring about restored devolution (BBC News Online, 6 November 2006), Sinn Féin convened a special party conference in January 2007 when 90 per cent of around 900 members voted to approve policing (BBC News Online, 28 January 2007). Sinn Féin President Gerry Adams declared that the positive vote "created the opportunity to significantly advance our struggle" and helped "further our primary objective of a united Ireland through the building of greater political strength." Following an Assembly election in March 2007, the parties moved towards the restoration of devolved government in May with the DUP's Ian Paisley as First Minister and Sinn Féin's Martin McGuinness as deputy First Minister (with their parties joined in the executive with ministers from the Ulster Unionist Party and the SDLP).

The time frame for the devolution of policing and justice powers to the Assembly subsequently became a protracted issue for the power-sharing executive. With disagreement over timing and the nomination or election of a Northern Ireland justice minister, the executive ceased to meet for several months. Throughout 2008 and into 2009, the DUP repeated its position that there was not yet "adequate public confidence" in the devolution of policing and justice powers. Despite ongoing talks, on occasion involving the British and Irish governments, a deal on the timing of devolution of policing remained elusive until February 2010. Following the passage of necessary legislation at Westminster, a Department for Justice for Northern Ireland was created in April. Alliance leader David Ford was voted justice minister with the required cross-community approval in the Assembly, the first local politician to take responsibility for policing and justice in 38 years (BBC News Online, 12 April 2010). The devolution of policing and justice powers marked the culmination of efforts on the part of the British government (encouraged by Dublin) and the local parties to transform security governance in Northern Ireland.

The establishment of power-sharing in Northern Ireland has brought about a significant security transformation. Despite the ongoing threat of dissident republican violence there has been tremendous progress, as borne out by the overall improved levels of security and the extent of security sector reform. Even though decommissioning was a frustratingly drawn-out process, we can argue that disarmament on the part of the paramilitaries would not have been possible without the establishment of inclusive power-sharing based on a peace agreement that allowed pro-agreement republicans to claim they were pursuing their objective of a united Ireland via an alternative path. Paramilitary decommissioning then facilitated the British government's progress on security normalization. In addition, even though reform of the RUC was difficult for unionists to accept, and a reformed police service was difficult for nationalists and republicans to support, Sinn Féin's historic vote to support the PSNI helped facilitate the restoration of devolved powers and ultimately provided for the devolution of policing and justice. Northern Ireland is a place very different than before the Agreement and before the ceasefires in the mid-1990s. As a measure of good governance, these security improvements arguably indicate the considerable progress achieved under power-sharing.

Delivering public services

Beyond security considerations, assessing the capacity of power-sharing in Northern Ireland to deliver good governance means evaluating the extent to which the political institutions have delivered for citizens in the form of effective public service delivery. Power-sharing theory assumes that elites will be incentivized to work together, that government will function based on elite accommodation via inter-communal bargaining and cooperation (McEvoy 2015). Empirically, we need to investigate the ways in which power-sharing, particularly consociation, impacts upon policy formulation, implementation and the overall pursuit of good governance. The evidence from Northern Ireland points to a mixed record in terms of governance as performance.

Under the Agreement, the executive is tasked to "agree each year, and review as necessary, a programme incorporating an agreed budget linked to policies and programmes, subject to approval by the Assembly, after scrutiny in Assembly Committees, on a cross-community basis" (Agreement 1998, 10). The three coalitions since 1999 (1999–2002, 2007–2011 and 2011–2016) point to the challenge of reaching a shared policy platform on social and economic policy. Due to the nature of inter- and intra-bloc party competition, and with no requirement for pre- or post-electoral executive formation negotiation (given the use of the d'Hondt procedure for executive portfolio allocation), there has been little in the way of parties sharing strategic policy priorities before assuming office. Once in office, producing a draft Programme for Government usually takes several months. Although the political dynamics of a divided society means that negotiating a shared policy platform may take some time, that the parties have been able to agree on successive policy programmes arguably indicates that power-sharing can at least facilitate executive intentions of realizing good governance. Moreover, it is worth pointing to the benefits of using d'Hondt as a sequential portfolio allocation mechanism, given that it helps avoid protracted negotiations over executive formation (as per political stalemate in Belgium, Bosnia and Lebanon in recent years) which may threaten political stability (McCrudden et al. 2016; McEvoy 2015).

Yet evidence from Northern Ireland highlights the challenge of making power-sharing 'work,' not only in terms of peace implementation but also with regard to the policy process. The potential of power-sharing to deliver good governance has been adversely affected by the start-stop nature of peace implementation with the operation of the institutions finally bedding down after May 2007. As Rick Wilford (2010, 134) notes, this "episodic existence has clearly hamstrung its policy achievements and constrained the extent to which devolution has made a difference to the daily lives of its population." Other research has indicated that the consociational arrangements have "accentuated the potential for fragmentation in public services" (Knox 2015, 24). Colin Knox (2015, 23) reminds us that the design of the executive to include a large number of departments to cover service provision for a population of 1.8 million (12 following the devolution of policing and justice) reflected the political requirement of establishing a sufficient number of portfolios to be shared between the parties in an inclusive coalition.[5] The parties committed to reducing the number of departments to nine, starting with the 2016 election, to provide more efficient service delivery (Northern Ireland Executive 2015). Perhaps owing to the rather large number of executive departments, efforts to promote "joined-up government," whereby different departments work together on cross-departmental policy issues, have been modest. There are, however, recent indications of a growing commitment on the part of departments to pursue a more joined-up approach to policy-making. For instance, the Office of the First Minister and Deputy First Minister created the "Delivering Social Change" initiative in 2012 as a framework set up to tackle poverty and social exclusion. With several ministerial sub-committees, the initiative seeks to streamline departmental efforts to undertake cross-cutting policy formulation and implementation, and has focused on a series of 'signature programmes,' including literacy and numeracy for children, social enterprise hubs, community family support and parenting programmes (see Knox 2015; www.ofmdfmni.gov.uk).

One of the major criticisms of policy-making in Northern Ireland relates to the power of individual ministers to impose policy decisions without achieving consensus with executive colleagues. In the absence of a requirement for the Westminster convention of collective cabinet responsibility, the institutional rules seek to promote consensus. Under the ministerial code, ministers are required to bring policy to the attention of the executive where any matter cuts across the responsibilities of two or more ministers; requires the adoption of a common position; has implications for the Programme for Government; or is significant or controversial. Yet, much attention has been applied to the capacity of ministers to embark on so-called 'solo runs' regarding non-legislative measures. During the first executive (1999–2002) several ministerial decisions further heightened intra-executive tension. For example, Sinn Féin Health Minister Bairbre de Brún took the decision to move maternity services from Belfast City Hospital to the Royal Victoria Hospital, next to the hospital for sick children. The decision was contentious given that the minister's preferred location was in her constituency and because the assembly's Health Committee had voted against the move. In late October 2002, Sinn Féin Education Minister Martin McGuinness announced his plans to end academic selection for entry to secondary education by 2004.[6] Unionist ministers protested at the timing of the minister's announcement, just days before the imminent suspension of the institutions. The future of academic selection continued to spark controversy. At the St Andrews negotiations in 2006, the DUP succeeded in preventing a ban on academic selection. Following the restoration of devolved government in May 2007, Sinn Féin Minister for Education Caitriona Ruane confirmed the abolition of the 11-plus transfer test without any executive agreement on its replacement. The political stalemate on the issue led to a "policy impasse" with grammar schools responding by setting up their own tests, a separate test for each community (Birrell and Heenan 2013). More recent examples include the decision of SDLP Minister of Social Development Margaret Ritchie to end funding to a loyalist community group in respect of paramilitary links, with a high court ruling later determining that the minister had breached the ministerial code (BBC New Online, 30 April 2009). In 2012, DUP Health Minister Edwin Poots maintained a ban on gay blood donation, and banned gay and unmarried couples from adopting children, prompting a row with his executive colleagues (BBC News Online, 22 October 2013). In light of these examples, one media commentator suggested that "ministers and parties operate in their own political cocoons, not just lacking consensus, but not even bothering to try to achieve it" (Curran 2013).

In addition to the issue of departmental 'silos,' some scholarship suggests that policy-making in Northern Ireland has been slow, that the executive has failed to adequately link economic and social policy, and that policy has followed a predominantly neo-liberal agenda (Horgan et al. 2012). In part, these limitations derive from the fact that the governing parties have different ideological standpoints. The DUP and UUP adhere to a neo-liberal agenda (the UUP has been formally linked with the UK Conservative Party), the SDLP is a sister party of the UK Labour Party and Sinn Féin claims to follow a socialist agenda. It is perhaps unsurprising that the formulation of innovative policy is difficult to achieve. To take one example, the parties failed to develop a community relations strategy for some time after 1998 (Nolan 2013, 115–117). During the suspension period, the direct rule administration sought to make progress in this area and published the document, *A Shared Future: Policy and Strategic Framework for Good Relations in Northern Ireland*. With no sense of ownership of the document, the post-2007 executive shelved it and launched the *Programme for Cohesion, Sharing and Integration* in 2010, subsequently assessed as reflecting "a lowest common denominator approach, with no radical policy innovations or special action plans" (Gray and Birrell 2011, 18; OFMDFM 2010). The Office of the First Minister and Deputy First Minister (OFMDFM) has since published the strategy document *Together: Building a United Community* and has recognized that it is time "to move from policy development to implementation and action" based on a series of cross-community initiatives around education, housing, sport, youth volunteering and interface barriers (OFMDFM 2013, 1).

A related issue to overall caution in public policy is the claim that there has been an underwhelming amount of legislation put forward by the executive. Wilford (2010, 147) refers to the "dearth of policy initiatives" and to a "legislative famine" since 2007. Paul Nolan (2013, 147–151) provides an overview of both legislative progress and logjam where the pace of legislation had begun to speed up during the 2007 to 2011 mandate but slowed down again post-2012 in the context of the flags dispute which dominated political debate.[7] An alternative viewpoint notes that the assembly has passed 82 pieces of legislation since 2007 (McCrudden *et al.* 2016). McCrudden and colleagues (2014, 50) claim that this is "hardly the picture of gridlock that the critics like to depict" and note that the Scottish Parliament passed only eight more pieces of legislation during the same period while enjoying the relative legislative freedom of a one-party government. Given the different political constraints faced by the Northern Ireland Assembly compared to other devolved regions in the UK, it will perhaps be more fruitful to compare Northern Ireland's legislative record over time.

In recent years, the pursuit of good governance has been thwarted by an ongoing inter-party row over welfare reform (particularly between the DUP and Sinn Féin). Even though social security is devolved to Northern Ireland, the 'parity principle' means that Northern Ireland is expected to adopt the same welfare reform changes as Scotland, Wales and England. As Ann Marie Gray and Derek Birrell (2011) point out, the difficulty of finding agreement on social policy sometimes reflects the context whereby some policy areas are determined by decisions outside Northern Ireland's political institutions, notably the UK government in London and the EU institutions in Brussels. Following the introduction of austerity measures by the UK government, the Northern Ireland parties have been divided over what form welfare reform should take. Ongoing stalemate eventually led to 11 weeks of inter-party talks, culminating in the Stormont House Agreement of December 2014. The Secretary of State for Northern Ireland, Theresa Villiers, sought to incentivize the DUP and Sinn Féin to reach an agreement on welfare reform, warning that failure to agree to reforms threatens the survival of devolved government in Northern Ireland as a whole. Following ongoing political wrangling during most of 2015, the implementation of the Stormont House Agreement failed to materialize. The inter-party tensions over welfare reform were then overshadowed by the murder of a former senior IRA member Gerard 'Jock' Davison in May 2015, followed by the murder of another republican, Kevin McGuigan, in August. The PSNI claimed that members of the

IRA were involved in McGuigan's murder and that IRA structures remained "broadly in place" (BBC News Online, 22 August 2015). In response to these developments, the UUP withdrew its executive minister and, after a Sinn Féin official was arrested for questioning (and then released), most of the DUP ministers vacated their posts, leaving Arlene Foster as acting First Minister. The Sinn Féin member was later released without charge and the DUP ministers returned to their executive posts in October following an official assessment of paramilitary activity which claimed that the IRA army council still exists but has a "wholly political focus" (BBC News Online, 20 October 2015). In November 2015, after ten weeks of new inter-party talks, the parties agreed to the Fresh Start Agreement, the terms of which saw the Northern Ireland Assembly vote in favour of a motion to allow Westminster to implement the welfare reforms (Northern Ireland Executive 2015).

Despite all of these challenges, power-sharing governance in Northern Ireland has not been devoid of policy achievements. Successes have included the creation of a Commissioner for Children and Young People; the introduction of free medical prescriptions; free public transport for those over the age of 60; the freeze on domestic tax rates; postponement of water charges; an eventual agreement on a community relations strategy and some progress on the reform of public administration. In setting out policy priorities in the Programme for Government (PfG), the executive has also been at pains to set out the benefits of devolution in terms of service delivery. For example, in the PfG for 2015/2016, the executive points to initiatives delivered in the previous mandate. These achievements included the devolution of policing and justice powers; significant foreign and local investment in jobs; the delivery of major infrastructure projects; the physical regeneration of cities and towns; the development of rural and urban communities, and the rollout of broadband networks (OFMDFM 2011). Overall, the record of power-sharing in policy formulation and service delivery is a story of both achievements and challenges. In one sense, the governance of Northern Ireland has been transformed; contemporary governance is far removed from the unionist government of 1922 to 1972 and more legitimate for the wider population than direct rule from London. Even though there may not have been much policy innovation, the parties have remained committed to power-sharing, progressing thorny issues through negotiation.

Conclusions

Research on power-sharing has focused on the capacity of such arrangements to promote political stability and to help avoid conflict recurrence. This chapter seeks to add to existing debates on the potential and limitations of power-sharing in deeply divided polities by focusing on the achievement of good governance under power-sharing structures. I suggest that if we are not yet sure whether and how peace agreements including power-sharing "may evolve into more enduring social contracts" (Sisk 2013, 7), the provision of good governance is an important element in such a transition. For power-sharing to be successful, citizens will need to be satisfied that politics delivers, certainly in terms of ongoing security (low levels of violence) but also that power-sharing can improve citizens' quality of life via tangible policy results.

How well have the power-sharing institutions in Northern Ireland exercised political power to manage the region's affairs? The good governance record in Northern Ireland may be assessed as a mixed bag of important progress amid ongoing challenges. The chapter offers a balanced evaluation of governance achievements and setbacks. The evidence points to the centrality of bringing about much-improved security levels, arguably impossible without power-sharing, and the importance of security sector reform in order to facilitate elite accommodation on wider policy issues. Decommissioning, state demilitarization and police reform are essential elements of the post-agreement political context and must be implemented in order to help provide the basis for progress on public service delivery. Without security transformation, the provision of public goods ranging from healthcare to education and economic development will likely flounder and will be beset with inter-party tensions.

This assessment of post-agreement Northern Ireland helps us consider the extent to which the design of power-sharing institutions helps facilitate good governance. This chapter has shown that the pursuit of good governance in power-sharing systems will likely be a complex task. As discussed above, an ongoing concern in Northern Ireland relates to the autonomy of individual ministers to take unilateral decisions on non-legislative matters without recourse to the wider executive, to operate within their respective departmental 'fiefdoms' and to pursue communal interests. That executive ministers will wish to shore up their party's position is hardly surprising, in whatever political context. In societies transitioning from conflict, it is unsurprising that ministers will seek to adopt policy positions with a particular communal hue. For parties to govern together in a spirit of compromise and for the good of the population as a whole, the further stabilization of the institutions will need to promote more joined-up working and the formulation of more innovative policy.

The Northern Ireland experience reminds us that power-sharing is not a quick fix and that institutional design is not a panacea in deeply divided societies. Power-sharing government established in the aftermath of violent conflict will be consumed with tackling constitutional and security issues as priorities. In defence of institutional design, power-sharing remains an appropriate political arrangement in deeply divided societies as parties are incentivized to take their ministerial seats (subject to sufficient electoral support) and in order to maintain power-sharing they need to deliver for citizens. Much depends, then, on the willingness of the governing parties to make power-sharing work. As Rotberg (2007, 153) writes, "Good governance does not occur by chance. [...] There is no good governance absent intentional, positive leadership." An important lesson from the Northern Ireland case demonstrates that the pursuit of good governance depends on parties' political willingness and ongoing commitments to maintain power-sharing even when they meet with (highly likely) political crises.

Notes

1 Security-related deaths are defined by the Police Service of Northern Ireland (PSNI) as "those which are considered at the time of the incident to be directly attributed to terrorism, where the cause has a direct or proximate link to subversive/sectarian strife or where the death is attributable to security force activity" (www.psni.police.uk/).
2 For security situation statistics since 1969, see the PSNI accompanying Excel spreadsheet to the 2014/2015 security statistics, available at www.psni.police.uk/updates_security_situation_statistics.
3 David Black in November 2012, PSNI Constable Ronan Kerr in April 2011, Constable Stephen Carroll in March 2009, and two soldiers, Patrick Azimcar and Mark Quinsey, also in March 2009.
4 The PSNI's 50:50 recruitment policy lasted up until March 2011 when then-Secretary of State for Northern Ireland Owen Paterson declared that Catholic officers made up 30 per cent of the force (BBC News Online, 22 March 2011).
5 The Northern Ireland Act 1998 devolved power (principally in economic and social policy) from Westminster to the Stormont Assembly. Schedules 2 and 3 of the Act set out the excepted and reserved matters to be retained by Westminster, including defence, immigration policy, taxation, national insurance elections, postal services, the national minimum wage and telecommunications.
6 Academic selection took the form of the '11-plus' exam, taken by (most) pupils in the final year of primary education. The test results were used to govern children's admission to secondary-level education with entry into grammar schools requiring a pass.
7 In December 2012 Belfast City Council voted to change its policy to flying the union flag on 18 designated dates rather than every day of the year. The loyalist community responded by staging violent protests across the city, leading to 201 arrests, 149 people charged, 146 police officers injured and a policing bill of £20 million (Nolan 2013, 160–165).

References

Adams, Gerry. 2003. *Hope and History: Making Peace in Ireland*. Kerry: Brandon Publishers.
Agreement. 1998. *The Agreement: Agreement Reached in the Multi-party Negotiations*. Belfast: Northern Ireland Office, available at www.gov.uk/government/publications/the-belfast-agreement.
Aughey, Arthur. 2001. "Learning from 'The Leopard.'" In *Aspects of the Belfast Agreement*, edited by Rick Wilford, pp. 184–201. Oxford: Oxford University Press.
BBC News Online. 2005. "IRA Statement in Full." 28 July.
BBC News Online. 2006. "SF Decides to 'Follow Agreement.'" 6 November.
BBC News Online. 2007. "Sinn Fein Votes to Support Police." 28 January.
BBC News Online. 2009. "Ritchie Case Cost Taxpayer £300k." 30 April.
BBC News Online. 2010. "David Ford Secures Justice Job." 12 April.
BBC News Online. 2011. "50–50 Policing to End in Six Days says NI Secretary." 22 March.
BBC News Online. 2013. "Court Rules Poots Cannot Appeal Gay Adoption Decision." 22 October.
BBC News Online. 2015a. "Timeline of Dissident Republican Activity." 16 December.
BBC News Online. 2015b. "Kevin McGuigan Murder: Provisional IRA Still Exists, says PSNI chief." 22 August.
BBC News Online. 2015c. "IRA 'Army Council' Still Exists but has 'Wholly Political Focus.'" 20 October.

Belfast Telegraph. 2013. "Northern Ireland Troop Levels to Return to Pre-Troubles Levels." 6 March.

Birrell, Derek and Deirdre Heenan. 2013. "Policy Style and Governing without Consensus: Devolution and Education Policy in Northern Ireland." *Social Policy & Administration* 47, no. 7: 765–782.

Curran, Ed. 2013. "Ministers are Operating in a Political Cocoon." *Belfast Telegraph*, 28 October.

Frampton, Martyn. 2012. "Dissident Irish Republican Violence: A Resurgent Threat?" *Political Quarterly* 83, no. 2: 227–237.

Frenett, Ross and M.L.R. Smith. 2012. "IRA 2.0: Continuing the Long War – Analyzing the Factors behind Anti-GFA Violence." *Terrorism and Political Violence* 24, no. 3: 375–395.

Fukuyama, Francis. 2013. "What is Governance?" *Governance* 26, no. 3: 347–368

Gisselquist, Rachel, M. 2014. "Developing and Evaluating Governance Indexes: 10 Questions." *Policy Studies* 35, no. 5: 513–531.

Gray, Ann Marie and Derek Birrell. 2011. "Coalition Government in Northern Ireland: Social Policy and the Lowest Common Denominator Thesis." *Social Policy and Society* 11, no. 1: 15–25.

Hartzell, Caroline and Matthew Hoddie. 2003. "Institutionalizing Peace: Power Sharing and Post-Civil War Conflict Management." *American Journal of Political Science* 47, no. 2: 318–332.

Hartzell, Caroline and Matthew Hoddie. 2007. *Crafting Peace: Power-Sharing Institutions and the Negotiated Settlement of Civil Wars.* University Park: Penn State Press.

Hayes, Bernadette C. and Ian McAllister. 2013. *Conflict to Peace: Politics and Society in Northern Ireland Over Half a Century.* Manchester: Manchester University Press.

Horgan, Goretti and Ann Marie Gray. 2012. "Devolution in Northern Ireland: A Lost Opportunity?" *Critical Social Policy* 32, no. 3: 467–478.

Horgan, John and John F. Morrison. 2011. "The Rising Threat of Violent Dissident Republicanism in Northern Ireland." *Terrorism and Political Violence* 23, no. 4: 642–669.

Independent Commission on Policing for Northern Ireland. 1999. *A New Beginning: Policing in Northern Ireland.* September, available at http://cain.ulst.ac.uk/issues/police/patten/patten99.pdf.

Independent International Commission on Decommissioning. 2001. *Report on the Third Inspection of IRA Weapons by Martti Athisaari and Cyril Ramaphosa.* 30 May, available at http://cain.ulst.ac.uk/events/peace/decommission/macr300501.htm.

Independent International Commission on Decommissioning. 2005. *Report of the Independent International Commission on Decommissioning.* 26 September, available at http://cain.ulst.ac.uk/events/peace/decommission/iicd260905.pdf.

Independent International Commission on Decommissioning. 2009. *Report of the Independent International Commission on Decommissioning.* 4 September, available at http://cain.ulst.ac.uk/events/peace/decommission/iicd040909.pdf.

Independent International Commission on Decommissioning. 2010. *Report of the Independent International Commission on Decommissioning.* 25 February, available at http://cain.ulst.ac.uk/events/peace/decommission/iicd250210.pdf.

Independent Monitoring Commission. 2010. *Twenty-Fifth Report of the Independent Monitoring Commission.* London: The Stationery Office, available at http://cain.ulst.ac.uk/issues/politics/docs/imc/imc041110.pdf.

Independent Monitoring Commission. 2011. *Twenty-Sixth and Final Report of the Independent Monitoring Commission, 2004–2011 – Changes, Impact and Lessons.* London:

The Stationery Office, available at http://cain.ulst.ac.uk/issues/politics/docs/imc/imc040711.pdf.
Independent Report. 2015. *Assessment of Paramilitary Activity*. Belfast: Northern Ireland Office, available at www.gov.uk/government/publications/assessment-on-paramilitary-groups-in-northern-ireland.
Knox, Colin. 2015. "Sharing Power and Fragmenting Public Services: Complex Government in Northern Ireland." *Public Money and Management* 35, no. 1: 23–30.
Lijphart, Arend. 1977. *Democracy in Plural Societies: A Comparative Exploration*. New Haven, CT, and London: Yale University Press.
McCrudden, Christopher, John McGarry, Brendan O'Leary and Alex Schwartz. 2016. "Why Northern Ireland's Institutions Need Stability." *Government and Opposition* 51, no. 1: 30–58.
McCulloch, Allison. 2014a. *Power-Sharing and Political Stability in Deeply Divided Societies*. London: Routledge.
McCulloch, Allison. 2014b. "Consociational Settlements in Deeply Divided Societies: The Liberal–Corporate Distinction." *Democratization* 21, no. 3: 501–518.
McEvoy, Joanne. 2015. *Power-Sharing Executives: Governing in Bosnia, Macedonia, and Northern Ireland*. Philadelphia: University of Pennsylvania Press.
McIntyre, Anthony. 2001. "Modern Irish Republicanism and the Belfast Agreement: Chickens Coming Home to Roost, or Turkeys Celebrating Christmas?" In *Aspects of the Belfast Agreement*, edited by Rick Wilford, pp. 202–222. Oxford: Oxford University Press.
Morrison, John F. and John Horgan. 2016. "Reloading the Armalite? Victims and Targets of Violent Dissident Irish Republicanism, 2007–2015." *Terrorism and Political Violence* 28, no. 3: 576–597.
Nolan, Paul. 2013. *The Northern Ireland Peace Monitoring Report: Number Two*. Belfast: Community Relations Council, available at http://cain.ulst.ac.uk/events/peace/docs/nipmr_2013-04_full.pdf.
Northern Ireland Executive. 2015. *A Fresh Start: The Stormont Agreement and Implementation Plan*. Belfast: OFMDFM, available at www.northernireland.gov.uk/a-fresh-start-stormont-agreement.pdf.
Office of the First Minister and Deputy First Minister. 2010. *Programme for Cohesion, Sharing and Integration*. Belfast: OFMDFM.
Office of the First Minister and Deputy First Minister. 2011. *Programme for Government 2011–15*, available at www.northernireland.gov.uk/pfg-2011-2015-final-report.pdf.
Office of the First Minister and Deputy First Minister. 2013. *Together: Building a United Community*. Belfast: OFMDFM, available at www.ofmdfmni.gov.uk/sites/default/files/publications/ofmdfm_dev/together-building-a-united-community-strategy.pdf.
O'Leary, Brendan. 2001. "The Character of the 1998 Agreement: Results and Prospects." In *Aspects of the Belfast Agreement*, edited by Rick Wilford, pp. 49–83. Oxford: Oxford University Press.
O'Leary, Brendan. 2013. "Power Sharing in Deeply Divided Places: An Advocate's Introduction." In *Power Sharing in Deeply Divided Places*, edited by Joanne McEvoy and Brendan O'Leary, pp. 1–66. Philadelphia: University of Pennsylvania Press.
Police Service of Northern Ireland. 2015. *Police Recorded Security Situation Statistics*, 12 May. Belfast: PSNI.
Pospieszna, Paulina and Gerald Schneider. 2013. "The Illusion of 'Peace through Power-Sharing': Constitutional Choice in the Shadow of Civil War." *Civil Wars* 15, no. 1: 44–70.

Richards, Anthony. 2001. "Terrorist Groups and Political Fronts: The IRA, Sinn Féin, the Peace Process and Democracy." *Terrorism and Political Violence* 13, no. 4: 72–89.

Rolston, Bill. 2007. "Demobilization and Reintegration of Ex-Combatants: The Irish Case in International Perspective." *Social and Legal Studies* 16, no. 2: 259–280.

Rotberg, Robert I. 2007. "On Improving Nation-State Governance." *Daedalus* 136, no. 1: 152–155.

Rotberg, Robert I. 2014. "Good Governance Means Performance and Results." *Governance* 27, no. 3: 511–518.

Schulze, Kirsten E. and M.L.R. Smith. 2000. "Decommissioning and Paramilitary Strategy in Northern Ireland: A Problem Compared." *The Journal of Strategic Studies* 23, no. 4: 77–106.

Sinn Féin. 2001. *Response to the Revised Implementation Plan on Policing*. 25 August, available at http://cain.ulst.ac.uk/issues/police/docs/sf250801.htm.

Sisk, Timothy. 2013. "Power-Sharing in Civil War: Puzzles of Peacemaking and Peacebuilding." *Civil Wars* 15, no. 1: 7–20.

Smyth, Marie. 2004. "The Process of Demilitarization and the Reversibility of the Peace Process in Northern Ireland." *Terrorism and Political Violence* 16, no. 3: 554–566.

Social Democratic and Labour Party. 2001. *SDLP Response to the Proposals for the New Police Service*. 20 August, available at http://cain.ulst.ac.uk/issues/police/docs/sdlp200801.htm.

Taylor, Rupert. 2009. "Introduction: The Promise of Consociational Theory." In *Consociational Theory: McGarry and O'Leary and the Northern Ireland Conflict*, edited by Rupert Taylor, pp. 1–11. London: Routledge.

Ulster Defence Association. 2007. "Remembrance Day Statement." 11 November, available at http://cain.ulst.ac.uk/othelem/organ/uda/uda111107.htm.

Villiers, Theresa. 2015. "The Northern Ireland Security Situation." Secretary of State for Northern Ireland speech delivered to the House of Commons, 26 February, available at www.gov.uk/government/speeches/villiers-the-northern-ireland-security-situation.

Weiss, Thomas G. 2000. "Governance, Good Governance and Global Governance: Conceptual and Actual Challenges." *Third World Quarterly* 21: 785–814.

Whiting, Sophie, A. 2015. *Spoiling the Peace? The Threat of Dissident Republicans to Peace in Northern Ireland*. Manchester: Manchester University Press.

Wilford, Rick. 2010. "Northern Ireland: The Politics of Constraint." *Parliamentary Affairs* 63, no. 1: 134–155.

11 Good fences make good neighbours
Assessing the role of consociational politics in transitional justice[1]

Kristian Brown and Fionnuala Ní Aoláin

This chapter reflects upon the relationship of transitional justice (TJ) theory and practice and consociational theory and practice to transitional solutions in deeply divided ethnic polities. We address the identity politics of transitional justice and the political forms that enable, define and consume transition with a particular hew to power-sharing and consociationalism-type arrangements in the aftermath of systematic atrocity or sustained repression. We provide a pragmatic, perhaps skeptical, account of the triumph of consociationalism as the preferred transitional accommodation, and point to the 'dark side' of governance arrangements in post-conflict settings with implications for understanding cycles of violence and repeat conflict patterns. We are particularly drawn to exploring the ways in which, despite substantive acknowledgement of the limits of consociationalism, it continues to be the preferred solution offered by internationally and bilaterally mediated peace negotiations as a means to address the governance crisis of deeply divided societies. We address a range of issues, including how transitional justice relates to different forms of power-sharing, the tensions in the *peace vs. justice* debates which are central to TJ theory and practice and how they interact with consociational forms of governance, the relationship between *community vs. individual rights* in consociational settlements, and how the emphasis on TJ theory and practice on 'bottom-up, victim-led' processes engages with consociational debate on *grassroots vs. elite interactions*. We map some of the positive and negative connections between transitional justice and consociationalism, and explore the meeting points between transitional justice, consociationalism and ethno-nationalism. We address some overlapping preoccupations that cut across both transitional justice and consociationalism, in particular their mutual engagement on elites, and explore how both could singularly and cooperatively benefit from a focus on the local.

Consociationalism and its critics: where sits transitional justice?

The critiques of consociational approaches are decades old and have already been addressed in this volume and elsewhere, but we will emphasize a key line of attack: namely that consociationalism entrenches segmental cleavages and leads to ineffective governance and political immobilism. That political freeze is especially damaging to rifted societies, particularly those where the risk of a return to communal violence is present. Centripetalists argue for mechanisms which incentivize inter-ethnic cooperation prior to government formation and encourage cooperation in government (Horowitz 1985; Sisk 1996), while those in the power-dividing camp favour a combination of checks and balances, powerful bodies to protect individual rights and a dispersal of power which is not open to capture by communal or ethnic groups (Roeder and Rothchild 2005). In response, consociationalists have not remained static, responding by nuancing their commitment to mutual veto, grand coalition, cultural autonomy and proportionality in governing structures via liberal consociationalism (McGarry 2007). This latter approach avoids processes of ascriptive identification, which arguably makes segmental cleavages more porous and allows for greater space to support parties built on cross-identity support. Liberal consociationalism is also less wedded to grand coalitions, deeming government representation of a plurality within each communal segment largely sufficient for governance purposes, though arguably this may not be an adequate and stable basis to maintain peace and security (McGarry and O'Leary 2007; O'Leary 2005). More recently, complex consociation has surfaced, employing a commitment to the bones of consociational theory while applying meat from centripetal and power-dividing strategies via commitments to rights protections and the avoidance of ascriptive identification (Wolff 2011).

Complex consociationalism presents itself as a hybrid, and if the Lijphartian (1977) genes remain dominant, it argues that it reflects the real-world accretions and evolutions that have taken place in the application of consociationalism in real-world settings. In particular, notions of sharing out power among segmental cleavages have become refracted through a burgeoning human rights discourse (McCrudden and O'Leary 2013). This rights discourse represents the confluence of two streams; one which looks towards emphasizing equality and protection in the present, and a second which underpins this through mechanisms seeking to deal with the poisonous legacy of large-scale human rights abuses in the past. In the former, human rights jurisprudence has shaped political choices through the insistence that governmental arrangements comport to fundamental norms of non-discrimination and procedural due process.[2] In the latter context, transitional justice, as its name implies, attempts to engage with transitional accountability during and after the realignment of power. As a result, the negotiation and content of TJ has a potential linkage with the power dispersal implicit in consociational deals struck to end or manage conflict. While notions of 'justice,' and thus 'law' beat in the heart of the realignment moment, in practice these lofty ideals must necessarily wade hip deep in the political waters of transition, uncertainty and indeterminate negotiation.

Transitional justice meets consociationalism

The positionality between law and politics will have implications for TJ processes when they must necessarily interact with consociationalism. The inevitability of that engagement is a critical juncture in understanding the overlaps and tensions that frame a transitional justice–consociationalism interface. Underneath their broadly similar interests in underwriting fresh peaceful forms for regulating conduct in conflicted societies, TJ and consociational arrangements differ in their respective ideological foundation. TJ has its origins in a discourse of human rights, which has emphasized protecting the individual against the abuse of power as well as the independent right-bearing entitlements of individuals. This is expressed in a cosmopolitan frame, which elevates a common universal humanity, intrinsic to all, the protection of which is a touchstone of proper social and political organization. TJ has embedded corner-stones of accountability and remedy that inevitably make claims upon political processes and political institutions. Thus, a central part of transitional justice processes involves institutional reform. Years or decades of large-scale abuses and/or conflict leave weakened state institutions that are often not capable of delivering truth, justice and reconciliation. State institutions also need to be reformed in cases where the entire state apparatus took part in or tolerated human rights violations, such as with the army or security forces. All these factors engage the local and international in change processes that criss-cross the lines between the political and the legal.

None of this need be inimical to consociationalism, but the latter's starting point is the group, and a recognition of the reality of associations which form lasting, authentic segmented cleavages. As such, the group (be it ethno-national, ethno-sectarian, or some other iteration of social boundedness) becomes its primary concern and default 'unit of analysis.' Therefore in transitional moments its sights are firmly fixed on group access to power, proportionality of groups in governance, group vetoes and a measure of autonomy for the cultural group. In some fundamental sense political groupings are not subject to any a priori exclusions, limitations or qualifications in a consociational framing; by contrast transitional justice increasingly defines the capacity to engage, negotiate and participate in political settlements through the lens of atrocity crime responsibility, the boundaries of amnesty law and the restrictions on the political participation of perpetrators.

This may imply that TJ and consociationalism will make an ill fit in any realignment of the political order. To be sure, it may seem that some centripetal approaches speak more readily to TJ's cosmopolitanism; Ben Reilly's model incorporates incentivizing actors to reach out for votes beyond their ethnic bloc *and* the creation of a space for centrist, aggregating parties (Reilly 2001, 11). A cosmopolitan discourse, which foregrounds civic and human rights, would provide a ready-made bridging framework. Likewise, power dividing (Roeder and Rothchild 2005), which draws from a well of constitutionalism and rights protections (being so heavily influenced by the US constitutional model) is more palatable to TJ's legal and universalist reference points. The power-dividing and centripetalist prescriptions, it has been noted, have been polemically attacked as somewhat patronizing and utopian, each underrating the authenticity and longevity of group identification (Tonge 2014) – would TJ deserve this pejorative label too? Given its insistence on the interrogation of some of the worst practices that humans, individually and in the name of the group, can inflict upon one another, there is reason to doubt that it lacks a cold-eyed stare. Consociationalism deals with the embeddedness of group identification as a hard fact, to be recognized and regulated; dissolution or realignment of 'groupness' is placed further down the track, rather off the political horizon. If TJ might be uncomfortable with an emphasis on group accommodation as the centre of gravity given its genealogy, nurture – the hybridity of its practical experience – has meant that it can attempt to work alongside consociational processes. There is no magnetic repulsion between the two, but there are a series of real or potential encounters which can both complement or complicate the goals of each.

Interactions between transitional justice and consociational theory? Mapping the positive and negative

Encounters between transitional justice and consociational theory will produce a range of interactions that may be complicated, and possibly exist in tension. Yet other points of intersection between TJ and consociationalism may produce complementary processes and even mutual reinforcement. We map them, not altogether neatly, into 'negative' and 'positive' interactions.

Negative interactions

If early motifs on transitional justice forcibly brought attention to the dilemmas of prosecution and the need for compromise (leading to practices of amnesty and forgiveness), there is now a greater contemporary reliance on the language of preventing impunity and the imperative to prosecute where possible. This is particularly evident in the trenchant emergence of international criminal law, the retreat from using amnesty laws and the emerging requirement that national legal systems perform a meaningful part in enforcing domestic criminal law, whether through the ICC complementarity regime or through the demands of universal jurisdiction for certain core atrocity crimes (Rome Statute; El Zeidy 2002). Other patterns are constant. These include the emphasis on a right to truth for victims, the value of victim acknowledgement and participation in legal processes addressing the past, and the need to provide repair and reparation to victims.

The first potentially negative interaction has been much discussed in the '*peace vs. justice*' debate and follows from these core focal points – the belief that TJ processes, which frustrate amnesties by invoking the need to avoid impunity through prosecution, will undo attempts to compose the elite accommodation necessary for power-sharing. Elite actors who face indictment for gross violations of human rights or humanitarian law will be unwilling to cut a deal which effectively grants power and legitimacy to the institutions which will lock them away; instead they are likely to act as spoilers, if they cannot leverage the deal to block prosecutions (Vandeginste and Sriram 2011). Multiple examples of this phenomenon have played out from the self-given amnesty of General Augusto Pinochet in Chile to the caution in providing for an International Criminal Court (ICC) referral by the Security Council to address the command-and-control responsibility of Bashar al-Assad for systematic human rights and humanitarian law violations in contemporary Syria. The argument runs that a commitment to prosecute will privilege justice for past wrongs at the expense of peace in the present and future; with the risk that a political vacuum will develop that may allow further violence to take place in the absence of a peace deal.

There are other potentially adverse interactions. Consociational institutions rely on a measure of *elite* control of segments, not just elite accommodation (Parry 2005; Lijphart 1977; Pappalardo 1981); the relative stability of the Northern Ireland consociation, for example, is in part due to the electoral dominance, and internal party control, of the Democratic Unionist Party and Sinn Féin. That control becomes highly problematized when elite leaders are identified as responsible for or tolerant of prior human rights violations. Jeremy Levitt among others has argued that once one adds human rights norms to peace agreements establishing power-sharing deals with warlords or chronic human rights abusers, the deals not only become meaningless but also take on a schizophrenic character (Levitt 2006). TJ processes may *kindle the grassroots* by picking at deeply held narratives of conflict, or by pursuing local actors who have strong local power bases. This 'bottom-up' TJ is often ignited by an emphasis on local harms, specific violations and the transformative effect on political mobilizing that can follow on from a rights-based awakening. Elite accommodation may exist at the top, but they may find that certain power levers are unresponsive or resistant due to this kindling at the base. TJ thereby creates unexpected blockages by engaging communities in the practice of ending impunity with unexpected downstream political consequences. Attempts to deal with the human rights violations of the past may simply become *displacement battles* for both elites and grassroots, as hard conflict becomes translated into a battle between narratives that may ultimately undermine trust and seep into the everyday working of consociational institutions. Biting at the heels of these political interactions are concrete national and international processes of criminal law accountability that increasingly populate the transitional justice domain, including criminal trials (e.g., Colombia), restorative justice practices (e.g., Rwanda) and administrative reparations programmes (e.g., Sierra Leone).

Allied to the previous two points, TJ reckoning may provide a usable *forum for ethnic entrepreneurs* who chastise a communal elite with backsliding, rather than supporting the narratives and interests of the group. More assertively, victimhood of their own group spotlighted by TJ may be used as a lever to advance narrow political goals. Either way, TJ can provide a space and resources for processes of ethnic outbidding.

TJ may also affect the *legitimacy* of consociational peace packages. It may act to partially corrode the legitimacy of the state institutions themselves, by continually shining a spotlight on mass violence, which created certain 'facts on the ground' from which a power-sharing peace deal developed. Institutional complicity has also increasingly become the focus of investigation for command-and-control responsibility by both civilian and military leaders, a fact that keeps the impunity spotlight on individuals who paradoxically turn out to be central to the delivery of functional politics in transitional societies. The ethnic cleansing and genocide committed in Republika Srpska, rightfully highlighted by the International Criminal Tribunal for the former Yugoslavia, is nevertheless used by Bosniak nationalists as proof that the Bosnian Serb republic is an entity whose legitimate power is compromised because it is built on genocidal foundations (Majstorović and Turjacanin 2013; Nettelfield and Wagner 2013). Yet if TJ is insufficiently searching in revealing rights abuses, this may eat away at the legitimacy of the consociational deal in total and can have direct repercussions for the functioning of power-sharing deals. Across multiple transitional societies, the long reach of accountability and its capacity to vault generations underpins the tenacity of justice claims in transitional societies, and their ability to hold moral and legal sway on the governance deals made. As Christine Bell argues, international rights bodies are more likely to challenge the workings of consociational mechanisms, if they perceive weakness in the legitimacy of state institutions and founding constitutions (Bell 2013). Moreover, the increased assertiveness of human rights courts in reviewing amnesty agreements, testing their conformity with due process rights, the 'right to truth' and guarantees of non-repetition mean that there can be little comfort that peace agreements or political settlements close the door to future legal claims of legal responsibility by state and non-state actors in transitional contexts.[3] The implications for consociational and power-sharing 'deal-making' are obvious.

Positive interactions

We can also map a series of possible positive interactions. There are a number of ways in which TJ might engage with identities that consociational deals tend to harden to the detriment of pluralism. By providing evidence of wrongdoing and allowing space for unheard stories, TJ may pick away at mythologies of conflict, self-regarding ethnic narratives that merely serve to validate a one-sided view of conflict. Thus it can *'get at the scripts'* of ethnic chauvinism, mitigating their excesses and creating a more complex mosaic from which political compromise and transformation may follow. In this way, specifically as TJ highlights the individualized harm of conflict and repression, the group hollows out, and the essential common vocabulary of loss, grief, damage, redemption and resilience can emerge.

By capturing and floating other narratives, TJ may serve to *humanize* the stories of conflict, opening out discourse about the past to encompass categories other than the major social and political cleavages. Narratives framed in terms of gender, youth, 'good Samaritans,' or smaller minorities that do not form part of the consociational package, may thereby partly *reflavour and complicate ethnic identities* and how communities interacted during periods of extremity (Arthur 2010). In consociations, which have an ascriptive approach to peoplehood when dispersing power, this may help shift societal (and ultimately institutional) discourse towards *validating non-ascriptive identities*, providing a crucial leavening that speaks to liberal consociationalism. TJ may also help *diminish ethnic fears*.

A key driver behind conflict is a sense of physical or cultural insecurity, something which the proportional dispersal of power in consociationalism attempts to address. By addressing large-scale rights abuses, and bedding down commitment to human rights and the rule of law in its discourse, TJ may thus help *reduce fear of further conflict*, or a belief that a group must remain subaltern and a target for future repression (Arthur 2010). A line is drawn; if violence accentuated the initial rupture in group relations, processes of justice attempt a further and cleaner rupture with the past, digging a deep trench that makes a return to the logic of battlefields less likely. As claimed above, TJ may provide space for ethnic entrepreneurs to engage in outbidding as they cherry pick the outworkings of truth recovery or prosecutions; but it need not go wholly their way. The criticism that injecting TJ into a peace process will produce a tension reflecting justice versus peace, that the question of amnesties or opposing impunity will act as a solvent on peacemaking, may also be flawed. *Calibrating amnesties*, introducing gradations and conditions, can mould TJ processes in a way that can attach to peace processing without either stifling peacemaking or accountability; there is evidence that this trend is underway (Mallinder 2008; Mallinder and McEvoy 2011). There is now effectively an outright ban on amnesty for certain egregious international crimes (genocide, crimes against humanity, certain war crimes); yet a defined legal space continues to exist that enables amnesty to apply to other breaches of human rights and humanitarian law. This legal enablement allows for 'deal-making' in the margins of conflict negotiation, and it provides elasticity to induce compliance with conflict-ending sequences (see, e.g., Belfast Guidelines on Amnesty and Accountability 2014). By supplying evidence that challenges or constrains ethnic myths of perpetual victimhood, and providing narrative room for more nuanced forms of identification, TJ may act to *constrain outbidding* if not erase it. Ethnic entrepreneurs could find simplistic one-dimensional narratives of group innocence and injustice, which could be used to mobilize ethnic constituencies, complicated by TJ's unearthing of unpalatable truths or contrasting testimony. The cherry picking of recent history for the purposes of mobilization thus becomes more problematic. Some cherries will remain out of reach, while others will prove as bitter as wormwood.

TJ has also attempted to reduce the ethnic appropriation of court judgments, by *individualizing crime* – projecting crimes against humanity as the result of individual criminal actions rather than the deeds perpetrated in the name of entire communities, something which would act as a splinter under the skin of any consociation. However, mass human rights abuses, by their scale and nature, contain an undeniable collective dimension. Such violations or certain patterns of abuse create a collective trauma and affect entire communities and society as a whole. There are countless instances in the Democratic Republic of Congo (DRC) of local communities being identified by reference to a massacre that took place during the war. As Théo Boutruche notes, the effect of a slew of atrocities committed by the Lord's Resistance Army (LRA) in the DRC, Uganda, South Sudan or the Central African Republic prompted international actors to talk of "LRA-affected communities" (Boutruche 2013, 308). In this context, while harms may be individual they have an undeniable communal dimension and to be effective TJ processes must address holistically this collective dimension. Invariably, there are tensions and trade-offs between individual and collective truth-recovery enterprises; one approach chosen over the other can lead to markedly different results in the legitimacy, breath and depth of truth-recovery processes. Efforts to establish the truth in the former Yugoslavia illustrate the complexity of collective truth-seeking and modalities of denial by local communities. As Janine Clark suggests, in Bosnia-Herzegovina,

> [T]here are essentially three ethnic versions of truth – the Bosnian Serb, the Bosnian Muslim and the Bosnian Croat – that quintessentially disagree on what happened during the country's three year war, on who were the aggressors and who were the principal victims.
> (Clark 2011, 248)

This, despite the trials at the ICTY. Clark further suggests that due in part to the persistency of denial, "truth in post conflict societies is a far more ambiguous and problematic concept than supporters of criminal trials and truth and reconciliation commissions sometimes appear to assume" (Clark 2011, 242). But this complex truth terrain is not divorced from the perceived (and actual) political success or failure of peace and political settlement.

Within this frame we determine a significant failure. The ethnic frame of society and politics more usually depicts acquittals of one's own group members or prosecutions of a communal 'other' as vindication for one's group. The successful pursuit of members of one's own group is often downplayed, or cast as proof of the inherent group bias against an ethnic community by international or domestic mechanisms. Ethnic identity is a strong adhesive, and in nationalistic forms proves effective in selectively marshalling the past to its purposes. Consociationalism recognizes the adhesive and mobilizing power of ethno-nationalism; yet TJ has something to add too, since it acts in the same ecology as ethno-nationalism – the contested past.

Thus, despite the theoretical occlusion of transitional justice theory from discourses concerning governance and government forms, this preliminary mapping demonstrates the ways in which transitional justice practice intrudes on post-conflict governance arrangements in contested transitional polities. Transitional justice, by virtue of its multiple forms and its indeterminate time lines, plays the role of consistently and unpredictably engaging collectives and individuals in ways that can both upend and reframe consociational politics. Transitional justice discourses, particularly those emanating from powerful 'bottom-up' voices, can force power-sharing arrangements to confront uncomfortable conversations in unexpected and intriguing ways. The impacts are not uniformly negative despite the discomfort they provoke. Discourses and practices of truth, reparation, guarantees of non-repetition and accountability are motifs that ultimately ground a rule of law-based society and ought to provide the basis for political and legal engagements in affirming and rule-sustaining ways. The challenge lies ultimately in managing these multiple discourses, and strengthening the capacity of legal and political processes to deliver transformation in conflict and post-conflict settings.

Consociationalism, ethno-nationalism and transitional justice: the mutual pull of the past

Consociationalism is an institutional approach to governance, which takes segmental cleavages seriously as authentic, deep-seated facets of social organization. In the most deeply divided societies in which consociational government has been tried, such as Northern Ireland, Bosnia-Herzegovina, Lebanon and (historically) Cyprus, these cleavages are organized around ethno-national or ethnosectarian communities. To be sure, not all deeply divided societies have an ethno-national or sectarian cleavage and not all consociations attempt to accommodate 'ethnic' splits. But we argue that in cases where ethno-nationalism is a factor, TJ may have a particular importance for consociational success or failure. As institutional structures of governance, consociations seem predisposed towards the present and less interested in picking over the past. But consociational thought and practice also grasps the importance of the cultural past as evidenced by their support for segmental autonomy. Ethnic cleavages crystallize around identities, which have been underpinned and shaped by the historical understandings that serve as warehouses of myth and symbol, and which also serve as route maps to the present and future. Ethno-nationalism draws readily upon these myth and symbol complexes from the past in creating boundaries between identities and fostering the narratives that foment or constrain group action. In the cases suggested above, we can see how ethnic narratives have prioritized mobilizing narratives of the past that spotlight boundaries and sharp contestation between ethnic groups. Here is the second point of strong contact between TJ and consociationalism: the question of legitimacy. Given that a key aspect of deeply divided societies is not only the existence of segmented political organization but also potential (often violent) contestation of the legitimacy of state structures, we can see how TJ, just like consociationalism, will be interested in mechanisms that bind ethno-national groups to a new, hopefully legitimate dispensation. For consociational proponents this legitimacy flows from appropriately and proportionally dispersing the levers of power; for TJ legitimacy flows from an accounting for past harms, the better to bed in new adherence to the rule of law. Each approach then has reason to take ethno-nationalism seriously. Noting this shared importance, and given that we seek to examine the interactions of TJ and consociational thinking, we should unpack TJ's relationship with ethnic cleavages.

Ethno-nationalism and TJ appear to be at opposite ideological points. The ethnic identities that form segmental cleavages are entities which draw up social boundaries and communicate in terms of the particular, not the universal. TJ is arguably a branch of the growing human rights discourse, which has a universal frame of reference. Yet if we examine ethno-nationalism and TJ in action we can discern structures that produce a similarity of focus. Each understands the influence and utility of the past as providing values, symbols and resources. It is seen as having a socializing, norm-creating role in the contemporary field of action. TJ and ethno-nationalism each understand the past as a number of things: a zone of contestation for legitimacy, a narrative guide for moral action in the present and a storehouse of mobilizing symbols. Each may instrumentalize the past as a force for contemporary policy; TJ may use the past to underwrite norms that dissolve impunity and promote acknowledgement and reparation for historic harms; ethno-nationalism reimagines narratives and events of the past to spotlight the endurance of identities and the necessity of group solidarity. This comparable reach for the past is not the result of an ideological similarity – there is no genetic link between TJ and ethno-nationalism: rather it is the outworking of each being formed out of the same historical and contemporary environment. The long twentieth century has seen rapid processes of democratization requiring mobilizing narratives (which the past is replete with), and violent and extended phases of state formation, warfare and decolonization, which have ensured that the 'past' remains sometimes emotive, in many cases politically 'unfinished' and still structuring relations in society. In recent decades the past's importance has been further amplified by a cultural 'memory boom' and a skepticism surrounding the future focused ideologies of the left or right (Torpey 2006; Nora 1989).

TJ and ethno-nationalism not only share a similar orientation in time, they can apply similar organizing frames in terms of narratives and individuals. Both place victimhood at their moral core. TJ processes must be 'victim-centred' or they are regarded as deficient; the extent to which victims sit at the heart of policy and implementation is used as a barometer of TJ's effectiveness and resonance with local populations. To be 'victim-centred' implies the empowerment and raising up of the silenced and excluded, fuller acknowledgement of harm, greater access to a range of experiences and greater access for social and legal remedies. But this approach to victimhood signals more than the rebalancing of power relations and a wish to open out justice meaningfully and democratically. It also has an emotional and symbolic connotation: the experience of traumatic suffering brings with it 'deep moral knowledge.' Victims may then be strategically essentialized as 'moral beacons' providing insight into not only the immorality of harms visited upon them but also the moral worth of their forbearance, resistance or forgiveness (Thomas 1999).

Transitional justice offers great hope to victims of serious human rights violations. It provides a new vocabulary of accountability and repair for those who have lost hope in the capacity of an ordinary legal system to provide meaningful redress. In addition to a vocabulary of harm, claim and repair, TJ also provides important institutions and structures to process crimes of mass atrocity, including truth commissions, lustration and vetting procedures, administrative and judicial reparations schemes and apologies. However, it is obvious that the scale of atrocity crime in most societies makes full repair, absolute accountability and meaningful redress highly elusive. For a variety of practical reasons, including budgetary constraints, TJ always works with partial capacity to meet the needs and expectations of victims. Accountability for those who are most responsible inevitably means that many will go unpunished. Limited resources mean that reparations will be partial or limited in their scope and reach. By virtue of the nature of the crimes committed, evidence will be difficult to produce, communities and individuals will be dispersed and making legal systems work in the aftermath of atrocity can be a limited exercise. All this goes to say that the burdens of expectation are high for transitional justice but some pragmatism and modesty is required given the real-time, real-life limitations of implementing transitional justice on the ground, a set of tensions that coexist with the lived realities of deals made with perpetrators that de facto compromise the expectations and needs of victims.

Victims also play a representational role within the discourse of ethno-nationalism. They are symbols and carriers of stories in relation to historic wrongs, witnesses to the perfidy of the communal 'other,' and the suppression of a community. If ethno-nationalism views the 'nation' as an organic natural entity, and can project it rhetorically as a great personhood, then victims become the metonyms for this national being – the national story in living miniature. They thus have a deeply symbolic existence within the ethno-national frame, often linked to the narrative of communal struggle and resistance. They also help shift the symbolic into the concrete; their stories provide often-verifiable evidence for the narrative and add to it an emotionally accessible human face (Smyth 2007).[4] For ethno-nationalism, the memory of victimhood has still more resonance. Nationalist narratives certainly encompass stories of heroes and victories; but still more significance is given over to martyrs, a category that usefully merges the status victim and hero. This provides a clue to an especially effective narrative type; nationalisms have an attraction to traumas and defeats.

We can offer four reasons for this lure towards the traumatic. First, it may underline a connection between the modern ethno-national grouping and the past and explains the dormant or politically unfulfilled status of the group. Second, it supplies an historical injustice around which a grouping can mobilize, and a 'sore thumb' with which to illicit international support. It also presents the community as a durable, tested entity in ways that narratives of victory or satisfaction cannot – the group demonstrates its steadfastness. Finally, it presents a narrative of the sacrificial, useful in channelling many forms of political resistance. Large-scale death becomes emblematic as group members died 'for' something; the trauma may even serve to carry a nationalistic narrative or moral obligation. The exemplary trauma of the past 100 years – genocide – has been used both as a driver within the universalist human rights discourse and as a mobilizing frame by ethno-cratic states and ethno-nationalist movements to reinforce their own nationalistic projects (Feldman 2008; MacDonald 2002). TJ and ethno-nationalism thus inhabit the same historical waters.

Consociational theory and practice understand that segmental cleavages are authentic, meaningful, valued and, most importantly, resilient. Because it understands this rootedness of identity, there is an implicit understanding of the power of the past. Consociationalism does not seek to 'engineer' cleavages out in the short or medium term. However, it does seek to manage tensions between blocs. Consociationalism's proportional allocation of power, and by implication resources, speaks directly to segmented communities' sense of security and just entitlement in the present; over time this may lead to a culture of cross-communal understanding and cooperation in the future. While the importance of the past (through schooling, religious and cultural practice) is given weight in the provisions for segmental autonomy (after all, can a community exist without a 'past'?), it is not consociationalism's largest concern. It is however very prominent in TJ, and clearly segmented cleavages themselves need the past to create a sense of self and difference from others. More problematically, narratives of the past may be used to mobilize for outbidding and disruption, to delegitimize peace agreements or provide a political rationale for spoiler groups. If TJ can have a role in augmenting consociation, it could be in providing a critical and searching public lens, which defuses the most violent mythologies, or at least complicates and balances partisan narratives.

Transitional justice in the grassroots: consociational complement or constraint?

Consociational structures operate at the elite level; the understanding is that each communal leadership will be able to manage its respective constituencies while meshing the gears of accommodation and cooperation at a higher level. A criticism is that in focusing on the elite level and in working to underwrite communal control via processes such as cultural autonomy, it is in fact entrenching divisions at a wider societal level right down to the grassroots. The argument is that elites will do little to undercut their own bases of support – communally framed political parties – and civic forms of representation are thereby squeezed. Indeed, proponents of liberal consociation do envisage non-ascriptive forms of identification finding room and hope that elite accommodation will eventually filter down to communities through a process of example-setting. Yet they do not provide a detailed understanding of how this may actually happen. This is understandable, given that in consociations such as Lebanon, Northern Ireland and Bosnia, civic forms of political representation remain minority undertakings. Even peaceful Belgium, at the heart of the European project, has witnessed increasing communalization rather than its withering and the ferment of extremist violence ('home-grown' terrorism) whose relationship with the underlying state political project remains uncharted. As recent research has argued, although consociationalism need not end in perpetual ethnic outbidding, a structure inhabited by ethnic tribunes may result in which, while there may be wider societal buy-in to the system and resource allocation may be more susceptible to moderation, issues of identity may still invoke intransigence (Mitchell *et al.* 2009); thus culture and symbolism may still combust and be far less amenable to accommodation. This appears to draw a thick question mark through the aspiration of power-sharing as an example of cooperation for wider society. Critics of a consociational elite focus have instead tended to shift the focus onto activating and nourishing civil society actors as a way of transforming social relations; civil society can act to challenge the narratives and identities of elite configurations and create the space for themselves to help evolve different civic forms of representation over time. This seems ambitious, but proponents critique consociationalists for their naivety in assuming that anything that entrenches segmented cleavages can produce a sustainable, workable system (Dixon 1997). Of course, the fact that in divided societies civil society groups are often themselves expressions of segmental cleavages, overloaded with bonding capital and exhibiting less in the way of bridging capital, means that it may also be simplistic to consider civil society as always providing a civic, transformative force.

Might TJ add something missing to the elite focus of consociational systems? We have argued that partisan ethnic cleavages are embedded in the local, and that consociational approaches, even in their liberal form, are not best placed to engage with these, given their elite focus and institutional strengthening of communal forms of representation (Brown and Ní Aoláin 2015). We will now consider whether processes of TJ can act to fill this gap between top- and bottom-level interactions, or merely circle that plughole. We address the turn to the 'local' in transitional justice as well as reflecting on what the 'local' might look like in a deeply divided society (given the inevitable plurality one should expect in divided polities).

Recent scholarship, whether seeking to establish new norms of interaction or supplying case studies of truth recovery and memory work, has shifted to a level of magnification that is designed to capture local processes of dealing with contentious pasts. Macro-level TJ, it is argued, may be too legalistic in its approach, preferring to 'see like a state' and in so doing failing to adequately engage with the complexities of transition at the local level; skipping over certain claims and narratives, failing to provide for meaningful, substantive input from victims, and ultimately losing relevance and legitimacy in the eyes of those at the grassroots (McEvoy and McGregor 2009). If we take the example of the states of the former Yugoslavia, we can see that evidence is mounting that higher level TJ processes can indeed be resisted if they threaten ethno-national narratives, be appropriated if they valorize the same or simply be ignored (Subotić 2005, 2013; Peskin and Boduszynski 2011). Releasing legalism and stepping away from the 'state-level' horizon of interpretation has thus been championed as a necessary way of increasing relevance for local communities by allowing a fuller examination of context, engaging them as actors and not merely as subjects and allowing voices to emerge which may have been previously screened out by elite level discourses, be they either judicial or ethno-national (Shaw *et al.* 2010; McEvoy 2007; Kent 2011; Bickford 2007). As Huma Haider warns, "Day-to-day lived realities in divided societies influence whether new narratives that may emerge from court decisions or truth commissions alter, reinforce or have no effect on dominant stories and myths" (2011, 185). It is necessary therefore for TJ to get access to the workings of ethno-nationalism in order to engage with its discourses, and this connection is ultimately and fundamentally connected to the success of the political project of agreed and shared governance. As argued above, it already wades in the waters of victimhood and the past; what is needed are locally based (and collaborative) designs, which can channel its norms and discourses into the local mix of a deeply divided society. Narratives that establish identity content and boundaries are very much like velcro, fastening to the local group and the individual as multiple hooks and eyes at the micro level (Hearn 2007). If identity content comprises hooks that fasten hostile, simplified narratives of militancy and threat, or boundaries that are over-communicated and encapsulating, neither macro TJ nor elite-level consociational approaches will be able to partially unpick it. We should not imagine that localizing TJ will be a simple case of a higher gear cog changing down and meshing with a lower one; the process produces friction and can cause the assumptions of macro TJ to fracture (Hinton 2011; Orentlicher 2007). Yet it can also throw open new and unforeseen possibilities (Shaw and Waldorf 2010). Grounded forms of TJ may enable understandings of the past that are more meaningful to communities, and can differ strikingly from higher political levels, foregrounding experiences that are at variance with the ethno-national elite focus on militarism and resistance, or international elite narratives of closure and reconciliation (Kent 2011). The process may thus be one of vernacularization where ideas and practices of TJ are shaped and communicated in a way that produces resonance with local values (Merry 2006). If there is a fear that locally based TJ could simply supply a displacement battlefield that could hinder the ability of elites to manage constituencies within a power-sharing framework, we should acknowledge that but also point out two facts of life within deeply divided societies. First, the 'local' may already be the happy hunting ground for ethnic entrepreneurs and 'spoilers' if they cannot yet acquire representation at governmental levels; and second, in matters of cultural and narrative contestation, the power-sharing elites may themselves tack to ethno-national scripts at the local level as a default position (Hayward and Komarova 2014).

Given the social capital of ethno-nationalism at the local level, reflecting resilience, authenticity and narrative depth, it would be foolish for TJ processes to attempt a foisting of predigested norms that will be regarded as lacking context, relevance and as something of an external intrusion. Rather, TJ could open up a space for *agonistic* debate, in which narratives and claims freely emerge, encounter one another but are also subject to challenge. Agonistic pluralism neither expects nor asks for a definitive end product to emerge; there need be no agreed narrative, full closure or final reconciliation. It does envisage a fundamental respect for other discourses, allowing a liberal circulation of narratives, but the ability of any narrative to be robustly contested is axiomatic (Mouffe 1999).

Rather than attempt to foist a series of norms that may be regarded as an intrusion or confection, and for which it lacks the ground-level social capital to transplant in any case, a different course could be navigated. Looking forward, we suggest that it may be that TJ should allow spaces for agonistic (as opposed to antagonistic) debate, enabling these narratives to encounter one another

(Schaap 2006, 2009; Bell 2008). It could work to facilitate these narratives in both the national arena and at local levels. But the process of engaging in this agonistic discourse should be predicated on respect, the free circulation of narrative and the ability to challenge those narratives. Rather than understanding reconciliation in terms of restoring a relationship between alienated co-members of a moral community, we should attempt to free up space to allow ethnonational orthodoxies to be routinely challenged, from both within and outside the community (Schaap 2006). It is thus a process of diffusion and complication, not of reconciliation between binaries; one which acknowledges "multiple pasts whilst offering the tools necessary to challenge all settled identity claims" (Bell 2008, 162).

This is the broad model, and other scholarship has advocated similar deliberative approaches that accept robust contestation and that have been skeptical of agreement as an outcome, even if they are not couched in a specifically agonistic frame (Payne 2007; Rangelov 2013). But such a model could however flip easily into simple antagonism where the past continues to pump into the present and local forms of ethno-nationalism just become adept at lawfare. We can certainly expect challenges around victimhood, so central to both TJ and ethnonationalism, to be particularly hot and recurrent. But to help prevent this model from toppling into *antagonism*, TJ can provide several avenues of approach. They include the following.

Rules of encounter. While agonism is non-prescriptive and open-ended, it does require a framework in which contested narratives and claims may productively interact. Examples may be usefully drawn from a range of truth commissions, which could assist in shaping the terrain in which agonistic actors can meet, and productively work out how narratives may be presented, engaged with and challenged. Narratives need not merely encounter one another in a quasilegal setting or in a truth commission format; local forms of agonism could adopt forms which more broadly based types of transitional justice have implemented, such as oral history projects, exhibitions or school curricula. The downstream impact of encounter is difficult to measure but we posit its capacity to prompt deeper inter-communal engagement and recognition on terms that ultimately (albeit sometimes painfully) advance the project of shared political practice.

Providing claims-making tools. In processes of memory-making, commemoration and shaping narratives of the past, law can be invoked in inventive ways. Statutes, international law, 'soft' law and declarations, even case law have all been creatively employed by actors outside of an obviously legal context (Savelsberg and King 2007). This could inflect claims which have relied on partisan and particularist frameworks and which have therefore closed off dialogue rather than opening it out to agonism. Law may also be used to open up archives and push new evidence into the wider public sphere; this could enhance agonistic processes and not just by adding extra facts to bolster argument. As new information emerges, perhaps confounding simplistic views of a conflict, fissures within ethno-national structures and discourses could develop. Within these openings there may be greater space for reflexivity, disruptive thinking and intersectionality. Increasingly too there is the recognition that opening up is cyclical; as discourses of post-transitional justice reveal, TJ may well be more of a loop than an end-point. A rapidly developing form of TJ has been that of memorialization and commemoration; as well as providing some measure of symbolic reparation, commemoration can serve as a sounding-board to articulate claims in public space. These may be 'single identity' but not expressly in an ethno-national frame, shifting robust, critical engagement into a different type of discourse (Brown 2012).

A means to draw out or test narratives. There is a strong role for historical commissions if they can be linked to local settings. Employing a broad range of historians, social scientists and lawyers, commissions might prove useful in testing the reliability and accuracy of locally based narratives, and also simply providing a circulation of these narratives, that provides them with a wider public space (Ingraor 2009; Gavrilović and Perica 2011). Feminist scholarship has much to add here, since it champions a willingness to detect and uncover silences, and provides a focus on the 'everyday,' thereby offering a different understanding of communal harms (Ní Aoláin and Turner 2007). An agonistic process precludes definitive verdicts on truth claims but militant or essentializing mythologies may be weakened by historical commissions. Alternatively, if group claims are accepted by agonistic actors as convincing, they may seep through ethno-national boundaries, having been provided with a degree of validation. We might imagine it in this way: the evidential standards of the academy, together with legal processes, are important validating resources to which an ethno-national actor is attracted; but in reaching for and using them, groups could well be obliged to moderate the particularism of their own truth claims. Notions of equality, fair dealing and respect for pluralism, which are often built into consociations, would thus be telescoped to the local level. It could also introduce pluralism at an intra-communal level. Ethno-national frames can put simplifying screen memories in front of intersectional claims of internal sub-groups and so any shift to universal norms may also provide a challenge to insider elites (O'Rourke 2013). TJ and historical inquiry may also be useful in illuminating patterns of harms that occur in ethno-national struggles; this could work to broaden the definition of harm in ways that disrupt simple ethno-national framing. TJ could also provide a simple but particularly helpful function: tallying the extent of harms accurately could work to dissolve mythologies of sole suffering and the outbidding instrumentalization of victimhood.

The need for caution and realism. When engaging with the 'grassroots' in a deeply divided society, level-headedness and realistic expectations are necessary. We can perhaps see this in consociationalism's unwillingness to commit itself to prescriptions far beyond elite management; it will settle for agreement at the top which will constrain conflict and just possibly set the mood music for deeper accommodation. The lessons of ethnic tribune politics (Mitchell *et al.* 2009) show that this music is often a contrapuntal rhythm and difficult to stay in step with. If we advocate a grounded focus for TJ as a way of addressing this, we do so in the full knowledge that the local ecology can be a thicket that can work to repel interlopers – hence the agonistic approach, which sees civil society as producing thorns as well as nectar.

We can speedily delineate the problems of engagement. West European and North American thinking on civil society frames it as promoting liberal democratic norms and creating a new civic space, one in opposition to particularist claims; this reflects an incomplete understanding of ethno-nationalism as being irrational, the product of scheming elites and which ignores the importance of ethnic bonds in societies (McGarry 1995). It is rather the case that civil society groups can be inflected by ethno-national memberships to a greater or lesser extent. In many instances, they may be more appropriately seen as particularist and not integrative, as *ethnic civil societies* (Alexander 1998; Haklai 2011). They may also be 'captured' by state institutions (Doyle 2015); less of a problem in a consociation, one might think, but if the power-sharing deal encompasses federalism then this leaves the possibility of capture by federal entities. Our agonistic approach, while factoring in endemic contestation, also requires certain fundamentals: a wish to engage, and an acceptance of reciprocal rights to be heard. These need not be forthcoming from the grassroots, where disagreement over equivalence, sequencing, time frames and overall intent of projects speedily work to dissolve local engagement (McCurn and Di Lellio 2012). More fundamentally, local dialogue may be greatly inhibited because, while in a more consensual society many interpretive horizons are accessible to citizens as part of their everyday lives, in a divided society "the capacity to choose from these interpretative horizons is constricted, both in terms of discourse and in terms of socially acceptable behaviour" (Hayward and Komarova 2014, 778). In other words, ethno-nationalism has powerfully narrowed what are deemed appropriate ways of looking at society, despite attempts to push past these boundaries. But it need not prevail in every case of engagement and interaction (Kovras 2012).

Conclusion

Within this discussion we have presented transitional justice as neither confection nor constraint but rather as a complement to consociationalism. We adopt a constructively critical approach to consociational structures, which acknowledges that they allow for the pursuit of claims at the elite level, but have avoided how sectional identities and claims play out at the local level. This has meant that any benefits of elite cooperation can fail to transfer to the grassroots – a major problem given that the 'local' is the forging house of ethno-nationalism in all its varieties, militant or otherwise. TJ, if properly attuned, can get at the local in ways that consociationalism does not. Consociationalism by necessity has an institutional focus, whereas TJ has a narrative sensitivity that is conversant with the power of historical accounts and attuned to the discourse of victimhood and trauma. The local model we have outlined, drawing upon a grassroots turn in TJ, is about robust engagement within a setting of coexistence rather than reconciliation; one that encourages pluralism and may defuse the worst of combustible mythologies, while allowing space for intersectional voices, and unheard stories to complicate simple binaries. It does not provide Potemkin village initiatives of brief, symbolic harmony. Expectations need to be set realistically. The environment is difficult. This is not reconciliation, but neither TJ nor consociationalism has been shown to assuredly deliver that. Both could however work together in a complementary fashion, providing a 'top' and 'bottom' engagement that acknowledges but is not subservient to group difference.

Notes

1 The authors acknowledge the support of the DfID Political Settlement Research Programme in enabling the completion of this research.
2 In Sejdić and Finci vs. Bosnia-Herzegovina, the European Court of Human Rights addressed the issue of a post-conflict power-sharing system and its compatibility with equality norms. The case raised issues under Protocols 1–3 and 12 and Article 14 of the European Convention on Human Rights. The court's decision was substantially rooted in the language and protections outlined in Protocol 12, and the court treated the matter as one of essentially straightforward discrimination on racial grounds: "a particularly egregious kind of discrimination" which required "special vigilance and a vigorous reaction" from the authorities.
3 The Inter-American Court of Human Rights has found in several cases that amnesty laws are in violation of Articles 1, 2, 8.1 and 25 of the American Convention on Human Rights. Barrios Altos vs. Peru, Merits, Inter-Am. Ct. H.R. (ser. C) No. 75 (14 March 2001); La Cantuta vs. Perú, Merits, Reparations and Costs, Inter-Am. Ct. H.R. (ser. C) No. 162 (29 November 2006); Almonacid-Arellano *et al*. vs. Chile, Preliminary Objections, Merits, Reparations and Costs, Inter-Am. Ct. H.R. (ser. C) No. 154 (26 September 2006).
4 Smyth (2007, 77) argues: "the construction of the narrative about the victim's experience plays a central role in both individual and collective identity formation" leading to a foisting of the role of "moral beacons" upon them.

References

Alexander, Jeffrey C., ed. 1998. *Real Civil Societies: Dilemmas of Institutionalization*. London: Sage.

Arthur, Paige, ed. 2010. *Identities in Transition: Challenges for Transitional Justice in Divided Societies*. Cambridge: Cambridge University Press.

Belfast Guidelines on Amnesty and Accountability. 2014. Available at http://peacemaker.un.org/sites/peacemaker.un.org/files/BelfastGuidelines_TJI2014.pdf.pdf.

Bell, Christine. 2013. "Power-Sharing and Human Rights Law." *International Journal of Human Rights* 17, no. 2: 204–237.

Bell, Duncan. 2008. "Agonistic Democracy and the Politics of Memory." *Constellations* 15, no. 1: 148–166.

Bickford, Louise. 2007. "Unofficial Truth Projects." *Human Rights Quarterly* 29: 994–1035.

Boutruche, Théo. 2013. "Seeking the Truth about Serious International Human Rights and Humanitarian Law Violations: The Various Facets of a Cardinal Notion of Transitional Justice." In *Armed Conflict and International Law: In Search of the Human Face: Liber Amicorum in Memory of Avril McDonald*, edited by Mariëlle Matthee, Brigit Toebes and Marcel Brus, pp. 303–326.The Hague: Asser Press.

Brown, Kristian. 2012. "'What It Was Like to Live through a Day': Transitional Justice and the Memory of the Everyday in a Divided Society." *International Journal of Transitional Justice* 6, no. 3: 444–466.

Brown, Kristian and Fionnuala Ní Aoláin. 2015. "Through the Looking Glass: Transitional Justice Futures through the Lens of Nationalism, Feminism, and Transformative Change." *International Journal of Transitional Justice* 9, no. 1: 127–149.

Clark, Janine N. 2011. "Transitional Justice, Truth and Reconciliation: An Under-Explored Relationship." *International Criminal Law Review* 11, no. 2: 247–249.

Dixon, Paul. 1997. "Paths to Peace in Northern Ireland (I): Civil Society and Consociational Approaches." *Democratization* 4, no. 2: 1–27.

Doyle, Jessica Leigh. 2015. "Civil Society as Ideology in the Middle East: A Critical Perspective." *British Journal of Middle Eastern Studies* 43, no 3: 403–422.

El Zeidy, Mohamed M. 2002. "The Principle of Complementarity: A New Machinery to Implement International Criminal Law." *Michigan Journal of International Law* 23, no. 4: 869–976.

Feldman, Jackie. 2008. *Above the Death Pits, Beneath the Flag: Youth Voyages to Poland and the Performance of Israeli National Identity*. New York: Berghahn Books.

Gavrilović, Darko and Vjekoslav Perica, eds. 2011. *Political Myths in the Former Yugoslavia and Successor States: A Shared Narrative*. Dordrecht, Netherlands: Republics of Letters.

Haider, Huma. 2011. "Social Repair in Divided Societies: Integrating a Coexistence Lens into Transitional Justice." *Conflict, Security and Development* 11, no. 2: 175–203.

Haklai, Oded. 2011. *Palestinian Ethnonationalism in Israel*. Philadelphia: University of Pennsylvania Press.

Hayward, Katy and Milena Komarova. 2014. "The Limits of Local Accommodation: Why Contentious Events Remain Prone to Conflict in Northern Ireland." *Studies in Conflict and Terrorism* 37, no. 9: 777–791.

Hearn, Jonathan. 2007. "National Identity: Banal, Personal and Embedded." *Nations and Nationalism* 13, no. 4: 657–674.

Hinton, Alexander Laban, ed. 2011. *Transitional Justice: Global Mechanisms and Local Realities after Genocide and Mass Violence*. New Jersey: Rutgers University Press.

Horowitz, Donald L. 1985. *Ethnic Groups in Conflict*. Berkeley: University of California Press.

Ingraor, Charles. 2009. "Confronting the Yugoslav Controversies: The Scholars' Initiative." *American Historical Review* 114, no. 4: 947–962.

Kent, Lia. 2011. "Local Memory Practices in East Timor: Disrupting Transitional Justice Narratives." *International Journal of Transitional Justice* 5, no. 3: 434–455.

Kovras, Iosif. 2012. "De-Linkage Processes and Grassroots Movements in Transitional Justice." *Cooperation and Conflict* 47, no. 1: 88–105.

Levitt, Jeremy. 2006. "Illegal Peace? Examining the Legality of Power-Sharing with Warlords and Rebels in Africa." *Michigan Journal of International Law* 27: 495–577.

Lijphart, Arend. 1977. *Democracy in Plural Societies: A Comparative Exploration*. New Haven, CT: Yale University Press.

MacDonald, David Bruce. 2002. *Balkan Holocausts? Serbian and Croatian Victim Centered Propaganda and the War in Yugoslavia*. Manchester: Manchester University Press.

Majstorović, Danijela and Vladimir Turjacanin. 2013. *Youth Ethnic and National Identity in Bosnia and Herzegovina: Social Science Approaches*. London: Palgrave Macmillan.

Mallinder, Louise. 2008. *Amnesty, Human Rights and Political Transitions: Bridging the Peace and Justice Divide*. Oxford: Bloomsbury Publishing.

Mallinder, Louise and Kieran McEvoy. 2011. "Rethinking Amnesties: Atrocity, Accountability and Impunity in Post-Conflict Societies." *Contemporary Social Science* 6, no. 1: 107–128.

McCrudden, Christopher and Brendan O'Leary. 2013. *Courts and Consociations: Human Rights versus Power-Sharing*. Oxford: Oxford University Press.

McCurn, Caitlin and Anna Di Lellio. 2012. "Engineering Grassroots Transitional Justice in the Balkans: The Case of Kosovo." *East European Politics and Societies* 27, no. 1: 129–148.

McEvoy, Kieran. 2007. "Beyond Legalism: Towards a Thicker Understanding of Transitional Justice." *Journal of Law and Society* 34, no. 4: 411–440.

McEvoy, Kieran and Lorna McGregor, eds. 2009. *Transitional Justice from Below: Grassroots Activism and the Struggle for Change*. Oxford: Hart Publishing.

McGarry, John. 1995. "Explaining Ethnonationalism: The Flaws in Western Thinking." *Nationalism and Ethnic Politics* 1, no. 4: 121–142.

McGarry, John. 2007. "Liberal Consociation and Conflict Management." In *Iraq: Preventing Another Generation of Conflict*, edited by Ben Roswell, David Malone and Markus Bouillon, pp. 169–188. Boulder, CO: Lynne Rienner.

McGarry, John and Brendan O'Leary. 2007. "Iraq's Constitution of 2005: Liberal Consociation as Political Prescription." *International Journal of Constitutional Law* 5, no. 4: 670–698.

Merry, Sally Engle. 2006. *Human Rights and Gender Violence: Translating International Law into Local Justice*. Chicago, IL: University of Chicago Press.

Mitchell, Paul, Geoffrey Evans and Brendan O'Leary. 2009. "Extremist Outbidding in Ethnic Party Systems is Not Inevitable: Tribune Parties in Northern Ireland." *Political Studies* 57, no. 2: 397–421.

Mouffe, Chantal. 1999. "Deliberative Democracy or Agonistic Pluralism?" *Social Research* 66, no. 3: 745–758.

Nettelfield, Lara J. and Sarah Wagner. 2013. *Srebrenica in the Aftermath of Genocide*. Cambridge: Cambridge University Press.

Ní Aoláin, Fionnuala and Catherine Turner. 2007. "Gender, Truth and Transition." *UCLA Women's Law Journal* 16: 229–279.

Nora, Pierre. 1989. "Between Memory and History: Les Lieux de Mémoire." *Representations* 26: 7–24.

O'Rourke, Catherine. 2013. *Gender Politics in Transitional Justice*. London: Routledge.

O'Leary, Brendan. 2005. "Debating Consociational Politics: Normative and Explanatory Arguments." In *From Power-Sharing to Democracy: Post-Conflict Institutions in Ethnically Divided Societies*, edited by Sid Noel, pp. 3–43. Montreal: McGill-Queen's University Press.

Orentlicher, Diane. 2007. "Settling Accounts Revisited: Reconciling Global Norms with Local Agency." *International Journal of Transitional Justice* 1, no. 1: 10–22.

Pappalardo, Adrian. 1981. "The Conditions for Consociational Democracy: A Logical and Empirical Critique." *European Journal of Political Research* 9: 365–390.

Parry, Geraint. 2005. *Political Elites*. Colchester: ECPR Press.

Payne, Leigh A. 2007. *Unsettling Accounts: Neither Truth nor Reconciliation in Confessions of State Violence*. Durham, NC: Duke University Press.

Peskin, Victor and Mieczyslaw P. Boduszynski. 2011. "Balancing International Justice in the Balkans: Surrogate Enforcers, Uncertain Transitions and the Road to Europe." *International Journal of Transitional Justice* 5, no. 1: 52–74.

Rangelov, Iavor. 2013. *Nationalism and the Rule of Law: Lessons from the Balkans and Beyond*. Cambridge: Cambridge University Press.

Reilly, Ben. 2001. *Democracy in Divided Societies: Electoral Engineering for Conflict Management*. Cambridge: Cambridge University Press, 2001.

Roeder, Philip G. and Donald Rothchild, eds. 2005. *Sustainable Peace: Power and Democracy after Civil Wars*. Ithaca, NY: Cornell University Press.

Savelsberg, Joachim J. and Ryan D. King. 2007. "Law and Collective Memory." *Annual Review of Law and Social Science* 3: 189–211.

Schaap, Andrew. 2006. "Agonism in Divided Societies." *Philosophy and Social Criticism* 32, no. 2: 255–277.

Schaap, Andrew, ed. 2009. *Law and Agonistic Politics*. Farnham: Ashgate Publishing.

Shaw, Rosalind and Lars Waldorf. 2010. "Introduction." In *Localizing Transitional Justice: Interventions and Priorities after Mass Violence*, edited by Rosalind Shaw and Lars Waldorf, with Pierre Hazan, pp. 3–26. Stanford, CA: Stanford University Press.

Shaw, Rosalind, Lars Waldorf and Pierre Hazan, eds. 2010. *Localizing Transitional Justice: Interventions and Priorities after Mass Violence*. Stanford, CA: Stanford University Press.

Sisk, Timothy D. 1996. *Power Sharing and International Mediation in Ethnic Conflicts*. Washington, DC: United States Institute of Peace Press.

Smyth, Marie Breen. 2007. *Truth Recovery and Justice after Conflict: Managing Violent Pasts*. London: Routledge.

Subotić, Jelena. 2005. "Hijacked Justice: Domestic Appropriation of International Norms." *Human Rights and Human Welfare Working Paper* No. 28.

Subotić, Jelena. 2013. "Remembrance, Public Narratives, and Obstacles to Justice in the Western Balkans." *Studies in Social Justice* 7, no 2: 265–283.

Thomas, Laurence Mordekhai. 1999. "Suffering as a Moral Beacon: Blacks and Jews." In *The Americanization of the Holocaust*, edited by Hilene Flanzbaum, pp. 198–210. Baltimore, MD: Johns Hopkins University Press.

Tonge, Jonathan. 2014. *Comparative Peace Processes*. Hoboken, NJ: John Wiley & Sons.

Torpey, John C. 2006. *Making Whole What Has Been Smashed: On Reparations Politics*. Cambridge, MA: Harvard University Press.

Vandeginste, Stef and Chandra Lekha Sriram. 2011. "Power Sharing and Transitional Justice: A Clash of Paradigms?" *Global Governance* 17, no. 4: 489–505.

Wolff, Stefan. 2011. "A Consociational Theory of Conflict Management." Available at www.stefanwolff.com/files/ConsociationalTheoryPaper.pdf.

12 Gendering power-sharing

Siobhan Byrne and Allison McCulloch

Power-sharing theory and power-sharing practices are gender-blind. While power-sharing may be an effective strategy for the democratic inclusion of minority ethnic groups, it has thus far failed to consider the gendered consequences of its institutional recommendations. Given the ascendancy of power-sharing theory in the conflict resolution field over the past three decades and considering its use in dozens of conflict transformation processes in diverse conflict zones around the world, we now have a wide-ranging sample of empirical cases which show that power-sharing institutions limit women's inclusion. Such persistent gender-blindness in power-sharing theory is particularly surprising given the growth, over the past decade and a half, of the women, peace and security (WPS) agenda. As articulated in UN Security Council Resolution 1325, this agenda challenges theorists and practitioners to improve the representation of women and gender in conflict transformation processes.

In what follows, we propose two possible points of alignment between power-sharing and WPS. We acknowledge that neither proposal, alone, would be sufficient for gendering power-sharing theory and power-sharing institutions. This exploratory exercise, however, does demonstrate that power-sharing and WPS norms need not be mutually exclusive processes. Whereas conventional feminist critiques tend to dismiss power-sharing processes as bad for women given the dismal record of women's inclusion in power-sharing institutions, we suggest that there are potential and hitherto unexplored avenues of analytic and practical engagement. Our aim is to dispel the view that, on the one hand, power-sharing is necessarily anti-feminist and, on the other hand, that the WPS agenda is irrelevant for the hard politics of peacemaking and post-conflict democratic governance in deeply divided societies.

Our first proposal is to align the locus of analysis. Power-sharing theory, as it is conventionally developed in the literature, is predicated on an underlying theory of identity which assumes that people's attachment to an ethno-national community – whether real or imagined – is the most important way in which they make meaning in their lives. Ethno-nationalism, thus, is the root of people's most important social and political claims, and, when threatened, can lead to the most serious forms of social friction and political conflict. Critical feminist scholarship on nations and nationalism, however, draw our attention to multiple and intersecting ways in which people make meaning in their lives. Ethnonationalism is but one mode of communal identification that functions in concert and conflict with gender and other social identities. While offering competing views on the relative weight and singularity of ethno-national identity, both power-sharing and feminist critics of power-sharing tend to agree that nationalism and ethnic chauvinism is politically destabilizing and potentially dangerous. We outline the possibilities and limits of aligning power-sharing and the WPS around a shared goal of taming divisive ethno-national politics.

Our second proposal is to reconcile the levels of analytical differences between power-sharing and WPS norms. Feminist critics charge that power-sharing processes advocate secret high-level political processes that favour elite male actors. Drawing on the principles of UNSCR 1325, we ask whether a process of gender mainstreaming at the elite level can facilitate a more gender-inclusive form of power-sharing. We show that power-sharing institutions, which tend to be constructed with strong and built-in commitments to democratic inclusion, can be gender-mainstreamed – at least in theory. As with our first proposal, however, there are limits to this approach as well, which we review.

Our argument is that building resilient democratic modes of conflict transformation requires the effective implementation of both power-sharing arrangements and the WPS agenda. In what follows, we propose the two possible strategies for bringing the goals of power-sharing theory and the WPS agenda into alignment. We focus on these two strategies because this is where the divides between power-sharing theorists and feminists are perceived to be widest. Before turning to these strategies of alignment, we first explicate why scholars of feminism and the women, peace and security agenda and power-sharing theorists find themselves at cross-purposes.

Contending norms of conflict transformation

The literature on power-sharing has been a central component of the Comparative Politics field since the late 1960s. Power-sharing may be implemented in a number of ways but it is most often associated with consociationalism, which is a system that brings together ethnic elites in grand coalitions and other forms of executive power-sharing, ensures groups are proportionally represented in key political institutions, like the legislature, executive and security forces, and which provides veto rights and autonomy arrangements for all major ethnic groups (Lijphart 1977, 2008). Scholars have elucidated compelling reasons for negotiating and implementing power-sharing provisions. Conflict actors are more likely to accept a peace accord that provides them with a share of power (Walter 2002); such provisions are more likely to facilitate a durable peace (Hartzell and Hoddie 2003); and they are often seen as a successful way of democratically accommodating difference and ensuring ethnic inclusiveness (McGarry and O'Leary 2009; Lijphart 2008; Norris 2008).

Initially, consociationalism was a model employed by plural societies, such as the Netherlands and Switzerland, without widespread ethnic violence or strong secessionism (Lijphart 1977). In the past 20 years or so, power-sharing has been reconceptualized as a way to end ethnicized conflicts, as in Bosnia-Herzegovina, Lebanon, Northern Ireland, Burundi, Kenya and Iraq (see Bogaards, Chapter 7, this volume). With this shift to war zones, the model has been revised from one that dealt solely with internal strategies of accommodation to an internationally driven model of conflict resolution (McGarry 2003; Taylor 2009). This "new wave" of power-sharing (Taylor 2009) includes a number of additional features beyond the traditional power-sharing institutions, such as provisions on security sector reform, refugee returns, the management of prisoners, the promotion of language rights, and, in some cases, cross-border institutions (McGarry 2003; O'Leary 2005; Wolff 2011). Power-sharing is increasingly seen as an attractive option by third-party mediators in peace processes.

The literature on women, peace and security is relatively new to the field of International Relations. It emerges out of local and transnational feminist advocacy work in the late 1980s, which culminated in the adoption of the groundbreaking UNSCR 1325 in 2000. This resolution requires member-states to include women in all aspects of conflict resolution and peacebuilding. Specifically, it calls for women's participation at all levels of decision-making, the adoption of a gender perspective in peace negotiations, and the protection of women from violence during and after conflict. The WPS literature focuses on the difficulties women face in their bid for inclusion in peace processes. As international legal scholars Fionnuala Ní Aoláin, Dina Francesca Haynes and Naomi Cahn write: "Women are the group most historically marginalized and excluded from the peacemaking and peacebuilding process across all jurisdictions and conflicts" (Ní Aoláin *et al.* 2011, 5). This is despite women's political and community engagement during periods of conflict and expectations that such political and social inclusion will continue or improve through peacebuilding periods (Byrne 2009; Bell and O'Rourke 2010). The feminist security studies literature also maps the ways in which women are active participants in conflict – including ethnicized ones – through careful case study analysis of, for example, female suicide bombers and women soldiers (see, e.g., Sjoberg and Gentry 2007; MacKenzie 2009; Sasson-Levy 2003). Women's roles in national conflicts are much more complicated, with multiple points at which women challenge traditional gender roles, even in hyper-masculinized and militarized contexts of war.

Feminist scholars stress the consequences of women's exclusion from peace processes. When women are excluded from peace talks, their issues and concerns are likely to be de-prioritized or go unaddressed altogether, allowing gender hierarchies to persist in the post-conflict period (Bell and O'Rourke 2010; De Alwis *et al.* 2013; Peuchguirbal 2012). This literature highlights the gendered effects of women's exclusion from peace negotiations and has advocated for the adoption of a gender perspective in a number of peacebuilding areas, including security sector reform and transitional justice processes (Ní Aoláin *et al.* 2011; Jacobson 2013).

Both sets of scholars perceive a gap between their respective equality projects (O'Leary 2005; Rebouché and Fearon 2005). Adrian Guelke (2012, 14), a leading scholar of ethnic conflict management, argues, "a society deeply divided on the basis of gender is practically speaking inconceivable." As feminist theorist Anne Phillips (1995, 15) suggests, the problem is that "no one really expects women to secede." Power-sharing theory assumes that in order to be considered a serious candidate for power-sharing, a group must have "a strong sense of itself" and be organized into political parties; this, Phillips suggests, means that power-sharing, and specifically consociationalism, misses the powerlessness and marginalization that occurs for those groups, like women, for whom political party formation is not the dominant mode of mobilization (Phillips 1995, 15–16). To the extent that this is true, feminists and consociationalists are talking past one another, employing different concepts of democratic inclusion.

As noted above, there are two major points of contention between feminists and power-sharing theorists. The first issue is that they focus on different identity structures. Much consociational theorizing, for example, is premised on a theory of ethno-nationalism wherein the nation is a "fact that cannot be wished away" (Lijphart 1985). Once mobilized, it is enduring and powerful (but not primordial – see McGarry and O'Leary 2009). Power-sharing scholars lament the destructive power of nations but they think it is "both fruitless and undesirable to attempt to abolish ethnic affiliations" (Horowitz 2000, xvii). The institutional recommendation is to bring competing ethno-national groups into the political fold (as "building blocks") in order to stabilize politics.

For feminists, the focus is not nations but gender. Of course, feminist scholars have much to say about the nation as well. Cynthia Enloe (2000) contends that nationalisms typically spring from "masculinized memory, masculinized humiliation and masculinized hope," while Anne McClintock (1997) goes further: "All nationalisms are gendered; all are invented; and all are dangerous." Starting from the position of ethno-nationalism, even if it is to tame it, risks reifying the nation and entrenching the gender hierarchies that go along with it. In this sense, what appears to be a source of contention is perhaps a consensus view on the dangers of the nation, a point we discuss further below.

The second issue is a level-of-analysis problem. Power-sharing scholars tend to focus on elite-level, often *in-camera* negotiations and elected bodies and other political institutions. Whether adopted through constitutional reforms or as part of a larger peace process, the adoption of power-sharing arrangements occurs in political arenas from which women have been historically marginalized. As John Darby and Roger MacGinty (2003, 3) note, peace processes are typically focused on a narrow understanding of the constituencies involved in the conflict:

> Those who held guns or the dominant position on the battlefield when a ceasefire was called become negotiating partners regardless of their ability to represent their community. Other voices, often those without firepower, tend to go unheard. This might help to explain why many peace processes are overwhelmingly male.

By contrast, feminist IR scholars have often focused on questions of grassroots activisms, transnational feminist peace activisms and accompanying beliefs in transparency and openness. Most consociationalists do not share this focus on civil society and informal political organizing; consociationalists, Brendan O'Leary suggests (2005, 10, emphasis in original), are "cautiously sceptical" of civil society as "*the* (or even *a*) vehicle of transformation, peace making and peace building." From this perspective, state building and political stability take precedence.

Nonetheless, the two norms do have some shared commitments. As Antonia Potter (2011, 8) notes, the topic of power-sharing "brings up all the questions about participation, voice and choice which tend to be already allied with the topic of women's representation and rights (and all sorts of other groups too)." That is, both feminists and power-sharing theorists begin with a similar concern – injustice and unfairness brought about by exclusion – and both often seek political inclusion as a remedy for injustice and non-democracy. The differences in analytical frames (elite–ethnic; grassroots–gender), however, means that while both prioritize democratic inclusion, they begin from different concepts of inclusiveness. Inclusiveness can mean either engaging belligerent groups and their leaders or it can be about "involving the main political and social groups affected by the conflict, including women, youth, displaced people and marginalized communities" (Potter 2011, 4). Power-sharing advocates often prefer the former and feminists the latter. We agree with Rachel Rebouché and Kate Fearon (2005, 168) who argue that "if divided societies are to succeed in their attempts to build a just and stable democracy, then that democracy must make room for everyone in society," but we stop short of their critique of power-sharing as unable to accommodate other identities. Instead, we propose that a policy of alignment between power-sharing goals and the women, peace and security agenda can facilitate the inclusive, democratic system which both seek.

Gender and nation: deconstructing the ethno-national foundation of power-sharing

The first strategy for assessing the alignment potential of power-sharing and WPS is to approach both policies at the same locus of analysis, which for power-sharing is a foundational theory of ethno-nationalism. Here we are referring to the theory that ethnicized national impulses – referred to as ethno-nationalism in the power-sharing literature – drive the most protracted conflicts today. The nation, in this sense, is the principal source of meaning-making: it explains the conditions that lead to conflict, it becomes the source for resolving conflict, and it serves as the foundation for a post-conflict body politic. Feminist theorists worry that national movements are deeply gendered political communities that are dangerous for women and women's interests (McClintock 1997; Enloe 2000; Yuval-Davis 1997).

While consociationalists and feminists may appear to hold competing views on the role nationalism should play in political institutions, they also agree that nationalism is a problem for political legitimacy. Consociational theory is deeply troubled by its apparent rooting in national identity; it is, in our view, imagined to allow for the ultimate transcendence of nationalism in a post-conflict political environment (albeit such transcendence is never explicitly theorized in the literature, only alluded to; see, e.g., Lijphart 1977; McGarry and O'Leary 2009). This has implications for identifying one possible path for alignment of power-sharing and the WPS agenda (although we have reservations about the critique of nationalism shared by consociationalists and feminists, discussed below).

The traditional view of consociationalism is that it is a theory that advocates (or is, at least, sympathetic to) national claims of self-determination. Many contemporary consociationalists ground their theorizing in an understanding of nationalism specifically developed by Walker Connor. Connor writes:

> The well-springs of national identity are more profound than are those associated with religion, class, and the like, and the presence of other shared characteristics may, therefore, not be sufficient to preserve the state. That the individual partakes of several group identities simultaneously is beyond dispute. But that these identities are not of the same order was the basis for Rupert Emerson's sage description of the nation as "the largest community which, when the chips are down, effectively commands men's loyalty," overriding the claims both of lesser communities within it and those which cut across it or potentially enfold it within a still greater society.
> (Connor 1994, 107)

It is the leaders of major national groups, after all, who are always included as the principal political figures in political power-sharing institutions. In Northern Ireland power is shared between Irish nationalists and British unionists. In Bosnia-Herzegovina, power is shared between the leaders of the Bosniak, Croat and Serb 'constituent peoples.' In Burundi, seats are reserved for Hutus and Tutsis; in Lebanon, Maronite Christians, Sunni and Shia Muslims have corporate representation and so on.

To be sure, consociationalism – in its liberal manifestation – resists reifying national groupings; this is in contrast with corporate consociationalism, which allocates political portfolios in power-sharing institutions based on ascriptive criteria (see McGarry and O'Leary 2007). The Northern Ireland version of power-sharing, for example, divides executive power between the largest elected *parties* to the Assembly, thereby theoretically allowing for a party based on any form of affiliation to fill a political post. Yet, it remains a form of governance specially modified for conflicts that are theorized to be rooted in ethnicized national divisions.

This is a troubling proposition for many feminists. We do not have to conclude that "a woman has no nation" (Nagel 1998) to recognize that other social and political identities have resonance in conflict zones – particularly when conservative ethno-national forces rigidly define the borders of who belongs to the nation, privileging sometimes sexist, elitist, heteronormative and other exclusionary values (Byrne 2009). The feminist critique extends beyond intersectional identities. Joanne Nagel writes:

> The project of establishing national identity and cultural boundaries tends to foster nationalist ethnocentrism. As a result nationalism and chauvinism seem to go hand in hand. Chauvinistic nationalism is often confined to the ideational realm in the form of attitudes and beliefs about national superiority. During periods of nationalist conflict or expansion, however, such ethnocentrism becomes animated. The result in modern world history has been for nationalism to display an intolerant, sometimes murderous face.
>
> (Nagel 1998, 248)

This view of boundary making, chauvinism and violence as the character of nations and nationalisms extends to institutional strategies for ethno-national accommodation. One might then anticipate that if nationalism is so ugly, particularly for women, it should not form the foundation of conflict resolution.

The work of Nira Yuval-Davis most clearly articulates the ways in which mainstream approaches to nationalism miss the importance of gender to the national project: nations and nationalism depend on particular constructions of manhood and womanhood. Central to Yuval-Davis's insight is the understanding that women are the biological, cultural and symbolic reproducers of the nation (Yuval-Davis 1997). Feminists also observe that nationalism most often serves men, typically to the detriment of women (McClintock 1977; Cockburn 1998). Nationalism is thus already gendered – marking particular roles for men and women. This has implications for political inclusion in power-sharing institutions. If the leaders of ethno-national groups are exclusively invited to the peace table and then form a new power-sharing government, the hierarchical relationship between men and women in national groupings remains intact. The attempt to provide a gender-neutral foundational theory of power-sharing is folly.

We can see, then, that power-sharing and the WPS agenda share a similar critique of nationalism. Feminists and consociationalists accept that nations are not primordial communities but also recognize that once established they can be resilient and have sometimes dangerous and violent political consequences. Both literatures, in this sense, are committed to solving problematic national movements. They also both aim to get to a post-conflict period of peace and stability.

This is a tempting foundation for a common alliance – reframing what appear to be contrasting positions on political identity as complementary perspectives. However, we have our reservations. This mutual suspicion of nationalism is based on a reified concept of political identity that establishes ever more boundaries: inside/outside; nationalism/cosmopolitanism. Nationalism in and of itself is not necessarily anti-feminist. Indeed, nationalist movements – particularly revolutionary and other anti-colonial movements against the status quo – can be radical spaces for politicization. Allowing for more boundary crossings and imagining more flux in our understanding of political identity is where we anticipate the most potential for alignment between power-sharing and the WPS agenda.

Consider, for example, Jill Steans's observation that while nationalism has had negative consequences for women, nationalist discourses can also serve as important sites of contestation in post-colonial contexts where the struggle for women's rights works in partnership with struggles for liberation (Steans 2013, 56–58). As Nahla Abdo writes:

> By taking an active role in their national liberation, and simultaneously bringing their concerns to the forefront of the agenda, women can contribute substantially to freeing the movement from its patriarchal structure.
>
> (Abdo 1991, 22)

Others, like Simona Sharoni (1995) and Kumari Jayawardena (1986), similarly recognize the emancipatory potential of revolutionary or anti-colonial nationalist movements. Women are not simply pawns of nationalizing groups, but are active political agents – sometimes challenging masculinist and patriarchal aspects of national political identity by exploiting gendered and nationalist tropes, and sometimes by organizing from a critical feminist standpoint within their national communities (Byrne 2014). Non-hegemonic national groupings, in particular, can tell us about abuses of authority and power; they can problematize hierarchical relations between peoples and can demonstrate how group relations both produce and resist domination.

As such, a gendering of power-sharing would also resist either/or thinking: *either* nationalist ideology is bad for women and peace *or* nationalism is a positive force for women's post-colonial liberation. Instead, a gendering would at once account for the emancipatory potential of nationalist movements, but also recognize the gender hierarchies which nationalist discourses, particularly in militarized conditions, may produce, and how these hierarchies are reproduced in power-sharing institutions.

Crossing boundaries and bringing together insights of both the literature on women in national revolutionary movements with critiques of nationalism will surely produce messy connections. Marysia Zalewski (2013) and other feminist IR theorists ask us to resist coherence, to accept reality as fragmented, and to withstand the impulse of neatness in our explanatory models. Consociationalism offers us an orderly, coherent story of the conflict that begins and ends with ethno-nationalism as the driving force. And yet consociationalists do recognize that ethno-national identities are not the only way people identify in conflict; rather they argue that it is just that these identities are the most salient (Lijphart 1995; McGarry and O'Leary 2007, 2009). They also recognize that attachments to ethno-national identities change over time and manifest differently depending on the context (i.e., some communities organize violently around ethno-national identity while others do not; the content of ethno-national identity changes, with language, territory and religion playing different roles in different places) (Wolff 2011). We might imagine, then, an openness to build in an explicit recognition of the importance of gender and other social identities, at least during periods of political stability under power-sharing formulas.

In power-sharing theory, stability is claimed as a pragmatic goal; consociational arrangements, for example, are seen as a kind of "necessary triage"

(O'Leary 2005). Stability, however, also does a tremendous amount of normative work. The upshot is twofold. First, we miss the feminist point that instability can be productive: creating space for new forms of politicization, new ways to resist the public/private divide and new ideas about how to constitute the state. For this reason, stability cannot be an end in itself. Second, when we prioritize stability, we assume that it works in a modular fashion, providing the conditions under which democracy and justice can be pursued (e.g., first stability, *then* democracy and justice). Stability, on this reading – often defined narrowly as the end of combat – will somehow create the conditions for social justice and greater democracy. It is also a commitment to nationalism defended on the basis of expediency and practicality: ethnicized groups cause violence and threaten political stability; therefore they must be included at the peace table and in post-conflict institutions.

There is optimism in consociationalism's theoretical foundations that the recognition of claims to national self-determination can produce safer, softer, more amenable nationalisms. This shared concern for the way in which nationalist movements can undermine democratic institutions is a possible basis for a gendered treatment of power-sharing. Such a reformulation could theorize the mechanisms by which power-sharing institutions and political processes might produce less antagonistic nationalisms in post-conflict contexts, at a minimum, and perhaps post-national futures, at a maximum. However, there are limits to such a move; still missing is the recognition in the feminist literature that instability through national revolutionary politics can produce emancipatory changes in unjust political contexts. Nationalisms – even violent ones – are not necessarily the problem that needs to be solved, but rather a popular vehicle to change unjust political contexts. What is more, such a reformulation would miss the insight that nations are not the only sources of meaning-making in people's lives. A commitment to include only ethno-national groupings in conflict-resolution processes does not capture the feminist emphasis on inclusion more broadly.

Gendering consociationalism

As a model that is focused on the direct representation of ethnic communities, consociationalism is likely to consider the counting of women in positions of elected power as the first yardstick for measuring inclusion. In this regard, leading contemporary consociations, such as Northern Ireland, Burundi, Bosnia-Herzegovina, Macedonia and Lebanon, do not fare well. When compared against the notion of critical mass, which is typically understood as 30 per cent of all representatives, only two legislative elections in Burundi and one in Macedonia pass the threshold. This threshold is often identified as a target in UNSCR 1325 National Action Plans and other quota strategies. If we take the global average of women's representation, which according to the Inter-Parliamentary Union is 22.2 per cent, Northern Ireland, Bosnia (save one anomalous election in 1998) and Lebanon miss the mark. Again, only Burundi and Macedonia exceed the average. Both Burundi and Macedonia have gender quotas in place; in

Macedonia they apply to candidates on party lists, whereas in Burundi the quota applies to the number of elected legislators.

Moreover, these numbers on women's limited political inclusion do not tell the whole story by glossing over structural and cultural considerations. For example, they do not explain why, while Northern Ireland is often celebrated as a consociational success story, it does a poor job of electing women when compared with the other devolved assemblies in the United Kingdom.[1] Likewise, these numbers do not capture why Bosnian women's political representation has suffered from electoral reforms, discussed further below, designed to encourage accountability and moderation (Borić 2004), and remains below the goal set in its UNSCR 1325 National Action Plan. Moreover, these data only consider post-conflict elections – they do not consider the input of women in the negotiations that culminate in power-sharing, a central concern for UNSCR 1325 and other aspects of the WPS agenda. Certainly, women remain woefully under-represented at the peace table: a UNIFEM (2010) study found that women account for less than 8 per cent in UN-mediated peace processes and less than 3 per cent of signatories to peace agreements. Power-sharing institutions – and peace processes more broadly – have not, on the whole, effectively embraced WPS norms.

The second strategy, then, for considering the alignment of the WPS agenda and ethno-political power-sharing is to approach both norms at the same level of analysis, which for power-sharing and specifically for consociationalism is the elite level.[2] Consociationalists concerned with women's inclusion might begin with the literature on gender mainstreaming, as promoted by UN agencies and as articulated in a series of WPS Security Council Resolutions.[3] Gender mainstreaming may be considered as a two-part phenomenon that begins with the adoption of a gender perspective (that is, "the process of assessing the implications for women and men of any planned action, including legislation, policies or programmes, in all areas and at all levels"), and which provides opportunities or "targeted interventions" for the narrowing of gender gaps between men and women (UN 2002). While there is a rich literature focusing on gender mainstreaming in peace processes and post-conflict reconstruction, there has been less theorizing on how to gender mainstream the power-sharing pacts that are often adopted in a peace agreement.

To start with, the first institutional feature on which WPS and consociationalist interests dovetail is proportional representation (PR) electoral systems. Consociationalists favour PR systems because they allow ethnic minority groups to articulate their own political identities (Lijphart 1995) and because they lessen the impulse to engage in strategic voting, instead allowing voters to vote for their most preferred party. These benefits are also believed to apply to women as political minorities (Lijphart 2012; Norris 2004). Pippa Norris identifies several reasons why PR is "women-friendly": parties are incentivized to create lists that "maximize their collective appeal" by including "candidates representing all the major social cleavages," it helps female candidates overcome the incumbency barrier, and it facilitates the development of "positive action strategies," such as voluntary or statutory gender quotas (Norris 2004, 187–191). Those concerned with the electoral representation of women thus share a predilection for PR with consociationalists.

Not all PR systems are created equally, however, and the kinship between feminists and consociationalists on PR should not be overstated. The distinction between open and closed lists matters, with little consensus as to which kind of list is better for women (or ethnic groups for that matter) (Htun 2004; Kunovich 2012; Matland 2005). Arend Lijphart (2008, 79) specifically advocates closed-list PR for ethnic representation because it encourages the formation of cohesive political parties and gives party leaders greater latitude in their bargaining and compromises with the leaders of other communities, making it easier to reach agreement; it also assumes that leaders are more predisposed to moderation than their followers. Open lists, on the other hand, are thought to empower individual voters, to cultivate greater accountability between voters and legislators, and to challenge party hierarchies (Belloni 2007, 82). This has made them an attractive option where leaders are seen as more intransigent than their followers; this is why, for example, Bosnia made the shift from a closed-list to an open-list PR system. However, this change was made without a gender perspective and had the impact of effectively 'demoting' female candidates, who experienced a 23 per cent drop in representation from the last closed-list election to the first open-list one (Borić 2004). The change has also contributed to 'leapfrogging'; for example, in the 2006 elections more than 30 women candidates lost seats to men who were ranked lower on the party lists (OSCE 2007). Open-list systems tend to privilege the more well-known candidates, who are likely to be male (Borić 2004).[4]

Other electoral strategies on which feminists and consociationalists may agree include legislative quotas. Some corporate consociations utilize quotas for ethnic groups; many UNSCR 1325 National Action Plans call for the implementation of legislative quotas for women. Gender quotas can be enacted in a variety of ways. They may be voluntarily adopted by political parties or they may be constitutionally mandated (Borić 2004; Norris 2008; Matland 2005). They can apply to candidate lists, as in Macedonia, or to the total number of elected representatives, as in Burundi. Gender quotas mirror consociational arguments about the proportional representation of ethno-political groups, and gender and ethnic quotas have worked alongside one another in several consociations.

As both feminists and consociationalists are aware, election to the legislature is often not enough to ensure the protection of rights and interests of the concerned groups. Access to the executive, where political priorities are set, is imperative for marginalized groups in divided societies. Women remain underrepresented from party leadership and executive positions. The adoption of executive quotas is one technique for greater executive representation; in Burundi there are constitutional provisions ensuring that 30 per cent of all cabinet posts are reserved for women (and which work in tandem with rules on ethnic representation in cabinet). While legislative and executive gender quotas cannot assume that women will necessarily take pro-women stances (Jacobson 2013; Pupavac 2005), they are often seen as a quick fix to increase women's representation. At least as it relates to executive and legislative strategies, points of engagement between consociationalists and feminists can be found.

The terrain becomes more complicated when considering the two remaining consociational institutions. Veto rights, which are meant to protect the 'vital interests' of minority groups, are typically enacted in one of two ways. Restrictive veto rights require the specification of which policy areas are open to veto use, which are then outlined in the constitution. Permissive vetoes can apply to any potential legislation. While not conclusive, there is some evidence suggesting that, in very divided settings, permissive veto rights encourage parties to take a hard line whereas restrictive veto rights would encourage more judicious use of the veto (Bieber 2005; Bahtić-Kunrath 2011). Yet restrictive veto rights run the risk of essentialism in that they would assume that "there is one fixed form of action or perception that captures the experience of all women" (Ní Aoláin *et al.* 2011, 42), and may restrict only so-called 'women's issues' to veto applicability. Rebouché and Fearon's argument that "women 'as a group' are unlike most others" is called to mind. They suggest that women "continue to be the target of widespread and systematic discrimination; yet the fact that their identities cut across almost all social, political, economic and cultural groups makes them enormously difficult to protect" (2005, 155). While women should have veto rights on issues of bodily autonomy and reproductive choices, there are plenty of other issues which concern women that may not be explicitly framed as gendered, such as land rights reform or the reconstruction of infrastructure. It may consequently become difficult for women to participate equally on these kinds of issues when restrictive vetoes are in play.

Permissive vetoes may therefore be the preferred option for gender protections. This could be implemented when a set number of representatives (potentially cross-party and cross-gender) argue that a proposed piece of legislation is against the vital interests of women (however defined), the veto can be exercised or, at a minimum, it can prompt a gender analysis of the proposed legislation to be conducted prior to a vote (similar to Belgium's alarm bell procedure for linguistic groups). A major challenge here would be to avoid strategies that expect female politicians to necessarily take pro-feminist, pro-women stances simply because they are women.

The final consociational institution is group autonomy, which may assume territorial or non-territorial forms (Lijphart 1977; Nimni 2007). A territorial division of power along gender lines is clearly problematic, given that gender groups do not exhibit territorially concentrated settlement patterns (Phillips 1995). Some non-territorial strategies, such as those that focus on resource allocation and funding for cultural institutions, may, however, be feasible. Those committed to gender equality could use consociational arguments on resource allocation and cultural autonomy to push for programme funding on gender issues. The challenge, as with vetoes, is to apply these provisions across gender groups and to not lock women – or men – into assumed gender roles.

There is a transformative core to gender mainstreaming that is often underestimated; "the generic demand is nothing short of the wholesale transformation of the institutions and processes of government in regard to gender, with the intention that this impacts on, works with, and change the wider society and polity" (Zalewski 2010, 7). Although, as Zalewski notes, the implementation of gender mainstreaming ideas has suffered a disconnect from feminist intentions and has been understood not as an opportunity for challenging patriarchal structures but as a mechanism for including more women in existing patriarchal establishments. Zalewski talks about this process as one of "suturing," whereas Susan Willett (2010), Ní Aoláin and colleagues (2011) and others employ 'grafting' in a similar context. The metaphors are apt. Gender mainstreaming power-sharing institutions does not challenge the core assumptions of the institutional design, it simply attempts to make room for women in existing structures. Gender mainstreaming is an 'add-and-stir' strategy.

While gender mainstreaming is one strategy for bringing power-sharing theory and the WPS agenda into alignment, there is reason for caution. The grafting of women's representation onto consociational institutions permits political elites to ignore patriarchal legacies and other structural-cultural impediments to women's political inclusion; that is, it can "introduce a conversation about 'gender' into policy-making practices and institutions" (Ní Aoláin *et al.* 2011), but it does not – and cannot, on its own – dismantle gender discrimination. Moreover, grafting provides an essentialist image of women as political minorities. It assumes that "women" is an uncontested category with high levels of internal homogeneity and is thus likely to expect female politicians to speak for all women, often across ethno-national and other identity lines. As Rebouché and Fearon (2005, 161) suggest, power-sharing may leave women in a double-bind:

> On the one hand, if they are to succeed politically, women may have to conform to an institutionalised identity that may be untrue to their particular experiences. On the other hand, this means that women may end up denying their own internal diversity as a distinctive group.

A gender mainstreamed version of power-sharing would also potentially reify "women's issues," making it difficult to see the gendered implications of other issue areas. Consequently, we may find that strategies for bringing the WPS agenda and consociationalism together exist, but the fit is awkward. According to Ní Aoláin and her co-authors, "inclusion of women alone is clearly insufficient without challenging the paradigms that have maintained their inequality and exclusion" (Ní Aoláin *et al.* 2011, 39). Policy alignment only works if we accept essentialist accounts of women and the nation, a proposition that is unsettling for feminists and for (liberal) consociationalists.

As with the limits of forming common alliances between power-sharing and WPS adherents around a shared skepticism of nationalism, there are limits here too. Attempting to gender mainstream power-sharing by way of adding women as an additional social group to power-sharing repeats the problem of group reification in the power-sharing formula: theorizing 'women' as a distinct constituency carries with it all the problems of theorizing ethno-national groups as distinct constituencies. People hold multiple and intersecting identities that cannot be fully realized in single-identity political units. Further, the broader feminist critique of elite-level political processes and the desire for broader inclusion is left unexplored. A gendering of power-sharing, thus, would require more than just the descriptive representation of women as either ethnic political party representatives or as separate political parties; it would challenge us to re-imagine an inclusive formulation whereby power is shared among a broader body politic.

Gendering power-sharing futures

In this chapter, we have assessed two sources of (perceived) tension between feminist and power-sharing priorities in political transitions and have found some surprising common ground between power-sharing and WPS. Both approaches tend to identify nationalisms as potentially dangerous and both are committed to inclusion as a foundation for democratic politics. We explored the potential to gender power-sharing – that is, incorporating WPS priorities into power-sharing theory and power-sharing institutions. On the face of it, there are some encouraging points of possible alliance which would require future work to design power-sharing practices that produce less ethno-nationally charged post-conflict futures and a potential reformulation of power-sharing institutions that build in explicit political mechanisms for women's inclusion in power-sharing processes.

As noted, however, we have some reservations about these proposals. First, in terms of the locus of analysis, a singular focus on a disciplined nation is incomplete because it does not fully capture how ordinary people make meaning in their lives. While it is ethno-nationalism that can motivate sharp and sometimes violent social divisions, this is not the only social cleavage that matters to political communities. What is more, social unrest and instability can also be productive, bringing into sharp relief important injustices suffered by particular communities. Feminist critics challenge us to begin with a politics of justice to guide democratic institutional design as opposed to a politics oriented around stability as a basis for democracy-building. Second, in terms of level of analysis, gender mainstreaming power-sharing institutions still leaves us with a focus on elite-level politics. In our view, this requires a modular form of thinking and a kind of essentialism that is discomfiting. Gendering power-sharing would require a more robust concept of inclusion, beyond elite level institutional design, that would build in mechanisms for greater social participation in political life.

While we have reservations about these two proposals for building common ground between power-sharing and the WPS agenda, we have also demonstrated that the gap between power-sharing and WPS is overdrawn in the critical feminist literature. Given a growing international preference for both power-sharing and WPS approaches to conflict mediation and peacebuilding, it is incumbent upon power-sharing and WPS scholars to think through how both approaches could work effectively together in theory and practice. The frustrating gender-blindness in power-sharing theory and institutions is untenable in a context where power-sharing and gender mainstreaming proposals are being applied simultaneously to conflicts around the world. New and sustained theoretical and practical engagements between power-sharing and WPS scholars and practitioners are needed to begin the urgent work of gendering power-sharing.

Notes

1 In the 2011 to 2016 Northern Ireland Assembly, 16 per cent of MLAs were women. In Scotland and Wales, the numbers are 35 per cent and 40 per cent, respectively. In addition, as a 2014 *Belfast Telegraph* article highlights, women in the Northern Ireland Assembly face a number of challenges to effective participation. www.belfasttelegraph.co.uk/news/politics/daily-humiliation-for-women-mlas-in-northern-ireland-assembly-30685614.html.
2 One may also argue that employing UN Security Council Resolutions as a means of facilitating greater political inclusion is similarly an elite-level strategy, thus suggesting some reconciliatory potential.
3 Beyond Resolution 1325, there are another seven Security Council resolutions – 1820, 1888, 1889, 1960, 2106, 2122 and 2242 – that address the women, peace and security agenda.
4 Other aspects of electoral system design also play a significant role. Female candidates, for example, benefit from larger district magnitudes, which lessens the "most broadly acceptable candidate" phenomenon that tends to reward male candidates.

References

Abdo, Nahla. 1991. "Women of the Intifada: Gender, Class and National Liberation." *Race and Class* 32, no. 4: 19–34.

Bahtić-Kunrath, Birgit. 2011. "Of Veto Players and Entity-Voting: Institutional Gridlock in the Bosnian Reform Process." *Nationalities Papers* 39, no. 6: 899–923.

Bell, Christine and Catherine O'Rourke. 2010. "Peace Agreements or Pieces of Paper? The Impact of UNSCR Resolution 1325 on Peace Processes and Their Agreements." *International and Comparative Law Quarterly* 59: 941–980.

Belloni, Roberto. 2007. *Statebuilding and International Intervention in Bosnia.* London: Routledge.

Bieber, Florian. 2005. "Power-Sharing After Yugoslavia: Functionality and Dysfunctionality of Power-Sharing Institutions in Post-War Bosnia, Macedonia, and Kosovo." In *From Power-Sharing to Democracy: Post-Conflict Institutions in Ethnically Divided Societies*, edited by Sid Noel, pp. 85–103. Montreal and Kingston: McGill-Queen's University Press.

Borić, Besima. 2004. "Application of Quotas: Legal Reforms and Implementation in Bosnia and Herzegovina." Paper presented at the International Institute for Democracy and Electoral Assistance (IDEA)/CEE Network for Gender Issues Conference, *The Implementation of Quotas: European Experiences.* Budapest, Hungary, 22–23 October, available at www.quotaproject.org/CS/CS_BiH-boric.pdf.

Byrne, Siobhan. 2009. *Women and the Transition from Conflict in Northern Ireland: Lessons for Peace-Building in Israel/Palestine.* IBIS Working Papers No. 89. Dublin: Institute for British-Irish Studies, University College Dublin.

Byrne, Siobhan. 2014. "Troubled Engagement in Ethnicized Conflict: Negotiating Difference among Feminist Activists in Israel/Palestine and Northern Ireland." *International Feminist Journal of Politics* 16, no. 1: 106–126.

Cockburn, Cynthia. 1998. *The Space between Us: Negotiating Gender and National Identities in Conflict.* London and New York: Zed Books.

Connor, Walker. 1994. *Ethnonationalism: The Quest for Understanding.* Princeton, NJ: Princeton University Press.

Darby, John and Roger MacGinty. 2003. "What Peace? What Process?" In *Contemporary Peacemaking: Conflict, Violence and Peace Processes*, edited by John Darby and Roger MacGinty, pp. 9–18. New York: Palgrave Macmillan.

De Alwis, Malathi, Julie Mertus and Tazreena Sajjad. 2013. "Women and Peace Processes." In *Women and Wars: Contested Histories, Uncertain Futures*, edited by Carol Cohn, pp. 169–193. Cambridge: Polity Press.

Enloe, Cynthia. 2000. *Bananas, Beaches, and Bases: Making Feminist Sense of International Politics*, updated edn. Berkeley: University of California Press.

Enloe, Cynthia. 2004. *The Curious Feminist: Searching for Women in a New Age of Empire.* Berkeley: University of California Press.

Guelke, Adrian. 2012. *Politics in Deeply Divided Societies.* Cambridge: Polity Press.

Hartzell, Caroline and Matthew Hoddie. 2003. "Institutionalizing Peace: Power Sharing and Post-Civil War Conflict Management." *American Journal of Political Science* 47, no. 2: 318–332.

Horowitz, Donald L. 2000. *Ethnic Groups in Conflict*, 2nd edn. Berkeley: University of California Press.

Htun, Mala. 2004. "Is Gender Like Ethnicity? The Political Representation of Identity Groups." *Perspectives on Politics* 2, no. 3: 439–458.

Jacobson, Ruth. 2013. "Women 'after' Wars." In *Women and Wars: Contested Histories, Uncertain Futures*, edited by Carol Cohn, pp. 215–241. Cambridge: Polity Press.

Jayawardena, Kumari. 1986. *Feminism and Nationalism in the Third World.* London and New Jersey: Zed Books.

Kunovich. Sheri L. 2012. "Unexpected Winners: The Significance of an Open-List System on Women's Representation in Poland." *Politics and Gender* 8: 153–217.

Lijphart, Arend. 1977. *Democracy in Plural Societies: A Comparative Exploration.* New Haven, CT: Yale University Press.

Lijphart, Arend. 1985. *Power-Sharing in South Africa.* Berkeley: University of California Press.

Lijphart, Arend. 1995. "Self-Determination versus Pre-Determination of Ethnic Minorities in Power-Sharing Systems." In *The Rights of Minority Cultures*, edited by Will Kymlicka, pp. 275–287. Oxford: Oxford University Press.

Lijphart, Arend. 2008. *Thinking about Democracy: Power Sharing and Majority Rule in Theory and Practice.* London: Routledge.

Lijphart, Arend. 2012. *Patterns of Democracy*, 2nd edn. New Haven, CT: Yale University Press.

MacKenzie, Megan. 2009. "Securitization and De-Securitization: Female Soldiers and the Reconstruction of Women in Post-Conflict Sierra Leone." *Security Studies* 18, no. 2: 241–261.

Matland, Richard. 2005. "Enhancing Women's Political Representation: Legislative Recruitment and Electoral Systems." In *Women in Parliament: Beyond the Numbers.* Stockholm: International IDEA.

McClintock, Anne. 1997. "'No Longer in a Future Heaven': Gender, Race and Nationalism." In *Dangerous Liaisons: Gender, Nation, and Postcolonial Perspectives*, pp. 89–112. Minneapolis: University of Minnesota Press.

McGarry, John. 2003. "Consociational Theory and Northern Ireland's Good Friday Agreement." In *European Yearbook of Minority Issues*, pp. 283–298. The Hague: Kluwer Law International.

McGarry, John and Brendan O'Leary. 2007. "Iraq's Constitution of 2005: Liberal Consociation as Political Prescription." *International Journal of Constitutional Law* 5, no. 4: 670–698.

McGarry, John and Brendan O'Leary. 2009. "Power Shared after the Death of Thousands." In *Consociational Theory: McGarry and O'Leary and the Northern Ireland Conflict*, edited by Rupert Taylor, pp. 15–84. London: Routledge.

Nagel, Joanne. 1998. "Masculinity and Nationalism: Gender and Sexuality in the Making of Nations." *Ethnic and Racial Studies* 21, no. 2: 242–269.

Ní Aoláin, Fionnuala, Dina Francesca Haynes and Naomi Cahn. 2011. *On the Frontlines: Gender, War and the Post-Conflict Process.* Oxford: Oxford University Press.

Nimni, Ephraim. 2007. "National-Cultural Autonomy as an Alternative to Minority Territorial Nationalism." *Ethnopolitics* 6, no. 3: 345–364.

Norris, Pippa. 2004. *Electoral Engineering: Voting Rules and Political Behaviour.* Cambridge: Cambridge University Press.

Norris, Pippa. 2008. *Driving Democracy: Do Power-Sharing Institutions Work?* Cambridge: Cambridge University Press.

O'Leary, Brendan. 2005. "Debating Consociational Politics: Normative and Explanatory Arguments." In *From Power-Sharing to Democracy: Post-Conflict Institutions in Ethnically Divided Societies*, edited by Sid Noel, pp. 3–43. Montreal: McGill-Queen's University Press.

OSCE. 2007. *Bosnia and Herzegovina General Elections 1 October 2006 OSCE/ODIHR Election Observation Final Report.* Warsaw. Available at www.osce.org/odihr/elections/bih/23945.

Peuchguirbal, Nadine. 2012. "The Cost of Ignoring Gender in Conflict and Post-Conflict Situations: A Feminist Perspective." *Amsterdam Law Forum* 4, no. 1: 4–19.

Phillips, Anne. 1995. *The Politics of Presence: Political Representation of Gender, Race and Ethnicity.* Oxford: Oxford University Press.

Potter, Antonia. 2011. "G is for Gendered: Taking the Mystery out of Gendering Peace Agreements." *Women at the Peace Table: Asia Pacific Opinion Series No 5.* Centre for Humanitarian Dialogue.

Pupavac, Vanessa. 2005. "Empowering Women? An Assessment of International Gender Policies in Bosnia." *International Peacekeeping* 12, no. 3: 391–405.

Rebouché, Rachel and Kate Fearon. 2005. "Overlapping Identities: Power Sharing and Women's Rights." In *Power Sharing: New Challenges for Divided Societies*, edited by Ian O'Flynn and David Russell, pp. 155–171. London: Pluto Press.

Sasson-Levy, Orna. 2003. "Feminism and Military Gender Practices: Israeli Women Soldiers in 'Masculine' Roles." *The Sociological Inquiry* 73, no. 3: 440–465.

Sharoni, Simona. 1995. *Gender and the Israeli–Palestinian Conflict: The Politics of Women's Resistance.* Syracuse, NY: Syracuse University Press.

Sjoberg, Laura and Caron Gentry. 2007. *Mothers, Monsters, Whores: Women's Violence in Global Politics.* London: Zed Books.

Steans, Jill. 2013. *Gender and International Relations*, 3rd edn. Cambridge, and Malden, MA: Polity Press.

Taylor, Rupert. 2009. "The Promise of Consociational Theory." In *Consociational Theory: McGarry and O'Leary and the Northern Ireland Conflict*, edited by Rupert Taylor, pp. 1–11. London: Routledge.
UNIFEM. 2010. *Women's Participation in Peace Negotiations.*
United Nations. 2002. *Gender Mainstreaming: An Overview*, available at www.un.org/womenwatch/osagi/pdf/e65237.pdf.
Walter, Barbara. 2002. *Committing to Peace: The Successful Settlement of Civil Wars.* Princeton, NJ: Princeton University Press.
Willett, Susan. 2010. "Security Council Resolution 1325: Assessing the Impact on Women, Peace and Security." *International Peacekeeping* 17, no. 2: 142–158
Wolff, Stefan. 2011. "Post-Conflict State Building: The Debate on Institutional Choice." *Third World Quarterly* 32, no. 10: 1777–1802.
Yuval-Davis, Nira. 1997. *Gender and Nation*. London: Sage.
Zalewski, Marysia. 2010. "'I Don't Even Know What Gender Is': A Discussion of the Connection between Gender Mainstreaming and Feminist Theory." *Review of International Studies* 36, no. 1: 3–27.
Zalewski, Marysia. 2013. *Feminist International Relations: Exquisite Corpse*. London: Routledge.

Conclusion

What explains the performance of power-sharing settlements?

John McGarry

Power-sharing theories, particularly consociational versions, are among the most influential in comparative politics. Consociational theory is also among the most criticized (for reviews and rebuttals see Lijphart 1985; O'Leary 2005). The criticisms are often sweeping and come from a broad spectrum of opinion, including from conservatives, liberals, socialists and feminists. Conservatives focus on what they see as consociation's inability to secure peace and stability, its alleged futility. Consociational settlements are said to be difficult to adopt because majorities will be unwilling to share power with minorities or because bitter rivals prefer disagreement to cooperation (Horowitz 2002, 194, 197). Even if such settlements can be agreed, they will be dysfunctional, gridlocked and incapable of providing good government (Horowitz 2014). Liberals claim that consociations, which tend to allocate office on the basis of ethnicity, discriminate against individuals, especially those from outside the privileged communities (Barry 2001; Brass 1991, 334).[1] Liberal lawyers concerned with transitional justice fault consociation for giving power to warlords and other leaders guilty of egregious human rights abuses, promoting a culture of impunity that allows its beneficiaries to "get away with murder" (Sriram 2013; Zahar and Sriram 2009). It allegedly creates perverse incentives by encouraging the conviction that violence pays (Tull and Mehler 2005). Socialists warn that consociation cannot deliver social transformation, the evolution of societies from benighted fixations on ethnicity and tribalism to a more progressive politics based on programmes and class (Taylor 2001, 2009; Hulsey 2010). A common feminist critique suggests that it is "bad for women given the dismal record of women's inclusion in power-sharing institutions" (Chapter 12; Rebouché and Fearon 2005). All of these critics worry that consociations entrench divisions, and some claim they cause such divisions, allowing elites to play ethnic cards (Brass 1991; Roeder and Rothchild 2005, 37, 29; Tull and Mehler 2005; van Schendelen 1984; Wilson 2005).

Given the frequency and persistence of these criticisms, we invited a number of scholars to subject power-sharing theory and practice to an in-depth analysis and critical evaluation. They were asked to focus on three questions: Do power-sharing arrangements enhance stability, peace and cooperation in divided places? Do they do so in ways that promote effective government? Lastly, do they promote justice, fairness and democracy?

The evidence presented here is mixed, and not just across cases, but in relation to different episodes of power-sharing within the same place, or different governmental functions and polices within the same episode. Cheeseman and Murray explain that the legacy of Kenya's temporary power-sharing pact (2008–2013) is "complex" (Chapter 2). It ended violence, provided political stability, facilitated reform of the security forces and constitutional change, but did little to counter corruption or impunity. It may have enabled the latter by facilitating alliances between perpetrators of violent crimes across the political divide. One such alliance – between Uhuru Kenyatta and William Ruto – comprised the winning ticket in the presidential elections that followed the end of power-sharing in 2013. In Northern Ireland, a power-sharing executive performed abysmally in 1974, failing to prevent violence (though it lacked security powers) and collapsing after only five months. In contrast, the power-sharing arrangements that followed the Good Friday Agreement of 1998 were associated with a dramatic and lasting reduction in violence (Chapter 3), which had begun in the run-up to its negotiation. After 1998, power-sharing in Northern Ireland went through two distinct phases: the years between 1998 and 2007 saw significant inter-party and intra-executive discord with the power-sharing institutions frequently suspended. In contrast, the second phase, from 2007 to 2016, has been one of relatively remarkable cooperation among the parties, particularly the hardline parties on each side, although this has not been without blips. Examining the period from 1998 up until 2016, McEvoy concludes that power-sharing has produced a "mixed bag of important progress amid ongoing challenges" (Chapter 10). Bose also identifies two phases of power-sharing in Mostar and Bosnia, roughly coterminous with the Dayton Agreement's first and second decades (Chapter 9). In his view, matters have regressed. The first phase "looks in retrospect almost like a golden era of peacebuilding compared to the second." Vandeginste describes the adoption of power-sharing in Burundi in 2000 and its survival as a "miracle," but adds that it is currently under threat as the country lapses into single-party authoritarianism (Chapter 8). Fraenkel has very little positive to say about Fiji's power-sharing experiment between 1999 and 2006, but notes a more "promising" experiment that began in April 2006 until its life was cut short by a military coup (Chapter 5). In the volume's final two chapters, which focus on transitional justice and feminism respectively, our contributors also emphasize consociationalism's mixed record, a welcome change from the unmitigated criticisms that usually issue from these quarters (Chapters 11 and 12).

Mixed evidence suggests that blanket critiques are out of place. It also raises the question: What explains variation in performance? Our contributors suggest that at least four variables matter: the role played by external actors in the making and implementation of consociational agreements; how security is structured and managed in polities that have been violently divided; how self-determination is addressed in polities that are nationally divided; and the precise institutions and rules used in each settlement. These variables supplement the structural and historical factors which Lijphart has emphasized as shaping the prospects for consociations, and which include group size, number of groups, size of the polity and historical traditions (Lijphart 1969, 1977).

Power-sharing and international intervention

In his classical statement of consociational theory, Lijphart suggested that the prospects for consociations were almost entirely influenced by factors internal to the state (Lijphart 1977: 53–103). Of the eight conditions listed as facilitating success, only one was external: rivals could be motivated to share power if they experienced a common external threat. The corollary was that an asymmetric external threat could have a negative effect on power-sharing, arousing fears about sharing power on the part of the threatened. Lijphart's views were shaped by his familiarity with the small Western European states of Belgium, the Netherlands and Switzerland, all of which had been threatened by powerful neighbours and all of which had successful consociations. Lebanon too had opted for power-sharing in 1943 in response to a common threat from the Free French who controlled the country and were unwilling to decolonize it. Its power-sharing regime collapsed in 1975 in part because of the intrusion of significant Palestinian forces into Lebanon, which destabilized its internal balance of power and unleashed a 15-year civil war (Lijphart 1985, 92).

It has since become clear that external factors may play a wider and sometimes more positive role than envisaged in Lijphart's early work. Northern Ireland's Good Friday Agreement shows that outsiders can facilitate agreements, and then help to implement and consolidate them (McGarry and O'Leary 2009, 37–44). This benign role of outsiders is confirmed by Cheeseman and Murray who emphasize the helpful part played by Kofi Annan and the Center for Humanitarian Dialogue (CHD), a Geneva-based NGO, in mediating Kenya's Serena Accord in 2008. This established a temporary power-sharing pact between Mwai Kibaki's Party of National Unity (PNU) and Raila Odinga's Orange Democratic Movement (ODM). Outsiders participated in a number of commissions and in a special court that was given exclusive jurisdiction to adjudicate matters concerning the making of a new constitution. The court's role was to "ensure impartiality and objectivity and that ethnic politics were not played out again in their deliberations." Personal ties between President Kikwete of Tanzania and Kenya's Kibaki were said to be useful in influencing the latter to accept power-sharing. Vandeginste explains that power-sharing in Burundi resulted from a "strong and lasting international involvement." The Arusha Agreement (2000) was brokered first by Tanzania's Julius Nyerere, and then by South Africa's Nelson Mandela, who had negotiated South Africa's temporary power-sharing constitution in 1994. In Vandeginste's view: "Mandela's moral authority came close to the 'divine' intervention that was required for the miracle of power-sharing in Burundi to become reality." Sanctions imposed by Tanzania persuaded Burundi's dominant Tutsi regime to enter negotiations. In the post-Agreement period, an International Monitoring Committee was established to supervise and coordinate the implementation of the Arusha Agreement, and outside peacekeepers were employed.[2] External diplomatic pressure helped defeat a proposal in Burundi's Parliament in 2014 that would have stripped the Tutsi of their legislative veto. Vandeginste believes that Burundi's current difficulties stem from a reduction in the international community's attentiveness. Relatedly, Fraenkel explains that the failure of Fiji's post-1997 power-sharing experiment may be partly attributed to an absence of external involvement.

In two of our cases, international actors have imposed power-sharing, and otherwise intervened in a heavy-handed and counterproductive way. These possibilities were not emphasized in early consociational theory, but there was a precedent in Cyprus in 1960. Lebanon's Ta'if Agreement (1989) was dictated by a neighbouring power, Syria, to local elites, and was facilitated by Saudi Arabia. Syria's role was made possible by the end of the Cold War and Syria's willingness to side with the USA in the buildup to the First Gulf War against Iraq. Power-sharing in Bosnia was dictated primarily by the USA at Dayton in 1995. The Dayton 'Agreement' was not even signed by the representatives of Bosnia's Serb and Croat communities, but rather by the leaders of their respective patron-states, Serbia and Croatia. Bose maintains that it is the external community's heavy-handedness that explains the deterioration of power-sharing in Bosnia and Mostar.

This nuanced evidence suggests that external actions can account for at least some of the positive and negative traits associated with recent examples of power-sharing experiments.

Security and power-sharing

The provenance of classical consociational theory within peaceful and historically neutral polities in Western Europe – Belgium, the Netherlands, Austria and Switzerland – led some critics to argue that consociations may work where they are unnecessary but not in the violently divided trust-devoid places where they are supposedly needed (Horowitz 1985, 573;[3] 2002, 256). Evidence here debunks this thesis. Three of our cases – Kenya, Northern Ireland and Burundi – were violently divided, on a genocidal scale in the last case; yet all three managed to negotiate broadly collegial executives, albeit often imperfect. In all three of these cases, consociational power-sharing has been associated with reductions of violence, which suggests that in this one crucial respect, consociation's record may be better than mixed. In Kenya and Northern Ireland, they have also been associated with important reforms to the security sector. Even in Lebanon and Bosnia, where power-sharing was imposed, it helped end civil wars. Vandeginste explains that far from needing trust to negotiate a consociation, Burundi's parties chose a consociation because it involved "mutually acceptable fear-reducing institutions, which [...] compensated for the lack of trust among the parties." Similarly, Bose argues that the bitter war in Bosnia produced such a profound mistrust that Bosnia needed consociation with its emphasis on good fences making good neighbours. War made integration unrealistic in Bosnia, not consociation.

Our contributors suggest that in violently divided places both political and security institutions matter, and that the fortunes of the former are tied closely to the management of the latter. McGarry and O'Leary explain that the relative instability of the 1998 to 2007 phase of power-sharing in Northern Ireland is largely attributable to difficulties with security issues such as policing reform, demilitarization and the decommissioning of weapons (Chapter 3). All of these issues were divisive, and none of them were immediately resolved by the 1998 Agreement. Failure to follow the wording of the Agreement and the recommendations of the commissions established by it, created an immediate crisis, and led to several suspensions, with the last occurring between 2002 and 2007. Stable power-sharing became possible only after the security issues were successfully dealt with in negotiations involving the Northern Irish parties and the British and Irish governments that took place between 2003 and 2006. Writing at the beginning of the last suspension in 2002, Donald Horowitz blamed the instability on consociational power-sharing itself, and insisted on reforms to the political institutions (Horowitz 2001, 102; 2002, 194, 197). This perspective fails to account for consociationalism's stability in the post-2007 period, even if this remains fragile (McCrudden *et al.* 2016).

Vandeginste stresses the importance of getting security institutions right in Burundi's power-sharing agreement. The military dimension was fundamental: "an essential and durable cornerstone of Burundi's transition to peace." Burundi's agreement was negotiated, and based on a rough balance of power between the majority Hutu and minority Tutsi (15 per cent). Given the record of Hutu violence against the Tutsi in neighbouring Rwanda in 1994, and in Burundi itself in 1993, Burundi's Tutsi regime could hardly have considered consociation unless Tutsi security needs were met, including the retention of significant representation in Burundi's army. As a *quid pro quo*, Tutsi leaders were prepared to accept a president who was likely to be Hutu. Other security provisions allowing for the inclusion of former rebels in the police and army were important for bringing on board the Hutu rebel group, the CNDD-FDD and other smaller Hutu paramilitary groups. As the current Hutu president, Pierre Nkurunziza consolidates his authority over political institutions, the survival of military power-sharing, in Vandeginste's view, stands between the country and disaster.

The failure to deal with an indigenous monopoly of posts in the security services in Fiji (95 per cent) was fatal to its political power-sharing experiment in 2000 (Chapter 5).[4] Although Fiji's accord provided for a consociational executive, it did not deal with the military, which remained under ethnic Fijian control. The 1999/2000 government fell to what was called a "civilian coup" because its leader, George Speight, was a businessman, but Speight was also an ethnocentric indigenous Fijian with the backing of the military's crack regiment, the Counter-Revolutionary Warfare Squadron. The core of the military first stood aside while the coup took place and then intervened to assume executive authority before handing office to a government of its choice, an action which the Supreme Court later deemed unconstitutional. A second straightforward military coup occurred in December 2006, led by the integrationist military commander Frank Bainimarama. Constitutional government was not restored until September 2014, but it was now shorn of its power-sharing provisions. Power-sharing in Fiji had more problems than an overbearing military (see below), but it is worth speculating if the coups could have been prevented and power-sharing saved if Fiji's parties had been able to adopt Burundi's model of a bi-ethnic military or agreed to military reforms aimed at coup-proofing their democracy.

McGarry argues that there will be no power-sharing settlement in Cyprus unless core security concerns are addressed in both the Turkish Cypriot and Greek Cypriot communities (Chapter 1). Turkish Cypriots fear a repeat of rights violations suffered at the hands of Greek Cypriots between December 1963 and the Turkish invasion of July 1974. Greek Cypriots wish to see the removal of some 30,000 Turkish troops from the north of the island and the end of Turkey's legal right of unilateral intervention under the 1960 Treaty of Guarantee, which it used to justify its invasion and partition of the island in 1974. A settlement that fails to address these security concerns will not be put to a referendum, and would not pass if it was.

Bose argues that the Office of the High Representative's decision in 2005 to push for policing reform that would take control away from entity jurisdiction in Republika Srpska and cantonal jurisdiction in the Federation of Bosnia and Herzegovina (FBiH), entrusting it instead to federal authorities, was needless and provocative. Policing had been improving in the post-war years, and normally belongs to the constituent entities of federations. Instead of addressing security dilemmas, the OHR's move increased them, especially in Republika Srpska, destabilizing Dayton's power-sharing architecture. The OHR's initiative was abandoned two years later.

Self-determination and power-sharing

Divided polities are riven not just to different extents but also in different ways. One meaningful twofold classification is between places that are reasonably nationally integrated but divided along ethnic, religious, linguistic or class lines and those that are nationally divided. The communities in these contrasting scenarios have distinctive aspirations. In the former, the groups behave like "communal contenders" (Gurr 1993), claiming a stake in their country's central government with proportionality and veto rights, and perhaps some (non-territorial) cultural autonomy. In the latter, the groups are 'ethno-national' communities with self-determination claims, including claims to partnerships between peoples within central governments, but sometimes with intense claims to territorial self-government, the recognition of their national symbols and institutional links with co-nationals in other states.

The difficulty with some power-sharing prescriptions is that they are more apt for communal contenders than they are for ethno-national communities (e.g., what Sisk (1996) has called "integrative" power-sharing but which most others recognize as "centripetalism"). Centripetalism suggests support for a politics that strengthens the 'centre' or moderate ground, but it also suggests a preference for a somewhat centralized state, achieved through a presidential system, electoral systems that undercut sectional appeals and local government boundaries which cut through ethnic groups rather than around them. Classical consociational theory, as McGarry and O'Leary have argued, may also be too centralized for ethno-nationalists (McGarry and O'Leary 2008, 2009, 2011). Because of its provenance in nationally integrated polities in Western Europe, it has tended to emphasize an approach focused on the central government over one based on self-determination claims.

Three of the cases considered in this volume involve ethno-national divisions: Northern Ireland, Bosnia-Herzegovina (and Mostar) and Cyprus. Northern Ireland's 1998 Agreement would not have been reached, or succeeded, if it had not dealt fairly with each of its two community's self-determination claims as well as providing executive power-sharing, proportionality and mutual veto rights (McGarry and O'Leary 2009). Although the 1998 Agreement was famously described by nationalist leader Seamus Mallon as "Sunningdale for slow learners" – a reference to where the failed power-sharing pact of 1974 had been negotiated – self-determination was addressed in a novel manner. The 1974 Agreement had been destroyed by loyalists who believed that Dublin (rule) was "only a Sunningdale away," and resented and feared Ireland's constitutional claim that Northern Ireland was part of its national territory and that Dublin reserved the right to rule it. In the 1998 Agreement, these concerns were addressed by constitutional amendments modifying Ireland's position to specify that unification would only occur through the joint and separate consent of both jurisdictions on the island. Nationalists were reassured in 1998 by, among other things, the British government's recognition of the right of the "people of Ireland" to self-determination, albeit in two jurisdictions, which had not been conceded at Sunningdale, and also by all-island and British-Irish institutional machinery that was more robust than that created in 1974 (for details, see McGarry and O'Leary 2009). Worryingly, the creative and balanced national self-determination package in the Good Friday Agreement may be fundamentally threatened by the June 2016 referendum vote in the UK and Gibraltar to leave the European Union – further evidence of how external actors can destabilize (and facilitate) power-sharing agreements. If this advisory vote is followed through it remains to be seen whether a hard international border between the two parts of Ireland will damage the 1998 settlement fatally, or undermine the current cooperation between the British and Irish governments, much of which has developed during their common membership of the European Union.

Bose's central argument with respect to Bosnia and Mostar is that the OHR damaged inter-communal relations by enforcing principles of 'integrative' rather than cross-national power-sharing. His chapter focuses on Mostar, which he sees as a microcosm of Bosnia, and which the OHR treated as such. During Dayton's first decade (1995–2004), Mostar was decentralized with several municipalities serving the Croat and Bosniak communities respectively. The overarching City Council was governed by what was effectively a co-mayor system, with one Bosniak and one Croat. In 2004, the OHR centralized the city by decree, abolishing the separate municipalities and replacing the co-mayors with a single mayor system. These reforms incensed Mostar's Bosniak minority and led to protracted conflict between Croat and Bosniak politicians. By 2009 the city was paralysed, with no mayor and no budget, both of which had fallen foul of procedures that required inter-communal cooperation. When local government elections were held throughout Bosnia in 2012, none took place in Mostar. The city continues to lack an elected council – there is a working administration accountable to no one. The OHR also tried to centralize Bosnia as a whole (for example, in relation to policing), this time incensing Croats and Serbs. Accession to the European Union was explicitly linked to integrative power-sharing, both with respect to the centralization of policing and a demand for reforms to Bosnia's three people's presidency on the grounds that it contravened the European Convention on Human Rights (McCrudden and O'Leary 2013). When it became clear that Bosnia's communities would not compromise their national aspirations for access to the EU, this 'conditionality' was dropped.

Bose believes that the international community should have employed an approach based on self-determination. The decentralized municipal structures in Mostar should have been left alone. Dayton's provisions for cooperation between Bosnia-Herzegovina and its neighbouring states should have been used more to foster linkages to Croatia and Serbia, transforming Bosnia from a 'prison' into a 'bridge' for its Croat and Serb communities. Instead of focusing on the centralization of Mostar (and Bosnia-Herzegovina) in 2004, the OHR should have taken up a proposal from the European Stability Initiative to transform Bosnia's federal structures. The proposal called for a federation based on Republika Srpska and the cantons of the FBiH with the FBiH Entity level disappearing. It was supported at the time by leaders of all three communities but ignored by the OHR. The proposal was the most feasible way to accommodate the Croat minority, the only one of Bosnia's three communities not to have its own federal entity or to be the dominant community in a federal entity.

McGarry shows that integrative models of power-sharing are inapplicable in Cyprus given its ethno-national divisions (Chapter 1). Just as Mostar's Bosniak minority resisted the one-mayor model, Cyprus's Turkish Cypriots consistently reject proposals for a single-person presidency in Cyprus. This is not just because they are a minority but because they see a co-presidency as consistent with their claim that Cyprus has two equal peoples. The Turkish Cypriots also object to an integrative federation of the sort recommended by centripetalists, in which their community is broken up across several "cantons," insisting instead on collective self-determination in one federal region. Like the ethno-national minorities in Northern Ireland (Irish nationalists) and in Bosnia (Croats and Serbs), Turkish Cypriots insist in any peace settlement on institutional links between them and their neighbouring co-nationals (in Turkey).

The prescriptive lesson is that if power-sharing is to work in nationally divided polities, it needs to address self-determination claims without an ethos of contempt or manipulation.

Power-sharing institutions and rules

As Brown and Ní Aoláin write, "consociationalism is an institutional approach" (Chapter 11). It is surprising, then, that critics of consociational power-sharing often avoid focusing on its rules, preferring general criticisms (Taylor 2001), or they criticize specific consociational rules without considering consociational alternatives. But as several cases in this volume show, it is the particular rules that are in place rather than consociation in general that may make the difference between success and failure. This section examines some of the institutional and regulatory complexity of power-sharing discussed in this volume.

Rules of inclusion

While power-sharing suggests inclusion, power-sharing executives are not equally inclusive. One of the most vigorous debates in power-sharing theory takes place between consociationalists who prefer broad inclusion, and centripetalists who seek to restrict coalitions to moderates. Horowitz writes that the choice between these two alternatives is the most important one facing policy-makers in deeply divided polities (Horowitz 2002, 213). O'Leary has shown that consociational arrangements may be differentially inclusive, including all major parties in grand coalitions, or majorities (concurrent alliances) or pluralities from each of the polity's different communities (O'Leary 2005). It would be surprising if these different degrees of inclusion did not have some effect on the performance of power-sharing governments, including their ability to deliver cooperation, peace and good governance. This volume discusses rules that facilitate the following three levels of inclusion: inclusive, or grand, coalitions; "concurrent" consociations; and coalitions of moderate parties.

In the first category is Northern Ireland's Good Friday Agreement (1998), Kenya's Serena Accord (2008), Fiji's 1997 Constitution and Burundi's 2000 Arusha Agreement. In Northern Ireland, every party that qualifies under the d'Hondt rule is eligible for a ministry. Since 1998, this has entitled at least the four largest parties, and the two largest in each community, to seats in the governing coalition, although the rules did not mandate participation in government and did not require any change to enable two of these parties to go into opposition in 2016. In Kenya, the Serena Accord stipulated that portfolios would be assigned in a manner that "at all times" reflected the representation of each party in Parliament and took account of "portfolio balance." Fiji's 1997 Constitution, taking its cue from South Africa's (interim) constitution of 1994, stated that any party winning 10 per cent of seats in the legislature was entitled to ministries "in proportion to their numbers in the House." In Burundi, the Arusha Agreement distributed between 50 and 60 per cent of portfolios to a coalition of predominantly Hutu parties (G7) and the rest to a coalition of predominantly Tutsi parties (G10) for a transitional period, originally 36 months. Burundi's 2005 constitution subsequently allocated a proportionate number of ministries to each party obtaining 5 per cent of the votes.

In the second category is the executive of the Brussels Capital region (Chapter 4) (and also Northern Ireland since the voluntary withdrawal of the UUP, the SDLP and the Alliance party from the executive in 2016). Apart from the minister-president, who is considered neutral, the executive includes four ministers, two of whom must be from the Dutch-speaking Group and two of whom must be from the French-speaking Group. The five are elected on a single list by a majority in Parliament, plus a concurrent majority of Dutch speakers and French speakers. There is also a default rule, which is discussed below.

In the third category is Northern Ireland's 1974 Sunningdale executive. According to the Northern Ireland Constitution Act of 1973, the executive needed to be comprised so that it was "likely to be widely accepted throughout the community" (S. 2 (1) (b)). This paved the way for a voluntary minimum winning coalition of moderate unionist and nationalist parties. The power-sharing proposals accepted by Cyprus's two communal leaders in 2008, although later rejected, were aimed at a (two-party) coalition of moderates (Chapter 1). The UN's Annan Plan for Cyprus (2004) similarly provided for a coalition restricted to moderates – a presidential council to be elected on a single list and approved by concurrent majorities of Greek Cypriot and Turkish Cypriot Senators. None of these models was formally restricted to moderates – their rules simply favoured moderates.

A popular and intuitive argument, associated with centripetalists, is that coalitions of moderates are more likely to be agreed on, and more likely to function, than more broadly inclusive coalitions which may include hardline rivals. This volume presents evidence to the contrary, although the record of inclusive coalitions like that of power-sharing in general is mixed. As McGarry shows, while Cyprus's two sides reached agreement in 2010 on a power-sharing agreement that would have favoured political moderates, the agreement lasted only a few months before collapsing. The reason is that agreement on a coalition that privileges moderates requires moderates to be in a durably dominant position within all relevant communities, a situation likely to be rare in deeply divided polities. Cyprus's agreement was initiated in 2010 because, for the first time in its history, moderates led both communities, but it quickly collapsed because this apparent strength was superficial. Using the Good Friday Agreement, McGarry and O'Leary show that even political moderates may support an inclusive coalition, and even if they have enough votes to adopt a moderates-only coalition (Chapter 3). The d'Hondt allocation mechanism was negotiated and agreed to by the moderate parties, without input from the hardline parties, which were either focused on other matters or boycotting the negotiations. The moderate parties saw the value of giving hardline parties a stake in government, believing that this was the best way to promote peace and stability.

McGarry and O'Leary also show that the GFA's broadly inclusive coalition has been much more successful than that of 1974, although it experienced early instability owing to unresolved disputes over security matters and, perhaps, the novelty of power-sharing. Since 2007 alone, it has lasted (so far) over 20 times longer than its Sunningdale predecessor. The Sunningdale coalition collapsed in part because it was restricted to moderates concerned about accusations of ethnic treachery from their excluded and more hardline intra-bloc rivals. Hardliners from both sides were against inclusion even if had been on offer and attacked the executive from outside, with loyalists eventually destroying it through a strike. In contrast, the more inclusive approach of the GFA led – eventually – to a moderation of hardline parties on either side. These parties, namely Sinn Féin and the DUP (Democratic Unionist Party), were given a stake in the system and rewarded with more ministries if they could broaden their support. This was more likely to occur if they moderated, given that there were no viable parties on their extremist flanks, and providing that their compromises did not give rise to the emergence of such parties (see also McEvoy 2015; Mitchell et al. 2009).

Not all of the inclusive coalitions in this volume have functioned well, but that invites inspection of the context and the relevant rules – not the assumption that they could never work. Fiji's new power-sharing executive established in 1999 quickly collapsed into acrimony, succumbing to a coup in 2000, but the legislature from which the executive was picked was elected by the alternative vote (AV), which delivered a grossly disproportional electoral result in relation to voters' first preferences. AV was recommended by Horowitz to Fiji's constitutional commission, but it contributed to the obliteration of the country's two main, and previously dominant, moderate parties – the indigenous Fijian SVT and Indian Fijian NFP – which had been responsible for the power-sharing constitution of 1997. The SVT won 38 per cent of indigenous Fijians' first preference votes, and 19.3 per cent of the total vote, but only 11 per cent of the seats in Parliament (8 of 71). The NFP won 32 per cent of the Indian Fijian vote, and 14.3 per cent of the total, but no seats in Parliament.[5] The SVT, the largest indigenous Fijian party, barely qualified for office and, in pique, attached conditions to its participation. Mahendra Chaudhry, the newly elected Indian Fijian prime minister (Fijian Labour Party – FLP) rejected the conditions, and the absence of the SVT produced the indigenous Fijian disquiet that led directly to the coup a year later. A more inclusive coalition, elected by proportional representation, would have been a much better bet. More indigenous Fijian ministers would have provided the government with coup-proofing capacities that Chaudhry's more narrow coalition lacked.

Kenya's 2008 to 2013 inclusive coalition model was "troubled by infighting and corruption accusations throughout its five-year existence," a record that prompted Kenyans to reject any form of executive power-sharing after the transitional experiment ended (Chapter 2). While the Serena Accord allowed parliamentary parties to receive a proportionate share of ministries, the coalition existed in what remained essentially a presidential rather than a parliamentary system. The cabinet's constitutional responsibility was "to aid and advise the president in the government of Kenya." The president, Mwai Kibaki, set the agenda, retained an executive veto, and made many decisions unilaterally. He was also a crook, almost universally believed to have stolen the preceding election with the assistance of a corrupt electoral commission, something that surely shaped Kenyans' impressions of power-sharing. Unlike Northern Ireland's inclusive coalition, neither Kenya's nor Fiji's included an essential feature of effective inclusion: a minority veto over majoritarian (or presidential) decision-making. Cheeseman and Murray write that "the legal framework developed around the deal [...] meant that under the power-sharing arrangement power was not really shared at all."

In Burundi, the constitutionally mandated inclusive coalition reassured the Tutsi minority's UPRONA party that it would be represented in government. But, like Kenya, Burundi's power-sharing coalition existed within a presidential system. Politics there has been destabilized by the incumbent president Nkurunziza's decision to exceed his term limit. In addition, in 2014 Nkurunziza's CNDD-FDD – based on the former Hutu rebel movement – effectively destroyed the purpose of the grand coalition provisions by splitting UPRONA into two factions, one loyal to the president and the other including most UPRONA MPs elected in 2010 and presumably backed by most of UPRONA'S Tutsi supporters. The former UPRONA sits in the coalition. As Vandeginste writes, "although formally Burundi still has a coalition government, in reality it became a CNDD-FDD single party government in disguise."

Rules of inclusion are also the focus of Chapter 6. Combining structuralist and situationalist theories of democratization, Bormann makes the case that under authoritarian conditions, multi-ethnic coalitions can increase the prospects for democratization. Two factors matter: how many ethnic groups are included in the coalition (diversity) and the proportion of the population that share their ethnic identity with political leaders in the coalition (representativeness).

Executive formation rules

The functionality of power-sharing agreements may be affected by the rules through which executives are formed. Executive formation through inter-party negotiations has obvious merits but runs the risk that agreement will not be reached in a timely manner, if at all. In Iraq in 2010 it took eight months after elections for a government to be formed, while more recently in Afghanistan, the president Ashraf Ghani and his chief executive Abdullah Abdullah took over three months of "squabbles and infighting" to form a cabinet, much to the amusement and advantage of the Taliban (*The Economist* 15 January 2015). Like Kenya, Afghanistan's power-sharing followed elections saturated in fraud.

In other cases, at least some of the difficulties that arise during executive formation may be pre-empted beforehand in a peace agreement or constitutional settlement. In Belgium, it is constitutionally mandated that the federal cabinet is made up of an equal number of French speakers and Dutch speakers. But this provision does not mandate which parties get which ministerial posts. As a consequence, Belgium regularly takes a very long time to negotiate executive formation – 176 days in 2007 and 541 days in 2010/2011 – a situation perhaps tolerable in a stable Western democracy where the previous government acts as caretaker. Similarly, in Kenya, the parties to the Serena Accord agreed on an allocation of cabinet portfolios proportional to the parties' representation in Parliament but not on which party got which positions. This shortcoming seriously destabilized Kenya in the months after the Accord. It later produced a bloated cabinet that helped undermine the popularity of power-sharing. Fiji's post-1997 executive formation rules and contributed directly to its power-sharing problems. The constitution required the prime minister to "invite all parties whose membership comprises at least 10 per cent of the total membership of the House to be represented in proportion to the numbers in the House." That is, the prime minister determined which qualifying parties got which portfolios. The wording produced squabbles over whether a party with, say, 10 per cent of MPs was entitled to only 10 per cent of ministries or to its proportion of the ministries that were allocated to qualifying parties, which could be much higher. The word "invite" was also not the same as "include." The combination of these rules and the disproportional AV electoral system led to the exclusion of the SVT from the 1999/2000 power-sharing government, with consequences fatal to power-sharing.

We have seen how executive formation rules that privilege moderates can produce opposition from hardliners that prevents agreement on power-sharing (Cyprus 2010), or that destabilize power-sharing coalitions once formed (Northern Ireland 1974). Some such rules may also prevent executive formation, even after there is agreement on power-sharing. Formal centripetal executive formation rules that require a candidate to win support from more than one ethnic community run the risk that no candidate will be elected – and usually require a default rule that is not centripetal (Chapter 3). In Northern Ireland between 1998 and 2007, the executive's first minister and deputy first minister (FM and DFM) needed to be elected by cross-community support (a concurrent majority of nationalists and unionist assembly members). The two offices were to be elected jointly, and the resignation or death of one automatically entailed the resignation of the other. When the unionist First Minister David Trimble resigned in July 2001, he and his nationalist counterpart Mark Durkan subsequently failed to be re-elected because they fell short of a majority on the unionist side. They were saved when three members of the Assembly, who did not identify as either nationalists or unionists, re-designated as "unionists," and a new vote was held. This concurrent rule used to elect the two premiers also contributed to the executive's dysfunctionality. Trimble's awareness of his precarious support among unionists encouraged him to threaten to resign on several occasions to influence the British government to intervene on his side, a tactic that made it more difficult to work with his nationalist and particularly his republican counterparts within the executive.

Our volume discusses executive formation rules that provide for a greater degree of "automaticity" and that arguably have a better track record than the alternatives used in Belgium, Kenya, Fiji, and in Northern Ireland in 1974. Northern Ireland's 1998 Agreement uses a sequential and proportional allocation method based on the d'Hondt formula for allocating portfolios among the executive, other than the first minister and deputy first minister. Sequential and proportional allocation rules allocate ministries based on preference intensities and parties' shares of seats in the legislature (see Chapter 3). A key advantage of such rules is that they are likely to reflect whatever balance of power exists in the polity in question, and to be seen as fair. They are likely, therefore, not just to contribute to agreement and executive formation but also to executive maintenance. Relatedly, sequential and proportional rules may encourage continuing participation in the executive, as boycotts lead to the reassignment of portfolios to other parties rather than to executive formation failure. The advantages over some of the other executive formation rules discussed in this volume are clear. Sequential and proportional rules would have avoided executive formation delay in Belgium, Iraq and Afghanistan and the disputes over which party was to get which portfolio in Kenya. If sequential and proportional allocation rules had been combined with their logical complement – a proportional electoral system – significant indigenous Fijian representation in Fiji's coalition in 1999 would have occurred, and eliminated the questions over what number and to what type of portfolios each party was entitled. Sequential and proportional rules would also have resolved the problems that arose with the concurrent voting rule used initially to elect Northern Ireland's first minister and deputy first ministers. Indeed, this was eventually recognized by the Northern Irish parties, and by the British and Irish governments, who agreed in the St Andrews Agreement of 2006 to scrap the concurrent majority election rule and instead to opt for a revised version of d'Hondt, as recommended by McGarry and O'Leary (2004). Under the Good Friday Agreement, Northern Ireland's parties must designate as either "unionist," "nationalist" or "other." The first minister is now the nominee of the largest party in the Assembly, while the deputy first minister is the nominee of the largest party in the largest "designation" other than that of the first minister, a formula that was necessary to prevent the first minister and deputy first minister from being both unionists or nationalists, and which opened the premiership, in principle, to the "others."

As Bodson and Loizides show, the Brussels Capital Region has an executive formation system that initially involves negotiation but is reinforced by a degree of automaticity as the default. The executive is first elected on a single slate by a majority of Parliament, including concurrent majorities of the French- and Dutch-speaking Groups, a method that effectively requires inter-ethnic negotiations to pass the twin thresholds. But if no executive is elected, the French- and Dutch-speaking members are each elected separately by their respective groups, subject to the approval of the legislature as a whole.

Corporate consociations versus liberal consociations

One common criticism of consociation is that it privileges particular ethnic categories, and that is said to be unfair to ethnic communities who are not included in the power-sharing institutions or who are included on an unequal basis, and to those who do not identify ethnically. One critic has even argued that consociation entails the establishment of an "ethnocracy" (Howard 2012), a term usually and more appropriately used to describe oppressive rule by one group over another (Yiftachel 2006).

These claims overlook the distinction between corporate and liberal consociations, even though consociationalists have stressed this distinction for decades (Lijphart 1995; McGarry and O'Leary 2007). Corporate consociations allocate offices and design protective rules on the basis of predetermined ethnic categories, arguably consolidating such categories while privileging them over the excluded others. Bosnia-Herzegovina (Mostar), Lebanon, Burundi and the Brussels Capital Region have strongly corporate consociational institutions. Liberal consociations, by contrast, largely allocate office on the basis of voter selection. In this volume, the power-sharing arrangements in Northern Ireland (both 1974 and 1998), Fiji and Kenya have at least some important liberal consociational components, particularly with respect to executive power-sharing, as did South Africa between 1994 and 1999. In Northern Ireland the d'Hondt formula rewards any party that qualifies with ministries, while under the changes introduced by the St Andrews Agreement the others can now win either of the two positions but not both, and are now equal in this respect to nationalists and unionists.

Liberal consociations need not privilege ethnic identities, and are *more* likely to create political space for previously weak and marginalized identity groups than conventional majoritarian systems of executive formation, whether parliamentary or presidential. Academic consociationalists have consistently expressed a normative preference for liberal consociations, have backed these where they are feasible, and have insisted on the maximum feasible protection for all groups and individuals where they are not.

Liberal consociations suffer from limitations. Minority groups that are in a position to insist on corporate protections, which offer formal guarantees into the future, are going to do so whatever feminists, socialists or liberals think. They are particularly likely to seek corporate guarantees in the aftermath of civil wars, when security fears abound (see Bogaards, Chapter 7; McCrudden and O'Leary 2013), or if they face a dominant majority community. Of the three cases in this volume that have some liberal consociational rules, two (Northern Ireland and Fiji) have communities that are similar in size while the other (Kenya) has several ethnic communities, none of which is in a majority. Relatedly liberal consociation is inconsistent with the formal *over*-representation of minorities (or majorities).

Degrees of proportionality and the presence or absence of quotas

Power-sharing agreements may be more or less proportional, which may have consequences for some of the criticisms targeted at them. Some proportionality rules benefit large parties or large communities at the expense of smaller ones, with negative or positive effects on stability and fairness. The d'Hondt formula used in Northern Ireland is less 'fair' to the 'others,' which are small, than would be the case with Sainte-Laguë or the Danish formula, and the initial executive of ten members, *ceteris paribus*, was less fair to the 'others' than if it had been more than ten. Similarly, Northern Ireland's proportional electoral system, PR-STV in six-member constituencies, is less fair (proportional) than if PR-STV were run with larger district magnitudes.

In two of our consociations, there is not even the pretence of proportionality. As Bodson and Loizides explain, the power-sharing institutions in the Brussels

Capital Region (BCR) are manifestly disproportional (and corporate). The small Dutch-speaking minority in the BCR, which comprises about 15 per cent of the total voting population, is entitled to at least two, or 40 per cent, of the BCR's five ministers. Dutch speakers are entitled to 17, or 19 per cent, of the 89 seats in Parliament, and the weight of each Dutch-speaking parliamentarian is greater than her French-speaking counterparts owing to corporate rules for executive formation and for passing laws. In Burundi, there is a similar disproportionality, this time favouring Tutsi, who like their BCR Dutch-speaking counterparts, comprise about 15 per cent of the population. Under the Arusha Agreement, the Tutsi are entitled to 33.3 per cent of the positions in Communal Administration, 40 per cent of the Council of Ministers, 50 per cent of the Senate and army, and one of two vice-presidents. Because of qualified majority voting, the Tutsi have a de facto veto in the legislature.

Normatively, a case can be made for some over-representation of minorities, particularly small ones, as proportionality offers little protection against an undivided majority. Thus it is an accepted principle in federations that small entities are entitled to disproportional representation in upper chambers to balance representation by population in the lower house and to compensate them for submerging their sovereignty in the whole. Significant disproportionality, on the other hand, is more difficult to justify, likely to be resented by the community correspondingly under-represented and to be a cause of instability. One of the reasons why Greek Cypriots rejected Cyprus's 1960 Constitution and sought to unilaterally transform it into a more clearly majoritarian system is because it significantly over-represented Turkish Cypriots. As Bogaards shows, Lebanon's power-sharing arrangements collapsed into civil war in 1975 in part because they under-represented the growing Shia community, and Muslims more generally.

As Bodson and Loizides explain, disproportionality is tolerated in the BCR for specific reasons, a useful reminder that context matters and that institutions which work in one place may not work in another. The French-speaking majority in the BCR accepts the privileged position of the Dutch-speaking minority in Brussels because French-speakers are over-represented in Belgium's federal institutions: it is part of an exchange. Bodson and Loizides observe that "protective disproportionality" can work elsewhere where such reciprocal trade-offs exist. As Bose argues, for example, protection for the Bosniak minority within Mostar's municipal institutions could serve as a *quid pro quo* for the Croat minority receiving commensurate privileges within the FBiH (or in Bosnia-Herzegovina as a whole). Vandeginste reminds us that without these trade-offs significant disproportionality can weaken power-sharing. In Burundi, elements in the dominant and mainly Hutu party, the CNDD-FDD, are increasingly making the argument that Burundi needs 'pure' proportionality, a step that would likely destroy what is left of consociationalism there.[6]

While feminists have generally criticized consociations as unfair to women, Byrne and McCulloch show that female inclusion in power-sharing institutions varies depending on the proportional rules in place (Chapter 12). While acknowledging that there is still debate on the question, they argue that closed-list PR, in which voters select a party rather than a candidate, is likely to be better for women candidates than open-list PR, in which voters can express a preference for a particular candidate on the party list. The latter is said to benefit the better known, who are likely to be male, and may also help men because of traditional views that politics is their sphere. Byrne and McCulloch also see quotas for women within the executive and the legislature as rules on which feminists and consociationalists can agree, and that liberal consociation is fairer to women than its corporate counterpart.

Other power-sharing institutions and rules

Many other institutions and rules affect the formation, functionality and fairness of power-sharing agreements. Vandeginste makes the simple point that one of the reasons why power-sharing has lasted in Burundi is because the Arusha Accord had no "sunset" clause: "Quite to the contrary [...] all dimensions of power-sharing were 'written in stone' in a post-transition constitution that can only be altered with a four fifths majority in Parliament." In contrast, Cheeseman and Murray explain that Kenya's parties were unable to develop norms of cooperation because power-sharing was formally temporary, and "provided little incentive for the elite accommodation that [...] is necessary for long-term stability in Kenya." Squabbling combined with corruption contributed to a popular rejection of power-sharing when it ended. Power-sharing with sunset clauses may be all that is agreeable in particular cases, but Kenya's record, and that of South Africa between 1994 and 1996, is not inspiring.

Another difficulty with power-sharing in Kenya, according to Cheeseman and Murray, was that there were no deadlock-breaking mechanisms. Deadlock-breaking mechanisms that allow one side to prevail over the other – usually the majority over a minority – are unacceptable from a power-sharing perspective, but agreed deadlock-breaking mechanisms may be possible, including, for example, placing outsiders in swing positions on supreme courts. Such external arbitration is never preferable to workable domestic and political alternatives, and does not function well when imposed, but it may have benefits if agreed and if it is used only as a last resort, when domestic political remedies fail.

By most accounts in this volume, centripetal institutions and rules do not fare well. Centripetalists generally advocate single-person presidencies, the alternative vote or electoral systems that require a regional distribution of votes, and a version of federation in which at least some ethnic groups are distributed across different federal regions. A single-person presidency is unadoptable in Cyprus because Turkish Cypriots (and their backer, Turkey) have a veto over a settlement. Cheeseman and Murray show that the concentration of power in the hands of a single person prevented power-sharing from working well in Kenya. In Burundi, Vandeginste explains that the main current danger to the continuation of power-sharing is the desire of the president to stay in office beyond his constitutional term limits. This is a common danger with presidential systems in countries with weak democratic traditions (Linz 1994). Regarding Lebanon, Bogaards cites Hanf, who argues that the Ta'if Accord "corrected the concentration of power in a one-person executive under the 1943 agreement into a collective executive that functioned in accordance with the principles of consocation." Bose argues that the OHR erred by converting Mostar's two-mayor system, which facilitated Croat–Bosniak power-sharing, into a single-mayor system that produced conflict.

Although the alternative vote was implemented in Fiji in 1999, the institutions to which it allocated positions fell victim to a coup within a year. In Cyprus, a centripetal electoral system that advantaged moderates was agreed in negotiations in 2010 but the agreement collapsed after its moderate backers found themselves outflanked by hardliners (Chapter 1). Consociational electoral systems which are based on proportionality, and which reflect the political balance of power, seem more feasible in deeply divided places (see also Chapter 3).

In two cases considered here, our contributors see value in centripetal institutions. Vandeginste praises the "intelligent design" of Burundi's electoral code, which requires Hutu and Tutsi parties to allocate one-third of positions on their party lists to Tutsi and Hutu, respectively. The purpose of such bi-ethnic lists is to encourage ethnic parties to moderate their platform to attract candidates from the other group, and by including such candidates, to further increase the party's appeal across ethnic lines. Bose argues that the OHR should dismantle the Federation of Bosnia-Herzegovina, one of Bosnia's two federal entities, leaving its cantons intact, while converting Republika Srpska from an entity into a canton. This would create a Bosnian federation of cantons, similar to that prescribed by centripetalists in which the Croats and Bosniaks would each be spread over a number of cantons.

These suggestions make sense as possible improvements on worst-case scenarios, rather than as ideal arrangements. If Burundi develops into a CNDD-FDD-dominated single-party state, it is desirable that the CNDD-FDD includes the Tutsi minority in its counsels as much as possible. But, given Burundi's polarization, the Tutsi would almost certainly prefer inter-party power-sharing involving the major Tutsi party, UPRONA, instead of having to support only Tutsi who are prepared to be candidates in a Hutu-dominated party–who may be read as co-opted clients. Bose's proposal for Bosnia would be welcomed by the Croats as an advance on current arrangements, in much the same way that Turkish Cypriots sought multiple autonomous cantons in the 1960s when the alternative was a unitary state. Turkish Cypriots will not currently accept multiple cantons because the status quo – autonomy within a single ethnically homogeneous region – is preferable. In this respect, their situation is directly analogous to that of Iraq's Kurds who had achieved an undivided region in 1992 and who fiercely resisted attempts by Arab parties and the Coalition Provisional Authority after 2003 to create an Iraqi federation based on 18 governorates and which would have dissolved the Kurdistan Region (O'Leary *et al.* 2005).

Consociationalism, feminism and transitional justice

Criticisms of consocation from a feminist or transitional justice perspective have been generally wholly negative. This volume baulks this trend, providing balanced and constructive critiques from each of these views (Chapters 11 and 12). Byrne and McCulloch argue that consociations can be "gender mainstreamed" (i.e., designed to include more women), although they are careful to note that this would not automatically entail feminist outputs.[7] They also argue that feminism and consociation are potentially reconcilable around a "shared goal of taming divisive ethno-national politics."

In addition to supporting closed-list PR and quotas for women in the executive and legislature, Byrne and McCulloch believe that veto rights and non-territorial autonomy can be designed to support women. They prefer 'permissive' veto rights that apply to all laws over 'restrictive' veto rights that apply only to some laws, because restrictive vetoes essentialize and homogenize women by suggesting that their concerns are limited to particular issues. If permissive vetoes are not accepted, they suggest "at a minimum" the use of 'alarm bell' mechanisms, such as those in use in Belgium (and South Tyrol and Northern Ireland). Under such rules, a number of representatives would be able to trigger a delay in the passage of legislation to allow it to be subjected to gender analysis before a vote is held. Non-territorial segmental autonomy, another consociational institution, is seen as potentially useful for resource allocation and funding for cultural institutions that cater to women's concerns.

Byrne and McCulloch's second point starts from their assumption that consociationalists see "people's attachment to an ethnonational community [...] [as] the most important way in which they make meaning in their lives," a view they contrast negatively with the feminist position that people make such meaning "in multiple and intersecting ways." They conclude that feminists and consociationalists should be able to coalesce against 'divisive' ethno-national politics. The conclusion is uncontroversial, but their grounds for reaching it may be contested. First, consociationalists do not necessarily assume that people's attachment to an ethno-national community is their most important identity, or even their most important 'political' identity. They accept that the extent of people's attachment to various identities is context-dependent. Ethnic and ethno-national identities, consociationalists believe, are likely to be primary in situations of deep division, a fact that can often be empirically verified. This formulation is consistent with people having multiple identities, and with some – though not most – having primary identities that are not national or ethnic. Consociationalists are just as able as feminists, who traditionally focus on gender, to draw attention to multiple and intersecting identities. Second, consociationalists do not actively seek any kind of "ultimate transcendence" of existing identities but will not oppose such developments if they occur voluntarily. Consociationalists seek to end violent division, and to build a community of communities, which is not the same as the assimilationist goal of seeking to transcend difference.

Brown and Ní Aoláin are constructively critical of consociational theory, although they often appear to be holding their lawyerly noses. They see relative virtue in liberal consociationalism which "avoids processes of ascriptive identification" and "arguably makes segmental cleavages more porous" than its corporate counterpart. They believe that transitional justice and consociational processes can complement one another, with the latter reducing conflict and insecurity while the former erodes the identities that consociationalism hardens. Most importantly, they stress a pragmatic approach in which transitional justice principles are pursued alongside consociationalism's emphasis on political dealmaking and on securing peace and stability through inclusion:

> [S]ome pragmatism and modesty is required given the real-time, real-life limitations of implementing transitional justice on the ground, a set of tensions that co-exist with the lived realities of deals made with perpetrators that de facto compromise the expectations and needs of victims.

They believe that amnesties can be 'calibrated' in a way that neither stifles peacemaking nor accountability, and that is consistent with outright bans on amnesty for certain egregious international crimes, including genocide and crimes against humanity. There is nothing here to which consociationalists would object.

Brown and Ní Aoláin nonetheless take consociationalists to task for focusing on groups rather than the individuals who are at the heart of transitional justice. The term 'groups' has the advantage of including nations as well as ethnic and other communities, but it is fallacious, albeit common, to think that a concern for groups (communities) means downplaying the rights of individuals. Groups, after all, comprise individuals who in certain contexts are deeply attached to their national, ethnic, linguistic, religious and other identities, and the state's treatment of these individuals may crucially affect their life chances (see Lijphart 1995).

Conclusion

The performance of consociational power-sharing institutions has been mixed, whether measured by ensuring stability, effective government, justice, fairness or democracy. This variation suggests that consociation is neither a panacea nor unworkable. Its performance, rather, is shaped by a number of variables, including the behaviour of external agents, the extent to which security concerns are addressed in violently divided places, the extent to which self-determination issues are resolved in nationally divided places, and, everywhere, the precise institutions and rules chosen and developed.

This perhaps obvious conclusion is not one that most critics of consociation accept. Early champions of consociation, well aware that it is not suitable everywhere, stressed different variables (e.g., the number and size of groups, the size of polities, or historical factors such as traditions of accommodation (Lijphart 1977, 53–103)). These factors are not irrelevant. McGarry and O'Leary show that Northern Ireland's grand coalition after 1998 and 2007 was facilitated by structural conditions: a balance of power between two blocs almost equal in size, plus an intra-bloc balance of power (Chapter 3). Vandeginste similarly explains that historic traditions in Burundi – primarily a political culture of one-party systems – is twisting its pluralist party system into a one-party system, which may work if the CNDD-FDD becomes an authentically consociational party (Bogaards 2014), but the prospects for that look slim. These structural and historical factors need to be combined with those summarized here to arrive at a more comprehensive explanation of the performance of consociations.

Our findings may be applied to any case where consociations have existed, are currently in place or are anticipated. Let us take Cyprus, a case which can absorb all of the insights in this volume. In its abortive power-sharing experiment of 1960 to 1963 the conventional wisdom of outside critics has been to attribute its failure to consociation per se (e.g., Frisch 2011, 175; Wilson 2005, 208). Cyprus was also infertile soil. It had only two communities, one of which was a large majority of 80 per cent. This majority believed that it could and should govern alone. Before its independence Cyprus lacked prior traditions of accommodation. These structural and historical problems were exacerbated by the fact that Cyprus's institutions were largely imposed upon Greek Cypriots by outside actors, particularly Turkey.[8] The crucial security issue of the establishment of an army was not settled in the 1960 Constitution. Disagreement over the role of the army led the Turkish Cypriot vice-president to use his veto, which destabilized the institutions,[9] and led to unofficial militias emerging, which helped produce the breakdown of consociation in December 1963.

The 1960 Constitution did not positively address the two communities' core self-determination aspirations for links to their national kin in Greece and Turkey, respectively. Instead it simply ruled out *enosis* (union with Greece) or *taksim* (partition, possibly followed by union of the Turkish Cypriot section with Turkey). The imposition of the constitution – with unamendable provisions – breeched self-determination principles. Treaties attached to the constitution, which could not be changed by the Cypriots themselves, allocated 'sovereign bases' to the former colonial power, the United Kingdom, and gave three powers, the UK, Turkey and Greece, the unilateral right to intervene in Cyprus to uphold the constitutional order. This right was used in 1974 by Turkey to intervene with massive military force to partition the island, and still remains a key obstacle to the creation of an agreed consociation. Greek Cypriots were also upset by provisions that handed the swing vote in Cyprus's Supreme Court to a foreign judge. Greek Cypriots concluded that they had achieved only a "fettered independence" (Soulioti 2006). For the Turkish Cypriots, the constitution lacked provisions that would have allowed them to exercise self-government, even at the municipal level. The inability to resolve the municipal question led to legislative deadlocks over taxation. Greek Cypriots feared that self-government would lead to partition, but it was their failure to accommodate the Turkish Cypriots that arguably produced partition (following an Athens-backed coup d'état by Greek Cypriot nationalists).

Foreign interference and a failure to address core security and self-determination issues were exacerbated by particular institutions and rules. Cyprus represented an example of the "protective disproportionality" explored by Bodson and Loizides, but without any *quid pro quo* for Greek Cypriots. The Turkish Cypriot minority of less than one-fifth was given at least one-third of all relevant political and public positions, including 40 per cent of positions in the police and army, and parity in the presidency and Supreme Court. Its representatives were given a legislative veto over tax matters and municipalities and an executive veto over foreign affairs, defence and security. The rules did not provide for mutually acceptable deadlock-breaking mechanisms, which made the dispute over taxation serious.[10] Greek Cypriot critics could argue, albeit with self-serving exaggeration, that the constitution was "unworkable" (Polyviou 1975, 26). The council of ministers selected by the Greek Cypriot president and the Turkish Cypriot president, respectively, was based on the idea of two ethnic monoliths, and failed to give expression to the ideological diversity that existed within each community and that might have promoted cross-cutting politics. The d'Hondt system that was used in Northern Ireland would have solved that problem by allocating ministries to different parties in each bloc (McGarry and Loizides 2015). The provisions were also corporately consociational, which may have reinforced bicommunalism.

It would be difficult to conclude from this flawed experiment that power-sharing itself was a bad idea, and yet this is exactly the conclusion that outside critics of Cyprus's consociation normally draw. The Cypriots, in contrast, know that the only joint future they have will require a consociation, although one that will avoid the mistakes of the past.[11] In Bosnia, 20 years after Dayton, most people would accept it again, warts and all (Morgan-Jones et al. 2015). Similarly, if Northern Ireland's power-sharing agreement was to collapse tomorrow, it would have to be replaced with something similar, with perhaps a greater emphasis on decentralization within the region. This brings us to the overall conclusion: deeply divided polities are likely to need consociational power-sharing to address issues of stability, peace, good governance, fairness and democracy. The fate of such consociations cannot be known a priori, but are shaped by the multiple and complex factors we have outlined here.

Notes

1 See also the reasoning of the European Court of Human Rights (ECHR 2009) in its decision on the Bosnian presidency (McCrudden and O'Leary 2013).
2 "Burundi confirms the correlation which Hartzell and Hoddie (2007) found between the successful use of power-sharing and the presence of an international peacekeeping operation."
3 Consociations, in Horowitz's view, are "more likely the product of resolved struggles or of relatively moderate cleavages than they are measures to resolve struggles and to moderate cleavages."
4 The military was also responsible for a coup that unseated an ethnic Indian government in 1987.
5 As Fraenkel explains, this result followed on from the fragmentation of the indigenous Fijian vote, but also from the decision of three indigenous Fijian parties, including a hardline ethnocentric party, to give their second preference votes to the victorious Indian Fijian Labour Party, rather than to either the SVT or the NFP, in a bid to punish the incumbents. This was facilitated by a provision in the electoral system that allowed voters to maintain control over how their lower preferences votes were assigned to the party of their first preference.

6 Both Lijphart and Horowitz have pointed to the structural problem for consociationalism posed by large majorities. Such groups are unlikely to accept consociations in any case, but their opposition is likely to be magnified if the consociation is based on significant disproportionality in favour of minorities.
7 This is similar to the concern consociationalists have about centripetal-type electoral systems, such as Lebanon's, that require ethnic quotas to be selected by cross-ethnic electorates. The person elected may be from a particular ethnic community, but may not represent its interests.
8 The Cyprus Constitution was negotiated in 1959 by the Turkish and Greek governments in Zurich and then completed by the UK, Greece and Turkey in London.
9 This notorious veto was used only once, which is not the impression one gets from reading critiques of consociationalism in Cyprus.
10 The previous budget could have been allowed to stay in place until agreement, or new elections held.
11 What such an agreement should entail is the subject of a paper currently underway.

References

Barry, Brian. 2001. *Culture and Equality: An Equalitarian Critique of Multiculturalism.* Cambridge, MA: Harvard University Press.
Bogaards, Matthijs. 2014. *Democracy and Social Peace in Divided Societies: Exploring Consociational Parties.* Basingstoke: Palgrave Macmillan.
Brass, Paul. 1991. *Ethnicity and Nationalism: Theory and Comparison.* New Delhi: Sage.
Economist, The. 2015. "Cabinet Joiners." 15 January.
European Court of Human Rights. 2009. Case of Sejdić and Finci vs. Bosnia-Herzegovina (Application nos 27996/06 and 34836/06). Strasbourg, 22 December.
Frisch, Hillel. 2011. *Israel's Security and its Arab Citizens.* Cambridge: Cambridge University Press.
Gurr, Ted. 1993. *Minorities at Risk.* Washington, DC: United States Institute of Peace Press.
Hartzell, Caroline and Matthew Hoddie. 2007. *Crafting Peace: Power-Sharing Institutions and the Negotiated Settlement of Civil Wars.* University Park: Pennsylvania State University Press.
Horowitz, Donald. 1985. *Ethnic Groups in Conflict.* Berkeley, CA: University of California Press.
Horowitz, Donald. 2000. "Constitutional Design: An Oxymoron?" In *Designing Democratic Institutions*, edited by Ian Shapiro and Stephen Macedo, pp. 253–284. New York: New York University Press.
Horowitz, Donald. 2001. "The Agreement: Clear, Consociational and Risky." In *Northern Ireland and the Divided World: Post-Agreement Northern Ireland in Comparative Perspective*, edited by John McGarry, pp. 89–108. Oxford: Oxford University Press.
Horowitz, Donald. 2002. "Explaining the Northern Ireland Agreement: The Sources of an Unlikely Constitutional Consensus." *British Journal of Political Science* 32: 193–220.
Horowitz, Donald. 2014. "Ethnic Power Sharing: Three Big Problems." *Journal of Democracy* 25: 5–20.
Hulsey, John. 2010. "'Why Did They Vote for Those Guys Again?' Challenges and Contradictions in the Promotion of Political Moderation in Postwar Bosnia and Herzegovina." *Democratization* 17, no. 6: 1132–1152.
Lijphart, Arend. 1969. "Consociational Democracy." *World Politics* 21, no 2: 207–225.
Lijphart, Arend. 1977. *Democracy in Plural Societies: A Comparative Exploration.* New Haven, CT: Yale University Press.

Lijphart, Arend. 1985. *Power-Sharing in South Africa.* Berkeley: University of California Press.
Lijphart, Arend. 1995. "Self-Determination versus Pre-Determination of Ethnic Minorities in Power-Sharing Systems." In *The Rights of Minority Cultures*, edited by Will Kymlicka, pp. 275–287. Oxford: Oxford University Press.
Linz, Juan. 1994. "Presidential or Parliamentary Democracy: Does it Make a Difference?" in *The Failure of Presidential Democracy*, edited by Juan Linz and Arturo Valenzuela, pp. 3–87. Baltimore, MD: Johns Hopkins University Press.
McCrudden, Christopher and Brendan O'Leary. 2013. *Courts and Consociations: Human Rights versus Power-Sharing.* Oxford: Oxford University Press.
McCrudden, Christopher, John McGarry, Brendan O'Leary and Alex Schwartz. 2016. "Why Northern Ireland's Institutions Need Stability." *Government and Opposition* 51, no. 1: 30–58.
McGarry, John and Brendan O'Leary. 2007. "Iraq's Constitution of 2005: Liberal Consociation as Political Prescription." *International Journal of Constitutional Law* 5, no. 4: 670–698.
McGarry, John and Brendan O'Leary. 2008. "Consociational Theory and Peace Agreements in Pluri-National Places: Northern Ireland and Other Cases." In *The Failure of the Middle East Peace Process*, edited by Guy Ben-Porat, pp. 70–96. London: Palgrave.
McGarry, John and Brendan O'Leary. 2011. "Consociation and Self-Determination Disputes: The Evidence from Northern Ireland and Other Recent Cases." In *After the Nation?*, edited by Shane O'Neill and Keith Breen, pp. 38–59. London: Palgrave Macmillan.
McGarry John and Brendan O'Leary. 2013. "Stabilising Northern Ireland's Agreement." *Political Quarterly* 75, no. 3: 213–225.
McGarry, John and Neophytos Loizides. 2015. "Power-Sharing in a Re-United Cyprus: Centripetal Coalitions vs. Proportional Sequential Coalitions." *International Journal of Constitutional Law* 13, no. 4: 847–872.
Mitchell, Paul, Geoffrey Evans and Brendan O'Leary. 2009. "Extremist Outbidding in Ethnic Party Systems Is Not Inevitable: Tribune Parties in Northern Ireland." *Political Studies* 57, no. 2: 397–421.
Morgan-Jones, Edward, Neophytos Loizides and Djorde Stefanovic. 2015. "Twenty Years Later, This is What Bosnians Think of the Dayton Peace Accords." *Washington Post*, 14 December.
O'Leary, Brendan. 2005. "Debating Consociational Politics: Normative and Explanatory Arguments." In *From Power-Sharing to Democracy: Post-Conflict Institutions in Ethnically Divided Societies*, edited by Sid Noel, pp. 3–43. Montreal: McGill-Queen's University Press.
O'Leary, Brendan, John McGarry and Khaled Salih, eds. 2005. *The Future of Kurdistan in Iraq.* Philadelphia: University of Pennsylvania Press.
Polyviou, Polys. 1975. *Cyprus: The Tragedy and the Challenge.* Washington, DC: American Hellenic Institute.
Rebouché, Rachel and Kate Fearon. 2005. "Overlapping Identities: Power Sharing and Women's Rights." In *Power Sharing: New Challenges for Divided Societies*, edited by Ian O'Flynn and David Russell, pp. 155–171. London: Pluto Press.
Roeder, Philip and Donal Rothchild. 2005. "Power Sharing as Impediment to Peace and Democracy." In *Sustainable Peace: Power and Democracy after Civil Wars*, edited by Donald Rothchild and Philip Roeder, pp. 29–50. Ithaca: Cornell University Press.

Sisk, Timothy. 1996. *Power Sharing and International Mediation in Ethnic Conflicts*. Washington, DC: United States Institute of Peace Press.

Soulioti, Stella. 2006. *Fettered Independence: Cyprus, 1878–1964*. Minneapolis: University of Minnesota Press.

Sriram, Chandra Lekha. 2013. "Making Rights Real: Minority and Gender Provisions and Power-Sharing Arrangements." *International Journal of Human Rights* 17, no. 2: 275–288.

Taylor, Rupert. 2001. "Northern Ireland: Consociation or Social Transformation." In *Northern Ireland and the Divided World: Post-Agreement Northern Ireland in Comparative Perspective*, edited by John McGarry, pp. 36–53. Oxford: Oxford University Press.

Taylor, Rupert. 2009. "The Injustice of a Consociational Solution to the Northern Ireland Problem." In *Consociational Theory: McGarry & O'Leary and the Northern Ireland Conflict*, edited by Rupert Taylor. London: Routledge.

Tull, Denis and Andreas Mehler. 2005. "The Hidden Costs of Power-Sharing: Reproducing Insurgent Violence in Africa." *African Affairs* 104, no. 416: 375–398.

van Schendelen, M.C.P.M. 1984. "The Views of Arend Lijphart and Collected Criticisms." *Acta Politica* 19, no. 1: 19–49.

Wilson, Robin. 2005. "Towards a Civic Culture: Implications for Power-Sharing Policy Makers." In *Power Sharing: New Challenges for Divided Societies*, edited by Ian O'Flynn and David Russell, pp. 204–219. London: Pluto Press.

Yiftachel, Oren. 2006. *Ethnocracy: Land and Identity Politics in Israel/Palestine*. Philadelphia: University of Pennsylvania Press.

Zahar, Marie-Joëlle and Chandra Lekha Sriram. 2009. "The Perils of Power-Sharing: Africa and Beyond." *Africa Spectrum* 44, no. 3: 11–39.

Index

Abdo, Nahla 257
Acemoglu, Daron 125, 134
Adams, Gerry 73
adoptability: meaning of 17; the question of for Cyprus 16–33 (*see also* Cyprus)
adoptability of institutions, domestic path dependency 33
adoption problem, power-sharing's 6, 8, 150, 174
Afghanistan 31, 69
Alston, Philip 53
Amin, Idi 128
Anastasiades, Nicos 21, 25
Annan, Kofi 43, 49, 52
Argentina 140–1
Arusha Agreement 166–8, 170–1, 173–4, 176–80, 182
Ashdown, Paddy 197–200, 203–6
al-Assad, Bashar 126, 232–3
asymmetric preferences 175
Austria 66, 148
autonomy: community 88, 93; cultural 230, 240, 261; group 88–9, 261–2; segmental 16, 27, 44, 149, 168, 190, 211, 213, 237, 240
autonomy provisions/arrangements, diversity of implementation 4
AV (alternative vote): benefits of for moderate parties 67; effects on inter-ethnic voting 22; Fiji's adoption 104
Azani, Eitan 158

Badran, Tony 157
Bainimarama, Frank 103, 113–15
Barkan, Joel 56
Bayer, Leanne 184
Baylouny, Anne Marie 157
Belgian Constitution 97
Belgium 32, 66, 69, 148; corporate segmentation 90; federal structure 88–90; territorial regions and language communities 88; *see also* Brussels Capital Region
Bell, Christine 234
Berri, Nabih 157
Birrell, Derek 222
Bodson, Thibaud 9–10, 281, 282, 283, 288
Bogaards, Matthijs 10, 283, 284
Bormann, Nils-Christian 10, 134, 279
Bose, Sumantra 11, 269
Bosnia-Herzegovina (BiH) 18, 31, 69, 148; Dayton Peace Agreement 116, 189–91, 193, 206–7; international peacebuilding and state-making interventions 191; local politics in Mostar 193–203; minority returns 190; Mostar and power-sharing 203–8; population and ethnic mix 208n1; power-sharing in post-war Bosnia 189–208; three ethnic versions of truth 236; *see also* Mostar
Boutruche, Théo 235
Brown, Kristian 12, 229, 286, 287
Brussels Capital Region: 'alarm bell' procedure 91–2; Belgian federal structure/state 88–90; consociationalism in 87–99; double-majority rule 91, 93, 95; effects of minority protection on PR 94–6; electoral process 90–1; legal validity of the minority protection model 96–8; main ethno-linguistic groups 87–8; minority protection mechanisms 90–3; parity requirements and consensus rules 93; Parliament, bilingual organization 90–1; Parliament, election of the government by 92–3; pre-determined competences, choosing 93; ratio of French/Dutch speaking populations 90

Burundi 31, 66, 148; achieves independence 167; adoption of power-sharing, explanatory factors 174–7; Arusha Agreement 166–8, 170–1, 173–4, 176–80, 182; assassination of Hutu President 168, 171, 175, 183; civil war 167; constitutional amendment process initiated 173; demonstrations and violence 173; elite behaviour 175–6; ethnic and non-ethnic dimensions of power-sharing 168–9; ethnic power-sharing, constitutional engineering of 169; ethnic power-sharing, post-election position 172; ethnic power-sharing and single party rule 180–2; founding of the kingdom 182; general election of 2015, aftermath 173–4, 178; general elections of 2010, opposition boycott 178; gradual erosion and future prospects of power-sharing 171–4; identity groups 167; international engagement 176; international peacekeeping operation 179; and Lijphart's favourable conditions 174–5; *longue durée* perspective of the dynamics of power-sharing 180–4; militarism 183; neo-patrimonialism 184; Peace and Reconciliation Agreement 166; political overview 166–7; political situation in the 1990s 175; post-colonial ethno-political violence 167–8; power-sharing dimensions 169–71; quota-based provisions 169; South Africa's inspiration 176; state centralism 182–3; survival of power-sharing 177–80
Byrne, Siobhan 12, 250, 284, 286

Cahn, Naomi 252
Canada 29
Cederman, Lars-Erik 139
Central African Republic 235
centripetal coalitions, requirements 66
centripetal federalism, Nigeria as working example 27
centripetal federation, potential for fragmenting divisive ethnic cleavages 26
centripetalism: vs consociationalism 26–30, 70–9; electoral options 5; function 5; Horowitz's recommendations 21; key prescriptive institutional mechanism 21; starting principle and primary focus 4–5
Chaudhry, Mahendra 109–12, 114–15, 118

Cheeseman, Nic 8, 37, 175, 270, 278, 284
Chile 232
Christofias, Demetris 21, 24–5
Clark, Janine 236
Clerides, Glafkos 21, 30
collegial executive, vs presidential executive 17–21
Colombia 66
community autonomy 88, 93
consociational power-sharing, favourable conditions 174–5
consociationalism: in BCR 87–99; centripetalism vs 26–30, 70–9; civil war and 149; the concept 148; consistency of collective/rotating presidencies with 18; contemporary examples of 148; following civil war 149–51; key institutions 4; liberal vs corporate 89, 281–2
consociations, typical requirements 64
Corm, Georges 157
corporate consociationalism 151, 255
corporate consociations 69–70, 89, 150–1, 260, 281
corporate power-sharing arrangements, vs liberal 6–7, 281–2
corporate vs liberal consociations 281–2
cross-voting schemes 23–5, 30, 67
cultural autonomy 230, 240, 261
Cyprus 67; the 'adoptability' question 16–33; bizonality perspective 30; cantonization proposal 29–30; centripetal federalism vs consociational federalism 26–30; 'co-presidency' proposal 19; demographic perspective 20; equality of veto power 16; ethno-political background 16–17; as example of failings of consociational power-sharing 17; Friends of Cyprus NGO 23; lessons of the stalemate 30–2; multizonal vs bizonal options 30; partitioning 16, 19; post-independence executive structure 19; presidential executive vs collegial 17–21; privileging systems vs inclusive systems 21–6; Turkish Cypriot federal region after adjustment 28; Turkish Cypriot opposition to conventional presidency 18; Turkish invasion and its impact 20, 30; weighted cross-voting proposal 23, 25

Dahl, Robert 135
Darby, John 253

Dayton Peace Agreement 116, 189–91, 193, 206–7
decommissioning and demilitarization, NI 215–17
Democratic Republic of Congo (DRC) 235
Denktash, Rauf 19
Denktash, Serdar 25
designing power-sharing 1–7; direct vs indirect 3–6; formal vs informal 2–3; liberal vs corporate 6–7, 255
devolution 37, 40–1, 44, 56–8, 218, 220, 223; constitutional objectives of 57
direct power-sharing arrangements, vs indirect 3–6
Donaldson, Jeffrey 78
Donno, Daniela 130
double-majority rule, BCR 91, 93, 95

Egypt 158
El Khazen, Farid 157
electoral college, US 18
electoral systems: Horowitz's recommendations 21–2; privileging vs inclusive 21–6; vote-pooling 6, 16, 18, 21–2, 25–7, 104–5; *see also* AV (alternative vote)
El-Husseini, Rola 156
elite behaviour, as a function of macro-economic forces 125
Emerson, Rupert 255
Enloe, Cynthia 253
Eroğlu, Dervis 24–5
Escriba-Folch, Abel 130
ethnic communities, benefits of inclusive electoral systems 21–6
ethnic groups, definition 127
ethnic minority regimes 128–9
ethnic power-sharing coalitions and democratization: context of study 124–7; democratization as cause of elite coalitions 137–9; key concepts 127–31; majority vs minority rule 129–30; model predictions 140–1; multi-ethnic coalitions vs mono ethnic 130–1; study conclusions 141–2; study data and variables 131–4; testing the hypothesis 134–7
European Union 18
executive formation, rules 279–81
executive power-sharing: areas of function 4; the debate 63; Fiji's formula 103; implications of mandatory rules 116; Kenyan model 36; role of in ending civil wars 124; *see also* Northern Ireland's power-sharing executive

Faulkner, Brian 71, 77
Fearon, Kate 254, 261
federalism, centripetal vs consociational 26–30
federations, benefits of 26
feminism, transitional justice and consociationalism 285–7
Fiji 66, 67, 69, 80; the 1999 election and 2000 coup 108–11; the 2001 election 111–13; the 2006 election 113–15; bicommunal polity, shaping of 105–7; consociational perspective 105; Constitution of 1997 107–8, 116; Constitution of 2013 115; coups 105, 107, 110–11, 114; defects in power-sharing arrangements 103; ethnic and political background 103–5; ethnic strife, history of 103; implications for power-sharing theory and practice 115–19; independence 106; location and history 105; mandatory power-sharing 103–19; multi-party cabinet experiment 115; proportional representation 107–8; strength of the power-sharing arrangements 116
Fitt, Gerry 71
Flanders 88, 90
formal power-sharing arrangements, vs informal 2–3
Fraenkel, Jon 10, 269, 271
Frampton, Martyn 214

Geddes, Barbara 131
gendering power-sharing: and chauvinistic nationalism 256–7; conflict transformation, contending norms of 251–4; consociationalist perspective 258–63; ethno-nationalist perspective 254–8; gender mainstreaming 251, 259, 261–3; gender quotas 260; gender-blindness of power-sharing theory and practices 250; and group autonomy 261–2; for post-conflict futures 263–4; and veto rights 261
Germany 66, 70
GFA 219
Ghana 126
Good Friday Agreement (GFA) 212–13; and the confluence of both inter- and intra-bloc balances 66, 72; consociational features 213; disarmament requirements 215; and dissident republican activity 214;

Good Friday Agreement (GFA) *continued*
inter- and intra-bloc balances,
confluence 66; negotiation of SPA
mechanisms 71; and security-related
incidents 214
good governance, overview of the NI
situation 211–13
grand coalitions: consociationalist
commitment to 230; facilitating
negotiations in multi-party ethnic blocs
66; feasibility and examples 66; and
group support 4
Gray, Ann Marie 222
group autonomy 88–9, 261–2
Guelke, Adrian 252

Haider, Huma 241
Hale, Henry 127
Hariri, Rafik 156
Hartzell, Caroline 2, 179
Haynes, Dina Francesca 252
Heath, Edward 71
Hezbollah 156, 158
Hoddie, Matthew 2, 179
d'Hondt divisor rule 65, 80n7
Horowitz, Donald 6, 8, 17–18, 63, 67, 75, 104, 124, 137, 174–5
Hudson, Michael 155
human rights: and amnesty provisions 235; European convention (ECHR) 97; transitional justice and 230, 233, 235, 238–9; violations of, implications for power-sharing deals 233
Hume, John 71, 73
Huntington, Samuel 128
Hunziker, Philipp 134

ICC (International Criminal Court) 232
inclusion, rules of 276–9
inclusive electoral systems, vs privileging systems 21–6
Indonesia 22
informal power-sharing arrangements, vs formal 2–3
inter-ethnic conciliation, centripetal vs consociation approaches 63–4
International Covenant on Civil and Political Rights 97
international intervention, power-sharing and 271
international peacekeeping operation, in Burundi 179
IRA (Irish Republican Army) 72
Iran 158

Iraq 31, 69, 128, 154; Kurdish position 28; post-invasion governance recommendations 27
Israel 70

Jayawardena, Kumari 257
Juma, Monica K. 48

Kaggia, Bildad 39
Kenya 22, 31, 36, 66, 69; achieved independence 38; assassinations of human rights activists in 53; constitutional review 40–1; electoral system 42, 56; ethnic groups 36; independence negotiations 38; Kenyatta/Ruto anti-reform alliance 51–2; leaders accused of crimes against humanity 37, 52; two main political parties 38; violence in 40, 43; Waki Commission 51
Kenya, power-sharing in 36–59; the agreement 43–9; choice of presidentialism 56; constitutional dispensation 55–8; criticisms of the agreement 46; culture of impunity 51–3; devolved government system 57; executive nature of the agreement 44–5; external monitoring project 48; impact of the arrangement on day-to-day politics 50; items on the mediation agenda 44, 49; the 'Kenya crisis' 42–3; 'majimbo' (regionalist) constitution 38–9; new constitution 54; overview 36–7; performance 49–51; politics of participation and control 39; protests 47; 'second coming' 41–2; security forces reform 53–4; subverting democracy 40
Kenyatta, Jomo 38–9
Kenyatta, Uhuru 37, 41, 51
Kerr, Michael 71, 152, 155
Khalaf, Samir 157
Kibaki, Mwai 36, 41–7, 49–50, 53–4
Knox, Colin 220
Koroi, Jokapeci 113
Kuwait 154

Laely, Thomas 182
Lagasse, Nicolas 95
Lebanon 148; civil war 70; civil war and the transformation of consociationalism 148–60; domestic dimension 156–7; external actors/international dimension 157–8; favourable factors for consociational democracy 153–4;

institutional flexibility 155–6; military power, the role of 158–9; peace process 154–5; political background 148; and post-war consociationalism 151–9; the stakes 152–3; Ta'if Agreement (National Pact) 152–9
liberal consociational institutions 70
liberal consociationalism 151, 230, 234
liberal consociations 69–70, 80, 89, 240, 281
liberal power-sharing arrangements, vs corporate 6–7, 89, 255, 281–2
Lijphart, Arend 3, 18, 94, 104, 124–5, 141, 148, 153, 155, 174, 211, 260
Linz, Juan 18
Lipset, Seymour Martin 125
Loizides, Neophytos 9–10, 281, 282, 283, 288
Lord's Resistance Army (LRA) 235
Lumumba, Patrick 52

MacGinty, Roger 253
majority rule 128
Makarios, Archbishop 20, 29
Malaysia 128, 139
al-Maliki, Nouri 69
Mandela 176–7; Nelson 176
Mara, Kamisese Kapaiwai Tuimacilai 106, 111
Mau Mau rebellion 38
McClintock, Anne 253
McCrudden, Christopher 89, 213
McCulloch, Allison 12, 151, 283, 284, 286
McEvoy, Joanne 11, 269
McGarry, John 6, 128, 148
McGuinness, Martin 75
Mehler, Andreas 8, 177
Mill, John Stuart 124
minorities, over-representation of 87, 94–6, 98, 169
minority protection: BCR mechanisms 90–3; effects on PR in Brussels 94–6; legal validity of the model 96–8
Moi, Daniel Arap 39–43, 50
Mostar, BiH: city council divisions (1996–2004) 194–9; demographic shift 197–8; destruction of the sixteenth-century bridge 189; early post-war atmosphere and the threat of violence 191–2; institutional integration and divisions 192–3; international peacebuilding regime 193; local elections 194; local politics 193–203; municipal structure 195; Old Bridge replica inaugurated 200; one city statute (2004–15) 199–203; Paddy Ashdown's role 197–8; political context 189–93; and power-sharing in Bosnia 203–8; power-sharing mechanisms 195; public sector strike 202; reform commissions 198; renewal of tourism 192
Mühlbacher, Tamirace Fakhoury 159
Muslim Brotherhood 158
Musyoka, Kalonzo 45

Nagle, John 159
nationalism, gendered perspective 253 (*see also* gendering power-sharing)
Ndadaye, Melchior 168, 171, 175, 183
Netherlands 148, 153
Ní Aoláin, Fionnuala 12, 252, 262, 275, 286, 287
Nigeria 18, 22, 26, 141; as example of centripetal federalism at work 27
Noel, Sid 7
Nolan, Paul 222
Norris, Pippa 172
Northern Ireland 115, 148; centripetal coalition experiment 64; decommissioning and demilitarization 215–17; d'Hondt-based executive proposal 73; dissident republican activity 214–15, 219; Fresh Start Agreement 223; policing and justice reforms 217–19; power-sharing and the pursuit of good governance 211–24; prison closures 217; public services delivery 219–23; security governance, improved provision 213–19
Northern Ireland's power-sharing executive: Anglo-Irish Agreement 73; centripetalism vs consociationalism (1973–2015) 70–9; challenges for 76, 78; coalition phases 74; comparative relevance of SPA 79–80; contribution of the SPA to stability 77–8; and the IRA ceasefire decision 73; key cleavage in NI politics 71; political context 63–4; Sinn Féin's participation 73–4; SPA mechanisms 64–70; St Andrews Agreement 76, 79; stability and success 75; suspensions by the UK government 74, 78; transfer of policing and justice powers agreement 75; Trimble's flexibility 74; *see also* Good Friday Agreement; Sunningdale Agreement; sequential and proportional allocation (SPA)

298   Index

Norton, Augustus 156
Noyes, Alex 54
Nyerere, Julius 176

Odinga, Oginga 39
Odinga, Raila 36, 41–2, 44–7, 50, 54
O'Leary, Brendan 4, 6, 89, 128, 148, 254
Olson, Mancur 80n2
Ong'wen, Odour 54
outflanking 66, 71, 73
over-representation, of minorities 87, 94–6, 98, 169

Paisley, Ian 72, 75
Pakistan 126, 140–1
Panama 140
parliamentarianism, vs presidentialism 18
Phillips, Anne 253
Pinochet, Augusto 232
positive discrimination 143n8
Potter, Antonia 254
Powell, G. Bingham 135
power-sharing: feminist perspective 253 (*see also* gendering power-sharing); the two main forms 16
power-sharing arrangements: corporate vs liberal 6–7, 281–2; international comparisons 115
power-sharing institutions/rules 275–85; corporate vs liberal consociations 281–2; executive formation 279–81; other institutions and rules 284–5; proportionality and quotas 282–4; rules of inclusion 276–9
power-sharing settlements, explaining the performance of 268–89
power-sharing solutions, Horowitz's preference 17
presidencies, collective/rotating 18
presidential executive: vs collegial executive 17–21; US system 18
presidentialism: claimed advantages 17–18; key difficulty according to Lijphart 18; Linz's writings 18
privileging electoral systems, vs inclusive systems 21–6
proportional democracies, vs majoritarian and consensual democracies 63
proportional representation (PR): basic aim 94; definition 94; effects of minority protection on in Brussels 94–6; Lijphart's preference 4; types of 4
proportionality and quotas, rules around 282–4

proportionality principle, function 4
protective disproportional representation: the concept 87; legality 96–8
Przeworski, Adam 135

Qarase, Laisenia 111–14
quotas, rules around proportionality and 282–4

Rabuka, Sitiveni 103, 107
Rebouché, Rachel 254, 261
Reilly, Ben 231
Richard, Anthony 216
Robinson, James A. 125
Roeder, Philip 8
Rolston, Bill 215
Rosiny, Stephan 159
Rotberg, Robert 212
Rothchild, Donald 8
Rustow, Dankwart 128
Ruto, William 37, 43, 51
Rwanda 31, 171, 175, 179, 183

Saddam Hussein 27, 128, 154
Šantić, Aleksa 192
Saudi Arabia 154
Schulze, Kirsten 215
Seaver, Brenda 157
security, and power-sharing 271–3
Seeberg, Peter 160
segmental autonomy 16, 27, 44, 149, 168, 190, 211, 213, 237, 240
Sejdić and Finci vs. Bosnia-Herzegovina 205, 246n2
self-determination: examples of 28; and power-sharing 273–5; Turkish Cypriots' claim to and insistence on 28–9
separation of powers, effects of in Cyprus 18
sequential and proportional allocation (SPA) 64, 76, 213; comparison with centripetal rules 68; comparison with other coalitions 69; contribution to Northern Ireland's political stability 77–8; the mechanisms 64–70; and the St Andrew's agreement 76, 79; *see also under* Northern Ireland's power-sharing executive
Sharia law 26
Sharoni, Simona 257
Singapore 128
Sisk, Timothy D. 167
Slater, Dan 128, 137, 139
Smith, M.L.R. 215

Somalia 143n9
South Africa 107, 148
South Sudan 235
Spears, Ian 177
Speight, George 110–13
Sri Lanka 18
Steans, Jill 256
Sullivan, Daniel 171
Sunningdale Agreement: the 1973 general election as referendum on 71–2; end of the experiment 72; establishment 66; Horowitz's account of the failure 72, 75; membership of the executive 71; ratio of votes won in preceding Assembly elections 71
Svolik, Milan W. 130
Switzerland 18, 29, 66, 148
Syria 31, 126, 128, 141, 154, 156–7, 233

Taiwan 128
Talat, Mehmet Ali 24–5, 67
Tanzania 49
Taylor, Rupert 8, 148
Thailand 140
transitional justice: centripetal approaches 231; claims-making tool provision 243–4; consociationalism, ethno nationalism and 237–40; consociationalism and feminism 285–7; feminist perspective 244; grassroots perspective 240–5; and human rights 230, 233, 235, 238–9; interface with consociationalism 230–2; locating in the consociational approach 229–30; narrative testing 244; negative interactions with consociational theory 232–4; positive interactions with consociational theory 234–7; role of consociational politics in 229–46; rules of encounter 243
Trimble, David 71, 78, 215
Tull, Dennis 8

Turkey 126
tyranny of the majority 96

Uganda 235
UN Security Council Resolutions: addressing the women, peace and security agenda 250, 264n3; and bizonal government 30
Uvin, Peter 184

Vandeginste, Stef 12, 269–70, 271, 272, 279, 284, 285, 287
veto rights/powers: BCA 93, 95; Belgium 89; BiH 190; Burundi 170–1, 173; consociationalist commitment to mutual entitlement 230; Cyprus 16, 19, 22; diversity of function 4; of elites 125; equality of 31; Fiji 118; implications of minority rights 96; Lebanon 149; NI 79; restrictive vs permissive 261
vote-pooling 6, 16, 18, 21–2, 25–7, 104–5
Voting Rights Act 143n8

Wallonia 88, 90
weighted cross-voting, proposal of in Cyprus 23–4
Whitelaw, William 71
Wilford, Rick 220, 222
Willett, Susan 262
women, exclusion from peace making/building 252 (*see also* gendering power-sharing)
Wright, Joseph 130

Yuval-Davis, Nira 256

Zahar, Marie-Joëlle 157
Zalewski, Marysia 257, 262
Ziadeh, Hanna 158
Ziblatt, Daniel 142
Zimbabwe 31, 36, 66, 69
Zisser, Eyal 158

Taylor & Francis eBooks

Helping you to choose the right eBooks for your Library

Add Routledge titles to your library's digital collection today. Taylor and Francis ebooks contains over 50,000 titles in the Humanities, Social Sciences, Behavioural Sciences, Built Environment and Law.

Choose from a range of subject packages or create your own!

Benefits for you
- Free MARC records
- COUNTER-compliant usage statistics
- Flexible purchase and pricing options
- All titles DRM-free.

Benefits for your user
- Off-site, anytime access via Athens or referring URL
- Print or copy pages or chapters
- Full content search
- Bookmark, highlight and annotate text
- Access to thousands of pages of quality research at the click of a button.

REQUEST YOUR **FREE** INSTITUTIONAL TRIAL TODAY

Free Trials Available
We offer free trials to qualifying academic, corporate and government customers.

eCollections – Choose from over 30 subject eCollections, including:

Archaeology	Language Learning
Architecture	Law
Asian Studies	Literature
Business & Management	Media & Communication
Classical Studies	Middle East Studies
Construction	Music
Creative & Media Arts	Philosophy
Criminology & Criminal Justice	Planning
Economics	Politics
Education	Psychology & Mental Health
Energy	Religion
Engineering	Security
English Language & Linguistics	Social Work
Environment & Sustainability	Sociology
Geography	Sport
Health Studies	Theatre & Performance
History	Tourism, Hospitality & Events

For more information, pricing enquiries or to order a free trial, please contact your local sales team:
www.tandfebooks.com/page/sales

The home of Routledge books

www.tandfebooks.com